QUALITATIVE METHODS in BUSINESS RESEARCH

SAGE was founded in 1965 by Sara Miller McCune to support the dissemination of usable knowledge by publishing innovative and high-quality research and teaching content. Today, we publish more than 850 journals, including those of more than 300 learned societies, more than 800 new books per year, and a growing range of library products including archives, data, case studies, reports, and video. SAGE remains majority-owned by our founder, and after Sara's lifetime will become owned by a charitable trust that secures our continued independence.

Los Angeles | London | New Delhi | Singapore | Washington DC

Päivi Eriksson
Anne Kovalainen

QUALITATIVE METHODS in BUSINESS RESEARCH

2nd EDITION

Los Angeles | London | New Delhi
Singapore | Washington DC

Los Angeles | London | New Delhi
Singapore | Washington DC

SAGE Publications Ltd
1 Oliver's Yard
55 City Road
London EC1Y 1SP

SAGE Publications Inc.
2455 Teller Road
Thousand Oaks, California 91320

SAGE Publications India Pvt Ltd
B 1/I 1 Mohan Cooperative Industrial Area
Mathura Road
New Delhi 110 044

SAGE Publications Asia-Pacific Pte Ltd
3 Church Street
#10-04 Samsung Hub
Singapore 049483

Editor: Jai Seaman
Assistant editor: James Piper
Production editor: Ian Antcliff
Copyeditor: Jen Hinchliffe
Proofreader: Derek Markham
Indexer: David Rudeforth
Marketing manager: Catherine Slinn
Cover design: Shaun Mercier
Typeset by: C&M Digitals (P) Ltd, Chennai, India
Printed and bound by CPI Group (UK) Ltd,
Croydon, CR0 4YY

Library of Congress Control Number: 2015937077

British Library Cataloguing in Publication data

A catalogue record for this book is available from the British Library

ISBN 978-1-4462-7338-8
ISBN 978-1-4462-7339-5 (pbk)

CONTENTS

PREFACE AND ACKNOWLEDGEMENTS

The first edition of this book was sketched on one cold and wintry evening during one of the national doctoral courses for business PhD students we held in Finland. We had been discussing the idea of the book based on our separate and joint teaching experiences several times. Since then, we have been teaching both in Finland and abroad.

Professor David Silverman's work on qualitative methods and his kind e-mail asking for our willingness to write a book on qualitative business research gave us a final push to move from long-time planning to action. We would like to thank David as the editor of the SAGE Qualitative Research Series for accepting our book to his series, and for his encouraging feedback during the process; it was extremely important to us.

We have both been teaching qualitative research, and using qualitative research methods and methodology in our own research for a number of years. In that process we have recognized a need for a clear and down-to-earth introduction, both to qualitative methods and to the whole research process and design. Therefore, we have written the book in a readable and student-friendly way by offering views not only of a wide range of useful methods that are available, but also to the whole research design, research ethics, varieties of data types, evaluation and writing process as key parts of any successful research project.

We are most grateful for the support from our Commissioning Editor Jai Seaman at SAGE and the whole skilled editorial team at SAGE. Anne Kovalainen would like to thank Academy of Finland for Minna Canth Academy Professorship and Gendered Economy project, both of which gave wonderful opportunity to research. Anne Kovalainen would also like to thank the University of Turku and Päivi Eriksson would like to thank the University of Eastern Finland for support.

The book project would not have succeeded without the support of our nearest and dearest. Anne would like to thank her partner, adjunct professor Seppo Poutanen, for his emotional and intellectual support, and also for his insightful comments specifically on the research ethics chapter and on critical realism. Päivi would like to thank her husband Tero Montonen and her daughters Tuusa, Saga and Pia for enduring inspiration and vital support throughout the process.

PART I

THE BUSINESS OF QUALITATIVE RESEARCH

1
INTRODUCTION

This chapter will provide information on:

- the purpose of the book
- qualitative business research
- the qualitative research approaches that are covered in this book
- how and for what purposes you can use the book.

THE PURPOSE OF THE BOOK

In this book, we want to show that qualitative business research is important, exciting and a highly rewarding enterprise. Qualitative business research gives you an opportunity to focus on the complexity of business-related phenomena in their contexts. It produces new knowledge about how people and things work in real life, why they work in a specific way, and how we can make sense of them in a way that may enable us to change something for the better.

We further suggest that qualitative business research is particularly relevant because it provides the possibility of adopting a critical and reflexive view about the social world of business and its core processes. This means that, as qualitative researchers, we are willing to ask ourselves what we are doing in our research, for what purpose, and with what kind of presumptions and consequences. Furthermore, as critical and reflexive business researchers, we are interested in how the decisions that we make during the research process shape what we see and find.

Just as with quantitative business research, qualitative business research also draws on more than one philosophical and disciplinary root, and it relies on several methods of data collection and analysis. This is why we consider that it is not fair to write about qualitative business research as one whole. We think that it is essential even for a novice researcher to acknowledge that there are a number of different qualitative research approaches, and even these have some variety in themselves in terms of their philosophical background, focus and research techniques. The main aim of our book is to open up this variety to a reader who wants to learn more about qualitative business research or plans to implement a qualitative research project.

Based on our 25-year experience of teaching qualitative business research, we feel that there is a need for a specialist book such as ours. Many business research books deal with both qualitative and quantitative research, and they do not cover the variety of qualitative research approaches. At best, the sections on qualitative business research in these books discuss only one or two approaches; most often this is case study research, and sometimes ethnographic, grounded theory, focus group or action research. The newcomers in business research, such as discursive, narrative, visual, critical and feminist research approaches, remain outside the scope of most introductory textbooks on business research. We have included all these into this book.

In comparison to the first edition of our book, this second revised edition includes new chapters on Qualitative Content Analysis, Visual Methods and Publishing. All chapters are updated with new content; knowledge, examples, exercises, readings and references.

WHAT IS QUALITATIVE BUSINESS RESEARCH?

Qualitative research is often described in contrast to quantitative research, which dominates the body of scientific work undertaken in social sciences, including business research. It is much easier to compare quantitative and qualitative research than to define them. The author of several qualitative research books in the social sciences, David Silverman provides an extensive discussion on the complexity of defining what quantitative and qualitative research is, and is not. This discussion shows appreciation of both quantitative and qualitative methodologies, and a reminder that both of them have a lot of internal variety, which makes any straightforward comparisons between qualitative and quantitative research inadequate (Silverman, 2011). However, there are some major differences. Silverman points out that quantitative research cannot deal with the social and cultural construction of its own 'variables'. This refers to one of the major interests of many qualitative research approaches, that is, understanding reality as socially constructed: produced and interpreted through social and cultural meanings.

Qualitative research approaches, therefore, are concerned with interpretation and understanding, whereas quantitative approaches deal with explanation, testing of hypothesis, and statistical analysis. Furthermore, in several qualitative research approaches, the collection of data and their analysis are sensitive to the social and cultural context aiming at a holistic understanding of the issues studied. Quantitative research is more prone to structured, standardized, and abstracted modes of collecting and analyzing empirical data.

Owing to the long-standing dominance of quantitative research, most business researchers are trained extensively in quantitative methods and less in qualitative methods. This may be one reason why business research textbooks typically introduce quantitative research as the one that provides more rigorous results, and qualitative research a somewhat suspicious affair, one that can be used as complementary when studying something that is expressed in words and cannot be translated into numbers. Indeed, this is the major way in which qualitative research has been used in social science and business research: as the first phase of study, which is then followed by a quantitative phase.

Another common way to use qualitative methods in business research is to use them as providers of a better understanding of issues that have remained unclear in quantitative studies.

Our book differs from this way of thinking because we consider qualitative business research to be an adequate method of knowledge production, without any link to quantitative research. This does not mean, however, that we would have any objections towards combining qualitative and quantitative methods of data collection and analysis in the same research project.

Business research project advisors easily accept that a student performs a purely quantitative research project, whereas a decision to undertake a qualitative research project may require more justification. Being able to justify these choices, however, should be just as important in both cases. Most research methods books teach that the justification should be primarily based on what you want to learn from your research, and not so much on other reasons. When the choice of methodology is based on its appropriateness in relation to the research aims, there is no point in claiming that quantitative methodology is the more desirable form of research and qualitative research is just complementary to it. Not many of us have enough knowledge and experience about both quantitative and qualitative research to be able to make fully justified decisions in relation to our research questions. However, this does not mean that we should not strive to do good research and find compatibility between our research questions and methods. Minimally, knowing the very basics of both quantitative and qualitative research helps you to identify what kinds of research questions and aims are more compatible with either methodology. However, for an enthusiastic 'qualitative person' it may be easier to reshape her research questions rather than to engage in quantitative research, and vice versa.

We want to emphasize in our book that making a justified decision between various qualitative approaches is just as important as choosing between quantitative and qualitative research. Making a decision on what kind of qualitative research you want to pursue requires an understanding of the specificities and finesses of different varieties of qualitative methods. This is the kind of knowledge that our book primarily provides – guidance on how to choose between various qualitative research approaches, and practical advice on how to proceed with the chosen one. Therefore, this book is most useful for students who have already made the decision to undertake qualitative research but who have not made a final choice about what kind of qualitative research approach would be the most appropriate in terms of their research aims.

QUALITATIVE APPROACHES INTRODUCED IN THIS BOOK

Our experience as teachers of qualitative methods has shown that business students have two major problems in doing qualitative research. First, many students think that qualitative business research means 'doing a case study with semi-structured interviews'. One reason for this is that, while there is plenty of information available on case studies, it is not easy to find similar information on the range of other qualitative research approaches that are suitable for business-related research. This information is scattered in a number of books and articles and it requires dedication for a student to assemble and make sense of it. Second, when a business student chooses to perform qualitative research other than case studies, it is even more difficult to find practical guidance on how to perform various qualitative research approaches, including the definition of the research questions, collection and analysis of empirical data, links between theory and empirical results and the production of conclusions.

Deciding on a research topic and refining it into research questions is an integral part of any research project. Choosing the most suitable methodology for each research question requires an understanding of the major advantages and possible limitations associated with different methods. Sometimes these limitations are philosophical by nature and sometimes they are more related to the data. In this book, we will cover the major advantages and limitations of each of the methods that we write about.

Throughout the book, we will show that there is plenty of choice in terms of how you can design and implement a successful qualitative business research project. The body of qualitative research approaches that we discuss in this book is wide but not comprehensive. The choice concerning what to include and what to leave out is based on a combination of theoretical and practical considerations. This means that some of the approaches have a well-established theoretical background (critical, discursive, feminist, ethnographic and research) and some do not (e.g. case study and focus group research).

In Part III of the book we introduce different qualitative research approaches that can be used in business research:

- case study research
- ethnographic research
- action research
- focus group research

- grounded theory research
- narrative research
- discourse theoretical research
- critical research
- feminist research
- visual research.

For each of these, we illustrate where they lead in terms of research questions, research designs, data collection and analysis, drawing conclusions and reporting a study. When introducing these qualitative approaches, we place particular emphasis on how to analyze empirical data and how to refine research questions and generate new ones from the data. Some qualitative researchers would call these approaches 'methods', but we prefer a wider definition because several data collection and data analysis methods can be used in most of the approaches that we write about.

Our aim is not only to enlighten the most common approaches used in business research, but also to give an overview on some approaches that have not gained wide popularity among business researchers as yet. We want to emphasize that qualitative research is a rich field of inquiry, which provides a vast number of approaches that can be adapted to the interests and contexts of business research. The qualitative approaches, and the specific versions within each of them, that we have chosen for this book, are all suitable for studying business-related topics, issues, and research questions, but they are not too demanding for graduate students or other novice qualitative researchers.

We have selected the qualitative approaches of this book with two aims in mind. Case studies, ethnographic research, action research, focus group research and grounded theory research have all been adopted by business researchers, which means you can find examples of their use in research books and scholarly journal articles. We also provide references to these examples in each of the respective chapters.

Narrative and discursive research, as well as critical, feminist and visual research, have not been so extensively used in business research as yet, but the interest in them is growing. We think that these approaches are highly interesting for two reasons. First, they widen the potential of qualitative business research beyond the more traditional choices. Second, they blur the boundaries of disciplinary fields within social sciences – for instance, the boundary between business research and sociology, business research and social psychology, and business research and cultural and media studies. Some of the approaches (e.g. focus group research) are more like research techniques and perhaps easier to adopt by novice researchers. Others might require prior understanding and interest in the philosophy of social sciences and epistemological and ontological questions. However, we have made an effort to write about these in a way that they can be read without extensive prior knowledge of the philosophy of science.

HOW TO USE THIS BOOK

We have designed this book to provide core reading for a graduate course on qualitative business research. It should also be useful for more specialized courses at masters and doctoral level studies as well as MBA courses focusing on certain qualitative research approaches, such as case studies or action research. To assist the reader in understanding the finesses of, and differences in, qualitative business research, we have included throughout the book several pedagogical features, such as chapter summaries and objectives, key points, name and subject indexes, and a glossary of qualitative research terminology. In addition, we provide lots of examples of published business research using different qualitative research approaches included in this book. We also provide a list of further reading and practical exercises at the end of each chapter.

The structure and the most central features of the book are as follows:

> Part I provides an introduction to the qualitative business research perspective. Furthermore, it describes the qualitative research process and its main concepts more generally. This part provides basic knowledge and practical advice on how to deal with research philosophical questions, how to focus and frame a qualitative business study, how to negotiate access and how to acknowledge research ethics. We believe that a qualitative business researcher needs to have the basic knowledge provided in Part I before making any justified decisions on data collection issues.

> Part II gives guidance on how to collect qualitative data for business research and how to learn to know your data. It covers the data collection methods that are most used in business research with an emphasis on interviews, observations and digital data. In addition to providing basic knowledge about how to collect qualitative data, Part II also helps the researcher in choosing a more specific qualitative research approach for the study at hand (if a more specific approach is needed).

> Part III introduces ten qualitative research approaches that can be used in business research. We first outline the approaches that are most common in business studies. Thus, Chapter 11 deals with case study research, Chapter 12 with ethnographic research, Chapter 13 with action research, Chapter 14 with focus group research and Chapter 15 with grounded theory research.

> Thereafter, we introduce the newcomers in business research. Accordingly, Chapter 16 focuses on narrative research, Chapter 17 on discourse theoretical research, Chapter 18 on critical research, Chapter 19 on feminist research, and Chapter 20 on visual research. Each chapter provides both the conceptual basis of the approach and practical guidance on how to perform the research.

We suggest that, for the purpose of conducting academic, rigorous and sophisticated qualitative business research, the qualitative business researcher should know the basics of qualitative research provided in the other parts of our book, but also be at least somewhat knowledgeable about the range of alternative, complementary, new and exciting qualitative research approaches to choose from that are outlined in Part III of our book.

Part IV

In addition to using the whole book as a course reading tool, it can also be read in parts. Parts I, II and IV can be read as a 'good-to-know' introduction to qualitative business research in cases where the reader does not necessarily intend to perform a qualitative research project of their own. Thus, these parts provide useful and easy-to-understand reading for a basic level introductory course on business research, or even for a course focusing on both qualitative and quantitative business research.

Furthermore, any of the research approaches introduced in separate chapters in Part III can be combined with the more general content in Parts I, II and IV. For example, if you already know that you will be doing either a narrative or a discursive study, you can concentrate only on those chapters in addition to reading the more general content provided in the book.

2

RESEARCH PHILOSOPHY

This chapter will provide information on:

- the relevance of philosophical issues in business research
- the key concepts and positions of the philosophy of science
- the logic of how theory and empirical analysis are related
- the role of reflexivity in qualitative research.

THE RELEVANCE OF PHILOSOPHICAL
ISSUES IN BUSINESS RESEARCH

There are several issues that you need to take into consideration when starting a research project. Some of these are more practical by nature, relating to the research design and process, the planning of the practicalities concerning data acquisition, access to the research site, gathering materials and analyzing them. We will valorize most of these issues throughout the book, and we will discuss in detail in Chapter 3 the entire planning process that relates in general to research design.

Among the issues that you need to consider at the beginning of your research project are the philosophical aspects and questions that lurk behind every research method and methodological approach. In order to gain a good understanding of what you can do with methods in your research, you should at least be somewhat familiar with the basic philosophical concepts, positions and traditions. All research methods are closely connected to research philosophy and to the ways it is possible to bring forward new knowledge through research.

Many practically-oriented business researchers do not explicitly state the philosophical viewpoints of their research. These are not always necessary to explicate. However, this often implies that they either find philosophical questions as non-relevant in their research settings, or take their own philosophical position as self-evident and known. The latter case is particularly prevalent in mainstream quantitative research.

In fact, it often happens during business research seminars, wherein philosophical discussions arise, especially in relation to qualitative business research settings. There can be several reasons for this. Qualitative research offers an alternative to the mainstream quantitative research approach, and it also often allows for the discussion of the taken-for-granted philosophical assumptions of quantitative research.

It is possible to do qualitative business research without much knowledge of the basic concepts in the philosophy of social sciences that concern various ways of doing research. We think that it is helpful for you to have knowledge of the basic philosophical concepts and ideas for research in order to be able to design a solid piece of study that delivers what it promises (Box 2.1). Statements – and clarity in thinking – about what constitutes your research phenomenon have implications for the ways in which it is possible to gain knowledge of it.

The exploration of philosophical concepts assists you in specifying your overall research design and strategy. These will in turn set the directions for your research, how to proceed from your research questions to the conclusions. You will need to make decisions about the type of empirical data you will collect, how you will analyze them, rules about how to interpret the analyses, and ideas about how to present your conclusions. The exploration of the basic philosophical concepts will also help you in making decisions about the issues that all have effect on your research design: what kinds of questions do you ask in your research, and in what ways can you answer those questions with your research?

BOX 2.1

The relevance of philosophical issues

Understanding philosophical issues provides you with a better understanding about:

- why researchers are interested in different topics and research questions;
- why qualitative research can be performed in many ways;
- why qualitative data can be collected and analyzed in many differing ways;
- why different methods are being used in analyzing the data.

Qualitative approaches attach to philosophical questions in different ways

It is particularly relevant for a novice business researcher to learn that qualitative research approaches can be related to the philosophy of social sciences in differing ways. Most research approaches are not related to only one specific tradition of the philosophy of science. This means that methods can be used within several philosophical traditions; therefore, you do not necessarily need to be an expert in the philosophy of science to get it right. For example, case study (see Chapter 11), action research (see Chapter 13) and focus group research (see Chapter 14) can be used in research with connections to several philosophical traditions.

On the other hand, some qualitative research approaches do sign up for specific philosophical thinking through their theoretical ideas and attachments. A good example of these approaches is critical research, which draws to a varying degree on critical theory (see Chapter 18). When you choose to follow these approaches in your research project, it is advisable to learn more about the philosophical questions and developments of that particular approach.

Reflexivity in qualitative research

With the constant growth of information and research knowledge, it becomes ever more important to assess the 'production process' of that knowledge and the knowledge itself. In practice, this usually means that you reflect on how you produce knowledge as a researcher, what kind of knowledge it is, and how you can relate this new knowledge to other knowledge you might already have. This everyday reflection is a way to think through your research project throughout the entire process.

In scientific thinking, reflection bears the same idea as in everyday life. It means careful reconsideration of knowledge: how it is produced, described and justified. Reflexivity is especially important when you think of your epistemological assumptions and commitments in research. On what basis knowledge is argued for and claimed is a question that is not solely related to qualitative research, but to all research knowledge. However, it is most often discussed and brought forward in a qualitative research setting, to add to the transparency of knowledge claims and sources of information, and to open up the relationships that exist between the knower, that is, you as a researcher, and your subjects of interest, that is, the economy, society, organizations, companies, firms and the people who work there.

KEY CONCEPTS OF THE PHILOSOPHY OF SCIENCE

Ontology, epistemology, methodology and methods are key concepts in the philosophy of social sciences. For many researchers, ontology, epistemology and methodology together can be related to each other as a unifying framework, or even one unified view that some researchers have called a paradigm (Burrell and Morgan, 1979; Guba and Lincoln, 1994). 'Paradigm' as a term has been diluted and come to signify different things in business studies, ranging from meta-theoretical aspects in research to different types of classifications made on the basis of theories, methods used, even empirical research topics.

All these concepts – ontology, epistemology, methodology and methods – relate to each other, but in various ways, depending on the more general philosophical position of your research. In this chapter we will introduce some key philosophical concepts and positions, and discuss their relation to the qualitative research approaches that we illustrate in this book (Box 2.2).

BOX 2.2

Some key philosophical concepts

Questions that the key philosophical concepts aim to answer:

Ontology	What is there in the world?
Epistemology	What is knowledge and what are the sources and limits of knowledge?
Methodology	How can knowledge about a given issue or problem be produced?
Methods	What are the specific ways of data collection and analysis that can be used?
Paradigm	What are the conceptual and/or methodological models that relate to a scientific discipline during a particular period of time?

Ontology

Ontology concerns the ideas about the existence of and relationship between people, society and the world in general. Ontological assumptions embrace all theories and methodological positions. Several of the qualitative approaches that we will introduce in this book are based on the ontological assumption in which reality is understood as being some form of subjectivism. This means that reality is understood to be based upon perceptions, and experiences that may be different for each person, and may change over time and context. However, the conceptual understandings of reality can be shared.

In comparison, in most quantitative research it is usual to assume that the social world exists for everyone as a distinctive and separate, that is, objective, reality. The division between objectivism and subjectivism is one aspect of ontology in philosophy, which refers to the study of conceptions of reality. Instead of subjectivism, the term constructionism is often used to describe the social nature of reality.

Objectivism as an ontological starting point assumes that the social world exists independently of people and their actions and activities. The objectivist view on ontology assumes that social reality has an independent existence outside the knower, that is, you as a researcher. Constructionism, on the other hand, assumes that social actors produce social reality through social interaction. This means that they also can change their views and understandings of social reality through interaction.

In other words, the subjectivist view on ontology (i.e. constructionism) assumes that the reality for a knower, such as you, is the outputting of social and cognitive processes. Therefore, two realities alike cannot exist. A focal point in the social constructionist view is that reality does not exist outside individuals; 'reality' is always about individuals' and groups' interpretations (Blaikie, 1993: 94).

When considering the ontological perspective of your research, you should think about what you see as the fundamental properties in the social world that are worth studying. This may sound rather difficult, because ontological assumptions are usually more or less taken for granted. Let us look at an example. If you are interested in studying what managers do and why, you must first decide whether you believe that they act, for instance, on the basis of biologically determined personalities, cognitively adopted attitudes, or socially constructed identities. All three interest fields can indicate very different world views in terms of what is considered as essential in existence and being, what should be studied, and how it can be studied.

Epistemology

In addition to ontology, which focuses on the question 'What is there in the world?', it is helpful to understand what epistemology in research means. Ontological claims in research are closely related to epistemological claims, and they usually are discussed together. Epistemology is concerned with the questions 'What is knowledge?' and 'What are the sources and limits of knowledge?'

As well, in epistemology there is an objectivist and a subjectivist view. According to the objective view in epistemology, it is possible that there exists a world that is external and theory neutral. According to the subjective epistemological view, no access to the external world beyond our own observations and interpretations is possible.

In addition, there are several avenues from which epistemology can be discussed (Box 2.3). These directions do not conflate to the qualitative–quantitative divide, but are based on the ways through which knowledge claims are made. We will take these up as an initial orientation to epistemic questions of research, and to show you the complexity that lies behind each method. In case you are interested in finding out more about the differences between epistemological directions, you can read specific literature or attend a course in the philosophy of sciences and social sciences.

Understanding the above-mentioned aspects, of what can be known that exists, makes it easier for any researcher to realize that whatever knowledge we produce in research, that knowledge is seldom based on one unified idea of science and research.

Instead, different and equally legitimate philosophically embedded views exist regarding how and in what ways we can know the world. This is the basic assumption concerning the methods and knowledge on methodological tools.

Within epistemology, there are several schools of thoughts that are associated with the main philosophical positions in social science, which we will introduce later in this chapter. First, there is empiricism, in which reality is constituted of observable material things. Empiricism is associated with the philosophical position called positivism. Second, there is subjectivism, which views reality as being socially constructed. This means that knowledge is available only through social actors. This epistemological view is associated with the position called interpretivism. Third, there is substantialism, which takes reality as material, but acknowledges that people interpret it differently in different times and contexts. This epistemological view is most often associated with the position called critical realism.

BOX 2.3

Foundation for different epistemological directions

The key division between different epistemological directions lies in three basic assumptions.

1. Epistemologies differ in terms of whether or not they can be considered as being 'foundationalist' epistemologies. Foundationalist epistemologies seek permanent and reliable criteria for knowledge that is produced in research.
2. Epistemologies differ in terms of the role that they give to the researcher. Is the researcher an autonomous and detached knower, or are they part of the knowledge production process, and if so, to what extent?
3. Epistemologies differ in terms of how they establish the relationship between idea and object, or concept and observation. The concept can be separate, it can be closely related and even corresponding, or it can be contextually different from observation (Schwandt, 2001: 71).

Methodologies and methods

Methodologies are concerned with how we come to know of the world, but they are more practical in nature than epistemologies. Epistemology and methodology are closely related: the former involves the philosophy of how we come to know the world, whereas the latter involves the same from a practical point of view. Methodology refers to organizing principles, which provide the procedure for guiding the research process and research design that you will learn about in Chapter 3.

Sometimes methodology is called the philosophy of methods. The focal point of methodology is to describe how a given issue or problem can be studied. David Silverman (2005: 4) writes that methodologies can be defined broadly and schematically (e.g. quantitative and qualitative methodologies), or narrowly and precisely (e.g. grounded theory, case study, ethnography).

Methodology is focused on the specific ways (that is, the methods) that we use in research when trying to understand our world better. Methods are often divided into methods of data collection (e.g. interviews, observation) and methods of data analysis (e.g. thematic analysis, narrative analysis). In the method chapters of Part III on qualitative research approaches and methods (Chapters 11–20), you will learn more about these. Although some methods are better suited to some methodologies (e.g. observation with ethnography, or in a broader sense with qualitative methodology), they are not rigidly bound to each other in the way that certain methodologies would rely on a very restricted body of methods.

Paradigm

Very often in research methods books, and even in textbooks, you will find the term 'paradigm'. The historian of science Thomas Kuhn gave the term paradigm the meaning that has become common and much used sometimes even misused within the research context. Kuhn referred to the set of practices that define a scientific discipline during a particular period of time. As a natural scientist, Kuhn did not consider the concept of paradigm to be appropriate for describing development in the social sciences.

Kuhn (1970), in his book *The Structure of Scientific Revolutions*, writes that he developed the concept of 'paradigm' so as to be able to distinguish the development of social sciences from the development within the natural sciences. He had observed that the researchers in social science were never in agreement on theories, concepts or methodologies. Therefore, he concluded that although there cannot be any paradigms in the social sciences, social sciences are in a pre-paradigmatic phase in the development of scientific knowledge. For a paradigm, researchers need to share not only theories, but also a shared basis for theory choice (Kuhn, 1977: 322).

Despite this, the concept of paradigm is widely used in social sciences and in business research. In this discussion, paradigm as a term has shifted away from the original remarks made by Kuhn, and can be defined as a world view or a belief system that guides a researcher in their work (Guba and Lincoln, 1994). Burrell and Morgan's (1979) model of 'four sociological paradigms for organizational analysis' gained wide popularity among business researchers in the 1980s and 1990s.

Even if Kuhn did not argue that paradigms would be invariable, they sometimes were mistakenly taken as such in the discussions. Also, the description of competing paradigms of inquiry that was introduced in 1994 by Guba and Lincoln is often referred to. They identify positivism, postpositivism, critical theory, and constructivism as the major paradigms that frame social science research. They also claim that these paradigms compete for acceptance as the paradigm of choice in qualitative research. More recently, management and business researchers have been more concerned about epistemological discussions than debating on paradigms (Willmott, 1997; Johnson and Duberley, 2000; Seirafi, 2013).

THE MAIN PHILOSOPHICAL POSITIONS

As is the case with many other terms and concepts, social scientists use the main philosophical concepts in somewhat differing ways. The issues that we discuss here under the title of 'philosophical positions' can be found in other methodology books under such titles as 'paradigms', 'epistemologies', or 'research philosophies' and 'research traditions'.

Also, the divisions made between philosophical positions vary in literature. Several textbooks label all qualitative research as being interpretative, but some prefer to make distinctions between various philosophical positions that inform qualitative research, including, among other things, postpositivism, critical realism, constructionism, and postmodernism. This is because some qualitative research is more inclined to follow the natural science model with hypothesis testing, etc. This is due to the differences in the epistemological and, more generally, philosophical positions of research settings. In the following, we will briefly describe the most common philosophical positions that business researchers rely on and describe how they direct research interests (Box 2.4).

--- BOX **2.4** ---

The main philosophical positions

Positivism: knowledge of the world is obtained through applying the scientific methods to experiences and to the empirical world.

Postpositivism: a reformed version of positivism, which also includes critique towards the basic assumptions of positivism.

Critical realism: combines some of the ideas in positivist and constructionist thinking; concerned with the identification of the structures of the world.

Interpretivism and constructionism: background in hermeneutics and phenomenology; concerned with subjective and shared meanings.

Hermeneutics: refers to the necessary condition of interpretation and understanding as part of the research process.

Postmodernism: rejects the positivist, rational and generalizable basis for scientific research, which would explain the world from an objective standpoint.

Post-structuralism: stands for the most extreme rejection of positivism within postmodernism.

Positivism and postpositivism

Management and organization researchers Johnson and Duberley (2000: 38) have suggested that positivism, also known as logical positivism, is the mainstream philosophical position of management studies. They propose that while management as science is fragmented and diffuse, positivism has been one programme to unify management research. Another additional explanation for the dominance of positivism lies in the nature of management and business knowledge. This knowledge is often functional by nature, and there is a desire for universal truth that would hold fast across industries, businesses, cultures and countries. Often, managerial implications in research are seen as important value added. These aspects can call for a positivist approach in research settings.

Positivism, a term coined by Auguste Comte (1798–1857), refers to an assumption that only legitimate knowledge can be found from experience.

According to the basic claim of positivism, research produces facts and accounts that correspond to an independent reality, is value free and prioritizes observation. Positivists believe in empiricism: the idea that observation and measurement are the essence of scientific endeavour. The key approach of the scientific method is the experiment in which the operationalization of issues that are studied is the prevailing idea: only things that are measurable can be dealt with.

There are also several directions within positivism. At first, positivism relied on empiricism as the foundationalist epistemology, but lately positivism has moved towards a non-foundationalist epistemology. Despite its several directions, positivisms in plural share some basic ideas of knowledge production, according to which the aim of research should be in finding causal explanations and regularities. Various versions of positivism find methodological unity in natural and social sciences, and sign for value-free science ideals. These elements of positivism can be found in most positivist research as the core orientation, and within qualitative and quantitative business research.

Positivism does have relevance in business research, but it is more closely related to the logic of, and ways for doing, quantitative research. Also, qualitative research can subscribe to some version of positivism, when hypothesis (or theory) testing is at the forefront in research. Further, older versions of the grounded theory approach accept some ideas of positivism in research (for more, see Chapter 15). Other philosophical approaches have more relevance for qualitative research than positivism.

Postpositivism (also known as postempiricism) has developed through the main criticism of positivism. It argues that the knower and the known cannot be separated (as positivism claims). It also questions the idea of a shared, single reality. It suggests that, although human beings cannot perfectly understand reality, researchers can approach it with rigorous data collection and analysis. Postpositivist thinking is influential within qualitative research, as it covers philosophical positions and methodologies as different as scientific and critical realism, grounded theory (Glaser and Strauss, 1967), and symbolic interactionism (Blumer, 1969). Furthermore, the detailed ways of analyzing qualitative data devised by Miles and Huberman (1994), for example, are often called postpositivist.

Critical realism

Critical realism agrees with positivists that there is an observable world, independent of human consciousness. At the same time, it suggests that knowledge about the world is socially constructed. Critical realism is closely related to the works of Roy Bhaskar and Rom Harré (Danermark et al., 2002). Critical realists use the word 'critical' in a particular way. This will be discussed in detail in Chapter 18.

In business research, Johnson and Duberley (2000), Reed (2005), Contu and Willmott (2005) and Delbridge (2014) suggest that critical realism provides one alternative for those studying management and organization. Johnson and Duberley (2000) have suggested that critical realism allows you to use multi-methodological approaches, which, in turn, enhance more detailed and accurate analyses when looking for causalities in companies' development, for example. Adoption of critical realism in business research is not, however, an easy or uncontested approach. Labeling research as 'critical research' does not yet cover the basic features of critical studies needed in critical research (Poutanen, 2016), as discussed in Chapter 18.

Interpretivism and constructionism

There are many forms of interpretivism and constructionism, but common to all of these is a concern with subjective and shared meanings. These philosophical positions are interested in how people, as individuals or as a group, interpret and understand social events and settings. As much of the qualitative research focuses on human action and understanding, interpretation is an important part of any analysis of qualitative materials. The philosophical base of interpretative and constructionist research is in hermeneutics and in phenomenology, which have an influence on the ideas of social construction of reality (Berger and Luckmann, 1967).

Interpretative and constructionist researchers start out with the assumption that access to shared dynamic, and changing and individually constructed reality, is only through social constructions such as language and shared meanings. This is why interpretative and constructionist research does not only focus on the content of empirical data, but also on how the content is produced through language practices. Furthermore, research done from these philosophical positions does not predefine dependent and independent variables, but focuses on the full complexity of human sense making as the situations emerge. It is also assumed that there are many possible interpretations of the same data, all of which are potentially meaningful.

Perhaps the dominant form of current interpretative research is social constructionism, which was introduced by Berger and Luckmann in their book published in 1967. Social constructionism seeks to understand how the seemingly 'objective' features, such as industries, organizations and technologies, are constituted by subjective meanings of individuals and intersubjective processes such as discourses. Since Berger and Luckmann, several versions of the social constructionism have been presented.

Vivien Burr (1995) identifies four basic assumptions of the social constructionist philosophical position. First, it takes a critical stance towards taken-for-granted knowledge, trying to open it up for discussion. It is assumed that the world does not present itself objectively to the observer, but is known through human experience, which is mediated by language. Second, the categories in language that are used to classify things around us are produced through social interaction within a group of individuals at a particular time and in a particular place. Third, knowledge is sustained by social processes and conventions of communication. Fourth, knowledge and social action go together.

In this view, reality is socially constructed by interconnected patterns of communication. Therefore, reality is not defined by individual acts, but by complex and organized patterns of ongoing actions. Schwandt (2001: 32) remarks that there are both weak and strong versions of social constructionism that differ in their views regarding the social construction of everything. For qualitative research, constructionist views on knowledge production are useful, as they emphasize the close relationship between researcher and researched field, interaction and understanding, as basic tenets of research. Reflexivity is one key part of constructionism.

Hermeneutics

Hermeneutics is a term that originates from Friedrich Schleiermacher (1768–1834). Also, the term 'interpretivism' is often used for hermeneutics. Hermeneutics refers to the necessary condition of interpretation and understanding as part of the research process: the inescapable action of interpretation (verstehen) taking place in all research. It is ontological by nature, but still, hermeneutics and interpretivism have given resonance to later epistemological developments in asserting that there is a fundamental difference between natural science's and social science's subject matters: human intentions are crucially moulding and changing the reality. Because of this, understanding of human intentions is needed, and it is the understanding of human actions that is the foundation for all knowledge in social sciences. Much of qualitative research focuses on human actions and understanding; therefore, interpretation is indeed an important part in any qualitative research.

Postmodernism and post-structuralism

Since the 1980s, postmodernism has attracted considerable interest among qualitative researchers. In terms of the philosophy of social sciences, postmodernism is a non-foundationalist epistemology. It rejects the positivist, rational and generalizable basis for scientific research, which would explain the world from an objective standpoint. The most extreme rejection of positivism within postmodernism is post-structuralism. It is derived from the idea of deconstruction (Derrida, 1978), which holds that there are no grounds for truth outside the text. Postmodernism in philosophy signs for epistemology with a small 'e'. This means that it rejects any common or shared ground for knowing. When doing this, it also rejects the 'knower' as an authority of any knowledge.

Postmodernism has had a strong appeal, especially within organization studies, culturally-oriented marketing studies, and strategic management research, especially in the early 1990s. Knights and Morgan (1991) presented a classic analysis of corporate strategy as discourse, and Hassard and Parker (1993) edited a comprehensive collection of the postmodern research in management studies. On the other hand, Alvesson and Willmott (2003) edited a book that took critical distance from postmodern research in management studies. It now seems that the direct influence of postmodernism is on the decline in business research, but it has had influence on the way research is done, not only through the emphasis on language and its role, but also by emphasizing the heterogeneity of researched issues and the ways the knowledge is understood in heterogeneous ways. As such, if we look at the ways the knowledge is produced in business studies, we can identify both a 'rational' and a 'social' approach (Longino, 2002; Poutanen, 2007). A good overall account of the influence of postmodernism in management studies can be found, for example, in Johnson and Duberley (2000).

BASIC ASPECTS OF INQUIRY

How to bring forward knowledge about the world in research? There are two basic models of social science research, called deduction and induction, that, to a large extent, cover the different general models of science according to which scientific knowledge is achieved. In addition, some researchers prefer to describe their study following the abduction logic. Inductive reasoning draws from observed cases more general statements or general claims about most cases of the same kind. Deductive reasoning is concerned with the formulation of hypotheses and theories from which particular phenomena can then be explained.

Even though a particular study may look like it is purely deductive (e.g. an experiment designed to test the hypothesized effects of some treatment on some outcome), most social research involves both inductive and deductive reasoning processes at some point in the same project. Therefore, it is good to keep in mind that labelling your research as deductive, inductive, or abductive does not, by itself, tell the reader exactly how your research process proceeded. Nor does it alone justify your methodological choices.

If you want to use these terms in explaining the logic of your research, you should be careful to describe in more detail how you have applied inductive or deductive reasoning in the course of your research.

Deduction

Despite divergent business disciplines, the idea of deduction in research has been by far the strongest way to build up the theoretical knowledge base. Deduction rests on the idea that theory is the first source of knowledge. On the basis of what is known about a phenomenon theoretically, the researcher is able to deduce one or more hypotheses. The hypotheses are then subjected to empirical study. The process of deduction is linear, following the logic of proceeding from theory to empirical research. The certainty in theory development is gained through hypothesis testing in empirical scrutiny. As multi-discipline approaches and differing ideas of the role and nature of theories in research have emerged, the strict deductive model of research is not considered suitable for most qualitative business research.

Induction

Much of the (quantitative) business research follows the logic of theory testing through hypothesis scrutiny in the empirical world. However, many business study researchers find this model lacking because they see theories as outcomes of empirical research, not prior to it. Theories can also be seen as corrective modes concerning findings or even publications that come forward during the research process (Johnson and Duberley, 2000; Alvesson, Hardy and Harley, 2008). Therefore, induction in research has gained a firm foothold. When you take the relationship between theory and empirical research as inductive, you follow the logic of proceeding from empirical research to theoretical results.

In other words, the research process develops, starting from empirical materials, not from theoretical propositions.

Abduction

These two 'ideal types' of research logic or traditions, deduction and induction, seldom exist as clear-cut alternatives. Many researchers use both induction and deduction in different phases of their study, which means that you move iteratively between these two during a research process. Some research methods books offer abduction as a way to combine deduction and induction in one research project. Abduction refers to the process of moving from the everyday descriptions and meanings given by people, to categories and concepts that create the basis of an understanding or an explanation of the phenomenon described.

Abduction, as defined by philosopher Charles Sanders Peirce, can be considered as the logic of exploratory data analysis. For Peirce, abduction referred to the process of generating new ideas or hypotheses. According to his idea, deduction can be used to evaluate the hypotheses and the induction for justifying them with empirical data (Staat, 1993; Schwandt, 2001). In practice, abduction is difficult to dissect from the iterative work taking place in all empirical research. Some researchers also talk about the hermeneutic circle in much the same meaning and relate abduction closer to interpretivism. In general, no single model of scientific research is used, as the whole research process most often consists of various forms of reasoning.

This chapter has briefly illustrated the complexity of the conceptual grid of philosophy that embraces the knowledge of and about the different research methods. You do not always need to explicate your philosophical position and commitments in great detail, nor do you need to know the most advanced philosophical conceptual discussions when you write a thesis on business-related issues. However, it is most often useful to be knowledgeable of the key concepts and background assumptions of each method.

Finally, research methods and their use change and develop over time. It is important to keep in mind that, if the qualitative research approach that you choose is based on, and shows an interest in philosophical questions, there is no excuse for you to be ignorant about them.

KEY POINTS OF THE CHAPTER

The key concepts, their content and relationships between ontology, epistemology, methodology and method are not fixed, and there are different ways of understanding and relating to each other the philosophical and methodological commitments in knowledge production.

The main philosophical traditions and positions that are relevant for qualitative business research are positivism and its different forms, critical realism, interpretivism and constructionism, hermeneutics, postmodernism and post-structuralism.

The concepts of deduction, induction and abduction clarify the way and direction for arguments and knowledge claims. However, although they can seldom be found purely presented, almost all qualitative research uses all three logics.

Reflexivity is an increasingly important part of any research design and can be related to the basic premises of knowledge production, theories and methods used and to the results of the research. It valorizes the modes of knowledge production we sign for in our research.

FURTHER READING

The articles 'Reflecting on Reflexivity: Reflexive Textual Practices in Organization and Management Theory', by Alvesson, Hardy and Harley (2008), and 'Multiplicity and Reflexivity in Organizational Research', by Davison, Steyaert, Marti and Michels (2012) both discuss the ways in which researchers think about and discuss their understanding of their own research field.

Understanding Management Research by Johnson and Duberley (2000) gives a balanced overview of the different paradigmatic views and research traditions within contemporary management research.

EXERCISE 2.1

Analyzing the philosophical and methodological choices of qualitative research

The purpose of this exercise is to learn to understand the relevance of philosophical commitment in qualitative research and their connection to the overall logic of the research.

Choose one recently published doctoral thesis. Read through the thesis by focusing on its philosophical background and the logic of the research in particular.

Answer the following questions:

1. What is the philosophical background of this research? How clearly does the researcher explicate their position?
2. What is the logic of the research? How clearly does the researcher explicate the logic of the research? Does it follow inductive, deductive or abductive reasoning? In what ways?
3. Do you find the philosophical background of the study compatible with its overall logic? Why? Why not?

EXERCISE 2.2

Analyzing the relationship between the philosophical and methodological choices of qualitative research

The purpose of this exercise is to learn to recognize the connections between philosophical commitments and chosen qualitative research methods and methodology.

Choose one recently published doctoral thesis that is using qualitative methodology. Read through the thesis.

Answer the following questions:

1. How and in what ways is the philosophical positioning of the qualitative approach and methodology chosen in the research shown in the dissertation?
2. Elaborate and explicate the connections between the philosophical concepts used and the methodology chosen.

3

RESEARCH DESIGN AND PROCESS

This chapter will provide information on:

- why research planning is so important
- what elements are needed in research design
- how to select the research topic, research question(s) and how to get started
- the role of theories and philosophies in your research project
- what linearity and circularity mean in the research process
- how to plan time use in the qualitative research process.

IMPORTANCE OF PLANNING

When planning your research project, you often start with the idea of the research topic that you have become interested in. Finding your research topic is important, but equally important is to sketch out the whole research design, which consists of the planning of your whole research project. You will need to think in several dimensions in relation to the research process before starting the actual research.

Research planning includes several decisions ranging from the selection of the topic for your research and drafting the work plan – that is, 'how to do things and in what order' – to planning the data analysis and writing phases. Research design also includes the basic ideas and the viewpoints for the theoretical framework of your project, the rough time plan for the whole project and for the different parts of it, the modes of data collection you might have available, and method choices you have available, given the research question(s), framework and the data you plan to collect. According to Yin (2014), you need to think logically through your rough research idea, outline the plan and think about the structure of inquiry for fulfilling that plan. When writing the research design, you are already getting started with the research and developing your rough research idea further (Silverman, 2013). A research plan helps you to think ahead, even if the actual research would not always follow the plan originally sketched.

Mixing together the ideas of the research design and the research method is a common occurrence, resulting in a certain amount of confusion; the simplistic division between qualitative and quantitative research that is sometimes presented as a decisive division between research types is perhaps to blame for that confusion. Many research methods present case studies, for example, that are only in relation to participant observation, and questionnaires that are only in relation to comparative cross-sectional surveys, even if different methods of data collection can be used variably with different types of research design.

What, then, does research design mean? De Vaus (2001: 16) states that research design refers to the structure of an enquiry. We need to identify the possible types of data and evidence needed for answering our research question(s) convincingly. This means that we do not only collect data or use theories that support our views and are in favour of our beliefs, but we also open up the possibility for various alternative ways of answering our research question. In practice, this means that different data collection types and methods can be applied in a variety of research design types, even if you should be aware that some methods are more used, or subscribe more closely to specific types of design. Therefore, you should not decide the method you aim to use in your study before you have developed your rough research idea further.

ELEMENTS OF THE RESEARCH DESIGN

Qualitative research does not usually follow a tightly woven plan. Owing to their philosophical and methodological commitments, most qualitative research designs allow for deviations and surprises during the research process in data collection and analysis, and changes in the research settings during the process. Even if the research design were not to be followed in the actual process of research, it is helpful for the process to recognize some key elements that should be planned beforehand. You will also need these elements of research design when you write your research proposal for your supervisor or for your sponsor or the funding body of your research.

Choosing your research area and identifying the research topic

The key guiding principle for you here should be 'researchability', that is, whether the idea you have for research is suitable and researchable or not. Often, a good test for researchability is to think whether the research topic can be studied empirically or not (De Vaus, 2001; Flick, 2002; Eriksson and Kovalainen, 2008), even if not all the research questions are empirical by nature. You may also be given a topic to research by your supervisor, but most often you should decide on the topic yourself. Sometimes an equally good criterion for your topic of choice is to think in terms of your own interests and priorities: you should have a genuine interest in the topic. A short literature review on any topic will also reveal to you something about the researchable nature of that topic: Is there already a vast amount of recent literature? Are there good journal articles available? Is the topic virtually unknown in the field of research? The research topic is the broad subject matter area that you are interested in; research question(s) define more precisely the issues you wish to explore in your project.

Formulating the research question(s)

After the topic selection, you may already have some ideas of the possible research questions in mind. Start with the purpose of the study; it does not have to be precise, but it is crucial to think through what kind of research you are doing. Why do you want to carry out the research? What is the purpose of your research and why is it worth doing? How will you explore the matters relating to your interest?

You can write down your ideas and then think them through: What type of research question(s) are you putting forward? You need to ask yourself, 'What type of question do I aim to answer in my research?' Is it a descriptive research question or an explanatory research question? The descriptive type of research question is suited to, for example, descriptive research designs, whereas the explanatory question type usually explores causes and/or consequences (e.g. 'the effects of mergers on income levels of middle management in banking'). Does the question you have in mind call for a longitudinal design, such as exploring or describing change or process over time (e.g. 'the change in organizational culture after mergers and acquisitions')? Or is it about a cross-sectional design that calls for descriptive analysis, such as in the case of market research, 'what types of people consume genetically modified food'?

It is important to keep in mind that the research problems and research questions drive your whole research project, and the choice of methods and theoretical frame. Initially, with a rough research idea or research topic, you start to reorganize your research topic into researchable question(s), and through literature reading you might refine and frame the original idea into more precise research question(s). This process is often iterative by nature.

Choice of appropriate method/s

The research method you choose should be appropriately relevant for answering the research question(s) you have formulated earlier. It is thus the research question that 'dictates' the choice of methods and the type of research setting, and not the other way round. In each chapter of this book you will find examples and arguments for each method. The guiding principle in choosing the method is the research question and its focus, but methods are also closely attached to different theories and theoretical ideas about research; therefore, weighing alternative methods in your research project can become important and should be related to the theoretical aspects of your research project.

Throughout this book, when reading different methods chapters, you will notice that methods are not developed or used in a vacuum in qualitative research. All research methods are loosely or closely interwoven into theoretical underpinnings of methodologies such as epistemological and ontological assumptions, which were discussed in the previous chapter. No method is thus a separate or mechanically added entity in a research project, but it should be closely related to the research question, the data acquired and the theoretical frame used in the project.

There are big differences between the various approaches in qualitative methodology, and the various approaches differ from each other in the way the relationship between the qualitative data, method, methodology and relation to theory in qualitative research is designed, and in the relational emphasis of these elements. The differences in the ways the relationship between data, method and theory are understood in the research show the vast variety of ways for doing qualitative analysis and research, and this is also visible within business research. These differences stem from epistemological differences between the various approaches that explain the differing emphases given in research. Epistemic differences are not always visible in research settings, therefore they cannot always be directly addressed.

In research settings, it is seldom sufficient to inform the reader that you are conducting qualitative research; it is more important to tell them about what kind of qualitative research you are doing. The importance of relating the details, materials, methodical tools and the ways you intend to use them gets more emphasis the more informed you become with the qualitative research methods. This is especially true with rather 'rigid' and rule-driven method approaches, such as the grounded theory approach, but is even more important in other approaches, where the rules regarding the knowing and knowledge production are not so clear.

Choice and role of appropriate theories

The correct choice of appropriate methods for research is crucial, as is the choice of the appropriate theories. How, then, can you be sure of the suitability of the choices? First of all, you need to think through your research question: Is it researchable empirically? Is it possible to obtain empirical data for solving your research question? Is it too wide or too narrow? These are questions you will need to think and rethink throughout your research process, as you might need to reformulate, change the wording in the question, etc. Therefore, it is good to start writing down the possible theoretical linkages that might help you in finding the answers for your research question(s).

Second, you need to think of your research question in terms of methods: your research interest and research question(s) should be determining factors for choosing a method, not the other way round. Sometimes, students choose a qualitative method research project for the wrong reasons. The research question they put forward calls for a quantitative research design. One example of such a research interest area and formulation of a research question that would call for, for example, a cross-sectional large survey research in several countries is, 'The prevalence of business start-ups in the service sector middle management in the UK, Finland and Germany'. Cross-sectional research design is possible in qualitative research, for example, through qualitative interviews or focus group analysis, but for this example you might need to rephrase the research topic, such as: 'starting your own business as a service-sector middle manager'. You would be able to do comparative studies and compare cases from three different countries, but would need to think hard why the country comparisons would be needed and in what ways you would take the country dimension into account in your research.

The role of theories in qualitative research is not one-dimensional or as predictable as in logico-hypothetical research, where theories are used for the purpose of hypothesis testing. The choice and use of theories in your work should be guided through your research purpose and research questions. The philosophical underpinnings of your research approach, as discussed previously in Chapter 2, might also have relevance for the theories you choose for your research and the ways you will use them. It is important to remember also that not all theories and approaches in the field of business research are compatible with the basic assumptions and tenets of every different epistemological approach.

Later on in this chapter you will learn about the circularity of the research process, where the role and place for theory in the research process emerges several times during the research process: you begin with your research idea or topic, review the theoretical literature and gather theoretical concepts that might be relevant in finding the answer, then you reconsider and redefine your idea, revisit your research design and re-examine your theoretical ideas, revisit the literature, and perhaps even redefine your research question(s) in accordance with your research idea. The circularity, or deepening spiral nature, of the qualitative research project is quite clear from this description: you can start with a rough idea, develop it through literature consultation and turn it into a researchable question which can shift and change during the research process.

Design of data collection

Research data can consist of a variety of empirical data, and research design also means designing the gathering of that data: what types of data, what ways to gather, how to gain access, how to document, how to plan the analysis, etc. Questions you need to think through concern the recording of data and in which situations to record, for example, will you be using a research diary throughout the entire research project or only during data collection? Will you make field notes or will you rely on your recorded, transcribed materials? Composition of data collection can also cover a variety of different designs, depending on the different data sets and materials you might be using in your research project.

As we mentioned in Chapter 1, the complexities involved in method selection and the vast amount of philosophical thinking that lies behind the methods lead us to a situation where we usually see methods at the same time as both practical tools for the analysis of the empirical data and frameworks for engaging with empirical analysis of data. This way of seeing methods is typical for qualitative approaches in social sciences and in business research. Even if we can disseminate the data-gathering and data analyzing processes from each other, they very often are closely related and interwoven with each other.

Qualitative research does not rely on unified theoretical and methodological concepts: a variety of different theories, methods and methodological thinking are possible in qualitative research, as you will notice when reading through the methods chapters in this book. However, there are some elements that are common to all qualitative research. One unifying element in the research process is reflexivity: you should view your part in knowledge production as an important one, and not exclude it from the research process or reporting. This means in practice that researchers are integrally part of the research process, not excluded from it as in logico-deductive analysis. The subjectivities of the researcher and of those who are studied are part of the interpretation, and documented in research diaries and protocols (e.g. Flick, 2007; Silverman, 2013; Creswell, 2014).

You may also need to think about your research topic in terms of originality. Will it be the topic of your research that is original, will it be carrying out empirical work that has not been done before, or will it be looking at areas that have not been looked at in your discipline before? There are multiple ways of being original: through ideas, data, methods, interpretations, or knowledge produced. You may also need to think of the different audiences for your research project, as they have their own conventions and styles (Box 3.1). We will discuss the different audiences and writing styles in more detail in Chapter 21.

BOX 3.1

Procedure for the research process

Steps to be taken in the research process after the initial project formulation:

- entry negotiations to data resources;
- entering the field and collecting data;
- analysis and interpretation of data;
- writing up the empirical results;
- writing up the literature review.

For most qualitative research projects in business studies, it is organizations, companies and corporations that are the sources and sites for research questions and for empirical data. It is far more crucial for qualitative research to negotiate and gain access to the field than it is in a quantitative research project. Participant observations, open interviews, focus groups and case studies require methodically either close or intense contact, or acquired access to the organization, institution, company or group in question. Securing collaboration and informed consent to participate in the research project is one of the challenges that the qualitative researcher faces when gathering data. Access to institutions such as companies can be highly problematic, as (from the company's point of view) the research consumes employees' time and can even pose safety problems in many ways, ranging from industrial health-and-safety regulations (case studies at industrial plants) to fears of industrial espionage and leaks of information. These questions will be discussed in detail further in Chapter 6, Ethics in Research.

The plan for analyzing and interpreting the research materials needs to go hand in hand with the method choices you will make and the research design of your study in general. Forthcoming chapters in this book will discuss in detail what ways to analyze materials and the appropriateness of the different methods. The form and design of any gathering of research materials needs to be cross-checked with the method and with the theoretical background of your study (Flick, 2007). Here we only take up the interrelatedness of writing up the empirical results and theoretical views, as Chapter 21 will deal with the general and specific issues of writing up qualitative research. You should not think of them as two separate issues and fields, but see qualitative research, the different parts of research design, as one interrelated process.

CIRCULARITY OF THE RESEARCH PROCESS

As mentioned earlier, in practice the research process is rarely clear cut, straightforward and linear. This is what makes research so exciting; you learn new things along the way. From the moment you start thinking about your research project, it is rare that you would be able to develop it directly into a straightforward research report, without correcting, revising or changing parts of the work, even changing your originally chosen methods, and finally, revising and correcting the original research question(s) and formulations, when writing up the final version of your project. The possibility of revisiting the research plan and reformulating the research design is one of the strengths of qualitative research.

Instead of a linear model of research, a more realistic picture of the research process is that of a circular process, where it is almost necessary to move back and forth during the different phases in the research process. The research process has many elements and tenets, as introduced earlier, ranging from formulating the research field, focusing on interesting themes or ideas, gradually defining the research problem and finding the right and precise enough expression for the research question(s), to empirical data collection after the entrance to the field, method selection, analysis, and writing up the results and literature review so that writing up the research report, be it a Master's or PhD thesis, shows your work, knowledge and skills.

Traditionally, and even today, students learn about research, and the planning and fulfilling of it, as if a research project were a linear process. This way of thinking about research relies heavily on the hypothetic–deductive idea of doing research. According to the hypothetic–deductive model, the researcher starts the research by building up a theoretical model based on the literature, previous studies on the subject and theoretical reading, where several relationships, relations and conditions might exist in the data. This modelling is based on earlier research and theoretical literature alone. The modelling usually leads to hypothesis setting, which is then operationalized and tested against empirical data gathered for the purpose through surveys or, for example, statistics. The empirical data are analyzed and looked at through the modelling developed earlier in the research process, and often with the help of hypotheses, where variable relations, causalities and effects are important. After the analysis, the research report writing process is relatively straightforward, even if small corrections in the model usually result from the analysis of empirical materials. Causes and effects, and simple or complex causal propositions, are usually the ways to analyze the data, especially when explanatory research design is in question (De Vaus, 2001). After the survey questionnaire is designed and completed, the corrective measures are not usually easy to make, and the iterative nature of the research process is missing.

Qualitative research only partially, and most often poorly, matches with the traditional linear logic of research as described above. Qualitative research settings do not operate on preset modelling on variables and their mutual correlational or causal relationships, but more on constant circularity and linking empirical analysis to a flexible literature review and theories. The relevance of empirical material to researched questions, rather than the existence of relationships in the earlier literature, is crucial. The way the researcher in qualitative research works their way through the empirical material is not based on preset existing connections between variables, but by taking into account not only the focus of the study, but also the context of the study. This inevitably increases its complexity.

Part of the circularity of the research process is the previously mentioned process of reflexivity: owing to the circularity of the research process, the researcher in qualitative research is compelled to reflect the research process as a whole and relate each step to previous ones, as they are not predetermined as happens in a linear research model. More specifically, reflexivity is especially related to the ways of doing fieldwork: researchers reflect their own biases, prejudices and position in relation to the researched object. More generally, reflexivity relates to interpretations made during the research process, positions taken, etc. Reflexivity is a means for critically inspecting the whole of the research process; and understood in this way, reflexivity is an important procedure for establishing the validity of the accounts of the phenomena studied (e.g. Schwandt, 2001). The different tenets in the issue of validity will be discussed in more detail in Chapter 22.

The circularity of the research process can also be related to the so-called 'hermeneutic circle'. The hermeneutic circle refers to the methodological process of understanding, constructing and deepening a meaning in the interpretative process during research activities. The prior knowledge is interpreted by the researcher and in that process the tradition (prior knowledge) can be modified and changed. The hermeneutic circle (originally by Schleiermacher and developed in the works of Heidegger and Husserl) is close to the German verstehende sociology, where the centrality of the language and meaning becomes important. In hermeneutics, objects are not fixed or given; rather, they are interpreted, contingent things. The process of interpretation involves an entering into the hermeneutic circle. The hermeneutic circle is thus not strictly taken as a method for uncovering meaning, but a way of conceptualizing understanding and the process of interpretation in which we as researchers participate and where we are situated. When we interpret, it is not without our own gender, experiences, culture and expectations. We interpret things, not in vacuum, but in a hermeneutic process. Can a researcher start with research and data gathering without any prior knowledge or literature review? The roles of and positions given to literature and theory are not so determined in qualitative research as they are in a logico-deductive mode: prior knowledge is also needed in qualitative research, but the prior knowledge could be regarded as prior understanding of, and the perspective on, the object being studied (Flick, 2007). These preliminary versions of knowledge then become further elaborated during the research process, through learning, analyzing and reading of materials. This is the hermeneutic circle mentioned earlier: as the researcher's knowledge base grows and changes, so also, therefore, does their position towards prior knowledge change. The process of working towards the meaningful interpretation and answering of the research question allows for corrective measures to be taken into account during the iterative research process.

TIME AND THE QUALITATIVE RESEARCH PROCESS

All research projects have a specific time span and limitations in terms of the maximum number of months or years they can take. All research projects have their beginning and their end. Therefore, it is important to learn to plan your project effectively in terms of the time that the different research phases require (Box 3.2). The research design and research plan also give you indications of the time frame needed for different activities: the time plan should be an integral part of your research design. Try to be realistic from the day you start planning your project. What type of research project are you aiming for? Getting access to texts in libraries is much less time consuming than trying to get access to executive CEOs of large companies and reserving interview time with them. Analysis of complex data, such as video and audio tapes of focus groups, needs more time to be allocated for transcriptions, coding and analyzing than data gained from structured interviews with individuals.

--------------------------------- BOX **3.2** ---------------------------------

Time use in the research project

The time plan for the research project should include the following elements:

Time for reading theories, research reports, and articles prior to gathering materials, in order to learn to know the field and find the focus for the research project. This reading time is needed throughout your research project on several occasions, not just at the beginning.

Time for research design, learning to develop, see new details as part of the whole, and think through the various detailed aspects and parts of your research project. This design time is also something that you need to reserve throughout your project in order to fit bits and pieces together.

Time for data gathering. This part could consist of, among others, the planning phase, access-negotiation phase, data-gathering phase, etc. This data-gathering time needs to cover all the time you need from initial contacts with your target organization, to gathering, sorting out, filling in, and adding new materials into your data.

Time for the data analysis. Before the analysis, you need to have a plan for the analysis that should be in relation to your research question(s). Do not underestimate the time required by the analysis phase. Sometimes, students think that the analysis and writing can go rather smoothly hand in hand, and even take place simultaneously, and the final version of the thesis is done while analyzing the materials. Most often this is not the case, so do reserve enough time for the analysis phase.

Time for writing up your report. Most often, with good planning and design, the writing process goes smoothly, even if you need to find your own style. Sometimes, though, you might find it necessary to turn the design of the whole work upside down, to make your argument(s) work better in the report. Thinking through the structure of the thesis and the way to report your findings and results takes time and is an iterative process throughout the research project. We will discuss the writing process in more detail in Chapter 21.

Time for dissemination/defence/inspection/re-entering the field. Depending on your project, you might need to reserve time for your viva defence, or inspection of your work, for the media when reporting your results, or to the community from where you have gathered your research materials. All these different activities are surprisingly time consuming.

You should start your research project by planning a preliminary timetable and discussing it with your supervisor. It is important that both of you have a similar kind of time frame in mind for your research. Remember that time schedules also need revisions during the research process. It is part of research design. When you face delays in your data gathering or reporting, do let your supervisor know about the delay and the reasons for it well in good time.

The scope and size of your research project inevitably has an effect on the time your project will need. Here, you need to think once again about the time and resources available and whether you can manage your research project. You might need to discuss with your supervisor about the time span: How much time do you have available for your project? What happens if you face delays in the data-gathering or analysis phase? Depending on time, you might need to limit the extent of data collection or find alternative solutions. Therefore, research design is important, as you can already think through the possible alternative routes to your destination beforehand. Very often time is also money, and the costs of research create alternative costs: you might need to postpone participation with other courses due to exceeding your time frame with your research project, etc. Therefore, limitations on your time frame underline the importance of planning ahead on paper in your research design, and scheduling different activities in your research project.

KEY POINTS OF THE CHAPTER

Research design is not just the research plan of the empirical part of the study; rather, it consists of multi-layered decisions and issues. Research design covers all issues from theoretical reading and the methodological choices, to the empirical data-gathering, analysis and writing processes. It is useful to plan your research project properly, as it gets easier for you to see details and their relation to the whole project.

The research process progresses most often through a circular process, not according to a linear model. Revising and revisiting your original ideas and thoughts, revisiting your plan and reading lists, and rewriting your chapters is an essential part of this circularity.

Time use is most often the most important frame for your project: all projects have a beginning and an end. Plan the different phases and different tasks of your project realistically from the outset. Find out about the time that the different data-gathering processes demand and plan your work time accordingly. You also need to estimate how much time the analysis of the data and writing up of the research results may take, in order to plan your time efficiently.

FURTHER READING

The book by Silverman (2013) *Doing Qualitative Research*, 4th edition, takes you through the different stages in the research process hand in hand with lots of examples.

Brewerton and Millward's (2009) *Organizational Research Methods* helps you in planning the research process in any organizational and business research setting.

EXERCISE 3.1

Finding a research question with a research design

Come up with a research topic that is close to your own research interests or disciplinary field that you are interested in. The research topic can also relate to an actual phenomenon in businesses or organizations. Write down as many different research questions that you can think of from that one research topic in a short time. What kinds of research designs would these different research questions require?

EXERCISE 3.2

Collaborative work for finding research questions

Alternatively, you can do this exercise with your research fellow or colleague: come up with one joint research topic and then separately write down as many research questions as you can and develop a research design for them. Discuss your results and find out how many similarities and differences you come up with in your responses. The collective form of this exercise gives you an idea of how many different kinds of research questions can be found, and how differently they can be designed into a research plan.

RESEARCH QUESTIONS AND LITERATURE REVIEW

This chapter will provide information on:

- the relevance of research questions in qualitative business research
- how to formulate and refine various types of research questions
- how to use theory in qualitative business research
- where and how to search for prior knowledge on your research topic
- how to write a literature review and position your study in the wider field of research that you have chosen.

THE RELEVANCE OF THE RESEARCH QUESTIONS

Business research often starts with an interesting and up-to-date business-related topic or a practical business problem. In this way, real-life phenomena can very well be the starting point of a good qualitative business study project. However, merely describing up-to-date topics or solving practical business problems are not enough for the purposes of scholarly research. Research is about producing new knowledge and relating this to the body of existing scientific knowledge about the topic that you are studying. As scientific knowledge is related to theories and theoretical concepts, you will need to study them as part of your research project. You will also need to formulate some methods in your research.

The key to success in a qualitative business research project, however, is not the use of theoretical concepts and methods as such, but your ability to formulate and reformulate scientifically relevant research questions. This does not take place only once, at the beginning of the research, but preferably several times during the research process. It is not uncommon to redefine the research questions of a qualitative study at the very final stages of the research project, or when making the last writing round of a research report. The spiralling research model presented in Chapter 3 is helpful in understanding that research is an iterative process. This means that the back-and-forth movement between research ideas, theoretical concepts, research design, methods of data collection and analysis, as well as the findings, is constant.

Defining your research ideas and research questions

In qualitative studies, you often start with identifying topics of wider interest and then try to come up with one or two more specific questions related to this. Ideas for topics can easily be obtained from printed and social media; practical and academic business literature; your personal interests, hobbies and work experience; your supervisors, fellow students, friends and family members; and research projects made by other researchers. For instance, your topic could be related to ongoing debates about corporate finance, changes taking place in work life or innovation in service sector companies.

When you become more familiar with the wider field of interest that you have chosen, you can start thinking about more specific questions. These questions may concern issues such as what is common knowledge within the field and what seems to be unknown, what kinds of arguments are given in favour, and what against some developments, and what surprises and puzzles you on the basis of what you already know about the topic. Choosing a specific point of view for your study often helps to narrow down its focus and define preliminary research questions. Think about whether you are interested in the management point of view, or the point of view of the employees, for instance. How about a historical point of view on your topic or a micro-political point of view?

Later in this chapter we will discuss how to search for the literature on your topic and how to write about it. It is good to keep in mind that prior to making a systematic literature review you must formulate one or more research questions. Otherwise, you cannot choose the literature in a focused way and you end up reading and writing a little bit about this and that. However, even when defining your research interests, we find it particularly advisable to read several Master's theses or doctoral dissertations written by other students. This is because, most commonly, the first set of research questions that a novice researcher formulates are often too complex and difficult to study. Reading other students' finished work gives you some idea about what level of complexity is manageable and which research questions can lead to a completed and coherent study.

Once you have developed your preliminary research questions, you should not forget to reformulate and redefine them during the research process with the aim of reducing the width and complexity of your study (Box 4.1). When reformulating your research questions, you must make sure that you are able to answer them from the point of view that you have chosen and with the empirical data that you have collected. It is important to remember that, although they may not remain the same, research questions do also have great value in the early phases of the study. With their help you can set the boundaries on your research project, giving it a specific direction and increased coherence (e.g. Silverman, 2013).

--------- **BOX 4.1** ---------

Refining your research ideas and questions

When starting to work with your research topic and ideas, try out the following steps:

- Choose a wider area of interest (e.g. corporate finance, changes in work life, service innovation).
- Explore this wider area by reading research done by students (theses) and other researchers (scholarly articles, research books); talk to your supervisor and your fellow students about your interests.
- Write a short description or a mind map about your research ideas and their interlinkages.
- Narrow down your interest area by choosing a specific point of view (e.g. management point of view, employees' point of view, historical point of view) for your study.
- Do some further research from the specific point of view that you have chosen.
- Formulate one or more preliminary research questions for your study (see Exercise 4.1 for a practical example of how to do this).

The crucial aspect in defining even a preliminary research question is that it is workable, which means that the research question should not be too broad or too specific. Silverman (2013), adapting from Punch (1998: 49), writes that a workable research question must be answerable, interconnected, and substantively relevant. An answerable research question means that we can see what type of data are required to answer the questions and how the data can be obtained. For instance, will the data be obtainable through archives, observation, or through open interviews? An interconnected research question means that in the case of several research questions (or sub-questions), these questions are related to each other in a meaningful way. Relevance in substance concerning research questions means that the questions are interesting and topical or timely, and especially worthwhile of research (Silverman, 2013).

VARIOUS TYPES OF RESEARCH QUESTION

What, how, and why questions are all typical of qualitative business research (Box 4.2). 'What' questions are descriptive and focus on exploring and describing states, situations and processes. 'How' and 'why' questions focus on causes and consequences; in other words, they aim at answering or explaining something in qualitative terms. In many cases, it is useful to work through your research topic with all these questions. For instance, if you were interested in fast-growing business ventures, you could first ask: 'What does it mean to be a fast-growing business venture? What are fast-growing business ventures like?' When answering these questions, you would describe their profiles and characteristics. Then you could ask: 'How do fast growing business ventures operate? How do they grow?' Here, you would try to provide an understanding of the way fast-growing business ventures operate and grow. Finally, you could ask: 'Why do companies aim towards fast growth?' When answering this question, you would try to explain why companies aim towards fast growth (e.g. instead of moderate growth or not trying to grow).

BOX 4.2

Three types of research question

'What' questions generate descriptions about states, situations and processes. For example: What does growth mean? What does fast growth mean? What does a fast-growing company look like?

'How' questions provide understandings of how something takes place, works, or interacts. For example: How does a fast growing company operate? How does it maintain its growth?

'Why' questions offer explanations for states, situations and processes. For example: Why do companies aim at fast growth?

You can also differentiate between research questions that are interested in outcomes and those that are interested in processes. Those research questions that are concerned with outcomes focus on entities as they are at a specific moment. The process-related questions are concerned with how these entities evolve or change over time. For instance, you can ask: 'What is the strategy of the organization?' This is a research question concerned with a specific entity (the strategy) with an interest in how the entity came about. But you could also ask: 'How has the strategy of the organization evolved during the last 10 years?' This is a processual question, which focuses not so much on the strategy itself, but on how the strategy came about. In addition to these types of research questions, business research projects may be based on generative research questions, the purpose of which is to discover and refine a number of new research questions. The objective of these new research questions is then to 'stimulate the line of investigation in profitable directions' (Strauss, 1987: 22).

If you find it difficult to focus and narrow down your research interests, then it can be helpful to generate a thesis statement for a research project. The thesis statement defines the core purpose of your study by a proposition or an argument that clearly indicates the point of the academic discussion that you aim to develop. For example, your thesis statement could argue that: 'Young start-up leaders empower their personnel.' This focuses your study on leadership and empowerment issues in start-up companies.

The thesis statement is particularly helpful in distilling the main point of your research into one or two sentences. In the beginning of your research project, the thesis statement helps you to focus your research efforts, and in the later stages it can be used to organize the ideas, materials and results that you are presenting. A good thesis statement is rather specific, as it takes a stand and justifies further discussion. It states what your research will be about and enables you to keep your study focused. A good thesis statement expresses, however, only one main idea for your research. If your thesis statement expresses several ideas, then you most probably are still developing the topic of your study.

THE USE OF THEORY AND THEORETICAL CONCEPTS

Although business research emphasizes practical business problems, you must incorporate into the study some theoretical ideas and concepts. In qualitative research this may happen at the beginning of the study or at later stages. In theory-driven research you pay a lot of attention to theoretical concepts right at the beginning of the study. In data-driven research you build the relationship between theoretical concepts and your data at later stages of the project. It is often helpful to make a distinction between theory (theoretical ideas and concepts) and prior research (studies dealing with empirical data). Both of these are needed in order to focus and frame your research project and to locate your research into a wider field of interest.

How theory directs research

There are two differing views about the role and position of theory in business research. The first view emphasizes the relevance of 'grand' theory, which is both consistent and stable and widely known and adopted among researchers. This view of theory is based on the idea that the main purpose of empirical research is to test existing theory and join in to the process of confirming and redefining it. This type of theory development takes place through small steps and setting of hypotheses and propositions.

The other conception of theory emphasizes the social nature of all scientific activity. Here, theory is defined in a more flexible way; it consists of preliminary and changing assumptions that direct the way of doing research. This understanding of theory opens up possibilities for gradual change, an influx of ideas, and the adoption of new ingredients in the construction of theory. This conception of theory suggests that theory need not be tested through hypothesis because it is constantly being challenged through the iterative nature of the research process. From this point of view, theory can be understood as a collection of ideas under ongoing redefinition instead of stable and rigid testable formalizations.

In qualitative business research, both conceptions of theory are valid. However, because qualitative research so often relies on a constant and close interplay between empirical data, interpretation and theory, the latter idea of theory as a collection of ideas in flux is often preferred. This conception of theory also gives you more freedom in terms of writing your theoretical framework and working your way through the connection between theories, concepts and methods.

Various ways of using theory

The use of theory differs within different qualitative research approaches, which we introduce in Part III of this book. The continuum idea, as used by Creswell (2012), offers one way of thinking about the use of theory in qualitative research. Creswell locates Grounded Theory research at one end of the continuum, because it aims at generating theory and theoretical concepts with the help of empirical research. He locates phenomenology and ethnography at the other end of the continuum because they always start with a theoretical commitment. Case studies and biographies are situated in the middle of the continuum because they rely on existing theory, using it in various ways at different stages of the research process.

Overall, in qualitative research, the question of how to use theory is often less clear during the first phases of the study compared with quantitative research. Theory often emerges through induction (see Chapter 2) during the phases of data collection, analysis and writing. Because of the interactive and iterative relationship between theory, method and data, the theory chapters of a qualitative business study (if there are any separate chapters) often get their final form after the data have been analyzed and the data and methods chapters written.

POSITIONING THE STUDY THROUGH LITERATURE

Novice researchers sometimes think that making a qualitative research project is an excuse to be ignorant about what other researchers have said about the issues under study. Some may even think that, when making a qualitative study, you do not need to use theoretical concepts to inform your study. This is not true. For any researcher, it is impossible to say anything of scholarly interest if you do not relate your findings, ideas and conclusions to what was already known prior to your study.

At some point of your research project, you must read yourself into the research field that you are interested in. Traditionally, this is done at the beginning of the research project, but in practice you should read other's work throughout your research process, because the idea is to clarify and sharpen your research questions during the research process. Therefore, you should reserve enough time during various phases of your research project. Theories, theoretical concepts, and research findings that you read about will assist you with positioning your study in relation to prior knowledge. This positioning takes place with the help of prior research and through the development of your own research questions.

THE RELEVANCE OF A LITERATURE REVIEW

The terms 'research literature' or just 'literature' refer to the body of research, both theoretical and empirical, that you must consult in order to develop, understand, investigate and evaluate your research ideas and the finished product. This literature is published in books, scholarly journals, electronic databases, and other outlets and you can have access to it through the library and the Internet.

In order to generate, develop and refine your research idea, you need to know what other researchers have written about the topic of your research project. Additionally, to be able to perform good research, you must be aware of the current knowledge in your topic area. Often, you are also required to demonstrate an ability to evaluate theoretical approaches and other researchers' empirical studies critically. This means that you have to search for and read a certain amount of research literature during your research process. This applies to all qualitative business research.

A literature review is often a separate chapter in the research report, but in qualitative research it does not need to be reported in this way. Wolcott (2009), an ethnographer giving practical advice on how to write qualitative research, recommends presenting prior research in interaction, or in dialogue, with your own research. In other words, the literature review can also be reported in smaller pieces in several chapters of your research report. Whatever choice you make in reporting prior research, it can be helpful to write a separate literature review at some point of your research project, just to clarify for yourself the main issues and viewpoints of prior research. If you do not report it in one chapter of your research report, you can use it as a knowledge base for several chapters.

Even when your aim is to pursue research through induction – developing theoretical ideas, questions and concepts from your empirical data – you must discuss your research in relation to other researchers' work. Furthermore, no research can start from scratch or without any prior theoretical or empirical knowledge. When working more inductively, you proceed through several cycles of reviewing the literature as your research questions become more specified. You can also pursue qualitative research through deduction, which means that you develop your research idea and questions directly from theories and prior research. In this case, it is extremely important to make a systematic literature search and an analysis of it before you start collecting any empirical data.

The purpose of a literature review

The purpose of a literature review is to explore, summarize, compare, and critically analyze what has been written by other researchers about the topic of your research (Box 4.3). In writing the literature review, the purpose is to explore what knowledge and ideas have been established on a topic, what approaches and viewpoints have been adopted, and what are their strengths and weaknesses. When you are writing a separate literature review, it is advisable to organize it into sections that identify research trends and present theoretical, empirical or methodological themes within the topical area of your study. However, it is good to bear in mind that an informative literature review should always be defined and guided by your research questions.

Sources for a literature review

Scholarly journal articles are excellent sources for the literature review. Research published in academic journals is peer reviewed for quality and appropriateness in relation to the purpose of the journal. Most academic journals are published in electronic form and they can be found in electronic databases. You can also find a good number of articles on the Internet and from Open Access journals. Professional magazines publish practically-oriented articles that are useful in generating research ideas, but they should not be used as sources of theoretical thinking and prior research results.

BOX 4.3

Characteristics of a good literature review

It deals with research that is relevant in relation to the research questions of your study.

It is organized around the research question(s) of your study.

It provides a summary, interpretation, evaluation and criticism of the literature.

It identifies areas of controversy and disagreement in the literature.

It helps in formulating new research questions for your study, or in refining those that you started with.

In addition to articles, research books provide very good references that you can study and include in your literature review. Textbooks on substantial issues are less likely to be useful because they are intended for teaching, not for research. However, they can offer a starting point from which to find more detailed sources. Master's theses and doctoral dissertations are useful sources. Many universities provide these in electronic form on their web pages. In addition, various types of research reports can provide a useful source of information, depending on your field of study.

Newspapers are intended for a general audience; therefore, the information they provide is of limited use for your literature review. Newspapers and professional magazines provide information on recent trends and discussions in economic life, or developments within specific industries and companies. In addition to scholarly articles that are provided for free on the Internet, it contains many other resources and a good number of various types of information. Compared with journal articles and scholarly books, this information has not been peer reviewed before publication. When using the Internet as a source for research results, you should be careful in critically checking the trustworthiness of the website.

In order to develop your own knowledge base about your research topic, it is important that you develop good referencing skills. These skills are needed throughout your research project. As soon as you find interesting research material, put the publication details into your own referencing archive, whether it be a notebook, note cards, computer text file, or a specific computer program such as Endnote. When considering what referencing system (i.e. in what form references are written in the reference list) you adopt in your research report, it is best to follow the advice given by your university. You can find details of the most common referencing systems (e.g. Harvard, Oxford, American Psychological Association (APA)) from the Internet.

Identifying key words

To be able to effectively search for the literature you need to generate 'key words' that are related to your research topic and research questions. Let us say that your preliminary research question is: 'How does organizational culture change within a merger process?' When doing the first rounds of literature search in the beginning of your study, you can use the words of your research question, such as 'organizational culture', 'merger' and 'change', as key words. The materials that you find will help you to familiarize yourself with the research field and the key words that other researchers use in this field. If you find one particularly relevant and recent article or research book on your topic, then you can find a long list of good references from this single source. This is why the best method for literature search is to start from the most recent sources and work backwards.

During the later stages of your study, you will probably need to perform a more refined literature search and use more specific key words, including ones that indicate the methodological choices that you are interested in. By now you might have focused your study on 'domestic mergers within the service sector' and your methodological alternatives to 'case studies' and 'narrative studies'. Using key words that connect these qualitative research approaches with your research topic produces a better defined list of references. However, you should not restrict your literature search only to qualitative research approaches. Even though you would be doing qualitative research, there might be plenty of relevant literature on your topic that has not used any qualitative methods.

Making a literature search

Two basic search strategies, identifying either key words or citations, help you in making a literature search. When using keywords, start with summarizing your research topic with one or two sentences. For instance, 'My research focuses on how institutional investors help small service companies to internationalize'. Then identify the most central elements that you have used in your summary. In our example these might be: 'help from institutional investors' and 'small internationalizing service company'. Then choose appropriate keywords for each element. For the first element 'help from institutional investors', you might use key words indicating different types of institutional investors in addition to the common words 'institutional investors'. These might include: 'bank', 'venture capitalist', 'business angel' combined with 'help' and 'contribution', for instance. For the second element 'small internationalizing service company', you might use key words such as 'small company', 'small business', 'service company' and 'internationalization'. Often, it is useful to include both common and scientific words, as this will increase the number of citations retrieved. When making subject searches, it is important to consider the relationships between the keywords, and use Boolean operators (AND, OR, and NOT) to connect them together.

The other strategy is to start searching for key citations, that is, references to earlier research. Starting with one recent good quality citation (an article or a book) a bibliography of research related to your topic can be easily created on the basis of their list of references. When searching for references from digital databases or from the Internet, the system may offer you other similar references or it may show you who has used a specific publication as a reference.

TWO WAYS OF DOING A LITERATURE REVIEW

Overall, in the literature review you should look for the key concepts, conclusions, theories and arguments that underlie research in your topic area. In addition, you need to describe how your study relates to previous theoretical and empirical research. The objective of the most simple literature review is to summarize the literatures that you intend to use in your research project and provide a short description of major research projects to which you are referring. Even when compiling a summary of the literature, you must decide what to take in and what to leave out. Consider carefully which ideas or pieces of information are important to your research, and which are less important and can be covered briefly or left out of your review.

In terms of advancing your research project, it is more helpful to make an evaluative and critical literature review than just a simple summary or a non-analytic description of the literature (Box 4.4). An evaluative and critical analysis of the literature includes comparing and contrasting the perspectives, viewpoints and arguments that other researchers have taken on your research topic and your research question. You should be thorough in analyzing particularly those issues in which researchers are in disagreement or present conflicting results. You can also describe exemplary studies and try to identify gaps in research approaches and questions. According to our experience, business students often forget to evaluate aspects of methodological choices that have been used in prior research. But methodological issues can be just as important as the substance. When analyzing methodological issues, you can already start to outline the methodology section of your own research project.

BOX **4.4**

Two types of literature review

A descriptive summary of prior research including theoretical approaches, concepts, methodologies and data used, and results presented:

- Provides short descriptions of major research projects and their results. Does not produce new knowledge, but compiles a body of existing knowledge and gaps in it.
- Can be very useful as a starting point of your research project, but is not the ideal way of developing your own research idea and the positioning of your study.

An evaluative, problematizing and critical analysis of prior research, which is built around your research idea, research questions and aims:

- Reorganizes and analyzes research approaches, theoretical concepts, methodologies and results of prior research.
- Produces new knowledge, which serves as the basis for focusing and positioning your study, as well as for generating and redefining research questions.

When reading the literature and preparing a literature review, it is important to keep the purpose of your own research tightly in mind. Do not let the interesting, strong and sophisticated arguments distract you from your own research agenda. Furthermore, before starting to read, take a few moments to consider exactly what it is you are expecting to find from your sources. Previewing or pre-reading can help you to focus your thoughts. Skim the headings and the abstracts of the source, or look at the first line of each paragraph and the conclusions and try to evaluate if the source is useful.

Finally, it is extremely enlightening to learn how to analyze and evaluate the rhetoric used in the literature. This means, for instance, that you pay attention to how evidence is presented through argumentation and how the truth value of presumptions and results is constructed in the text. This may be difficult when you first start reading and writing, but should become easier the more you investigate the research in your topic area. However, being critical towards other researchers' ideas, arguments and results is not the same as being disrespectful. Therefore, remember to be fair when detaching the research of others and when presenting them. Chapter 6 on research ethics and Chapter 21 on writing discuss some issues concerning this in more detail.

KEY POINTS OF THE CHAPTER

Research questions are essential in focusing and framing a qualitative business study right from the start, but they are most often specified, narrowed down and sharpened during the entire research process.

Your research must be linked to theory and theoretical concepts, and you need to position your study in relation to prior research. This is why you must know what other researchers have written about the same issues.

At some point of your research project, you will need to perform a systematic literature search and write about the literature in one way or another. An evaluative and critical literature review is more helpful than a simple summary of prior research.

FURTHER READING

Ridley's (2012) book *The Literature Review: A Step-by-Step Guide for Students* is a practical and reader-friendly presentation of how to write your literature review.

Jesson's (2011) book *Doing Your Literature Review: Traditional and Systematic Techniques* discusses several alternative ways of comprising the literature review.

EXERCISE 4.1

Producing and refining research questions

This exercise uses free association and writing techniques to produce research questions and redefine them. You can repeat the process as many times as you find useful.

Choose a topic area of interest, for example, gendered business networks, changes in consumer culture or the development of accounting practices.

Use ten minutes to write down as many questions concerning your area of interest as you can think of. Do not evaluate the questions, but write them down in their spontaneous form.

Read the list of questions that you have produced and pick out the most exciting and interesting one.

Try to answer the question that you found to be most interesting on the basis of what you already know about the issue. Use 15 minutes to do this.

Use your answer to redefine the question that you started with and produce new ones related to it.

EXERCISE 4.2

Evaluating preliminary research questions

The purpose of this exercise is to learn how you can evaluate your research questions at the beginning of the research process. Choose a topic and formulate two or three research questions that you might be interested in studying. Then work through the following questions to evaluate the suitability and workability of these research questions.

Do your research questions deal with an issue that will sustain your interest throughout the research process?

Are the questions researchable in terms of theoretical knowledge, empirical data and methods, and the resources that you have in your project?

What theoretical knowledge, empirical data and research methods do you need to be able to answer these research questions?

Is the scope of the knowledge and data reasonable to you?

Given the nature of the theoretical knowledge and empirical data that you will need, is your question too broad, too narrow, or suitable for the aims of your research project, your resources, and your timetables?

What data sources will provide the information that you will need to be able to answer your research questions (e.g. academic journals, books, Internet resources, documents, people)?

Can you access all these sources with reasonable effort?

Can you think of a suitable methodology and methods that you can use to study your research questions?

Given all the answers to the above questions, do you find your research questions suitable and workable enough to produce good quality research? If not, what should you do next?

––––––––––––––––––––––––– EXERCISE **4.3** –––––––––––––––––

Analyzing literature reviews

The purpose of this exercise is to learn to understand how various types of literature reviews are composed. Also, the exercise develops your ability to identify good quality literature reviews.

Search for three to five high quality scholarly articles in your research area, which include a review of prior research. This is a section that might be titled 'Prior research', 'Theoretical starting points', 'Theoretical background', or similar. The section is sometimes part of the Introduction, but most often it is the second section of the article. Read through the articles concentrating on the literature review. Then work through the following questions to evaluate the style and quality of the literature review.

How does the author set the goals for the literature review?

Is the review descriptive or evaluative and critical?

How comprehensive is the review?

How up-to-date is the review?

Is some relevant research missing from the review?

What are the results and conclusions from the review?

In what way does the author plan to use the review in her own research?

Given all the answers to the above questions, do you find that the literature review is well done and of good quality? Why is it of good quality or why is it not? Give groundings for your conclusions.

You can do the same exercise by using finished master's or doctoral theses.

5

ACCESS AND RELATIONSHIPS

This chapter will give you information on:

- how to identify organizations and individuals as research participants
- how to gain access to organizations
- how to gain access to individuals
- how to make research agreements
- how to develop the researcher-participant relationship.

IDENTIFYING RESEARCH PARTICIPANTS

Qualitative business researchers often use people as sources of information. If you do not rely primarily on existing research materials (e.g. documents, archives, interviews made by others), then you will need to identify which organizations, groups and individuals could participate in your study. How can you do this?

As qualitative research does not aim at statistical generalization, specific sampling methods that are designed for this purpose are not required. Identifying research participants for qualitative research is purposeful rather than representative and random, as is the case in quantitative studies.

Thus, instead of using sophisticated sampling methods, appropriateness of the data and access to them are central issues. The aim is to have access to rich data, which enables fine-grained and in-depth analyses as well as provides an opportunity to learn from the phenomena under study.

Despite some challenges described later, we find it worthwhile to consider if you can conduct your research in an organization and with people with whom you are already familiar, or at least have some direct or indirect contact. Therefore, you should consider approaching an organization with which you have had an internship or a work contract, for instance. Or think about organizations that have given visiting lectures on your courses. Also, it may be a good idea to use the contacts of your supervisor and your university department if they allow it. Your topic may, however, require access to organizations and individuals as yet unfamiliar to you. For example, if you want to make an ethnographic research of women-controlled ethnic businesses, then the first thing you need to do is to figure out how to identify suitable companies for your study. Depending on your goals, finding just one suitable company may be sufficient. When you need more than one participant, then snowball, chain and network sampling techniques (see e.g. Patton, 2014) are useful. To put it briefly, this means that you interview one person (e.g. one female CEO of an ethnic business company) who knows others that could become participants in your study. As part of your interview, you can ask the first participant to name others that you could include in your study.

Depending on your goals, you may also want to identify a larger population of organizations or people in order to make a purposeful sampling of either unique (in which the phenomenon under study is rare), or representative cases (in which the phenomenon under study is very common), for instance. For doing this, you can use several sources of information, such as company directories, web pages, industrial associations, and business experts. If you are lucky, you can find a list of organizations or individuals to choose from. If not, you may need to combine several of these sources to produce a list of organizations.

ACCESSING ORGANIZATIONS

Business research typically involves gaining access to organizations. Issues of access are highly important in qualitative business studies because the quality of access has a direct effect on the results of the study (Feldman, Bell and Berger, 2003). After making initial contact with the organization you will often need to maintain this contact during the whole research project. Therefore, instead of treating contact as a one-time event, taking place at the beginning of your study, it is important to consider it as a continuous process that may extend to the final stages of your research (Gummesson, 2000).

Organizations as gatekeepers of research

Business research projects often require the permission of an organization or a central person in that organization (e.g. the CEO) for the collection of empirical data. A gatekeeper, whether an organization or a person, has the power to allow or deny access to data.

This means that it is gatekeepers who will decide if data can be collected and on what terms this can take place. Therefore, selling your research idea to the gatekeeper is crucial. Among other things, your success in selling your ideas will depend on how understandable your research aims are for the gatekeepers.

Particularly large business companies recognize their power as the gatekeepers of business research. Global companies, such as Starbuck's, Audi and Samsung, have their own policies towards research, and any proposals from individual researchers most probably need to accommodate these. Even smaller companies may wish to influence the aims and structure of your research project, the methods that are used, the form of reporting the study, and whether it will be publicly available for others to read. From the researcher's point of view, doing research with business companies can require compromises between what is ideal and what is possible.

Common concerns

When thinking about useful contact organizations, it is helpful to understand why organizations do or do not want to participate in research projects. Some of the common concerns of organizations are related to the confidentiality of the information concerning them. Business companies and business people can be very concerned about confidentiality of all information that has a link to their management, business operations or future plans.

When negotiating access you must have a clear idea about how you will safeguard the confidentiality of the data. Safeguarding may involve, for instance, keeping the tapes in a safe place for a certain period of time, or destroying the tapes after the study has been finished. These issues are discussed in detail in Chapter 6.

Using pseudonyms for people and organizations in publications and reports is also safeguarding them. Using pseudonyms is common practice in business research, particularly when extracts of interviews or conversations will be used in the research report.

Another reason for the unwillingness to participate is that research always requires resources from the participants, most often time and information from the people who will be interviewed or whose work will be followed. Being clear about how much time and other resources will be required from the participants makes it easier to negotiate access.

Finally, it is easy to understand that an organization does not want to participate if it does not see how your research project would benefit it. This is why you need to consider how to 'sell' your research project to an organization that you would like to study.

Persuasive arguments are needed to sell your proposal, but often you will need to offer more than that. Minimally, you should offer a follow-up letter giving the main results of the study along with a more comprehensive research report. Another alternative is to suggest arranging a short meeting or a seminar in which you can present and discuss the results of your study with the participants.

Introducing your research project

When you approach an organization that you have had no prior relationship with, you need to take extra care in introducing your research project properly and to the right person. The right person is the one who can either grant you the permission to perform the study or forward on the issue for others to decide. When making the initial contact, it is good practice to send out a short outline of your research proposal by mail or e-mail, indicating that you will contact the person by phone within three to four days. This leaves the company person some time to consider your offer and, most importantly, does not require any effort on their part.

The larger the organization, the more worthwhile it is to use some time for finding the right person to send the outline to. Making a phone call to the organization to ask who takes care of marketing research issues or who takes care of employee training programmes often works best.

The research outline for introducing your research project is your 'business card', and it should include your 'sales arguments'. When writing the outline for this purpose, it is essential that you consider the question of 'who is the audience?' For this outline, the audience is not academic, nor necessarily research oriented, but more or less practically oriented. A business company representative often wants to know quickly and efficiently about issues such as:

- What is the relevance of your research from a practical point of view?
- What kind of resources does it require from the participants?
- What is the direct benefit for the company?
- What can you do to ensure confidentiality?

For this purpose, your outline should not be too long: one page or 300–400 words is usually enough. When writing the outline, make sure that it clearly communicates your research interests and intentions; it should be both systematic and informative. In addition, the outline should be polite and it should include your contact information.

If your research request is met with interest, then it is common that you will be asked to visit the organization to discuss the details of your research project and the resources it requires from the participating organization.

Because the visit may determine the destiny of your relationship with that organization, it is advisable that you prepare yourself thoroughly. Study all the written information about the organization that you can find (e.g. media texts, annual reports, web pages) in order to show that you have a genuine interest in the organization and that you can work in a professional manner. Think in advance about what type of agreement you can make with the organization in question, but also leave some flexibility for accommodating the suggestions that the organization might make.

ACCESSING INDIVIDUALS

Once you have the organization's agreement, you still need to convince the individuals within that organization about the relevance of your research. An individual's participation in research is always voluntary and needs to be negotiated separately, either by the researcher or the organization. You also need to negotiate access to individual participants even if your research project does not include any organization. For example, if you wish to interview consumers in a shopping centre, you must get their permission, and this involves explaining what your research is about, how it will be used, and by whom (for more details, see Chapter 6 on Ethics in Research).

Some business people think that participation in a scholarly study is a waste of time. Some may also have reservations towards qualitative studies. Why should they participate? Why should they be interested in talking to a researcher? Just as in the case of convincing the organization to allow your research, it is your job as a researcher to also convince the individual participants by telling them what the benefits of your research are. For example, let the participant know that, as a part of your study on 'changes in managerial work during rapid growth', you are attempting to provide answers to the question of how their business could grow more profitably by reorganizing and clarifying the tasks that the managers are performing.

Individual participants of your study have a right to receive adequate information about what their participation entails in practice. It is essential that you tell people whether you are asking for one single interview lasting about 60 minutes, or whether you are asking for permission to observe a person for a week. If giving this type of detailed information about your research leads to a refusal, it is much better to hear this before the study has started than during the later stages of your project when losing your data would compromise the whole study.

MAKING RESEARCH AGREEMENTS

Larger companies routinely require written research agreements, including details about anonymity, confidentiality, ethics, property rights, timetables, publications and resources required from the company (for details, see e.g. Collins and Hussey, 2003: 35–41). A written agreement often starts with a summary of the purpose of the project and includes details of the type of information that the researcher wants to compile and whether participants are offered something in return for their participation.

Even if a written agreement is not required, it is a good idea to make detailed notes about what you agreed upon with participants. Consider making a memo about the first meeting with each participant and giving it back to them for comments and confirmation. Bear in mind that the participants of your study have a right to know who is responsible for the research and who can be contacted for additional information. The main sources of funding also need to be revealed to the participants. Overall, you should be honest about your research project and let the participants know what you are doing with the information that will be given to you. Only in this way can you get their informed consent to agree to participate in your study. You can find more information on these issues in Chapter 6 which focuses on ethics in research.

Dealing with limitations

It is not unusual for organizations to negotiate some limitations to a research project in which they will participate. These may concern issues such as who you can interview or observe, what meetings you are allowed to attend, or what types of documents you can read. Albeit showing due care in dealing with all potential limitations at the beginning of the research process, more can pop up during the process and you will need to be able to handle them. Finally, it is up to you as a researcher to consider what kind of limitations you can accept and yet be able to pursue a good-quality study.

The participants must be allowed to read your research plan if they wish and it is good practice to offer them the opportunity to read your final research report before it becomes publicly available. You may get lots of useful feedback from the participants if they are interested in your research. It can also happen that the participants are not comfortable with what you are writing or aiming at. Open discussion and willingness to search for satisfactory compromises usually works best in these situations. In cases of disagreement over your results and conclusions, however, it is good to remember that you have a right to make your own interpretations and draw your own conclusions even though the participants may not agree with them.

THE RESEARCHER-PARTICIPANT RELATIONSHIP

When doing quantitative business research, you typically keep your distance from the participants. In qualitative business research, this distance is often diminished. This means that the participants of your study can become intensively involved in your research process in a multitude of ways depending on your goals and research approach (see e.g. Shank, 2002: 50–70).

The variation in involvement can range from the participants and the researcher meeting only once, to them being involved in intensive interactive interviews and serial open-ended discussions. The exceptions are qualitative studies that use existing research materials (e.g. media texts, documents, annual reports, web pages), although sometimes you can also develop a relationship with the people who are present in the materials or who have produced them.

Particularly in ethnographic, action and case study research, it is common that you meet with the participants of your study often and over a longer period of time, which leads to a closer than usual relationship with them. The goal of becoming an insider in the culture under study in ethnographic research requires the development of close relationships. A close relationship can evolve, however, even though it may not be a goal of your study. When a close relationship has developed, whether planned or not, the participants may be more inclined to give feedback to the researcher on their empirical analysis, research writing and conclusions.

Reasons for diminishing the distance between the researcher and the participants

There are several reasons for diminishing the distance between the researcher and the participants. First, it can be taken as a starting point for the study that the participants are the best experts to talk to about the subject matter. Second, qualitative research often aims to include the participant's perspective in the research process, which demands an increased familiarity and understanding between the researcher and the participants. By including the participants in the process, you can assume that the empirical materials will be more representative of their social worlds.

Third, in qualitative research projects, the researcher is the primary instrument of the study. This means that the research process is mediated through your speech and writing rather than through technical equipment. Within the qualitative research tradition the researcher is considered an active agent, whose age, gender, class, race, ethnicity, orientation, history and experiences can play a significant role in shaping the research process.

Insider and outsider positions

A business researcher can be either an 'insider' or an 'outsider' of her research (Eriksson and Rajamäki, 2010). For example, when you do research in a company where you also work, you are an insider in the organization and you are familiar with the issues that you study. In a similar way, when you do your research on issues that are not familiar to you and in an organization that you are not familiar with, you are an outsider. It depends on your research approach and your goals as to whether it is better to be an insider or an outsider. Also, it is not uncommon that you start your research as an outsider and, during the process, become an insider.

As an insider you can have easier access to the organization and the individuals, and a better chance to develop close relationships with the participants. This is because you have an understanding of the cultural norms and social relationships that inform the issues and situations within the organization. Being or staying as an outsider can give you a better opportunity to be analytical, and even critical, towards the organization and its people, as well as to the issues and situations that you are examining.

Challenges of the insider position

Being an insider, is a fruitful position, but it can also be a challenging position for a novice researcher. According to our experience, a common problem is caused by confusing what you know (or think that you know) intuitively and what you know on the basis of your research evidence. Furthermore, novice business researchers easily rely on and replicate normative beliefs about how to make business or how to manage a company without any consideration about how these beliefs have come about. This is why an insider business researcher should try to reflect upon her beliefs and presumptions, analyzing where they came from and how they came about.

When the research topic and the context are very familiar to you, another piece of advice that the more experienced researchers give is to try to develop a way to look at it in an unusual manner, or as an outsider. For example, if you are a young female employee in the company that you are studying, try to look at the company from the point of view of an older male employee. Or, when you have been working in the customer service function and you are doing a study on 'how teamwork is performed in customer service', try to look at things from the point of view of the customer.

Other researcher roles

Besides being an insider or an outsider, you can also have other roles in your research project (see e.g. Glesne, 2010). A novice business researcher can easily act like a student who wants more experienced business people to teach her. The more confidence you will have with your research project, the easier it is to act like an academic scholar, expert or teacher.

Critical business researchers, for instance, can take a political stance and serve as advocates of a less powerful group of people in society (e.g. young female entrepreneurs or employees with ethnic backgrounds), which is a very specific role for a researcher. It is also possible to act as a collaborator with the participants, even allowing them to participate in making decisions about your research. When the researcher is an insider, they can also act as a friend to the participants.

In any case, you should take responsibility for the research process and be in charge of the work. In a similar way to social life in general, friendships can cause problems in research settings. Often, these concern issues such as loyalty and confidentiality.

Being reflexive about the researcher's role

It is not always possible to position yourself initially in a desired role. Also, you are not always able to develop a role that you wished for at the beginning of your research process. Despite this, it is good to keep in mind that you negotiate roles with the participants of your study. This means that your role as a researcher and their roles as participants can change, sometimes several times, during the research process. For example, as your confidence grows, you may first move from a student role to an expert role and, later on, from an expert role to a teacher role.

Overall, it is relevant to reflect on your role and your relationship with the participants as your research progresses. One reason for the importance of reflexivity is that every role entails differing power relationships between you and the participants and this affects your study and its results in one way or another. Being reflexive about how power relationships are involved in research, for instance, how you make interpretations and suggestions, improves your chances of making a well-grounded and trustworthy piece of research. Novice researchers are not spontaneously aware of the power issues in research, and this is why you should pay some attention to this.

KEY POINTS OF THE CHAPTER

In qualitative business research, you often need to gain access to both organizations and individuals, and the organizations often act as gatekeepers of your research. It can require time and energy to convince the organization and to come to an agreement on the details of your research.

There are several benefits in choosing organizations and people that you already know to be research participants, but you can also use various types of purposeful and convenience sampling techniques.

Although the positions and roles of the qualitative researcher are many and they can change during the research process, it is typical that the distance between the researcher and the participants is diminished in qualitative business research.

FURTHER READING

Feldman et al.'s (2003) book *Gaining Access: A Practical and Theoretical Guide for Qualitative Researchers* outlines the process of access in great detail and discusses both theoretical and practical issues in social science qualitative research.

Bryman's (2013) book *Doing Research in Organizations* provides a collection of chapters by different researchers, outlining their experiences in various aspects of doing social science and business research in different types of organizations.

—————————————— **EXERCISE 5.1** ——————————————

Identifying participants and introducing research

The objective of this exercise is to learn how to communicate persuasively about your research to a potential participant of your research project. Work through the following three steps:

- With your research topic and preliminary research question in mind, consider who (organization, group, individuals) could be a good participant in your study. Make a list of all potential participants, considering their pros and cons, and then choose one to three of the most promising ones.
- With the chosen participants, think through and make notes about how you could sell your research project to them: what would be interesting for them in your project and how it could benefit them; what you could promise to give in return for their time; how you could ensure confidentiality, etc.
- On the basis of your notes, write a one-page research outline for each potential participant. Pay special attention to the clarity, novelty and practical aspects of your outline.
- Then let a fellow student, researcher, or a friend working in an organization read your outline and give comments. With the help of these comments, rewrite your research outline.

—————————————— **EXERCISE 5.2** ——————————————

Insider and outsider positions

The purpose of this exercise is to evaluate the pros and cons of insider and outsider positions in research:

- Choose a topic of research and think about some preliminary research questions that you could study in an organization or with people who are familiar to you. If you do not have any close contacts to business organizations, you can think about your own university department as a site of your research.
- Make a list of the advantages and disadvantages of performing your study as an insider. If you find it difficult to imagine the situation, read another researcher's description about being an insider in their study (e.g. in Bryman, 2013).
- Then consider doing the same research as an outsider; in an organization or with people that you do not have a relationship with. Make a list of the advantages and disadvantages of performing your study as an outsider.
- Compare the lists. Consider which position would better help you to answer your research questions. Which position would you be more comfortable with and why? Could it be possible to combine these positions in order to have the advantages of them both? How could you do that?

6

ETHICS IN RESEARCH

This chapter will provide information on:

- the general rules and regulations concerning ethics in research
- the possible problems present specifically in business research settings
- what concepts such as confidentiality, anonymity, and different forms of consent mean
- where to find information on the general ethical guidelines in research
- the issues of plagiarism in research.

THE IMPORTANCE OF ETHICS IN BUSINESS RESEARCH

Ethics pervade the way we live our lives. The dos and don'ts are only part of ethics and moral issues. Society and the economy are regulated by numerous written and unwritten laws and regulations, and new issues for ethical regulation emerge as societies – and science especially – become more complex. In all social research, such as business research, ethical issues require taking into account questions that go beyond ethics. These issues are related to the ways we constitute legitimate and justified knowledge of the social life. The ethical principles, such as informed consent, the avoidance of deception, harm or risk, and Kant's universal principle of respect, treating others always as ends and never as means, all go hand in hand with the ways we see the researcher as related to the researched topic, or knowledge production, in a more general way. The ethical principles mentioned govern all research activities, irrespective of the researcher's own approach to knowledge production. Research ethics covers the ways in which research is conducted and reported. In addition, more complex issues, such as research bias, ways of quoting other authors and researchers, and even the question of silencing other researchers in the research community, all have their place in research ethics and will be discussed (Box 6.1).

One of the fundamental parts of research is the issue of trust created in the research community. This trust within the research community, that all research and all researchers are following ethical principles and guidelines, is in principle based on the generally accepted notion of ethics, which at its most fundamental is about 'right' and 'wrong' in society, and in this specific case, in research. In general, the standards, codes, normative principles and regulations are needed in order to make the ethical principles and guidelines known and accepted as a code of conduct in the research community. They are also needed in order to create a procedure for handling possible problem situations.

The common understanding of 'right' and 'wrong' is present in the legal and in regulatory societal systems, as well as in those voluntary codes that are commonly accepted in societies and in our everyday life and behaviour. Ethics, however, concern all aspects of our life. New issues and concerns come forward, both in everyday life and especially in research, where new topics, issues, methods and materials make it possible to explore questions not previously studied or even thought of. As new issues and questions arise in society, the rules and regulations also need to be readdressed, rejustified and readjusted. This also applies to the research ethics and code of conduct in research. During recent years, new ethical questions have especially emerged with new possibilities and development within the fields of medical and biosciences. In business and the economy, business ethics has brought up issues of misconduct in the economic sphere that have also become of interest from a research ethics point of view (Clegg and Rhodes, 2006), especially so after the global financial crisis of 2008.

BOX 6.1

Why are ethical rules important in science?

Why are ethical rules specifically needed in research? Even if it is often said that ethics is about drawing the line between 'right' and 'wrong', ethics has a natural justification of its own as a disciplinary field. Most, if not all, scientific research questions have some ethical aspects: if not directly related to the research questions, then they might be related to research practices, processes or to the overall research field, or the ways we understand the relationships between the researcher and research topic and communicate about the research. Questions of an ethical nature come up very easily in medical and bioscience research, but they are also present in the humanities and social sciences, due to the complexity of the fields.

Research ethics is often only thought of in relation to empirical data gathering. Alternatively, it is thought of as adding credibility to research, as the following quotation shows where the researcher is urged to 'address these issues [ethics] in the methods chapter, thus adding to the credibility of the research process' (Zalan and Lewis, 2004: 520). It is perhaps unnecessary to add that an instruction such as this might not increase the credibility of the research process unless the researcher has not followed ethical rules and does not know them before starting the process, does not adapt them during the actual research process, and the method book at hand does not properly address the issues.

At the same time, business bribery and forging scandals in globally known cases such as Enron and Siemens have become widely known and have increased the general interest in the research of ethics in business. Business as a research field has also drawn attention from scientists other than management researchers, who, perhaps more easily, have brought the issues of ethics into focus. Thus, research in business ethics has increased. Yet, achieving information and getting access to businesses includes several aspects where the general rules of research ethics might come into play, for example, in how to get access, what kind of information is available, whose interests might be served, etc.

Research ethics in qualitative business research is most often only related to ethnographic data-collection processes and interview processes in ethnography or case study, not to any other part of the research process and procedure, such as the general research settings or to other features discussed later in this chapter. Therefore, a larger view into research ethics is provided in this chapter. In the following, you will be guided through the variety of topics most often related to research ethics, keeping in mind the economy as a research field and opening up the key concepts.

DIMENSIONS OF RESEARCHER-PARTICIPANT RELATIONSHIPS

As mentioned, surprisingly little attention is given to the research ethics and relationship between researcher and the researched person or group in methods books.

Most often, research ethics is discussed only in relation to 'entering the field'; that is, in relation to access to ethnographic materials, observations and interviews in general social science research methods books (e.g. Silverman, 2013), and, most often, the emerging questions are taken up through examples. Indeed, in qualitative research, the question of obtaining data is crucial; therefore, discussion of research ethics tends to centre around the question of so-called informed consent, which will be discussed later in this chapter. Research ethics is, however, a much larger field and concerns more principle-level questions in research than just material gathering or interviewing. Research ethics concerns the whole research process, starting from the relationship between researcher and research object and ending up with writing up and publishing the report.

The general relationship between researcher and researched can vary in at least three different ways, and this variation gives differing perspectives on the ways the information flows, confidentiality, consent and other research-ethics-related questions are discussed (e.g. Elliott, 1988):

A. The researcher can be detached and remain neutral and distant to the research object; researched are subjects, data sources and respondents in a research setting.

B. The researcher can be marginally participant (participant-observer) in the research, and researched are informants.

C. The researcher can actively participate in activities and enable changes to take place, perhaps also making changes, as facilitator, change agent or enabler. Those researched are collaborators in research (e.g. action research; for more, see Chapter 13).

All three of these relations and variations between these types are possible in qualitative research. Some methods and types of research call for a specific type of relationship, such as, action research calls for a C-type relationship between researcher and those researched, whereas a case study can subscribe to any type of relationship described above.

Schwandt (2001) proposes that, in the A-type relationships, the researcher often thinks of the possible ethical obligations of research as simply contractual ones: a written agreement is thus needed between the two parties that explicates the purpose of research, the involvement, the treatment of subjects, details in the research relationship, publications and various questions on, for example, anonymity and confidentiality. This contractual model of ethics is most often also assumed in boards and institutional settings that review and advise on ethical questions in universities and research institutions. A contract is thought to formalize the research relationship and create a situation where most issues concerning research are known to both partners. The contractual model can cover many aspects in research; however, many times in social science research, situations or even conflicts arise that cannot be governed by the contractual model beforehand.

In the B- and C-type relationships between researcher and researched, all aspects described above are present; but, in addition to the contractual approach to ethics between the researcher and researched, for example, Schwandt (2001) proposes several special obligations for the researcher that arise due to the extended and often complex dealings between the researcher and researched that safeguard the position of the researched person or group. These dealings occur specifically in ethnographic research, but also in action research and other types of qualitative research, where close relationships develop during the research project. Researchers can become friends with their informants, and close relationships extend over into free time, for example. In these types of research, it becomes of importance for the researcher to pay attention specifically to the following aspects: to guard the anonymity of informants, and to create a trusting relationship that will not be violated during the research process. This also includes aspects such as confidence creation within the researched field and sensitivity to and respect for the values and interests of those studied persons and/or groups.

In business research, the ways to handle the trust situations can be easily problematic. The trust relationship might become an issue when, for example, the researcher has interviewed employees in a company where access and consent has been granted by the management, and the interviews bring forth evidence of great mistrust towards the leadership skills of the manager who is the contact person for the research project in the company. How best to guard the anonymity of employees and present the research results to the management so that the information will not create difficult situations later on for the employees, is the dilemma the researcher needs to consider thoroughly in order to maintain the ethical standards present in their research.

SPONSORSHIP AND RESEARCH ETHICS

In qualitative business research, where companies, corporations, organizations and firms are being studied, it is relatively common to have a close working relationship with the companies or organizations in question: to have access to a firm or company or to its materials, people or premises usually means that close working relationships are being built around the mutual trust and ideas of common goals, both for the researcher and the company. Often, besides the mutual interest in the joint project, this can mean some financial compensation for the research work and report, or compensation for training, practical problem solving, etc. for the researcher. In research, the concept used is sponsorship, which should be made publicly explicit in the research.

The sponsor can be the host organization (such as a university), the specific research funding body (fund), corporation or company, or the employer of the researcher. Sponsorship, in practice, is usually related to the research project where the sponsor pays for or supports the specific research financially and also gives access to the company (premises, materials and people) and in response expects some form of written report or presentation from the research project. Sponsorship usually also actively offers some specific research question for the researcher to be studied. Usually, these relationships are contractual by nature, where the contract regulates and covers the issues of research interest, the research question, sometimes methods, and always the forms of reporting, material and/or immaterial compensation, and intellectual property rights questions regarding the data themselves, the usage of the data, and the rights to and ways of publishing the material.

Sponsorship does not usually create problems when both parties (sponsor and researcher/research group) making a sponsorship contract regarding a research project know, agree upon and consent to the contracted issues, respect each other's positions in the contract and agree upon the mutual benefit of the research done through sponsorship. Not only does the researcher have a role and responsibilities in research, but so also does the sponsor (Box 6.2). Both parties might need to assure the wider audience or other parties of the scientific quality of the proposed research, and, if such an institution exists, ensure the research ethics committee's approval of the plan, where such approval is needed for the research.

This latter type of ethical problem, however, relates more generally to issues of ideal types and categories concerning the best possible research model, and is not necessarily related to sponsorship in research. Ethnographers have especially remarked that they have been losing out in competition over general research funding due to the prevailing natural science model of research (e.g. Brewer, 2000). This may or may not be true, but differences in research paradigmatic orientation and the ways these differences are recognized in research funding might bring up the differences in how various kinds of research and its information are valued in the scientific community and by research funding bodies.

BOX 6.2

Sponsorship and freedom of research

Does sponsorship create ethical problems in relation to freedom of research? The question of sponsorship in research and ethics in sponsorship can relate to problems in research ethics in at least two ways. Sponsorships can force unwanted limits to research, either in relation to research setting and data collection or in relation to restricting or censoring the results and their reporting and publishing. This sort of censorship is ethically unsustainable, as it deals with the integrity of the researcher and research project. More generally, if not taken care of, sponsorship (and external funding in general) can possibly promote a more general bias in the research paradigm if it favours some specific type of research setting, data or method choices only, instead of a balanced and wide view on science. Such bias can occur when favouring, for example, one methodical approach over others.

WHAT IS GOOD SCIENTIFIC PRACTICE?

For any individual researcher, research ethics most often concern the practical-level 'line drawing' between 'right' and 'wrong', but this line drawing is strongly embedded in the ways 'right' and 'wrong' in general can and should be defined in society.

Research often concerns very complex issues and concern over using human beings and animals as research objects. Research, like any activity in human life, can contain direct frauds, lies and wrongdoings. Misconduct and fraud in science have serious consequences for the whole science community and science field; therefore, normative guidelines and codes of ethics and rules are needed in social sciences specifically in order to protect the rights of persons being studied or researched. They are needed in order to govern the integrity of scientific endeavour and to create ways for academic institutions and organizations to handle misdoings. Most academic and professional organizations such as universities and associations have their own ethical standards, ethics approval standards and procedures and codes of conduct, for example, see Academy of Management Code of Ethics and ISA Code of Ethics.

Even if certain ethical principles are more or less universally accepted, other ethical issues and questions are not always so clear-cut. What belongs to good scientific practice and what are the means for identifying wrongful or harmful actions and misconduct, or even a biased way of behaving and acting in the scientific community, are under debate in different fields of science and different parts of the world: stem cell research is a good and topical example of such a research field, where strong differences and ethical standpoints prevail concerning what kind of research can and should be allowed, and for what purposes and from what sources can stem cells be obtained for medical and biomedical research. The seemingly simple question of stem cells and where to obtain them widens up to an individual's own and to society's general moral beliefs and values.

Ethical guidelines and ethical review boards

Most scientific organizations have developed instructions in order to establish good ethical standards for scientific research and raise issues concerning, for example, informed consent, privacy and confidentiality in the research processes. Whereas certain ethical principles are more or less universally accepted, other ethical issues are not so clear-cut. Science is one of those societal fields where complex ethical challenges clearly exist and come forward continually. Therefore, written guidelines for good scientific practice are being established, developed and published. These guidelines usually also include guidelines on how to draw the line between different ways of working through the research practices and how to handle possible problem cases (e.g. APA Ethics Code, 2006; ISA Code of Ethics, 2006; there are also renewed editions available).

With the help of professional and institutional guidelines and codes of conduct, cases of misconduct and fraud in science can be identified and dealt with. At present, the guidelines most often already exist, as the scientific domain at large is already governed by strong ethical codes. Many social science fields refer to international institutional guidelines written and published by international professional associations such as the American Psychological Association (APA) and the International Sociological Association (ISA). The ever-changing nature of science, however, means that regular, and often rapid, reviews and revisions are also needed in the associated rules and regulations. In social sciences, the earliest questions of the need for ethical rules were most closely related to the issues of covert research setting and the gathering of data in such settings.

There also exist written general ethical rules and principles, such as the Charter of European Fundamental Rights (European Parliament, 2006), which has established the general ethical principles (and more) as fundamental rights in Europe. In the case of research and science, the principles include the need to ensure freedom of research as one of the key aspects of the freedom of expression, and the need to work in the interests of the physical and moral integrity of individuals. Similar rules and principles exist in most countries.

The question of research ethics is pervasive and, therefore, not only a question of personal or individual concern, or even of the choice of the individual researchers themselves, even if many times discussed in such an individual manner in research methods books. Even if individual researchers need to be aware of and make decisions by themselves, they do not have to play it by ear. Most scientific associations that canonize the disciplinary field as well, for example, research councils and ministries that fund research, and universities and organizations that fund, organize or associate in some ways with research, have all written rules of conduct that give directions to good scientific practice. These bodies most often also have ethical review boards that take up issues and give statements on research proposals that include ethical concerns, ranging from the issues of research design, the use of individuals in research, and other issues.

The practice of ethical review boards and committees varies between countries and universities. In some countries and universities, all research proposals need to go through the ethical committee when considered for funding; in others, only those involving some ethical considerations, such as tests with human beings or with animals, require this.

The regulations concern the basic respect in scientific research, and they usually emphasize several issues. The key element in regulations is the principle that all research should be conducted with respect for the welfare of all persons. Especially important in this respect is when persons might benefit from or be otherwise affected by the research and its dissemination, including individual participants and the systems and organizations in which they function. Research should also be conducted with respect for knowledge and evidence. This refers to collegial information and results by other researchers, as well as acknowledging colleagues' work. Respect should also be shown for the law and civic values of the host culture, in the case where multi-cultural research is being done. Universities and research institutions may have written codes of practice that help researchers to uphold scientific standards, comply with the law and avoid social and personal harm.

The following examples of good scientific practice, rules and ethical codes come from several professional and institutional sources, which mainly adapt the codes established by the ISA (ISA Code of Ethics, 2006), the APA (APA Ethics Code, 2006) and the American Sociological Association (ASA Code of Ethics, 2008). The APA Code of Conduct (2010) focuses also on research where individuals are used as 'test materials', and these rules might be relevant for those researchers in business research who work with similar types of research settings as in psychology (tests, focus groups).

Many universities have established specific research governance frameworks that define the broad principles of good research practice and ensure that research is conducted to high scientific and ethical standards. The aim with standards and practical procedures is to bring together the existing legislation and guidance for researchers and other parties in research that concern, for example, data protection and maintenance, legislations and regulations.

Relations with and responsibilities towards research participants

Several issues relate to the responsibility of the researcher when conducting research in social settings, be it among individuals, groups, companies, corporations or other organizations (Box 6.3).

BOX 6.3

Basic rule of responsibility towards others

You should follow the modes of actions and procedures approved and supported by the research community in general. These actions and procedures or rules most often include accuracy, thoroughness and integrity in conducting research, ranging from research design and planning the research setting, to gathering the data, analyzing the data and presenting the results. This also includes the ways the research is judged. One of the key elements in all ethical guidelines is the protection of participants in research.

Voluntary participation

People only need to participate in the research on a voluntary basis. Therefore, they should not be led to believe that they are required to participate in a study, because of their position, etc. This aspect of voluntary participation and protection of partici-pants is vitally important in business-related research, where, for example, employees in the company might be instructed to participate in interviews, tests or experiments in a study contracted by the management of the company, without prior knowledge of how the results will be used.

Participants (be they employees or other participants) should know that they can withdraw from the study at any point, and that this information (whether a person is participating or refusing to participate, or withdrawing from participation) should not be given to the employer. This aspect of voluntarism is very important in situations where the context in which the request to participate is made can make participants feel that they cannot withdraw from the study. What kind of situation could this relate to? A teacher using their own students as participants in research is a classic example of this situation. It is rather more usual to set test questionnaires or collect research materials using students, the classroom or other audience as informants in business research. This might, however, impose a coercive situation for a student where the student cannot really choose whether to participate or not, as participation in the course where the research is being conducted might be crucial for studies and refusal might put the student in an unfavourable position.

All research has a responsibility towards its subjects. Respect should be thought of in terms of human life in general, human dignity and the integrity of the person, but also, more generally, for prohibition of inhuman or degrading treatment and for the support of different aspects of equality, as well as cultural, religious and linguistic diversities. The respect for privacy and the protection of personal data, and genetic data, are basic features of responsibility towards the research subjects. Issues such as the protection of consumers might be relevant for business research, using, for example, focus group analysis or interview data on consumer experiences of business products. For an individual company, it might be valuable to know more of even very personalized information about the consumers; but for a researcher, the revelation of identities or the personal data of consumers should not be a possibility.

Informed consent

Informed consent is closely related to voluntary participation. The basic information of the study available to the audience should include facts such as the purpose of the study and its basic procedures, the roles and identities of researchers and their possible sponsors or other beneficiaries, such as external financers, and the use of data. Often, facts such as a description of why specifically certain participants were selected for the study and information regarding the possible future uses of the data should also be made public. The promise of replying to all possible questions in relation to research is also worth bringing forward publicly. Most often, the basic information and the offer to answer further questions are important in order for the possible participants to create their opinion about their participation and get further information at any time they need to.

Ethics boards in universities, hospitals, ministries and research institutions usually require that consent is obtained before participation (see covert research later in this chapter). Researchers also share responsibility for the ethical treatment of research participants with their collaborators, assistants, students, employees and with other researchers. A researcher who believes that another researcher may be conducting research that is not in accordance with the principles above should encourage that researcher to re-evaluate their research procedures.

Professional integrity

Is it possible to 'open up' your data and the qualitative analysis you have conducted to outsiders and expect them to understand, follow the logic, accept and get a reliable picture of the analysis presented in qualitative research? The answer is yes. It is important to show the logic of your analysis, the logic in your arguments and the logic of reporting the analysis in the research report, and to keep a record of the proceedings and procedure of your analysis in order to be able to inspect the process later (Box 6.4).

The aspect of professional integrity is crucial when you (by doing research) also learn to become a member of the research community. In particular, even if competition in academic life is very tough, research should be open in the sense that, after you have published your research, information about your research project should be part of the common knowledge and background of the scientific community. Therefore, it is open to comments and criticism to which researchers should be allowed to react (ISA Code of Ethics, 2006).

BOX **6.4**

Basic guidelines for professional integrity

You should plan, conduct and report your research in detail and according to the standards set in general for scientific research. This can mean in practice that your data materials and the ways you have conducted the data gathering, analysis process and analysis reporting should be available for scrutiny and inspection by your research community.

Research should not bring harm to participants

Perhaps more so in medical or psychological research than in business research, the experiments might include elements that are potentially harmful or distressing, and these should be avoided. Sometimes, even with the best of intentions, there might be harmful or negative consequences of experiments or trial tests. Therefore, it is important to protect the participants from any form of direct or indirect harm by anticipating these possibilities. Anticipation of possible negative consequences is a part of professional integrity, irrespective of the disciplinary field in question.

You should apply ethically sustainable data collection, research, use of materials and evaluation methods conforming to general scientific criteria. Protecting the integrity and confidentiality of the data generated by the research is an important part of this point.

Problems of covert research

A responsibility concerning informants exists even if the research were so-called covert research. Covert research in ethnography means that the researcher does not reveal themselves to the research subjects. Even if covert research is often described as an exciting, new and novel way of acquiring information, the methodological decision to attain such information is not new. Ethically, however, covert research and methods are very problematic ways of doing research, in spite of some positive reasons such as avoiding certain difficulties, for example, changes in the behaviour of the participants when they know they are being studied.

The problems with covert methods and research are that they violate the principles of informed consent and may even invade the privacy of those being studied. Many codes of conduct and codes of ethics by professional associations state that, as in the ISA Code of Ethics (2006): Covert research should be avoided in principle, unless it is the only method by which information can be gathered, and/or when access to the usual sources of information is obstructed by those in power.

In business research covert studies can be very problematic and put forward several ethical problems. Consumer behaviour and buyer–salesperson interactions in shopping situations are two examples of research situations where covert research is possible. De Vaus (2001) takes up an example of covert research concerning sexual harassment: a researcher might undertake the research by obtaining a job with the company and covertly observing what goes on in the working environment. In this case, obviously, the ethical issues of deception and failure to obtain informed consent beforehand would most probably arise, but the possibility of getting information on the sensitive and hidden issues might otherwise be impossible.

On the other hand, observing public behaviour (as long as individuals are not identifiable), such as behaviour in shops (which consumables raise a buyer's interest, etc.), raises few ethical problems, as there should not be any danger of harm to participants. As De Vaus (2001: 246) remarks, if the behaviour is public, then there is hardly any invasion of privacy of those persons. The observation of people in demonstrations, in meetings or in the shopping centre, without informing them, is thus not problematic, as long as individual persons are not identifiable.

Anonymity, privacy and confidentiality

The anonymity of individuals and/or groups participating in the research should be the first priority of the researcher and be respected in research. Personal information should be kept confidential and, where possible, threats to the confidentiality and anonymity of research data should be anticipated. The identities and research records of the participants of the research should be kept confidential. In practice, all data should be stored in such a way that no unauthorized access is possible; removal of personal identification from the data is also essential.

Silencing

You should respect your colleagues' and other researchers' research work, publications and scientific achievements by giving them the credit and weighting that belongs to them in your own research. The misconduct in not giving credit to your collaborators and colleagues when they are entitled to it could lead to 'silencing' other researchers, 'forgetting' to refer to their research results, or giving them a minor role or no role in a joint research project. You should mention the intellectual origins of your project, if you owe it to somebody. When publishing, you should determine authorship on the basis that, with their consent, all those contributing substantially to the research are listed in the authorship of the publication, in relation to relative contributions in leadership, creativity and effort expended. The alphabetical order is most often used in social sciences where an equal amount of work is being conducted. Give due credit to all collaborators, acknowledging also the less substantial contributions to the research.

Referring in a right and proper way to other researchers' scientific input and results, and acknowledging their intellectual property rights, is an important part of academic research activity. Silencing the voice of other researchers is one of those grey areas of ethical misconduct, where it is difficult to prove or show wrongdoings. Another form of misconduct might be that colleagues within the same research field are not credited for their work or input within the field. These issues of research ethics are more difficult, as many times novice researchers may find out about other research reports similar or closely related to their own only after they have finished their work. However, with more powerful search engines and library services, finding out about your own research interest and publications within the research field is easier than ever before.

Still, we must be careful of dismissing other researchers' views or results as unimportant, as it can be a way of silencing alternative and opposing perspectives, and silencing other researchers. According to research ethics, it is always important to acknowledge the intellectual ownership and scientific contributions of collaborators; this is especially important in collaboration projects, where several researchers contribute to the project.

Plagiarism

The core of all scientific work is about sharing, but much of the scientific work is also about competition. Competition, time pressures and even laziness have been used as possible excuses for breaking the law, bending ethical rules and committing plagiarism.

Plagiarism is seldom thought of as 'crime' in legal terms within the research community, but in most countries it is regulated through copyright laws, and in this sense it can also be considered a 'crime'. Plagiarism is an intellectual crime as well. What does plagiarism mean in practice?

At its simplest, you plagiarize when you do not give acknowledgement to other researchers' ideas, inventions, research work, written texts and publications, but use them and present them as your own and produce work of another person without expressly crediting that person. You should not claim credit for other people's ideas, intellectual property and research.

One of the questions often put forward by the student is when a citation should be used. A layman's answer to that is: whenever your eyes rest longer on the text you are citing, than on the keyboards when writing down the citation, you need to carefully cite your source by using citation marks (van Leunen, 1978). If unsure, do cite and use references very conscientiously. To get a citation formally right, excellent source books on citation and referencing exist. Reference to author and acknowledgement of authorship or intellectual source is an important part of research work.

In detail, whenever you wish to quote somebody word for word, or use quotations or paraphrases, the citation is vital. Another vital point where a citation is to be used is when you use an idea that someone else has already expressed or formulated, or whenever the idea developed by somebody is critical in developing your own idea. And whenever you refer to a specific piece from other people's work, citation/ referencing is needed.

The simple rule is always to be careful with writing up references when coming across an interesting idea or thought or article. Developing your thoughts and ideas around the interesting work done by others, and acknowledging that work by others, while relating your own work to it, is part of the process of how to become a member of the research community and intellectual community that is worldwide. Check with your university or institute whether they have ethical guidelines in use; if not, ask if there is a specific reason for not having ethical standards established in written form.

Copying other people's work and words has never been so easy as it is today, with access to the Internet providing a lot of information, books, chapters, articles, debates and papers of any topic, quality and nature can be found very easily. Copying and then forgetting the citations and references can take place sometimes even uncon- sciously, or without knowing the 'right' rules for referring to and citing other people's work. Plagiarism involves the omission of the citation and reference to the author and owner of the idea or text, thus breaking the ethical rules of research and also the legislation concerning copyright ownership.

KEY POINTS OF THE CHAPTER

The area of research ethics concerns all kinds of research and covers the whole research process, not just empirical data collection. Research ethics govern the issues of research ideas, collaborative work, intellectual ownership of ideas and even all issues ranging from empirical work and materials to writing and publishing.

Treating other people as ends not as means, and a responsibility towards other researchers, the science community, informants and your colleagues should be the guiding principles for your behaviour as a researcher.

Basic issues about confidentiality, informed consent, and protecting your informants are important cornerstones for empirical data gathering in business research. For writing and research collaboration, similar cornerstones are the knowledge of how to cite and quote other researchers, how to treat your colleagues and collaborators, how not to silence your research fellows and how to recognize and avoid plagiarism.

FURTHER READING

For example, the ASA Code of Ethics is available at www.asanet.org. It covers the most essential ethical codes and norms in social sciences research. The APA Ethical Principles for Psychologists and Code of Conduct is available at www.apa.org; this takes up several aspects of research activities and ethical code of conduct. Almost all professional associations have their code of ethics published, and their guidelines follow similar logic, regulations and recommendations.

EXERCISE 6.1

Putting ethical rules into practice. What issues do you need to take into account?

You are writing your PhD thesis on conflict management as part of personnel policy in small and medium-sized companies, and have gained access to one company where your intention is to interview a large section of the personnel. In the early part of your interview period, a major conflict situation between the personnel and managing director in the company emerges in relation to layoffs. You have secured access to the company only through the managing director, not through personnel. How will you handle the situation so that you are able to follow the research ethics as described above?

EXERCISE 6.2

Putting ethical rules into practice. What issues do you need to take into account?

You are doing your research project on strategic change in organizations. You are doing a large number of interviews in several organizations and would like to use the transcribed interview material in your teaching class. When conducting the interviews for the research project, you did not ask for permission to use the interviews for teaching purposes. Can you use the transcribed interview materials for teaching?

PART II

WORKING WITH QUALITATIVE DATA

7
INTRODUCTION TO QUALITATIVE DATA

This chapter will provide information on:

- the nature of qualitative research data
- ways of collecting the data
- what kinds of qualitative data exist
- some key definitions.

WHAT COUNTS AS QUALITATIVE DATA?

The book has so far introduced you to the key aspects of qualitative research in business studies. Both Research Philosophy (Chapter 2) and Research Design and Process (Chapter 3) have underlined the importance of consistency in research. The idea of research, planning phases, and the processes related to the data planning and gathering, and the possibilities you will have with different research methods all relate to the ways you know your topic and your data. This chapter will highlight some general aspects that relate to data gathering, irrespective of the method chosen for the analysis of the data. The chapter will also guide you through a few easy exercises that show you the potentiality of your data.

Most business researchers collect empirical data for their research projects and use various types of data collection methods for this purpose. Each of the data collection methods requires some specific knowledge and skills that you can learn by studying, experimenting, rehearsing, and by reflecting on your aims and practices in collecting the data for your study. Also here, the general purpose of your research, the research approach you choose, and your research questions should be the guiding lights in terms of deciding what kind of empirical data are most useful in your study. The circularity of the process, as described in Chapter 3, emphasizes the fact that you may modify your decisions regarding the data and selection you may already have, and you can gather additional data, in order to finalize your research in the process.

In methodology textbooks, empirical data collected by researchers themselves are often called primary data. The division between 'primary data' and 'secondary data' relates to the slightly arbitrary division between the researcher-designed and researcher-gathered data, and between prior existing data in sources such as data archives, libraries, etc. Researchers can collect empirical data for their research project by interviewing and observing and by asking the participants to write (e.g. diaries, stories), draw, or present in some other way (e.g. drama). This would be considered as primary data.

Empirical data that already exists somewhere are commonly called secondary data. These include both textual data that exist without any specific collecting activities (e.g. documents, histories, newspapers, diaries, memos, stories) and visual materials (e.g. video recordings, television programmes, movies). In qualitative research, these types of materials can also be called 'naturally occurring materials' (e.g. Silverman, 2011) because they exist irrespective of the researcher's actions and intentions.

In this chapter we will give a general overview of the ways to collect different types of qualitative data that are commonly available for business researchers. This chapter aims to shortly introduce you to how to collect various types of data, and you can find more detailed information on how to analyze data from the viewpoint of different methodological approaches in Chapters 11–20. You will find a more detailed description on qualitative interviews and observations in Chapter 8, on digital materials in Chapter 9, and on ways to learn to know your data in Chapter 10.

INTRODUCING DIFFERENT TYPES OF QUALITATIVE DATA

Qualitative data (or research material, as some methodology books call it) are varied: there is not just one type of qualitative data. A usual way to define qualitative data is to contrast it with quantitative data and define it through differences: qualitative data is any information that can be captured that is not numerical in nature, that is, not measurable data. Hence, often the divide between numbers and words is seen as a difference. But even words can be quantified and counted, and their frequency, presence or absence may allow for interpretations. Thus the division is not clear-cut.

One common feature for qualitative data is that it is either the textual, verbal, audio material or visual material that allows for interpretations and descriptions and does not focus on measurements. Even quantitative research uses qualitative data, and the definition there often follows the definition given in statistics for qualitative data: data collected about a categorical variable is qualitative.

It should be clear though that for any data, the importance of interpretation and the analysis of the data are crucial. Your research question should give you possibilities and indicate directions for recognizing the possible data sources, obtaining the data and thinking of possible alternatives, if your original plan for data gathering fails. The great thing about qualitative research design is that the research design is seldom built on one data source alone.

From interviews and observations...

There are different types of data available and depending on your research questions and methods chosen for the analysis, the data may be treated similarly or differently in the analysis. We can distinguish interviews, observations, texts, documents and other written materials, visual materials and even digital materials from each other, as they are differently acquired and require different types of data-gathering strategies. However, the analysis does not necessarily differentiate the data in a similar manner. Within each of these (interviews, observations, textual materials, visual materials, digital materials) there are differing categorizations and classifications for the materials, different ways to acquire data and procedures for the analysis. Therefore, throughout the book we encourage you to take exercises and practice the use of different data in your research projects.

Most often interviews are thought of as being qualitative material, and sometimes even exclusively introduced as the only qualitative research material. It is indeed the case that in the 'interview society' (Gubrium and Holstein, 2001; Silverman, 2013), interviews are used extensively by the mass media and professional services (consulting, counselling, therapy) as well as by practical and academic researchers. The popularity of interviews in qualitative research is overwhelming. Therefore, a good number of textbooks and book chapters are available for a novice researcher who plans to conduct interviews in their research project (e.g. Spradley, 1979; Fontana and Frey, 2000; Gubrium and Holstein, 2001; Wengraf, 2001). We will discuss interviews in a more extensive manner in Chapter 8.

In general, interviews consist of talks organized into a series of questions and answers. Qualitative interviews may also resemble open, everyday conversations, in which the distinction between the interviewer and the interviewee is not so evident, the materials and issues dealt with throughout the interviews are not so organized, they do not follow each other chronologically and are more or less quite messy.

Interviews most often take place face to face, but they can also take place over the telephone, or online using computer-mediated technologies (see Chapter 9). Most interviews are conducted between two people (the interviewer and the interviewee or the participant), but interviews made in groups of two or more participants are also common in business studies (see Chapter 14 on Focus Group Research).

Qualitative interviews, as used in scholarly research, are research vehicles, the purpose of which is to produce empirical materials for the study in question. In contrast to how you conduct everyday conversations with fellow students, teachers or business managers, a good qualitative interviewer most often prepares at least some of their questions in advance, and later analyzes and reports results in a specific way. The interviewer also focuses the interview on particular issues that are related to the topic and research questions of their study. Although you might think that qualitative interviews are easy to do, they are not. In Chapter 8 you will find examples of how to distinguish research questions from interview questions and how to organize your interviews for the analysis. There are different ways of making and gathering observations. There are also several ways of transferring observations to analyzable data: in principle they can range from systemic written notes to photographing and videoing activities. These two latter in turn require visual analysis methods (Chapter 20). All qualitative data can be analyzed in several ways and this also concerns observations (for more, see Chapter 8).

... to textual and digital data

Texts and textual data can in principle be defined as all written materials and transcribed interviews. Texts can be organized and analyzed in different ways and also with different nuances: individual words, whole sentences, meanings, activities, actors and intertextualities, connotations, rhetoric, and several other aspects can all be traced down in texts. The texts can be analyzed through counting words but also through densities, translations and meaning-makings. The several methods chapters in the following part of the book will exemplify more of the uses of textual materials. Organizing the data for the analysis is part of the research protocol and concerns all research materials, such as interviews, observations, visual materials, documents or other texts.

Much of our social life is currently mediated by written texts. In fact, society would not function without written laws and regulations, the financial system would not work without written rules and regulations for monetary transfers, and the educational system would not function without books. This is why various types of text provide increasingly relevant research data.

Textual materials that are used for research purposes include both texts that you collect for your research project (e.g. transcribed interviews, stories and jokes in written form) and texts that already exist prior to your research project (e.g. annual reports, media texts). As was mentioned at the beginning of this chapter, the first types of text are called primary data and the second types of text are often referred to as secondary data.

Besides primary data, secondary data most often provide excellent opportunities for qualitative business research. For instance, in case study-oriented accounting and organization research, published texts are studied as 'artefacts' (Ryan, Scapens and Theobold, 1992, 2002; Belk, Fischer and Kozinets, 2013). These texts can include tangible items such as formal reports and statements, minutes of meetings, informal records, personal notes and memos.

Texts as representations of reality

The concept of textual data refers to all empirical materials that exist in textual form, be they produced through writing or through transcription from speech. The usefulness and relevance of textual data in qualitative business research is traditionally based on the idea of transparency. This means that texts are considered to represent directly what is being studied. In other words, texts are treated as suitable objects of analysis because we believe in their ability to tell us about the people and issues that they represent.

Post-structuralist view on texts

Another way of understanding texts is provided by post-structuralism, in which all human action is treated as text. This means, for instance, that interviews, when they are transcribed into texts, detach from the individuals interviewed and their social settings, and become artefacts in their own right. According to this view, the text has several distinctive characteristics that differ from the more common positivist and realist viewpoints on texts and their role in research. Post-structuralism signs for views, according to which:

1. texts do not transparently reflect or refer to the social world to be perceived in a similar way by everybody;
2. texts are not transparent and similarly read by every reader, they are open to various interpretations;
3. every text is related to other texts through intertextualities.

The production process of a text can be one relevant part of research. However, it is often useful to think about texts in a post-structuralist way and treat them as detached from the people who wrote them, or who were interviewed. By doing this, you can more easily focus your attention on the form and structure of the text and the meanings circulated by it, not on the people who produced the texts.

This, in turn, helps you to get away from 'the sin of "trying to get inside the head" of the author' of the text or the person who was interviewed by thinking that 'surely she must have meant this, but she just did not say or write it'. What happens here in that process is that you start over-interpreting the materials and you start talking about intentions, what was meant by the interviewee or by the author, instead of focusing on written or spoken texts.

Texts as artefacts

The ways to understand texts are several, ranging from realist to post-structuralist viewpoints. In qualitative research the texts are understood mostly as artefacts: gathered and related to the research topic for a specific reason. Intertextuality exists also not only through researchers' interpretations and re-readings but also increasingly, through the Internet, where any search for information gives, creates and re-creates new linkages and intertextualities. In this sense, all textual data are artefact: assimilated and related through and with the help of various interests. For research purposes, texts – gathered either through traditional interviews or through Internet data mining and net-observations – are culturally compiled and usable research materials.

WAYS OF DOING TEXTUAL ANALYSIS

In general, the varieties of and possibilities for textual analysis are abundant, as you will see in Part III of this book. The specific methods of analysis vary from content analysis to conversation analysis and from narrative analysis (Chapter 16) to discourse analysis (see Chapter 17). While content analysis is more concerned with the content of the text, and even frequencies within the text (e.g. number of words and expressions), conversation, narrative and discourse analyses are more concerned with the form, structure and meanings of the text. Internet and digital interviews, textual materials, online observations, etc. offer increasing and rich data sources for qualitative analysis.

One way of thinking about the variety of methods available is through your research questions. Does your research question call for very detailed and sophisticated methods of analysis? If qualitative materials are complementing other materials, such as quantitative data used in the study, an informal approach may be the best choice of method (Peräkylä, 2005: 870).

Johnson and Duberley (2000: 59) identify three approaches to textual analysis that they call positivist, linguistic and interpretative approaches. In each of these, the nature of the text, the role of the researcher, and the research method vary in a more detailed manner compared with the division between the more traditional and the post-structuralist views of texts. In the positivist approach, the nature of the text is objective and the research method is close to identifying the non-random variation in the material. The role of researcher is that of an outsider. In the linguistic approach, the text is considered to be emergent and again the role of researcher is that of an outsider. This approach differs from the positivist because it investigates the relationship between language and reality, that is, how language produces reality. However, in the interpretative approach, the text is considered subjective, the role of the researcher is that of an insider, and the research method focuses on the cultural influences of the text.

From a qualitative research point of view texts are also always artefacts and new ways in Internet data mining may also produce interesting contextualized qualitative data in the future. The recording, organization and governing of the data becomes even more important when the use of the Internet as a source for data has become more common, as webpages change and expire, and their content changes and disappear. Keeping a log, copying and keeping data records, with various versions, detailed data gathering of information and recording is a crucial part of using the Internet as a data source, as also for all data and diaries of various kinds. This importance of documenting concerns also the progress in data gathering, and the various steps taken in the analysis and reporting of the data. Detailing this to one's own use is beneficial if and when you need to re-visit earlier decisions made in the progress of the research. Revisiting earlier deci-sions concerning data gathering can often help in further decision making, and help in explicating various steps taken in the data-gathering and analysis processes. The diaries are not necessary if the research questions do not require complex or complicated data, or several analyses. The more complex the research topic, the data gathered and the analyses planned are, the more decisions need to be made in the process that concern the data and their forms and functions, so keeping a diary is immensely helpful in the record-keeping process.

Prior to the steps into the analysis, in the initial data-gathering phase, it is also good to think about and recognize when to stop gathering the data. As this is dependent on the research questions you have, the types of data you have planned to collect and the ways you have designed your research, there is no universal or unequivocal answer to this question. The circularity of the research process gives you more possi-bilities to be flexible about the start and end processes. For case studies, where a case can consist of several types of data, you may need to think more carefully about what type of data you require, and from which sources you gather that data. In case studies you may also pay attention to designing the exit, that is, when and how to exit the data gathering process.

THE CIRCULARITY OF DATA GATHERING AND ANALYSIS

In qualitative research, the initial research design is crucial for the data-collecting process. Your research questions should indicate what type of data you require and how much you would need to gather. After the initial design, you may have decided to do interviews, perhaps gather documentary materials, or gather observation data. You may have originally decided to do six to eight interviews, gather a few years' documentary materials and for one week gather on-site observation data. Yet, the design may fail you, and if you feel, after the initial analysis, that you have not enough research material, it is very often possible to re-think your research design and/or gather additionally more data. This can happen, for example, if you have not taken into account or if you have not been aware of all those crucial aspects that may affect the quality of the data you gather. Thus, 'going back' to gather more data is sometimes necessary in qualitative research. The circularity of the research process in qualitative research makes it easier to revisit your initial research plan, if needed.

The sequencing of data gathering and analysis may also be part of the initial plan. This means in practice that you gather data, and then analyze them in order to gather more data. This type of circularity or sequencing of the gathering and analysis may prove to be helpful, especially if you do processual research or action research with time span. Unfolding complex questions in the analysis may also require this type of layering of data gathering and data analysis. Thus, thinking rigidly in terms of 'sample size' and 'saturation' prior to the analysis (e.g. Charmaz, 2003, 2006) proves many times more difficult, if not impossible, as qualitative research most often is complex and the results of the data analysis are not known prior to the analysis.

Sample size

In qualitative research the sample size simply explains the possible size of the empirical materials and sources. The term 'sample size' originates from quantitative, exact sciences and refers to the accuracy of defining the data collection source and materials prior to the collection. But as we know, one interview is never like another: the amount of information or data you are able to obtain is not known prior to the interview. Thus, defining the qualitative research sample size equivalent to x number of interviews works against the qualitative research logic. For this reason, the term 'sample size' is not regularly used in qualitative research, and when used, it is with the general understanding of its nature. In practical terms the number of interviews is used to give an approximate size of the study, or time needed for interviews, but not as a predetermined pool of data.

Even if you would not use term 'sample size' there are factors that affect the potential size of the empirical materials gathered. First, in your research design and research question do state whether you aim for in-depth analysis of one case, for example, or comparative analysis of several questions using several criteria for data collection. Thus the intensive vs. extensive design, and the type of data collection methods you will use have an effect on the potential source of the data. Additionally, the practical questions of budget and the resources you will have for use for the study are important. You can have several other selection criteria that you will need to take into account, depending on your research design.

Saturation

The much-used term, 'saturation', relates to the similar type of setting as the 'sample size'. In this type of qualitative research the factual orientation is the starting point, and the researcher wants to find out about facts. In such an approach, the term 'saturation' makes sense: interviews are not interesting for research as sources of discourses or narratives, for example, but as statements with facts or issues with a factual purpose. Still, the point of saturation of the data is difficult to define as new data will always add something new to the existing data. Saturation is not used when the purpose of the qualitative study is not factual. When qualitative research is concerned with meanings and not with making hypothesis statements, then the term 'saturation' is not useful, and some researchers even argue it is inappropriate (Dey, 1999). In Grounded Theory, for example, Strauss and Corbin (1990) argue that saturation is a matter of degree. For them, the issue of time is crucial, as they argue that the longer researchers take to learn about and know their data, familiarize themselves with and analyze their data, the better the results are as there will always be the potential for 'something new to emerge' in the analysis. Our suggestion is that if and when using the term 'saturation', it is necessary to know the type of qualitative research it relates to, as it is not used in all qualitative research.

KEY POINTS OF THE CHAPTER

There is an abundance of qualitative research data that you can use and combine in qualitative business research; the appropriateness of each type of data for your own study should be evaluated on the basis of its ability to provide answers to your research questions through analysis.

Although qualitative interviews are the most common type of qualitative data gathering in business research, you should consider using other types of relevant data as well; there are also different types of qualitative interview, and it is your job to choose the most relevant type for your own study.

Each of the data collection methods requires specific skills and attention to different types of issues, you can learn from these by experimenting, rehearsing and being reflective about what your aims and practices concerning data collecting are.

FURTHER READING

The Handbook of Interview Research. Context and Method, edited by Gubrium and Holstein (2001), is a comprehensive compilation on the subject of interviewing containing a number of excellent articles by well-established qualitative researchers.

DeWalt and DeWalt's (2002) *Participant Observation: A Guide for Fieldworkers* is an excellent and easy-to-read source book on how to do participant observation.

Belk, Fischer and Kozinets' (2013) *Qualitative Consumer and Marketing Research.* London: SAGE presents online observations as part of the consumer research.

EXERCISE 7.1

What annual reports tell us about the company

The purpose of this exercise is to familiarize you with the analysis of textual and visual materials and to show their potential and usefulness in business research.

Choose two or three annual reports of business companies or other organizations. You can either use print versions of them or download them from the Internet. Try to choose companies or corporations that are competitors in the same business sector.

Look at the pictures used in the annual reports, read the texts and analyze both the text and the pictures. You will find more information on the visual analysis in Chapter 20. Use the following points as your guideline when making the analysis:

- Categorize the images of the pictures in some way (e.g. according to type: human beings, products, interaction situations, buildings; according to focus of the picture: faces, interactions, groups of people, products, landscapes; according to colour schemes used; age, ethnicity and gender of people in pictures, etc.).
- Analyze the ways the images relate to the text and/or the production or services of the corporation.

Do this exercise with all two or three annual reports.

Then compare the visual materials used in annual reports and write down in what ways the materials are similar to and/or deviate from one company to another.

EXERCISE 7.2

Research questions that use various types of data

Develop a research topic for the exercise purpose. You can, for example, pick up a contemporary economic news article from a daily newspaper. Gather three types of data in relation to your research topic: short interview of colleague; social media online observation on the topic; newspaper article. Now come up with three different types of research questions that can in principle be answered by using any available data you have. Do you find restrictions that come up with the data?

8

INTERVIEWS AND OBSERVATIONS

This chapter will provide information on:

- qualitative interviews
- how to design and perform them
- what observation is
- how you can collect and use observational data.

QUALITATIVE INTERVIEWS

The purpose of qualitative interviews is to produce research data. In contrast to how you conduct everyday conversations with fellow students, teachers or business managers, a qualitative interviewer prepares themselves for the interview in advance. Also, the interviewer focuses the interview on particular issues that are related to the topic and research questions of their study.

Qualitative interviews, however, come in various forms. In some cases, they can even resemble everyday conversations, in which the questions or their order have not been predetermined. In these cases, the interview is more about interaction and dialogue between two people rather than merely transferring information from the interviewee to the interviewer.

Three types of qualitative interview study

Silverman (2013) provides a typology of interview studies that he calls positivist, emotionalist and constructionist. These focus on different types of research questions; therefore, they also require different types of interview questions.

Positivist (also called naturalist or realist) interview studies are interested in 'facts'. This is why they contain a lot of information questions (Stake, 1995, 2005). For instance, when studying 'a process of organizational change' you would want to collect as accurate information as possible about what happened in this process. You would probably ask the participants the same questions concerning who were involved, in which ways, what events took place, what were the consequences of these to various parties, etc. Your analysis could be focused on putting the pieces from the interviews together and checking across the participants (and perhaps across other sources of information) about the 'true' picture of what happened in this process.

'Emotionalist' (also called subjectivists) interview studies consider interviews as a pathway to the participants' authentic experiences. In this case, you would be studying how people experience the process of organizational change. The interview questions would not focus on information and facts, but on people's perceptions, conceptions, understandings, viewpoints and emotions. You could ask, for instance, 'What happened to your work when this process started?' and 'What did you think about the changes in your co-worker relationships?'

'Constructionist' interview studies focus on how meanings are produced through the interaction that takes place between the interviewer and interviewee. Whereas interaction is the focus here, the interviews often resemble everyday conversations in which the researcher can take a more or less active role as the other party of the conversation. It is quite evident that there is less interaction if the interviewer is passive, as is often the case in standardized and structured interviews. One important point in these kinds of interviews is that the researcher uses their pre-designed questions as initiators of conversation, which can then flow into many directions, depending on how the interaction proceeds.

From research questions into interview questions

The first two types of interview studies described above (positivist and emotionalist) are more interested in research questions starting with the word 'what', and the third one with research questions starting with the word 'how'. Holstein and Gubrium

(2004) point out, however, that the best research is often done by combining 'what' and 'how' research questions. This would actually mean combining different types of interview questions in the same interview.

The main issue is that your interview questions should provide data that will help you answer research questions starting with words 'what' and 'how'.

Therefore, you need to have at least some preliminary research questions before you can start designing your interviews. Then, you should consider what type of interview data allows you to perform the sort of analysis that provides answers to your research questions. For instance, if your research question is 'How do entrepreneurs narrate their experiences concerning financial problems?', your interview questions should focus on generating data that allow you to analyze 'narration'. For this purpose you would need interview data that have allowed the interviewees to describe their experiences rather freely. Structured interviews would not be appropriate for this, so you would need more open interviews.

Inexperienced researchers are often confused about the difference between research questions and interview questions. Here is a simple rule: interviewees can never answer your research questions directly. If they could, there would be no need for analysis, and no need for research.

Different types of qualitative interview

As you can see from the above, both your research approach and research questions should guide the interviews. This includes decisions about what type of qualitative interview (Box 8.1) and what type of interview questions are appropriate in your study. Just as with any other data collection method, you should ask yourself if interviews really are the best way of collecting data for the purposes of your research project. Instead of interviews, it could be relevant to use naturalistic recordings of conversations (see e.g. Silverman 2011, 2013), for instance.

--- **BOX 8.1** ---

Different types of qualitative interview

1. Structured and standardized – same standardized questions for all participants, mostly 'what' questions.
2. Guided and semi-structured – outline of topics, issues, or themes, but variation in wording and sequence; both 'what' and 'how' questions.
3. Unstructured, informal, open and narrative interviews – some guiding questions or core concepts to start with, but freedom to move the conversation in any direction of interest that may come up; both 'what' and 'how' questions.

A common reason for the use of interviews in business research is that they are an efficient and practical way of collecting information that you cannot find in a published form. But there are also other reasons, such as the aim to study people's experiences as seen from their points of view, or the social construction of knowledge concerning the chosen topic. It is good to keep this in mind when considering what type of interview and interview question would be most appropriate for your study.

Structured and standardized interviews

Interviews made with a positivist 'what' question in mind tend to be structured and standardized. This means that, the interviewer adheres to a pre-designed script with little flexibility in the wording or order of questions. A structured and standardized interview is considered 'qualitative' when the responses given by participants are open-ended. These types of interview are efficient in terms of collecting information about 'facts' (e.g. what happened, when and how; who were involved and how). They are also useful when it is necessary to reduce variety caused by several interviewers involved, when interviewers are less knowledgeable, or when it is important to be able to compare the information provided by the participants in a systematic manner.

Structured and standardized interviews can be a good choice if you must rely on volunteer or inexperienced interviewers, or if you have limited time and money available for your research. The major drawback is that the interviewer has little flexibility to respond to the particular concerns of the interviewee, and there is no guarantee that the questions asked focus on the issues that are most relevant in the social context that is being studied. It could be argued that standardized interviews are too restrictive to be used as the main source of data in qualitative research.

Guided and semi-structured interviews

This type of interview can be used to study both 'what' and 'how' questions. When making a guided or semi-structured interview, you take a pre-designed outline of topics, issues, or themes with you, but still have the possibility to vary the wording and order of questions in each interview. The major advantage is that the materials are somewhat systematic and comprehensive, while the tone of the interview is fairly conversational and informal.

This type of interview works well when you have some interview experience or prepare yourself thoroughly. A major challenge is to take care that all topics on the outline are covered and, at the same time, be prepared to probe for more in-depth responses. Keeping too close to the pre-designed questions can prevent important topics from being raised by the interviewee. While this format is systematic to a certain extent, it may still be difficult to analyze and compare 'facts' because the interviewees are allowed more freedom than in structured interviews in choosing what they want to talk about and how.

Unstructured, narrative, informal and open interviews

Qualitative interviews can also be unstructured, informal, open, and narrative in nature. This type of interview is useful for exploring the research subject in depth and from the participant's point of view. Unstructured interviewing differs from structured interviewing in several ways. First, a formal interview protocol is not used although you may have some guiding questions. Second, you are free to move the conversation in any direction of interest that may come up.

Further, these interviews rely to a great extent on what the interviewee talks about. In narrative interviews, the main purpose is to produce a narrative. In her study, Hytti (2003) encouraged entrepreneurs to construct their life histories in order to be able to study their entrepreneurial identities. While narrative interviews are pre-designed to a certain extent (e.g. the topic of the interview has been defined beforehand) a conversational interview may occur more spontaneously. In the latter case, the interviewee may not consider this to be an interview, but needs to be told that the researcher will use the conversation as data. In both cases, the more specific content of the interview emerges from the immediate context, or is defined by the participant. This is why the focus of the interview is not strictly predetermined by the researcher.

The advantage of an unstructured, informal, open, or narrative interview is that it is highly individualized, contextualized, and relevant to the interviewee – not just the researcher. This type of interview is likely to produce insights that a researcher could not have anticipated. Conducting such an interview requires good interpersonal skills, which means that you need to know how to interact with the interviewee.

Designing and performing interviews

In accordance with different types of interview, there are a variety of question types that you can use (Box 8.2). Although it is quite common to use the same types of questions throughout the interview, you can also combine them. If you do, you should carefully consider their order. For example, if you ask structured and closed questions first then it may require extra effort to encourage the interviewee to talk more freely later in the interview.

Open and closed interview questions

Interview questions can vary between very open-ended, such as 'Tell me the story of your professional career', to very closed, such as 'Do you have work experience in this business or not?' There is also an option in between these two, such as 'Give me three events in your career that have been most exciting and motivating'. Open-ended questions give the participant more control over what is talked about and usually produce more detailed responses.

BOX 8.2

Interview questions

Open and closed: open questions encourage more speech.

Simple and complex: simple questions are easier to understand and answer.

Neutral and leading: neutral questions leave more choice for the participant.

Direct and indirect: indirect questions are more suitable for sensitive issues.

Primary and secondary: a combination of both can be used when it is necessary to get a more complete account.

Simple and complex interview questions

Making several simple questions one after the other usually works better than using one complex question. For instance, it is better to ask 'How did the merger process start?', 'Who were involved at the beginning?' and 'How did the CEO react?' than 'Can you describe to me all the details: opportunities, problems and consequences of this three-year merger process?' The more complex your question, the more likely it is that the interviewee finds it difficult to answer.

Neutral and leading interview questions

Neutral questions try to avoid pre-assumptions and pre-given typologies. A leading question, such as 'You would like to be a strategic manager, wouldn't you?', clearly indicates the response the interviewer expects to get. Less obvious leading questions typically provide the interviewee with a typology that they are expected to use in their response. For instance, asking 'Have your experiences as a woman manager been good or bad?' encourages the interviewee to categorize her experiences as 'positive' and 'negative'. Furthermore, the question emphasizes the gender of the interviewee as something exceptional (in some cases, this may be done on purpose). A more neutral question would be 'What experiences have you had in this job?'

Direct and indirect interview questions

Usually, a direct question produces more talk than an indirect one. However, it is not wise to ask overtly direct questions if you suspect that the interviewee might be offended, hurt, or embarrassed by this. One technique is to use a series of related questions approaching the issue that you would like to discuss. You can also ask the interviewee to speculate about how others in their situation think about the issue and then move to their own views about it. For example, gender issues are often a sensitive topic in business research. Let us consider that you wanted to interview women board members about their experiences and include gender as a central topic in your study. You would not go ahead and start the interview by asking direct questions such as 'How does it feel to be the only woman on the Board of Directors of this company?' Instead, you could start by asking 'Tell me about what happened in the last board meeting?' Depending on what kind of description the interviewee produces, you can ask for more details such as 'What did you do?', 'What kind of point of view did you take', and 'How did the others react?' In this way, you can make room for the interviewee to talk about gender issues, and later on ask about them directly.

Primary and secondary interview questions

When you offer the interviewee a question and get a response, you may want to continue the discussion and elaboration of their response instead of moving into the following question. It might be a good idea to try to discuss each question and response as far as possible by asking 'Can you tell me more about that?' or 'What do you mean when you say…?' During the interview, it may also be necessary to ask reflective questions that provide you with the possibility to check your understanding about a specific response, or give the interviewee an opportunity to add in or correct some details. It is quite common to make some clearing questions at the end of the interview to find out whether there are other issues that the interviewee would like to discuss, for example, 'Can you think of anything else that would be important to you when considering your relationship with the customers?'

Recording and transcribing

There are several ways of recording interviews: notes written on the spot, notes written afterwards, and taping the interview with a tape recorder. You can also videotape interviews if you wish to analyze interaction between yourself and the participant. Writing notes on the spot interferes with the process of interviewing, and notes written afterwards easily miss out details. In situations when the topic of the interview is very sensitive (e.g. negative feelings towards co-workers or the success of strategic decisions), the research participants may prefer that you take notes instead of tape or video recording. In most cases, the participants agree to have the interview tape recorded. When doing this, it is essential to use good quality equipment, which you have studied and tested beforehand.

Transcribing tape-recorded interviews takes quite a lot of time, but it is a very good way to familiarize yourself with the interviews. You can also have a professional to transcribe the interviews. In both cases you should decide how the transcription is made (Poland, 2001). This depends on your research questions and on the nature of the analyses that you plan to perform. In business research, it is most often enough to have a transcription that includes all the words that have been said, and maybe pauses also. However, for discourse analysis and particularly for conversation analysis this is not enough. You can find detailed instructions of how to transcribe tapes for these purposes from methodology books such as Silverman's *Interpreting Qualitative Data* (2011).

Interviews with business people

Rather than interviews being a taken-for-granted method of collecting empirical materials, which is often the case in business research, we advise you to consider carefully the virtues and limitations of qualitative interviews in your research project. In any case, you should give a reason for the use of interviews and, furthermore, for the use of certain types of interviews in your research report.

In addition to learning about the various types of interviews that you can choose from, it is useful to pay attention to some practical issues concerning the art of interviewing business people. These are outlined in Box 8.3.

BOX 8.3

Undertaking interviews with business people

Do your homework well. Agree on the timetable well in advance, have all the materials you need ready, and make sure that you will find the place where you will make the interview.

Be there on time. Most preferably, arrive somewhat in advance to have some slack time to relax and quickly go through the most important issues of the interview.

Dress appropriately, considering both your position as a student-researcher and the dress code of the organization that you are visiting.

When you meet the research participant, introduce yourself briefly. Then explain how you wish the interview to proceed and how long it will take.

Ask for permission to use a tape recorder.

End on time. If you need more time, ask if it is possible to continue the interview for a fixed time (e.g. 20 minutes).

As you leave, thank the participant for their time and make sure that you have agreed on what the participant will receive as feedback from your research. The feedback can be a draft of your research report that can be commented on or the final report.

Afterwards, it is polite to write a thank you note or e-mail.

PARTICIPANT AND NON-PARTICIPANT OBSERVATIONS

Observation is a key social science method of collecting empirical data in which the researcher may or may not have direct contact with the people and events being observed. Various observation techniques can be distinguished along at least four dimensions:

1. Participant and non-participant observation, depending on whether the researcher is part of the situation they are studying, or not.
2. Obtrusive and non-obtrusive, or disguised and non-disguised observation, depending on whether the research participants know that they are being observed, or not.
3. Observation in natural and contrived settings, depending on whether action is observed where it occurs 'naturally' without the researcher's involvement, or in a contrived setting.
4. Structured and non-structured observation, depending on whether a checklist determines what is being observed, or not.

Participant observation

Participant observation is a demanding way of collecting empirical materials and is mostly used in ethnographic research (see Chapter 12). It requires that the researcher becomes a participant in the culture or context being observed. The literature on participant observation discusses how to enter the context, the role of the researcher as a participant, the collection and storage of field notes, and the analysis of field data. In business research, participant observation requires weeks and months if the research context is familiar to the researcher (if you are an insider), or even years if you enter a context that is not familiar to you (if you are an outsider).

Non-participant observation

A non-participant or direct observer does not try to become a participant in the context they study; instead, they try to be as unobtrusive as possible. In direct observation, the researcher is watching rather than taking part; therefore, technology is often used to collect the data. The researcher can, for instance, videotape action or events, or observe from behind two-way mirrors. Direct observation can be focused on more specific issues compared with participant observation because you are able to revisit the observation several times (e.g. on a videotape or in the form of photographs). The business researcher could, for instance, observe clearly defined situations such as meetings, or specific people such as consumers, rather than try to become immersed in the context. Direct observation often takes a shorter time than participant observation.

Advantages and limitations

One distinct advantage in making observations is that it records action as it takes place. This is different from people describing afterwards what they said or did, or what they believe they will do or say in the future, as people do in interviews. In some cases, it may even be the focus of research to compare observed activities with the statements given about them. For instance, when the activity studied is subject to social pressure (e.g. the manager giving positive feedback to employees), making observations in addition to interviews can be useful.

Observation does not provide any insights into what a person thinks about the action or what might motivate it. This information can only be obtained by asking people. When people are being observed, whether they are aware of it or not, ethical issues arise that you need to consider. For instance, advanced technologies, such as hidden cameras and microphones, have made it easy to collect empirical data about the verbal and non-verbal activities of consumers, customers, employees and managers. Collecting data while people are unaware invades their privacy and can even be considered abusive.

What to observe and how?

When you plan to make observations, it may at first seem difficult to make a decision on what to observe. However, there are several things that you can observe (see Box 8.4). Often, the researcher starts out with observing the setting, such as a company meeting room, employee coffee room or a shopping centre. In addition, you would pay attention to the human and social environment, which includes characteristics of people (e.g. gender, ethnicity, age group, appearance), as well as patterns, frequency and direction of interaction and communication.

Both business professions and business organizations have their own vocabularies and ways of talking and communicating. You can also observe these and become familiar with them. Knowing the language enhances your understanding about what happens in the setting that you are observing. Non-verbal communication is just as important as verbal communication. It includes body language, facial expressions and ways of behaving.

───────────────────── BOX **8.4** ─────────────────────

What can be observed in a research setting?
(Modified from Spradley, 1980)

Space. What is the physical space like? For example, what is the size of the office, what are its location, architecture, colours and smells?

Actors. Who is involved? For example, women, men, children; company people, citizens; young, old, middle-aged. How do these people look? How do they relate to each other?

Activities. What are people doing? For example, are they having a formal meeting, daily coffee break, or ad hoc conversations? Are they explaining, negotiating, or arguing?

Objects. What objects and artefacts are present? Where are they? Do they look much used or new?

Events. What kind of event is it? For example, is it a board meeting, feedback session, training seminar? Is it crowded, well-planned, professional?

Goals. What do the people involved try to accomplish? For example, do they arrive at an agreement of schedule, resolution of conflict, or exchange of opinions?

Feelings. What is the mood of the group of people or individuals involved? For example, are they anxious, sad, relieved, or energetic?

As a business researcher you would be interested in business-related settings and events, such as management team or board meetings, negotiations of mergers and acquisitions, and sales negotiations. When studying events like these, you may observe one or several of the following issues:

- Who initiates the event and in what way?
- What happens during the event?
- Who is present? Who is involved?
- What are the participants' verbal and non-verbal reactions?
- What is communicated, both verbally and non-verbally?
- What are the signals indicating that this activity is about to end?
- What is communicated regarding such signals, both verbally and non-verbally?
- How is this particular activity related to the other activities that are observed?

It can also be revealing for a researcher to turn their focus on observing things that do not happen instead of what does happen. As an example, imagine a company training programme which, according to the brochures, intends to be 'participative'. What you observe in the training sessions is that the employees do not speak up, nor do they volunteer in describing their own perspectives, expectations or experiences. Instead, you notice that the educator controls interaction top-down; doing most of the talking in the form of directives and suggestions. Noticing and recording that an intended event did not happen may be just as important as recording that it did happen. This observation can spur both new research questions and further investigations as to why intended outcomes are not occurring.

KEY POINTS OF THE CHAPTER

Although qualitative interviews are among the most common types of qualitative data in business research, you should consider if they are suited to your study aims.

Qualitative interviews come in many forms; it is your job to choose which forms suit your study aims.

Observation data are typically combined with other data in business research in which participant observation is more typical than non-participant observation.

FURTHER READING

InterViews. Learning the Craft of Qualitative Research Interviewing by Brinkmann and Kvale (2014) offers a thorough and practical introduction to interviews.

Participant Observation: A Guide for Fieldworkers by DeWalt and DeWalt (2010) is an easy-to-read source book on how to do participant observation.

--------- EXERCISE 8.1 ---------

Styles and techniques used by the interviewer

The purpose of this exercise is to learn about different ways of performing qualitative interviews, and to teach you the importance of considering your own style and techniques.

- Start with a videotaped interview. You can use your own interviews (or perform one for the exercise), or take one from the media.
- Make a detailed analysis of the style and techniques used by the interviewer. Analyze one or more of the following issues:

  - Interview questions – how can you describe these? What questions could the interviewer have posed instead of those that were used?
  - Way of posing the questions – what is the style, frequency, and relation of a new question to the answer of the previous question?
  - Content of interview – what is the topic and the themes or issues dealt with in the interview, and what can be learned about these on the basis of this interview?

○ The roles of the interviewer and the participant - how can you describe these, and do they vary as the interview proceeds?

○ The flow of the interview - what is interaction like; what is the order of questions; what kind of pauses are there; does the interviewer let the participant talk freely?

- Reflect on how well you succeeded. What could you have done better?

EXERCISE 8.2

Non-participant observation

With this exercise you will learn to collect observation data without being a participant in what you are observing.

- Choose a building that you have convenient access to such as a library, church or store.
- Make a list of about five things that you can observe in and around that building without participating in any of them (see Box 8.4). These might include the architecture of the building, how it is used by different people, how people work in the building, how people meet each other in the building, etc.
- Visit the building and observe the things you listed one by one and write down your observations.
- You can also take photographs or make drawings on your observations.
- Go through your observation data and reflect on how well you succeeded in your task.

EXERCISE 8.3

Participant observation

This exercise develops your skills in planning and performing observations as a participant of what you are observing.

- Choose an activity that you do regularly with your friends or family members. These might include some sports activities, going to the movies or having a dinner at a restaurant.
- Tell the other persons participating that you will perform an exercise and observe what you are doing together.
- Make a list of about five things that you would be able to observe at the same time as participating in them. For all five things, consider how you can store your observations; will you be able to record your observation with a tape recorder or a video camera? Will you be able to write them down immediately or afterwards? Can you take photographs, etc.?
- Participate and make observations in the way you planned.
- Go through your participant observation data and reflect on how well you succeeded in your task.

9

DIGITAL DATA

This chapter will provide information on:

- the value of digital data
- what existing digital materials are available for researchers
- how digital materials can be collected
- how computer software can be used in analyzing digital data.

THE RELEVANCE OF DIGITAL RESEARCH

Since the 1990s, digital technologies have transformed the way we live, work and do business. Although not all people are able or willing to rely on digital technologies, they have a direct or indirect impact on us. For many, it is difficult to imagine leading a business enterprise, working in an office, on a service counter or a hospital, or studying and doing research without computers, smart phones, e-mail and the Internet.

Simultaneously with the growth of other digital applications in companies, digital research has flourished for purposes such as market analysis, product planning, testing of consumer preferences and segmentation. Within companies, digital materials and methods are used to monitor organizational culture, plan and implement strategies, and collect new business ideas, for instance.

Digital technologies offer a variety of novel ways of doing qualitative research (Paulus, Lester and Dempster, 2013). Terms such as 'Internet research', 'virtual research', 'electronic research', 'e-research' and 'online research' refer to the increasing use of digital data and digital tools, such as computers, tablets, smart phones and video cameras, in scholarly research projects. As a result, you can find an increasing number of specific methods books on digital research in the social sciences (e.g. Dolowitz, Buckler and Sweeney, 2008; Fielding, Lee and Blank, 2008; Hine, 2012; Paulus et al., 2013).

Although digital tools can have an effect on every step of the research process, we will focus this chapter on various types of digital research materials relevant for business research, and the use of computer software packages in empirical analysis.

THREE CATEGORIES OF DIGITAL RESEARCH DATA

For business researchers, three categories of digital research data are useful in various types of research projects:

- research literature published in digital form
- existing digital data, not initiated by the researcher (e.g. annual reports and other company documents, e-mails, blogposts and other social media materials)
- digital data produced by the users of digital technologies for research purposes (e.g. e-mail interviews, digital focus groups, virtual ethnography).

Digital research literature

Research literature is increasingly provided in digital form, either as complementary to articles and books in print form or by itself, without printed versions of the same. An increasing amount of digital research literature can be found on the Internet for free. In addition, literature can be searched from commercial databases.

University students, teachers and researchers have access to a vast amount of digital materials through their library. These include digital books, digital journals, various types of database, library catalogues, and digital services for saving and organizing citations and full text materials. Because the services offered and the methods used for searching may vary, it is wise to find out from your library how the system works and what services are available. In addition to having good web pages, libraries offer tutorials that give specific advice on how to use their services.

There is some difference between the literature that you will find on the Internet and that you will find in the digital services provided by libraries. While the library databases include literature that has been exposed to various academic evaluation systems, all materials published on the Internet have not. This is why it is your job as a user to evaluate what digital literature would be relevant and appropriate to be used in research.

When using literature published on the Internet, it is important to evaluate the sites and web pages that you intend to use critically. In particular, if you use simple key words and a search engine such as Google, providing hundreds of web pages by one click, it can take considerable time and skill to evaluate which are good sources in terms of the goals of your literature search. We advise you to start evaluating business research-related sites and web pages with the following general questions focusing on who has produced the content and for what purpose.

Who?

- Whose web address is it (e.g. is it a university address, company address, online journal address; in which country)?
- Who is the author of the information presented on a site or a web page (e.g. academic author, market researcher, consultant, teacher, political activist)?
- For whom was the information written or compiled (e.g. researchers, business people, students, consumers)?

What?

- What is the purpose of the site or web page (e.g. informing, entertaining, advertising)?
- What is the content of the site or web page (e.g. information, advertisements, public opinions)?
- What is the currency of the information (e.g. publication years of the references, last update of the site)?
- What is the accuracy and completeness of the information (e.g. how many references are given)?

Existing digital data

There is an enormous amount of existing data in digital form dealing with industries, companies, products and services, as well as managers, experts and consumers. As we described in Chapter 8, existing empirical data are texts and other materials that a researcher has not produced for research purposes.

The biggest challenge for a business researcher is not the shortage of existing digital materials, but rather their relevance and quality. Just as in searching for digital research literature, the key is figuring out in advance what kinds of material you want to find. Are you looking for basic information on the airline industry, strategies of global service companies, diaries or blogs of business writers, or do you want to know what types of patents European pharmaceutical companies have?

Basic business information is rather easy to find from business portals and from the web pages of industrial associations and large companies. More specific information may require specialist skills in formulating key words and using directories as well as databases. Personal materials, such as home pages, diaries and blogs, are easy to find, but locating specific ones can be more challenging.

Both the Internet and the library are good places to start looking for existing empirical data on industries, companies and business people. Libraries have subscription-only databases. Industry and company information is available online from many databases such as Business Source Premier and ABI Inform. All these databases, for example, contain current articles from trade journals and they can be searched by key words and subject headings. There are also a great number of online public records databases.

You can find a good amount of useful information on the web pages of large companies, non-profit organizations, associations and other organizations such as research institutions, universities and science parks. Besides the information provided, these types of web pages provide a lot of cultural and visual materials (e.g. stories and discourses; photographs and pictures; colours and symbols) that can be used in qualitative business research.

A typical organization website contains basic information about the organization: its goals and operations and the people running the organization. Similarly, company websites offer the basics of the company profile. The web pages can also provide a description of the company mission and vision, as well as key people and customers. Sometimes, a history of the company is included, perhaps with a vivid and memorable story about how the company was established by the founder. Large companies may also provide biographies of CEOs and the owners, or owner-families.

If you are lucky you can find such items as press releases and even copies of company magazines on the websites of organizations, corporations and companies. These are useful as sources of information that may never make it into the media and may also include insider articles about people and events, as well as the norms and values of the company. Press releases serve as a primary source for official company positions, claims and arguments that are used discursively to produce a certain version of company reality. Many global companies put lists of their factories, offices and other facilities on their web pages, including their location.

A good example of an informative company website is provided by The Body Shop (www.thebodyshop.com; website read 07/09/2015). The *About Us* section provides basic information on the company, its environmental values, history and the founder, Anita Roddick. The section named *Our Values* contains information on what the company believes in and how these beliefs are demonstrated in its business. The section contains detailed information on issues such as community trade principles, animal testing principles, human rights, ethical trade and more. The section called Careers describes the work opportunities that The Body Shop provides worldwide.

An important source of information for a business researcher is provided by annual reports, which you can find both from company web pages and from specialist websites. Annual reports typically include information about strategies, business operations, products and services, financial results, management and organization structure. Most of them include statements written by the CEO about the business, the company and its future visions.

Many organizations and individuals are active in social media (Fuchs, 2013) and use it for marketing and recruiting purposes, for instance. External corporate and organization blogs are also published on the Internet to enhance interaction with a network of stakeholders. Internal blogs, published on the intranet of the organization, are used for internal communication, identity building and organization development purposes. For instance, managers and employees can post their suggestions on more effective marketing practices on the blog and anyone can read and comment on them.

Personal materials on the Internet are created by an individual as opposed to organizations and companies. Personal pages may contain any kind of textual material of personal interest, including information, opinions, stories, poems, jokes and lyrics. They often include photographs, videos and links to other web pages.

Digital diaries and journals are used by people to write entries arranged by date, reporting on everyday events. Many people use these as a medium with which to chronicle their lives to a worldwide audience. A personal blog is a website that is operated by an individual for personal purposes. Often, it serves as an extension of an online diary, because entries are made in journal style and displayed in chronological order. In the same way as personal home pages, blogs can combine text and images, links to other people's blogs and pages, as well as links related to the topics that are described in the blog (e.g. movies and TV shows, shopping, dieting, etc.). Besides storying personal lives, blogs often provide commentaries on news and politics. In fact, blogs are rather popular among politicians. A central part of many personal blogs is that readers can post their comments on the blog.

A researcher should approach materials on the web with a similar kind of critical attitude as they would any other research materials. Critical assessment is particularly relevant when you use web materials as sources of information. However, when you use digital materials as cultural texts, their quality as information is not the main issue. In this case, digital materials on the Internet are valid in representing a culture whether they are truthful or not. For example, a company website or a personal blog represents and constructs a specific version of reality whether it is true or not.

COLLECTING DIGITAL DATA

The general methods of collecting qualitative data, ranging from interviews and focus groups to observation, have been adapted for digital materials. When you consider the suitability of initiating the collection of new digital materials specifically for your research project, it is important to keep in mind that relying on digital technologies, such as computers, smarts phones and tablets, limits your research to individuals and groups who have both access to them and competence in using them. However, using digital methods in business research may also democratize the study (see Box 9.1). For instance, undertaking e-mail interviews in a global company allows a number of people from different countries and cultures to participate; or, by conducting online focus groups with young people, you are able to reach those who live in remote areas and would not be able to travel long distances just for one focus group discussion. Another advantage is that digital research allows participants to take part in your research in a familiar environment (e.g. home or office), which may make them feel more relaxed in expressing themselves and in responding when and how they feel comfortable.

BOX **9.1**

Some advantages of using digital data in business research

- Access to geographically dispersed population (e.g. employees of a multi-national company in different countries).
- Access to individuals or groups who are difficult to reach with any other methods (e.g. executives, members of the board of directors).
- Savings in costs (e.g. receiving materials in textual form, no need for transcription).
- Flexibility (e.g. participants can choose when they will write their responses).

Digital interviews and focus groups

Digital interviews and focus groups resemble their traditional counterparts to a great extent. However, owing to the technologies used in designing and pursuing them, they are divided into two main types: synchronous and asynchronous. The main difference between these is that synchronous interviews and focus groups take place in real time, whereas asynchronous interviews do not (Kivits, 2005; Lokman, 2006).

Synchronous digital interviews and focus groups resemble face-to-face situations, in that all parties are digital and interact simultaneously. Real-time virtual interaction needs to be facilitated technically, either with a software package that all participants can access and learn to use, or by using services provided by social media, for instance.

When conducting asynchronous interviews and focus groups, the researcher sends out interview questions to the participants by e-mail or some other media. Compared with synchronous and face-to-face situations, the advantage of asynchronous e-mail interviews and focus groups is that the participants can write their responses to the questions at their convenience and take time in considering how and what to answer to each of the questions. This can be a real advantage when dealing with busy business people, such as managers, experts and entrepreneurs. Another advantage is that the participant can edit their responses until satisfied with them.

Recruiting for digital interviews and focus groups is done in multiple ways, including individual requests through e-mail or personal websites, invitations through social media, as well as snowballing (Hamilton and Bowers, 2006). When considering the collection of new digital materials, you should plan this carefully to increase the willingness of the potential interviewees to participate in your project. What makes a big difference is how accurate the instructions are, how many questions there are, and how easy they are to understand and discuss. One common problem with recruiting is that many people routinely ignore these due to the overload of digital research requests.

Virtual ethnography

Virtual ethnography refers to fieldwork that takes place in virtual groups, communities, or networks. Virtual groups of people interact on various types of interactive websites. Studying virtual business teams and consumer groups, for instance, benefits from this version of ethnographic research. The ability of virtual ethnography to transform the traditional localized 'field site' into a 'cyberspace' that can be anywhere is an aspect with great potential value in business research, which addresses global and cross-cultural research problems.

Despite its new features, virtual ethnography attempts to safeguard the central aim of ethnographic studies, that is, the immersion of the researcher into the lives and culture of the participants (e.g. Hine, 2005). Although interactions within a virtual group form the central body of research materials, virtual ethnographers use any digital material to make observations about the group of people that they are studying. This may involve both non-participant and participant observation. The difference between these is whether or not the researcher participates in the production of the materials.

In marketing, Kozinets (2010) uses the term 'netnography' to adapt ethnography to the study of digital consumer communities. In his article, he develops a marketing research technique for providing consumer insight and to provide information on the symbolism, meanings, and consumption patterns of digital consumer groups. Kozinets (2010) also discusses how a researcher can acknowledge the digital environment, respect the inherent flexibility and openness of ethnography, and provide rigour and ethics in the conduct of marketing research. Providing a living example, the researcher describes and analyzes a digital coffee newsgroup and discusses its marketing implications.

Ethical issues with digital data

Although digital research methods are unlikely to replace any traditional research methods, the development of digital technologies provides new opportunities and can even have surprising methodological consequences. Accordingly, digital research has some ethical aspects of its own, and there are potential problems in using digital materials in business research (see Box 9.2). Overall, business researchers need to plan and execute studies using digital materials with caution and reflexivity.

─────────────── BOX **9.2** ───────────────

Some potential problems with digital research materials in business research

- Lack of interest and motivation (e.g. business people and consumers receiving too many invitations to provide digital materials for researchers).
- Distrust in confidentiality (e.g. is a research project based on data collected from social media respectable?).
- Distraction of the participants while providing data (e.g. writing responses at a meeting or while watching the television).
- Technological issues (e.g. access to digital technologies; competence in using them).
- Identity verification (e.g. how can you know that a company blog was written by the CEO and not their media assistant?).

As with any other method of collecting qualitative materials, it is essential in digital research that you provide the participants with accurate information about your research and get their informed consent. In addition, you, as a researcher, need to ensure that you can protect the privacy of participants and maintain confidentiality of the materials you collect. A minimum requirement is that you strip all identifying information (names, e-mail addresses, personal page or blog addresses) from the materials when using and storing them. You can find more detailed discussion on the ethics of digital research from many sources (e.g. Heider and Massanari, 2012; Rogers, 2013).

COMPUTER SOFTWARE FOR DIGITAL DATA

Besides literature searches and data collection, digital technologies have also changed the ways qualitative data analysis can be made. Technologies for recording, videoing, saving, creating databases, mapping and handling data have all fed into the development of software programs for handling qualitative data and performing data analysis. These software programs are referred to as QDA and CAQDAS. QDA is an acronym for qualitative data analysis and CAQDAS is an acronym for computer-assisted qualitative data analysis, and both refer to the ways of using computer programs available for the analysis of qualitative data.

Computer software packages for qualitative research are widely available and will help the researcher with large amounts of qualitative data. The possibilities for using computer software packages range from making notes in the field, writing up or transcribing notes and interview materials, editing, coding, attaching key words and tags to segments of text to storage, search and retrieve commands, data linking, memo and report writing. All these activities are easier to handle and keep in mind with the help of the software programs, which are especially designed for organizing and analyzing, in various forms, large amounts of qualitative research data.

For a business researcher, CAQDAS can be useful, but they are not a standard requirement. When considering the use of CAQDAS, it is important to remember that even if data analysis software can help you with data management, organization and analysis, it does not provide any theoretical or analytical frameworks. It is still the job of the researcher to decide what theoretical and methodological concepts and ideas frame the study. This is something that a novice business researcher sometimes tends to forget.

It is also good to keep in mind that the theoretical framework you have chosen might or might not suit the type of analysis that you are able to make with a specific software package. When choosing the software, it is good to carefully consider what kind of analysis will be used for the study. Is it exploratory or confirming analysis, or perhaps descriptive analysis? Do you plan to develop a coding scheme through induction, or do you plan to use a predefined scheme? How do you want to present the data in your research report, etc.? All these questions relate to the analytic framework that you must develop yourself, prior to using any software programs.

Characteristics of CAQDAS

There are several software packages on the market, and they follow the same principles of helping a researcher to perform various procedures. In the following, we will describe these briefly. We do not present any specific software packages; instead, we will provide an overall understanding of how software can be used in qualitative business research. Good overviews and comparisons of the key features of CAQDAS software packages can be found in Silver and Lewins (2014). Bazeley and Jackson (2013), in turn, provide experience-based knowledge concerning one of the most used software packages – NVivo.

In principle, all available software packages take a qualitative approach to qualitative data. This means that the software packages do not focus on the kind of content analysis in which frequencies of words or expressions are counted. Thus, the software packages do not 'force' qualitative data into quantitative mode. However, many of them can be used for combining quantitative and qualitative data.

The following questions can be used to assess the suitability of a specific software package for your research (for more details, see Silver and Lewins (2014)):

- How much and what kind of data do you have or plan to collect?
- How do you want to handle the data in your research?
- What kind of theoretical framework do you have for your research?
- What kind of methodology have you planned for your research?

Overall, we think that if your university or research institution offers access to software, it is useful and educating to have a try with it (Box 9.3). As you become more experienced and adept with the use of software, you can find new adaptations of the programs that open up ways to handle and present your qualitative analysis in a meaningful way.

BOX 9.3

Some advantages of CAQDAS in business research

- It can help in handling large volumes of qualitative data.
- Search and retrieve functions make data management easier than word-processing programs, especially with large volumes of qualitative data.
- Offers team research possibilities in comparative research and large multi-site research projects (e.g. projects where data come from different countries, on the basis of multi-site data collection).

The disadvantages and limitations attached to the use of CAQDAS are often related to their technical qualities. When planning to use CAQDAS, you should think about questions and issues such as whether there is a major difference between what you can do with the software and with the word-processing programs. Do you plan to take advantage of the specific functions of the software package, or would you use it in a similar manner to word processing? Also, keep in mind that not all analyses gain as much as others in the use of software.

The specific functions of most CAQDAS programs, such as Atlas.ti, NVivo, the Ethnograph and others, make instant access to data easy and code generation simple and flexible. As some of the much used programs, such as Atlas.ti, have been developed with a specific relationship to the grounded theory approach (see Chapter 15), they also carry limitations in terms of their usability. In particular, these limitations concern the analysis of small data extracts, which is common in some forms of discourse analysis (Chapter 17) such as positioning analysis (see e.g. Katila and Eriksson, 2013) as well as conversation analysis and semiotic analysis.

How can you use computer software in qualitative business research?

Even if software offers many possibilities for qualitative analysis, ranging from storage, management and coding to content analysis, memoing and theory building, not all data analysis proceeds in a similar way. Kelle (2000), for instance, elaborates on two different strategies of using software in qualitative research. The first is closely linked to the Grounded Theory approach (see Chapter 15). Here, the analysis starts with developing codes inductively from the empirical data through six specified steps (Kelle, 2000: 295):

Step 1: formatting textual data for the analysis

Step 2: coding data with ad hoc codes (so-called open coding)

Step 3: writing memos and relating them to specific segments of the text

Step 4: comparing segments of the text to which the same codes have been attached

Step 5: integrating codes and, if needed, attaching memos to codes

Step 6: developing a core category.

The second strategy has an interest to link qualitative data to quantitative data through the development and analysis of a data matrix. This strategy has nine steps and it is more formalized than the first one. Here, the code scheme is developed at the beginning of the analysis process (Kelle, 2000: 296):

Step 1: formatting textual data

Step 2: defining a code scheme (e.g. from theory)

Step 3: coding data with the help of the code scheme

Step 4: linking memos to the codes during the coding process

Step 5: comparing text segments to which the same codes have been attached

Step 6: developing (possible) sub-categories from the comparison

Step 7: recoding the data with the sub-categories

Step 8: producing a numerical data matrix

Step 9: analyzing the data matrix with IBM SPSS statistics or some other statistics program.

Both of the strategies are ideal types that the user can develop to suit the objectives and aims of their research. Thus, the software does not design any specific data analysis for you, but it offers pragmatic tools to choose in between a variety of analysis strategies.

Overall, CAQDAS is useful for performing the practical procedures of analyzing empirical data, such as searching and retrieving data segments and maintaining links with codes. However, you should keep in mind that it cannot perform an in-depth contextualized analysis by itself, such as is required in discourse and narrative research (Silverman, 2013) and in intensive case studies and ethnographies. With this type of analysis, researchers' interpretative and reflexive skills are emphasized and they cannot be replaced with computer software. Therefore, developing knowledge about specific methods of analysis, their philosophical backgrounds and requirements is still an essential task in terms of performing a successful qualitative study, with or without the help of computer software.

KEY POINTS OF THE CHAPTER

Digital research, including digital materials and data, as well as software for making the analysis, provides new ways of conducting qualitative research in business studies.

While using digital research literatures is a basic skill required of any researcher, there is a growing need to consider the relevance of various types of digital data and the specific research methods designed for them, as well as the need to use software packages for analysis in qualitative business research.

Using software for the analysis of your data can be beneficial, but it does not mean that you can stop thinking about your choices concerning the research design and the link between the research questions, analysis and results. The computer software packages do not perform this work for you.

FURTHER READING

Digital Tools for Qualitative Research by Paulus, Lester and Dempster (2013) provides an overall view of the effect of digital tools on the whole research process.

Hewson and Laurent's (2012) book *Research Design and Tools for Internet Research* is a comprehensive guide to conducting research, particularly on the Internet.

EXERCISE 9.1

Searching for the research literature from digital sources

The purpose of this exercise is to learn how to search for digital research literature in a systematic way from the two main sources that are most often available to a business researcher. You will also learn about the differences between the databases and the Internet sources of digital research literature.

Use your own research topic or choose a new one about which you would like to know more. You can define your topic rather widely; for instance, 'brand management in SME-businesses' or 'strategic management of women-owned businesses'.

Plan a search strategy and make a list of key words that you can start with. Conduct your search:

- on the Internet;
- at the digital databases of your library (one or more).

Read and compare the literature that you found from each and consider the usefulness of both searches. Are they different? And if they are, then why is it so?

Use the literature that you found to reconsider your search strategy and the list of key words. Can you find new key words from the literature? Did you find the pieces of research that seem to be widely referred to by the authors? Where can you locate these if you did not find them on your first round?

EXERCISE 9.2

Searching and evaluating digital research materials

The objective of this exercise is, first, to learn to search the Internet for secondary or supportive information that you can use in your research and, second, to learn to evaluate this information critically.

Choose an organization (a business company or some other) that you find interesting in terms of your research topic and aims, or by some other criteria. Try to choose an organization that you think is widely represented on the Internet.

- Plan a search on the Internet through which you think you will find the most information about the organization. Think about where you should start your search and how to proceed? What kinds of key words can you use? How you can find different types of material (e.g. not just produced by the organization itself)?
- Conduct your search on the Internet.
- Evaluate the materials that you found with the 'who, what and where' questions given in this chapter. Which materials are most useful for your research and why? Which ones would you not use and why?

10
QUALITATIVE CONTENT ANALYSIS

This chapter will provide information on:

- What qualitative content analysis means
- How qualitative content analysis can be done
- How qualitative content analysis relates to the qualitative research approaches.

WHAT IS QUALITATIVE CONTENT ANALYSIS?

In this chapter, the term 'qualitative content analysis' refers to the ways of analyzing the content and meaning of different types of qualitative data. As the term indicates, this type of analysis focuses on the 'content' of the data with an emphasis on 'what is said' and 'what is done' in the data. Furthermore, the word 'qualitative' indicates that there is also an increased interest in the contextual meaning of the data with an emphasis on 'how something is said and done' and 'why in this particular way'. Thus, the prefix 'qualitative' indicates that the aim is to increase the understanding of the phenomenon under study in its proper context. This aim differentiates 'qualitative content analysis' from the more traditional 'content analysis', the purpose of which is to transform qualitative data into variables that can be analyzed with quantitative methods. In this chapter, we will not discuss traditional 'content analysis' about which you can find more information from methods books such as Krippendorff (2012).

Qualitative data used for doing qualitative content analysis are either texts (e.g. transcribed interviews, written documents, minutes of meetings, etc.) or audio-visual data (e.g. video recordings, movies, pictures, etc.). One purpose of qualitative content analysis is to produce a holistic and factual description, which provides the 'big picture' about the phenomenon under study. Another purpose is to produce a detailed, rich and nuanced interpretation of the contextual meanings of the data. When interpretation is emphasized, a factual description often serves as a useful first step of the analysis especially for a novice business researcher who wants to learn to know the data before undertaking more sophisticated analyses.

Systematic coding is an essential part of traditional content analysis, which aims at the quantification of qualitative data. Various coding procedures can also be applied in qualitative content analysis. In its simplest form, coding means tagging or labelling parts of the data (e.g. words, phrases, sentences, themes, etc.) with descriptive names such as 'change initiative', 'change agent' and 'new idea'. In this way, parts of the data become classified into categories which have specific names as their codes.

Coding is a relevant part of qualitative content analysis when the researcher wants to categorize the data for the purpose of writing a factual description of the data. When coding the data, the researcher tries to be objective in such a way that other researchers could repeat the coding process and analysis and ultimately come up with the same research results.

The role of theory is among the main differences in coding between traditional content analysis and qualitative content analysis. While the first one relies on predefined coding schemes derived from theory, the latter emphasizes the contextual nature of qualitative data, the analysis of which requires that the coding scheme is generated with the help of the data. This type of coding scheme provides the possibility of generating new theoretical and conceptual ideas. Thus, when doing qualitative content analysis, the coding categories are typically derived inductively from the data. Alternatively, when using theory-driven codes, the researcher is flexible in revising the original codes on the basis of the data.

It is also good to remember that qualitative content analysis does not necessarily require any coding. When coding is not used, the researcher relies on other procedures such as intuition, mind mapping, memo writing, as well as close reading of the text leading to direct interpretation. These procedures emphasize the role of the researcher as a subjective and self-reflective interpreter of the data. Related to this, some qualitative researchers favour the idea that qualitative researchers' interpretative capability is the most central asset of the research process and that mechanistic procedures such as coding should not be part of qualitative research. Despite this, and especially in business research, qualitative researchers do use various types of coding procedures in their research projects. Coding can be done in many different ways (see e.g. Saldaña, 2012; and e.g. Chapter 15 – Grounded Theory Coding), some of which are more mechanistic than others. Choosing between no coding and coding, and deciding which way of coding is appropriate should be done in relation to the research aims and research questions. What is the procedure that is able to meet study goals and provide good ground for answering the research questions?

HOW QUALITATIVE CONTENT ANALYSIS CAN BE DONE

Although many types of qualitative content analysis exist in the field of social sciences and humanities (Schreier, 2012), their common interests are in describing and interpreting the data at hand. In this section, we will discuss two general types of qualitative content analysis in more detail. The first one focuses on categorizing the data with the aim of providing a holistic and factual description of the phenomena under study. The second focuses on intensive interpretation with the aim of understanding the meaning of the issues under study. While categorization of the data requires coding to take place, interpretation can be done with coding or without them.

There are a few things that you should consider before deciding on the use of the two types of analyses that we will introduce. First of all, you can use various types of 'qualitative content analyses' for the purpose of learning to know your data better or you can use them as the main analyses in your research. For learning purposes you can experiment with alternative goals and research questions, but for a goal-oriented research process you should check to see if some form of qualitative content analysis is appropriate for your research, considering the goals and the preliminary research questions of your study. Does the analysis of the content of the data allow you to answer your research questions? Do you need to continue the analysis with some other methods of analysis? For instance, if your goal is to study how corporate identities are rhetorically constructed, or how processes of branding evolve over time, you should consider other types of analysis instead of, or in combination with qualitative content analyses.

If you find qualitative content analysis appropriate for your research purposes, the next step is to identify the body of content that you will deal with in your analysis. When you want to analyze certain content (e.g. consumer behaviour or managerial decision making), what are the data that you should include into your analysis? The content you are interested in could be found in documents but not in interviews, for instance. For learning purposes you can choose more freely what data you will analyze, but for the main analysis of your study you will need to think carefully whether the data are representative of the phenomenon and issues that you are interested in. If you have a very large data set, you may have to do sampling according to some criteria (e.g. theoretical, data-based). You can also do the analysis in two steps: first analyze the whole data with a more general objective, and then zoom-in to specific sections of the data with the help of specific research questions. Qualitative computer software described in Chapter 9 is particularly helpful when doing qualitative content analyses for large data sets.

Most commonly, the data for qualitative content analysis are in text form, including transcribed interviews, documents, brochures, annual reports, articles in newspapers and magazines, memoranda, web pages and social media materials, job descriptions, minutes of meetings, client records, etc. Other forms of data include audio and video recordings, radio and television programmes, movies, photographs, paintings and other works of art. When preparing the analysis, it is advisable to take examples of the content to be analyzed and check that they represent the intended content. For instance, if you want to study the mutual relationships of leaders and employees, check that the articles in company magazines that you intend to analyze contain data about those relationships. Both good and bad examples of the content can be valuable.

In the following, we discuss two general types of qualitative content analysis in more detail: categorization and interpretation of the data. While categorization is based on systematic coding of the data, interpretation does not necessarily require formal coding. Categorization aims at describing the content of the data in a manner that provides a general and holistic picture of the phenomenon under study. Interpretation aims at understanding the phenomenon from a meaning-making perspective in a given context.

Categorization

When coding is an essential part of the analysis, you should first select the coding units which capture the data in the best possible way in terms of your study goals. Words, often called key words, are the smallest unit of analysis you can use. Phrases and sentences are also relatively small and easily definable units of analysis. Key words, phrases and sentences are fairly easy to classify, although they can have very different meanings in the data. Themes are wider and more complex units of analysis, explicating a conceptual domain or an idea such as 'innovative action' or 'democratic leadership', for instance. Identifying themes involves the analysis of several passages of the data and, thus, it can be rather challenging for a novice researcher.

Analyzing key words, phrases, sentences and themes focuses on the existence of certain content in the data and thus provides a rather static conception of the content. Compared to words, phrases, sentences and themes, the units of analysis can also be more dynamic in nature such as 'actors' and 'actions' or 'processes'. This shift in attention provides a different picture of the content. It is also good to keep in mind that you do not need to limit your analysis to one coding unit only. Using several coding units and comparing, for instance, less dynamic (focusing on key words, phrases and sentences and themes) and more dynamic (focusing on actors and actions) approaches will give you different perspectives to your data and will also help you to specify and revise your research questions.

For categorization, the next step is to develop a coding scheme (see Box 10.1) including all coding categories. These determine the quality and reliability of your analysis. Coding categories can be derived from theory and from data. Thus, a combination of theory-driven and data-driven codes can also be used. When developing data-driven coding categories, a preliminary analysis of the data must be done in order to be able to define the categories. Good coding categories are exhaustive enough that all content can be categorized, mutually exclusive so that data will be placed in only one category, and independent so that putting data into one category does not affect other procedures in the process.

─────────────── BOX 10.1 ───────────────

Developing a coding scheme

Developing a coding scheme includes at least the following steps:

- Define labels or names for the codes.
- Write down specifications of what each code concerns (i.e. what content or meaning each code describes).
- Write down instructions about how to identify proper content and meanings for each code.
- Write down criteria of how to decide on exclusions of the data.
- Write down examples of excluded sections of the data.

When you have your coding scheme ready, you need to actually code the data. In this process it is advisable to allow for flexibility in generating new categories and revising the original ones when the researcher finds this necessary. Because assigning content into the codes is an interpretative process, it is essential to write down for yourself the rules according to which you will make the decisions on how to code the data (see Box 10.1). These rules should also be written down in the research report so that the reader can follow your coding logic.

When you have categorized the data into codes, you can check if any codes are overlapping or if they have too little content to be relevant on their own. Alternatively some codes might be too wide and include a lot of content. In these cases you can merge categories together or divide them into parts. The analysis of categorized data involves the search for trends, patterns and relationships between the categories as well as summarizing these in order to provide a description of the big picture.

Interpretation

Categorization and descriptive analysis emphasize the explicit content of the data, focusing on what is said and what is done in the data. The data are treated as factual information about the issues studied. Even though all research processes necessarily involve interpretation, for instance, when deciding to which coding category a specific piece of data can be assigned, the main purpose of categorization and descriptive analysis is typically not on interpretation, which focuses on the implicit meanings emerging from the data.

Interpretation as a method of analysis is concerned with how meanings come about and why. Looking at the relationships between the concepts indicating specific content (e.g. key words, phrases, sentences, themes, actors, action, etc.) guides the analysis, focusing on how things are said and done and what is the meaning of it all. In this type of analysis, researchers are not so much interested in the general meanings of concepts, but on the local and context-specific nuances of the content produced through the relationships that the concepts have with each other.

When analyzing meanings, it is relevant that your study aims and research questions guide the analysis. Although you can revise your research questions throughout the process, you will need a research question from the beginning in order to guide the analysis. Without a research question, the possibilities of meaning-making relationships that you can study even in a small piece of text are easily too many. Therefore, the first step of the analysis is to define at least a preliminary research question. This may come from the data, either through memo writing, direct interpretation or some other form of preliminary analysis the main purpose of which is to generate alternative research questions.

Categorization of content may also precede the analysis of meanings because this provides an opportunity for the researcher to become familiar with the data and to explore the fruitfulness of different types of research questions. Categorization of content may also be needed as a first step of qualitative content analysis because the analysis of meanings is rather challenging. A novice business researcher, in particular, benefits from starting with the categorization and description of the data, and can thereafter more easily proceed to interpretation and the analysis of meanings.

The next step of interpretation and analysis of meanings may involve systematic coding in a similar manner as with categorization. The difference is that here the unit of analysis is the relationship between concepts, and several issues can be analyzed from that. First, you can analyze the existence and non-existence of relationships between two or more concepts. There might be a relationship or there might not, and the absence of a relationship can be just as important as its existence. Furthermore, the relationship can be positive, negative or neutral, and all of these have a different bearing in terms of how they shape the meanings of the concepts and the relationships themselves. The strength of the relationship, indicated by its frequency or centrality in the data, for instance, is an important indication of the power of specific relationships. It can also be useful to look at the direction of the relationships between various concepts. For instance, relationships can be unilateral or bilateral and these may induce different types of meanings.

When analyzing meanings and writing about them, the main focus is not so much on describing the content as it is, but on how this specific content comes about and is understandable in this specific context. Compared to categorization for which the researcher can more easily produce clear rules and follow them, interpretation requires more intuition, flexibility and creativity from the researcher. In this way, it is also more challenging and benefits from experience.

QUALITATIVE CONTENT ANALYSIS IN RELATION TO QUALITATIVE RESEARCH APPROACHES

The two types of qualitative content analysis that we have discussed in this chapter have connections to the wider qualitative research approaches that we will introduce in Part III of this book. Both forms of analyses can be used for the purpose of learning to know your data and for the purpose of generating or revising research questions. This might happen before the researcher has made any decisions concerning the wider research approaches that the qualitative research in question might benefit from.

Also, in a situation when the researcher has already made a final decision about the research approach to use, categorization and interpretation can be useful and can serve as the main methods of analysis for several research approaches including case study research (Chapter 11), ethnography (Chapter 12), action research (Chapter 13) and focus group research (Chapter 14). In case study research, categorization is useful in extensive case studies while intensive case studies as well as ethnographies put more emphasis on interpretation. In addition to categorization and interpretation, many other methods of analysis (e.g. critical incident analysis, time series analysis) are suitable for case studies. Some of these will be explained in more detail in the respective chapters in Part III of the book.

As will be explained in Chapter 15, Grounded Theory research has its own specific procedures for the analysis with several rounds of coding. Also, narrative research and discourse theoretical research have their own procedures and methods of coding and analysis although qualitative content analysis may also be used here for the purpose of learning to know the data.

Some of the qualitative research approaches introduced in Part III of this book do not rely on any specific methods of analysis and therefore, qualitative content analysis can be suitable or not. As we will explain, feminist and critical research approaches are umbrellas for a wide range of different types of research projects that can benefit from various methods of analysis, depending on their research questions.

Finally, it is good to note that the two forms of qualitative content analysis that we have discussed in this chapter do not automatically focus attention on some specific aspects of research such as time and process. When these aspects are at the core of the research (e.g. how do entrepreneurial processes evolve over time?), the researcher needs to consider if qualitative content analysis can be performed in a way that keeps the researcher's attention on time and process, for instance.

Overall, various forms of qualitative content analyses do offer an excellent opportunity for any qualitative researcher to learn to know their qualitative data in a detailed manner whatever qualitative research approach they will decide to use and whatever more specific methods of analysis they want to use later on. This is why every qualitative researcher benefits from knowing the basics of doing qualitative content analyses.

KEY POINTS OF THE CHAPTER

Qualitative content analysis is not the same as content analysis, the purpose of which is to quantify qualitative data and transform them into variables.

Qualitative content analysis can be based on coding the data or it can rely more on direct interpretation.

Categorization is a basic form of qualitative content analysis, which requires systematic coding. The purpose of categorization is to produce a holistic and factual description of the content.

Interpretation is another basic form of qualitative content analysis, which can be based on coding but does not necessarily require it. The purpose of interpretation is to understand contextual meanings.

FURTHER READING

Qualitative Content Analysis in Practice written by Schreier (2012), provides a thorough guidance of the coding process used in qualitative content analysis, with a good number of research examples included.

───────────── EXERCISE **10.1** ─────────────

Analyzing content and relationships

The purpose of this exercise is to illustrate how simple, but systematic, analysis of textual data can be rehearsed. It also shows that changing your analytical focus from key words and phrases to key actors and action can produce very different outcomes.

Choose an article from a business magazine that tells you about a company, an industry, or a current topic in the business world. Read the article and mark words and phrases, as well as actors and action, that:

- occur frequently in the text
- are central and crucial to the text in some way
- have different meanings in the text.

Then draw two mind maps of your findings, one for key phrases and words and the other for key actors and action. When drawing the mind map, consider:

- what the relationships are between the key words or phrases or between the key actors and action, and
- which words and phrases, as well as actors and action, you want to put in the middle of your mind map, and why?

You can make this exercise in the classroom with one (or more than one) group of students doing key word and phrase analysis and the other (one or more than one) group doing the actor and action analysis. By comparing the maps drawn by each group you can illustrate:

- what difference it makes as to whether you focus on words and phrases or actors and action, and
- how different researchers (within a group and across groups) interpret what is relevant, essential and central - and what is less so.

PART III

QUALITATIVE RESEARCH APPROACHES

11

CASE STUDY RESEARCH

This chapter will provide information on:

- What is specific about case study research
- How case study research can be done
- What is 'intensive' and 'extensive' case study research
- How to collect and analyze empirical data for case studies
- How to write and evaluate case studies.

WHAT IS CASE STUDY RESEARCH?

Case study research has a long history across academic disciplines, such as psychology, medicine, law, political sciences, anthropology, sociology, social psychology and education (David, 2006). Also, some of the classic organization and management studies are classified as case studies (Dyer and Wilkins, 1991), which have enjoyed a steady popularity in business research. A central feature of case study research is first defining and then solving the case.

In our view, case studies are excellent in generating holistic and contextual in-depth knowledge through the use of multiple sources of data. Overall, case study research aims to make room for diversity and complexity and, therefore, avoids overly simplistic research designs. Despite this, the boundaries of the case should be identifiable. From this point of view, it is critical that the researcher pays attention to the criteria that they use in defining their research cases (Box 11.1).

─────────────────────────────── BOX 11.1 ───────────────────────────────

Two definitions of case studies

According to Creswell (2012), a case study is an exploration of

- 'a bounded system' which can be defined in terms of time and place (e.g. an event, an activity, individuals or groups of people)
- over time and through detailed, in-depth data collection
- involving multiple sources of information that are rich in context.

Yin (2014) defines a case study as an empirical inquiry that

- investigates a contemporary phenomenon within its real-life context, when
- the boundaries between the phenomenon and the context are not clearly evident, and in which
- multiple sources of evidence are used.

Case studies from a methodological point of view

Methodologically, classic case studies are connected to the interpretative, ethnographic and field-research traditions (Dyer and Wilkins, 1991; David, 2006). They are different from the experimental, quantitative, and deductive research traditions in business research that aim to produce statistical generalizations.

Despite the qualitative spirit of classic case study research, quantitative data can also be used. There is actually no limit on the empirical data used in case study research. Also the methods of data analysis of case studies can vary considerably depending on study aims. This means that case study research should be understood more as a research approach or research strategy than a method. In several business research methods books, case study research is presented as an alternative research strategy in a situation when quantitative methodologies are not appropriate. We want to emphasize that case study research is not only a second-best substitute to quantitative business research, but it is valuable as such when the aim is to understand the logic of the case rather than generate causal explanations for it.

Business-related case study research

The popularity of case studies in business research is no surprise considering that there is a long tradition of using real-life cases in business teaching. Companies also use case histories that address business problems as well as business successes and failures, mostly for training purposes. Overall, you can easily find exciting and educating real-life cases in the world of business.

One reason for the popularity of case study research is its ability to present complex and hard-to-grasp business problems in a practical, accessible, vivid, personal and down-to-earth format. This often has a better appeal to business students, managers, political decision makers, and business researchers than statistical and survey research. However, the practical real-life dimension is also a source of criticism against case study research. Case studies are sometimes labelled anecdotal descriptions, which lack scientific rigour.

In addition to being practical, business-related case studies can also be normative. You can, for example, decide to study a quality management project that is either problematic or exceptionally successful. With the results of your study, you will be able to say something about how to perform a successful project, or how to avoid some problems, at least in one particular organization or in a specific business context.

Normative and practical case studies have been criticized for their managerial concerns, that is, their aim to help managers and decision makers gain better operational control over business organizations. However, as Humphrey and Scapens (1996) argue, case study research can be used to gain a better understanding of mundane and changing business practices in their social contexts in a way that is not dominated by the managerial perspective.

WAYS OF DOING CASE STUDY RESEARCH

There are several ways of doing case study research, depending on the purpose of the study, the nature of the research design, including the number of cases to be studied, and the research philosophical background of the study (see e.g. Stake, 1995, 2005, 2013; Thomas, 2010). Stoecker (1991) has suggested that there is a key difference between intensive and extensive case study research (Box 11.2). Intensive case research explores one case (or a few cases) in-depth whereas extensive case research maps common patterns across several cases (Eriksson and Kovalainen, 2008, 2010). We find this division particularly useful in trying to describe the different ways of doing case studies in business research. Furthermore, we think that the differences between intensive and extensive case study designs make it understandable why the terminology used for describing case study research varies so much.

──────────────── BOX **11.2** ────────────────

Intensive and extensive case studies

- Intensive case study research aims at understanding the case from the inside by providing a thick, holistic and contextualized description and interpretation.
- Extensive case study research aims at advancing or generating theory by comparing a number of cases to achieve generalization.

INTENSIVE CASE STUDY RESEARCH

Intensive case study research draws on qualitative and ethnographic research traditions, emphasizing the interpretation and understanding of the case as well as the elaboration of cultural meanings and sense-making processes in specific contexts. The main aim is to understand and explore the case from 'the inside' and develop an understanding from the perspectives of the people involved in the case. This does not mean that this understanding would not be theoretically informed or that the case could not be used to elaborate theory. On the contrary, as Dyer and Wilkins (1991) argue, classic case study research is also theoretically informed and capable of developing theory. However, the key interest is in the case itself, not in testing the pre-given theoretical propositions.

Imagining one unit or an individual as a 'case' is a simple way of trying to understand what is specific about case studies compared to other qualitative research approaches (see also Stake, 2005). Let us think about an example. An intensive single-case study could focus on one individual, for example, a service counter employee at the local hotel of an international hotel chain. The reason for studying this employee would be that they are somehow exceptional and unique, and that we want to learn more about their uniqueness. They might be one of the very few that have been moving between hotels in different countries, or they might be among the very few local employees that the hotel has employed. Or they might have exceptional training, language skills or a handicap, which makes them develop new practices for that job. To be able to study this case, we would need to talk to them, to their co-workers, supervisors and customers (informal or formal interviews), observe them doing their job, and read documents about the hotel and its business concept, customer structure, etc. This way we should get a rich and illuminating body of empirical data telling us something about this unique case.

When proceeding with the analysis of these data, we might have some preliminary research questions, but we would also remain open to what is specifically interesting in their work from a research point of view. To be able to know what is interesting or new, we would need to know what other researchers have said about work in general and service counter work in particular, organizing and doing work at hotels, the relationship between work and other spheres of life, management of hotels, employee–customer relationships, etc. Only by knowing what other researchers have said about the same issues can we know what is interesting and new. Therefore, prior research, empirical findings and theoretical ideas are constantly intertwined in our own research.

Contextualization and interpretation

The aim of intensive case study research is to learn how a specific and unique case works. This is done through the contextualized and 'thick description' (Geertz, 1973) of one or a few cases. Thick description does not refer to a voluminous, idiosyncratic, or artistic description, but to a verbalized interpretation that is able to crystallize the reasons behind the rich and multi-faceted details of the case. Therefore, the purpose of thick description is to provide an interpretation that makes the meanings embedded in the case clear to the reader (Shank, 2002: 74–6).

A distinctive characteristic of any qualitative inquiry is its emphasis on interpretation. Although there is interpretation in all research, the main purpose of intensive case studies is to offer interpretations on the case made by the researcher, and sometimes by the business actors involved in the study. Accordingly, the business researcher is an interpreter who both constructs the case and analyzes it, focusing on the perspectives, conceptions, experiences, interactions and sense-making processes of the people involved in the study.

The overall purpose of intensive case study research is to construct a narrative, 'a good story worth hearing' (Dyer and Wilkins, 1991). This means that the case is explored in its economic, social, cultural, technological, historical and physical setting. In business research, the economic or business context is often the most evident, but other contexts may also be important, depending on the research issues and questions.

Intensive case study research may be carried out with a static, cross-cut research design, but dynamic designs, looking at development over time, or exploring time-related issues are quite typical. Stoecker (1991: 97) even suggests that case studies in the social sciences should be defined as 'projects, which attempt to explain holistically the dynamics of a certain historical period of a particular social unit'. Indeed, intensive case study research often extends over time, which has been considered an advantage of case studies in business.

We have lots of good examples of intensive, longitudinal, process-related and even historical case studies. Pettigrew (1985) examined organizational change in one chemical industry corporation, ICI, over several decades, focusing on organizational events and managerial action. Gibbert (2004) also traced the strategic management of Siemens over a long period of time. Eriksson and Räsänen (1998/2012) studied how various combinations of managerial logics of action shaped the product mix of a Finnish confectionery company during 1950–1990.

The role of theory

A typical challenge for intensive case study research is to relate theoretical concepts with empirical investigations that engage their readers to learn and take action. However, the difficulty for the goal-oriented business researcher is often not to jump to generalizing conclusions too soon. Having accomplished a first version of a thorough description of the case, the researcher is better placed to try to figure out what the most interesting research questions are, as well as to understand and conclude what happened and why. This is why the research process is best described as a continuous interplay or dialogue of theory and empirical data. Dubois and Gadde (2002) provide one illustration of this process in their article on an abductive approach to case research in industrial marketing. Humphrey and Scapens (1996) also provide convincing arguments on how theory is always integrated with the investigation of empirical data in case study research in accounting.

Generalization in intensive case study research

The main focus of intensive case study research lies in the workings of the case itself. Stake (1995, 2005) describes such a case study as intrinsic. The aim of intensive case studies is not to produce knowledge that could be generalized to a larger population as with statistical methods. The objective is to explore and understand how the chosen case works. In intensive case study research, the case is considered as unique, critical or extreme in one way or another, and it is the researcher's key task to be able to show these features to the audience of the research. In this way, the exceptional nature of the chosen case is not a problem, but a key issue of research interest and the specific nature of the case at hand justifies the appropriateness of the intensive case study approach.

EXTENSIVE CASE STUDY RESEARCH

Extensive case study research relies more on the ideals of factual, quantitative and positivist research. It focuses on mapping common patterns, mechanisms and properties in a chosen context for the purpose of developing, elaborating or testing theory. The real-life cases and their detailed descriptions are not the focus of interest per se. Cases are seen as instruments that can be used in exploring specific business-related phenomena, and in developing theoretical propositions that could be tested and generalized to other business contexts or to theory. This does not mean, however, that all single-case studies would be interested in the inner workings of the case itself, and could not have a primary focus on certain phenomena, or that all multi-case studies would be aiming at theory testing.

Testing and extending theory

The objective of extensive case studies in business research is to test or extend prior theory (Hillebrand, Kok and Biemans, 2001), or to build new theory (Eisenhardt, 1989; Woodside and Wilson, 2003). Thus, the main interest lies in investigating, elaborating and explaining a specific phenomenon, not the cases themselves. With the empirical knowledge generated from the cases, the researcher is assumed to be able to add something new to the existing theory, or conceptual model, or to develop new theoretical constructs.

Eisenhardt (1989, 1991) promotes theory building as the primary goal for case study research. She suggests that this should be done with multi-case and comparative research designs that include the development of testable theoretical constructs during the study process. Her approach is inspired by the grounded theory approach (Glaser and Strauss, 1967, also see Chapter 15 this volume), which focuses on developing substantive theories from the empirical data and transforming these into formal theories that apply to other contexts.

Eisenhardt argues that a priori formal propositions can inhibit exploration of the cases and development of novel propositions, and supports the development of tentative theoretical constructs to inform the study, and an iterative process that links data to the emerging theory. This approach requires using multiplicity of evidence from each case in order to produce well-defined and measurable theoretical propositions or constructs. Each proposition should then be tested afresh against each case. Confidence in the propositions increases if replication of findings occurs across cases. She also proposes that the research design should include a phase of testing the theoretical propositions that emerge from the study against the literature, both supportive and contrary.

Multiple, cumulative and instrumental cases

When doing an extensive multiple (Yin, 2014) case study research, with an instrumental interest (Stake, 1995, 2005), not all the features of the cases are necessarily analyzed in similar detail as in the one-case, intensive research designs. Furthermore, most often the themes, issues and questions to be studied are more or less predefined in some way. They can be planned deductions of prior research or based on the pre-given theoretical interests of the researcher. The cases are not studied in every detail because the researcher has a specific predefined research interest. Some might even call these 'mini-cases' because of their well-defined, even restricted nature, and lack of everyday detail (Stoecker, 1991). Johnston, Leach and Liu (2000) give a detailed example of using systematic multiple-case study designs to test or confirm existing theory in business-to-business research.

Multiple cases may be sampled for several reasons: they extend emergent theory, fill theoretical categories, provide examples of polar types, or replicate previously selected cases (see Box 11.3). Eisenhardt (1989) advises that multiple cases should follow a replication rather than a sampling logic, which is characteristic to survey research.

Unlike statistical sampling methods, there is no single rule concerning the minimum number of cases that should be selected for a given multiple-case research project. The number of cases is influenced by the study aims and the research question. Each case within a multiple-case design can incrementally increase the ability of the researchers to generalize her findings. However, Eisenhardt (1989) suggests limiting the number of cases to the point where the incremental contribution of extra cases is only marginal (e.g. four to ten cases). She also suggests retaining flexibility to add more cases if necessary.

———————————————— BOX 11.3 ————————————————

Sampling cases

Patton (2014) describes several ways of sampling cases, for instance:

- extreme or deviant case sampling is used to identify a sub-group within a culture;
- typical cases provide a cross-section of a larger group;
- maximum-variation case sampling identifies units that are able to adapt to different kinds of contexts and conditions;
- critical case sampling looks for units representing the most 'critical' or relevant cases for transfer of findings to other related cases;
- sensitive cases are used to investigate important issues through the use of individuals or groups who have particular viewpoints.

Generalization in extensive case study research

Even extensive case study research cannot produce generalizations that would hold for a certain population, that is, produce statistical generalization. One way to generalize beyond empirical findings is that of generalization to theory, which Yin (2014) calls analytic generalization. Extensive case study design can be based on a well-grounded theory and a set of testable propositions. Findings are then generalized to that theoretical base according to the degree of support the findings provide to the original propositions. When the empirical findings support the chosen theory, or a rival theory, theory testing and development takes place. Hillebrand et al. (2001) provide a detailed discussion on various possibilities to generalize the findings of multiple-case study research.

COLLECTING AND ANALYZING CASE STUDY DATA

Case studies are considered more accurate, convincing, diverse and rich if they are based on several sources of empirical data and their analysis.

Collecting data

Case researchers can collect empirical data from a variety of sources (Box 11.4) and use both qualitative and quantitative data in their research. In business research personal and in-depth interviews have been typically used as the primary data. Other types of data are commonly used as complementary, and for triangulation purposes.

BOX 11.4

Empirical data for case studies

Existing empirical data:

- documents – minutes of meetings, letters, agendas, progress reports, annual reports, statistics;
- archival records – service records, organizational charts, budgets;
- media texts – articles in newspapers and professional magazines, print advertisements, brochures;
- organization members' personal diaries;
- digital materials – various types of web pages, chat conversations, e-mails;
- physical artefacts – trophies, framed photographs, signs, artworks, furniture, awards, and memorabilia.

Some of these are publicly available (e.g. media texts, annual reports, web pages), but some can be difficult, or even impossible, to access. When existing data are used, you should consider the original purpose for which they were produced to be able to evaluate their value.

Data produced for the research project in question:

- interviews – typically open-ended, but focused and structured are also possible;
- surveys – mostly mini surveys to collect focused data;
- protocols – transcriptions of participants talking aloud about what they are doing as they do it;
- instructed stories and diaries written by the participants of the study;
- direct observation – formal or casual; useful to have multiple observers;
- participant observation – assuming a role in the situation and getting an inside view of the events.

Some of these are less resource consuming to produce (e.g. interviews, surveys, instructed stories and diaries), but some are very time consuming and may even be non-accessible (e.g. observation, protocols).

Using data from different sources enables cross-checking the content, which is called data triangulation. Case study researchers often use other modes of triangulation in addition to triangulating their data (for method, researcher and theory triangulation, see Chapter 22). This is expected to provide a multi-dimensional but also more 'objective' analysis of the case. Overall, case studies are considered more accurate, convincing, diverse and rich if they are based on several sources of empirical data.

Analyzing cases

The case study researcher starts the analysis of the data very early on in their research. Even if methods books (this one included) present data collection and data analysis as separate processes, in practice they seldom are so clearly separable from each other. In spite of this, there are some steps that are useful to take in the beginning of the analysis, such as designing a case record, deciding on your analytic strategy and thinking about if coding is needed.

The case record

The construction of the case often begins with organizing all empirical data into a primary resource package, which is called a case record. This is advisable when you are using lots of unedited empirical data from several sources. The case record can be assembled either thematically or chronologically, the most important feature being its manageability. This is where you should find all the information about the case in an edited form, which means that various bits and pieces of information from various sources are fitted together with some kind of logic. Various types of computer software can be useful in organizing and managing a large case record (see Chapter 9).

Two strategies of analysis

Yin (2014) also distinguishes between two main strategies of analysis. The first one is based on pre-formulated theoretical propositions and a respective coding system. The second one is based on the development of a case description, which would then form the basis for emerging research questions and a framework for organizing the case study. The latter alternative needs to be based not on a formal coding procedure, but more on direct interpretation of the research materials (Stake, 1995).

Several business researchers are in favour of the latter, more inductively-oriented strategy of case material analysis (Eisenhardt, 1989; Dyer and Wilkins, 1991; Fox-Wolfgramm, 1997). This implies that the case researcher is interested in the themes, categories, activities and patterns that they find and extract from the natural variation of the empirical data, not from a pre-given theoretical framework or a set of pre-formulated propositions. It also means that the research questions are either formulated or at least refined and refocused in the process of the analysis procedure. Stake (1995) suggests using issue questions in refining research questions. Issue questions define the case study conceptually, whereas information and evaluative questions are used for collecting empirical data. It is helpful to keep in mind that information and evaluative questions such as 'Who made this decision and when?' can be asked from various informants, but issue questions such as 'What are the meanings attached to decision making in this organization?' are posed to the empirical data.

Coding

Every attempt to recode, organize and label your empirical data includes some kind of interpretation, which can be more or less systematic (see also Chapter 10). Whereas all qualitative researchers pursue everyday coding of their empirical data when making field notes and compiling their data record (Silverman, 2011), thematic coding can also be used as a planned and systemized activity from the beginning of the study. In general, coding means that the features, instances, issues and themes in empirical data are classified and given a specific label, which is called a code.

In case study research, pre-planned systematic coding is most often used when the research is grounded in existing theory and attempts to improve the theory, or to test it. In this form of research, you would have predefined propositions, which would give a basis for a predeveloped thematic coding scheme to be used when collecting and analyzing the empirical data. The codes would be derived from theory, not from the empirical data as such. Another way to use systematic coding would be to develop a coding system from your own empirical data, as is done in grounded theory approaches (see Chapter 15).

Sensitizing concepts

Using an inductive strategy of analysis does not mean that concepts from prior theory could not be used when analyzing the data. Although the analysis of the case is not based on a pre-given theoretical framework, researchers do use theoretical concepts to sensitize empirical data, that is, to give 'a general sense of reference' into the analysis (Blumer, 1969: 148; see also Eisenhardt, 1989). When using sensitizing concepts, you look for a theoretical concept from prior research that helps you to describe and analyze the central organizing features of empirical data and the meanings invested in them. This type of approach is often called abductive logic (Dubois and Gadde, 2002).

Besides using sensitizing concepts in the analysis, intensive case study research often includes an interest in analyzing indigenous concepts, that is, concepts that are used by the participants of the study. In a similar way, you can develop both indigenous (or emic) typologies and analyst constructed (or etic) typologies for analyzing the case (see e.g. Eriksson and Rajamäki, 2010; Laukkanen and Eriksson, 2013).

Analytic techniques

Regardless of whether the researcher has chosen a single-case or a multiple-case design, the analysis begins with the analysis of each individual case separately. This is called within-case analysis. In multiple-case studies, this phase is followed by cross-case analysis, which entails some kind of comparison of the cases in the search for similarities and differences across cases and in contrast to theory. Besides coding, the individual case analysis often includes drafting a general description of the case, which may be structured either in chronological order (emphasizing events, actors and action, and processes) or in thematic order (emphasizing themes, issues, problems and conceptual categories). The main purpose of this description is to construct for meaning by linking empirical patterns (themes, events, processes) to each other to form a holistic configuration – the case (Stake, 1995: 78).

Yin (2014) distinguishes between five different analytic techniques that can be used in case study research. The first four are suitable for both single-case and multiple-case studies, and the fifth is for multiple-case studies only. Yin calls the first technique pattern matching, although the other ones also involve a search for and matching of some type of pattern.

The first technique includes finding patterns from empirical data and comparing them with the propositions pre-developed on the basis of existing theory. Explanation building is a second technique. This includes an iterative search process for causal links in the empirical data, which are then presented in narrative form. The third technique is called time-series analysis, and it focuses on the detailed tracing of events over time. Building chronologies is a special form of time-series analysis. Logic models are a fourth technique. Here, the focus is on complex chains of events, which are staged in repeated cause–effect–cause–effect patterns. These are then compared with the theoretically predicted events. The fifth technique is cross-case analysis, which treats each single-case study as a separate study. In this way, it does not differ from any other way of doing a synthesis by aggregating findings across several studies.

WRITING AND EVALUATION OF CASE STUDIES

Case study research reports come in many forms although the classic ones follow a narrative structure. Methods books offer a variety of reporting options, which vary according to the underlying differences in meta-theoretical assumptions and research traditions in various disciplinary fields.

The narrative form and other structures

The classic form of an intensive case study report is a narrative similar to the ethnographic research tradition (Dyer and Wilkins, 1991). Here, the research report presents a detailed and vivid narrative of the actual and realistic events in their context. This narrative has a main research question, a plot, exposition, context, characters and sometimes a dialogue. However, business-related case study reports, and particularly those presenting extensive case studies, may follow very different lines of reporting.

Stake (1995, 2005) argues that storytelling should only be part of the case study report. Storytelling can be focused on case vignettes (short descriptive pieces of text) that illustrate vividly what is going on in the case. He suggests that the case study report can be written following three different paths (see also van Maanen, 2011: a chronological development of the case (a realist tale); a researcher's view of coming to know the case (a confessional tale); and a one-by-one description of several major components of the case (an impressionist tale).

Yin (2014), in turn, outlines five different ways of reporting case studies. First, the linear-analytic structure starts with an outline of the problem formulation and research questions, then reviews the literature and describes the theoretical frame-work, proceeds to the methodology section and analysis, and ends with presenting the findings and conclusions. This structure is suitable for many business-related case studies. However, it is not appropriate for intensive case studies relying on the narrative logic or research.

Second, comparative structures present several cases one after the other, com-paring them. They may also explore just one case from a variety of theoretical, explanatory, or actor perspectives and then compare these. This structure is suitable for extensive case studies in particular, but also for intensive case studies with a multi-perspective design.

The third alternative, the chronological structure, presents evidence in chrono-logical order, each section describing one phase of the case study research. This is suitable for case studies aiming at an explanation by linking issues together through time.

Fourth, the theory-building structures are built around the theory-building logic of research. These are suitable for extensive case studies in particular, but also for intensive case studies developing new theoretical constructs.

The fifth one, the suspense structure, starts with the outcome of the study and then reveals empirical evidence incrementally, step by step. This is the inverse of the linear-analytical structure and most suitable for intensive case studies.

The last alternative, the unsequenced structure, means that the ordering of sec-tions and chapters follows some other logic than the previous ones. This can, for instance, be a specific type of narrative logic, such as a detective story, fairytale, folk story or legend. This structure suits intensive case studies best.

Whatever the structure of the research report, case study reports are often exten-sively descriptive, with the most problematic issue then being the determination of the right combination of narrative description, more formal analysis and theoreti-cal insights. In any case, you should address each step of the research process and give the reader as much contextualization as possible for the decisions you made concerning your research questions, research design, analysis and the conclusions.

Appreciating the real-life setting of the case

We think that an important issue to keep in mind is that, at its best, the case study report is able to take the reader into the real-life setting of the case but also to the mysteries of the theoretical issues in question. Whatever form and structure the case study report takes, the main task is to keep in mind the research question and follow the logic of providing an answer to this question throughout the entire report in a way that builds a solid relationship between argument and evidence. Furthermore, regardless of the research approach taken, the researcher has an obligation to explain how the excerpts of empirical material were selected for inclusion in the case report and how the evidence was interpreted.

Contextualization

Contextualization includes a detailed explanation of several issues. First, you should be explicit about your theoretical position and describe how theories drove the inquiry you made and led to research questions that you ended up with. Second, you should give enough information on the case environment (e.g. company, industry, historical developments), participants' backgrounds and the processes of data collection. Finally, you should make the connections between your empirical data and the conclusions you made as evident as possible. You can also include the reactions of the participants to the whole study or to your conclusions. These are particularly relevant when the purpose of your study is to elaborate issues and questions from the inside.

At the end of a business-related case study research report you often have a section focusing on the need for further research, on the development of business practices, and on teaching issues. This section elaborates on what the new questions and ideas raised by the study are, that other researchers should address in the future. You may also want to outline the practical and pedagogical ramifications of your findings for business people and for business teachers.

Thinking about the audience

The researcher does not always know the readers of their report. Most probably, some academic people will read the report. However, for a business student it is important to think about how and to what extent the researcher wishes to acknowledge the business practitioners and their stakeholders as the readers of their study, and to what extent it is assumed that there is a difference between these audiences. Case studies are often pursued because of their potential to appeal to and benefit the practitioner; therefore, the researcher should think carefully about how to make the report interesting, readable, and understandable from the point of view of business practitioners in addition to academics.

Evaluation of case study research

In principle, case studies can be evaluated in much the same way as any other research (see Chapter 22). However, there are also specific evaluation criteria developed for case study research. Yin (2014) describes the qualities of a good case study in great detail (see also Stake, 1995, 2005). Case study researchers emphasize that a good case study must be significant in one way or another. A case can be unusual, unique or of general interest. Furthermore, the issues that are studied should be interesting and relevant, either theoretically or practically. The case study must also be complete. This means that you have given explicit attention to the definition of the case and its context and that all relevant evidence has been investigated (including contradictory evidence). A case study should come to an end only because it has reached a convincing result, not because the researcher runs out of money, time or energy.

A good case study considers alternative perspectives, which involves the examination of evidence from different perspectives, not from a single point of view alone. Triangulation can be helpful in doing this (see Chapter 22). You should also look at the evidence that most seriously challenges your research design and results. It is quite clear that a case study needs to display sufficient evidence for its research questions.

Overall, you should present critical pieces of evidence in such a way that the reader can reach an independent judgement regarding the merits of your analysis and conclusions. It is not advisable to include only such evidence that supports your conclusions, but instead to present both the supporting and the challenging evidence.

Finally, a case study must be composed in an engaging manner. A good case study report is so engaging that the reader cannot stop reading until reaching the end. Usually, this entails familiarity with the audience and clarity of writing; but there is also the researcher's enthusiasm, that conveys that they have something extraordinary to say to the readers.

KEY POINTS OF THE CHAPTER

The most important feature of case study research is the construction and solving of one or more 'cases' (e.g. individuals and groups, organizations, events, processes). You can use a variety of data sources and methods of analysis for solving the case. Therefore, case study research is best described as a research strategy.

There are several ways of designing and performing business-related case studies, with more emphasis on either theory development and testing or providing a good story worth reading. 'Intensive' and 'extensive' case studies pursue differing aims, goals and objectives, and they are most often based on different conceptions of reality.

You can choose from a variety of ways to report a case study, varying from traditional and chronological structures to narrative and suspense structures. Case studies can be evaluated on the same types of criteria as other qualitative research, but there are also specific criteria for case studies in particular.

FURTHER READING

How To Do Your Case Study by Thomas (2010) is an inspiring general introduction to various kinds of case studies.

Case Study Research for Business by Farquhar (2012) is a practical and easy-to-read book that, in particular, discusses several key aspects of business-related case study research.

Case Study Research, the classic book by Yin (2014), elaborates in detail what we call in this chapter 'extensive case studies'.

EXERCISE 11.1

A mini case study

The purpose of this exercise is to learn about the case study process as a whole by performing all the steps with a mini case study. The exercise also helps to understand the specifics and challenges of constructing 'a case' that is worth studying.

Think about a business-related case that is:

- interesting to you and to a wider audience;
- easily accessible through public sources (company annual reports, autobiographies, articles in professional magazines, research reports written by other researchers, etc.);
- manageable enough for a small exercise (a mini case study).

Your case could be one individual, such as a manager, an entrepreneur, an expert, or an employee; a group of people (e.g. a business team); a popular brand or a product (e.g. Omega watches, Audi cars); or an event (e.g. a merger of two companies, the launch of a new product or service). The availability of the empirical data will help you to define your case to be manageable for this exercise.

When starting with your mini case study, you may or may not have some preliminary research questions in mind. For example, you could be interested in how cultural background shapes team dynamics. To be able to study this research question, you would need to focus on a team with people from different cultures. On the other hand, you could have an interest in new technology, but not any specific research question in mind. Following your interest, you could choose a case in which new technology is relevant and start to look at the case to find out what is unique about it, and then develop this insight into a research question to be studied.

- Begin your case study by collecting some easily accessible material, then organize your materials, develop a research question, and start analyzing the case. You can ground your analysis on some theoretical framework, or work more inductively. During the analysis, refine your research question and try to answer it on the basis of your analysis.

- Write a short case report (about five pages) including all relevant parts of your case study research (introduction to the case and the research question, description of the materials and analyses used, analysis and interpretation of the case, elaboration of the results and conclusions). Think carefully how you structure your report, and tell the reader what the logic of your report is.
- Pay particular attention to justifying your choices, considering research questions, analysis and evidence, and making the report work for the readers (also consider who they could be).

─────────────── **EXERCISE 11.2** ───────────────

Intensive or extensive case study?

The goal of this exercise is to learn more of the applicability of intensive and extensive case studies through analyzing published articles.

- Start with making a literature search on recent articles using the case study approach (e.g. articles published during the past five years). Extend your search outside business research into social sciences, education, health care, for instance. Use key words such as 'case study', 'case research', 'comparison of cases' and focus your search on empirical articles.
- Pick up around ten articles, half of which deal with one or a few cases in depth and half of which study more than two cases.
- Analyze the articles to see the differences in their case study strategies.
- Make a comparison (e.g. a table) of the aims and research questions of the articles and their results and conclusions. What kinds of similarities and differences can you find?
- Make a comparison in the methodological literature use in the articles. What kinds of similarities and differences can you find?

12

ETHNOGRAPHIC RESEARCH

This chapter will provide information on:

- What is specific about ethnographic research
- How the ethnographic research process proceeds
- What are the methodological and ethical principles of ethnographic research
- How to do ethnographic fieldwork
- How to analyze and interpret ethnographic research materials
- How to write and evaluate ethnographic research.

WHAT IS ETHNOGRAPHIC RESEARCH?

Ethnographic research takes a cultural lens to the study of people's lives within their communities (Hammersley and Atkinson, 2007; Fetterman, 2010). The roots of ethnography lie in anthropological studies that focused on studying social and cultural aspects of small communities in foreign countries. The researchers lived among the inhabitants with the purpose of understanding the culture that these people shared. Thus, the classic anthropologists were foreigners in their field sites. It often took years for them to get into the culture of the community that they were studying. In order to do so, they had to learn the language necessary for socializing with the inhabitants and understanding their daily habits, rituals, norms and actions.

In the 1930s, the critical sociologists of the Chicago school introduced a new stream of ethnographic studies when they started to explore their own street corners just as if they were unknown places (Deegan, 2007). Currently, the fieldsites of ethnographic research can be anywhere, including familiar settings. Ethnographic research can take place in many types of communities including formal and informal organizations such as workplaces, urban communities, fan clubs, trade fares, shopping centres, and social media. In addition, the research is often performed in the native language of the researcher. The main aim of the ethnographers, however, remains about the same: to observe and analyze how people interact with each other and with their environment in order to understand their culture (see Box 12.1).

The emic and etic perspectives

Ethnographers seek to gain an emic perspective, or the 'native's point of view' of a specific culture (Hammersley and Atkinson, 2007). This means that they try to look at the culture under study from the inside; through the meanings that the members of that culture live with. Therefore, ethnographers avoid imposing conceptual and theoretical frameworks on empirical data at the beginning of the research process.

According to our experience, understanding the emic perspective is difficult for a novice business researcher who is more familiar with what is called the etic perspective. Etic perspective means that the researcher looks at the culture mostly with theoretical conceptions. Although researchers tend to combine emic and etic perspectives at some point of their research, you can still emphasize them in different ways throughout your study. For an example of this, see the Laukkanen and Eriksson (2013) article in which they discuss various ways of combining emic and etic perspectives when studying managerial cognitions.

While ethnographers are interested in the emic perspective, that is, how members of a culture give meaning to the world, they are also interested in language practices. This is also true in business-related ethnographic studies; for good examples, see Kärreman and Alvesson (2001) and Samra-Fredericks (2003). In ethnographic research, language is conceptualized as a social practice: what people say and what they keep silent about produce meaning and value in social life. Language practices are socially constituted because they are shaped by social and historical forces, which are beyond the control of individuals. At the same time, however, language practices constitute people's lives together by specifying, creating, maintaining and changing the frames of their action.

BOX 12.1

Key elements of ethnographic research

Ethnographic research entails:

- an interest in cultures, cultural understanding, and meaning-making;
- looking at the culture from the 'inside', with the emic perspective;

- being attentive to language practices;
- being close to the field and collecting first-hand experience.

Different versions of ethnographic research

Ethnography exists in many forms and ethnographers continuously debate about what counts as ethnography, and 'how to represent the field' (van Maanen, 2011). As a result, there are distinct versions of ethnographic research that have their own epistemological backgrounds and varied research practices (Atkinson et al., 2007). This is why, if you plan to do an ethnographic study, you will need to specify what kind of ethnographic research you wish to perform. Besides the basic approach outlined in this chapter, there are also more specific alternatives.

Critical ethnographies (Castagno, 2012) and feminist ethnographies (Pillow and Mayo, 2011) are examples of theoretically informed approaches relying on the principles of critical theory (see Chapter 18) and feminist theory (see Chapter 19). Autoethnography (Adams, Jones and Ellis, 2014) refers to an approach where the researcher's personal and reflective perspective is part of the analysis.

The expansion of the Internet and social media has boosted researchers to perform virtual ethnography or netnography (see e.g. Hine, 2010). Virtual ethnography rests on the argument that the ethnographer should experience the social life of the research subjects regardless of how those experiences are mediated. Related to this, ethnography can be global, multi-sited and mobile in the sense that researchers follow people around physical and virtual places (Epstein, Fahey and Kenway, 2013).

Business-related ethnographic research

Workplace, industrial and organizational ethnographies (Eberle and Maeder, 2011; Yanow, Ybema and van Hulst, 2012) provide in-depth descriptions on a wide range of topics within the field of management and organizations, such as managerial action, organizational cultures, interaction of professional groups, work behaviour and co-worker relations, emotional labour, and sexual harassment. For exemplary empirical studies, see Watson's (1994) research on company managers; Ram's (1994) study on working lives in small firms; Bruni, Gherardi and Poggio's (2004) research on gender and entrepreneurship; and De Rond's (2012) research of teamwork in Cambridge university's boat rowing team.

In marketing, Arnould and Wallendorf (1994) have encouraged researchers to understand the marketing professionals' point of view of the market (for an example, see Schweingruber and Berns, 2005) and to explore the cultural meanings of marketing outputs such as a brand or service quality from the consumer's perspective (for an example, see Bradford and Sherry, 2013). Mariampolski (2006) provides wider insight into the extensive use of ethnographic approaches in marketing research.

With these developments, business companies have noticed that they can benefit from ethnographic research through which culture-based business problems can be addressed (Abrams, 2000; Sweet, 2001; Elliott and Jankel-Elliot, 2003).

Corporate anthropology (van Marrewijk, 2014) has also been pursued for several decades, and the interest in it is increasing. Issues that have been studied relate to all fields of business research. Thus, examples can be found in accounting (e.g. Kornberger, Justesen and Mouritsen, 2011), international business (e.g. Moore, 2011) and small-business research (e.g. Wapshott and Mallett, 2013).

But is the research done by business researchers really ethnography? Some would say it is not. It is not long-term fieldwork in a community context. It is much more likely to be short term and multi-sited with multi-researchers (for an example, see Eriksson, Henttonen and Meriläinen, 2008). Ethnography that deals with business issues often involves shorter periods of participant observation than the classic ethnographies. Despite this, ethnographic business research can still be informed by a theory of cultural interpretation.

METHODOLOGICAL PRINCIPLES

There are three methodological features of ethnographic research, which have differing philosophical backgrounds. 'Naturalism' has its roots in the realist research tradition, which seeks to discover a true or authentic description of the world. Understanding and induction, in turn, are related to the social constructionist research tradition, which suggest that there are several descriptions, or versions, of the reality, the trustworthiness of which depends on what we believe is true, and how relevant the description is.

Naturalism

According to naturalism, the aim of research is to capture the objective nature of naturally occurring human action (Lincoln and Guba, 1985; Hammersley, 1992: 43–54). The argument is that this can only be achieved through intensive, first-hand contact and not through what people do in experimental and artificial settings, or by what people say in interviews. This is why ethnographers carry out their research in natural settings, which exist independently of the researcher. They also try to explain social events and processes in terms of their relationship to the context in which they occur. According to naturalism, objective description requires you to minimize your influence on the activities of the people that are studied.

Understanding

A counter argument to naturalism entails that you can explain human action only if you have an understanding of the culture in which action takes place (Rosen, 1991). This is rather obvious if you study something that is completely alien to you. However, some ethnographers argue that it is just as important when you are studying more familiar settings. Indeed, when a setting is familiar, the danger of misunderstanding is especially great. You should not assume that you already know other people's perspectives, because specific groups and individuals develop distinctive world views. This is especially true in large complex societies; therefore, it is necessary to learn the culture of the group that you are studying before you can give explanations for the actions of its members. This is why participant observation, conversations and open interviews are central to ethnographic research.

Induction

Ethnographers argue in favour of inductive and discovery-based research processes focusing on 'local interpretations' (Geertz, 1973; Fetterman, 2010). It is argued that if the researcher approaches a community with a set of predefined theoretical models, concepts or propositions, they may fail to discover the distinctive and contextual nature of it. This is why ethnographers typically start their research with just a general interest in a community, group of people, type of social action, or a practical problem. The research problem will then be refined, and sometimes even changed, as the research project proceeds. Similarly, theoretical ideas are developed over the course of the research process. These are regarded as valuable outcomes of the research, not as its starting points.

Ethics

One of the strengths of ethnographic research, but also one of its challenges, is the reflection on the relationships that the researchers build with the participants in their studies. Carrying out ethnographic business research differs from many other qualitative research approaches. Doing ethnographic research means getting to know people (e.g. managers, employees, customers, consumers), gaining their trust, and perhaps committing oneself to long-term friendship relations. Or, as van Maanen (2011) puts it, in your research project you are 'part spy, part voyeur, part fan, part member'.

All research is supposed to protect the people who participate in the study. This includes letting them know the risks of the research, protecting their identities and, more generally, paying extra attention to the decisions that you make during the research process (Vanderstaay, 2005). You need to make your research goals and objectives clear to the members of the community under study, and gain the informed consent of these people prior to starting your research project.

Ethics in research also includes ensuring that the study participants are given the opportunity to decide whether you can use their real names or pseudonyms in your research. You also need to discuss whether participants would want to read and comment on the drafts of the research report. Overall, you must be sure that your research does not harm or exploit individuals or groups of people that you are studying. For more details, see Chapter 6 for research ethics.

HOW TO CONDUCT ETHNOGRAPHIC RESEARCH

The concept of 'field' implies that the research is carried out in the real world. The field site is the place in which your research happens, such as a small enterprise, a department in a larger company, or a shopping centre.

Choosing the field site

Ethnographic research often starts with choosing a field site. Thereafter, you generate a guiding research question appropriate to that specific site. It is also possible, however, to start with a theoretically derived research question about a certain cultural process and to find a site where that question might be appropriate. For example, Girod (2005) tested a pre-given theoretical model in her ethnographic study in retail branding.

Either way, setting up a research project can work as long as the site and the question are relevant to one another. Whatever way you choose to proceed, be careful that your research questions touch upon something important about social and cultural life in the field site.

Once a potential field site has been selected, you need to negotiate access (see Chapter 5). This involves getting permission from the people on the site to visit the site for research purposes during a certain period of time. Getting permission often means that you need to convince a gatekeeper (e.g. the CEO of the company) about the relevance of your study. Also, you need to find some key participants, that is, people who you think are central in terms of the research question that you have in mind.

When doing an ethnographic study in a business company, it is often crucial that the researcher can offer to the company involved in the study, some concrete benefit in exchange (for example, see e.g. Ram, 1994; Fletcher, 2002). This might include working for the company, providing consultation services or business training, or some other exchangeable services.

Ethnographic fieldwork typically begins with participant observation, which is later complemented by other data (e.g. interviews and documents). Keeping field notes is a key activity performed by the ethnographer. Everyday events are recorded along with the participants' viewpoints and interpretations. Initial observations focus on the general, open-ended collection of materials derived from learning the basic cultural rules and language used at the site. This initial orientation process is important for providing a background for a more focused investigation. It also helps the researcher to gain a rapport with the participants and test out whether the original research objectives are appropriate in the local situation.

Ethnographers engage in participant observation in order to gain insight into the culture in which they are interested. These insights develop over time and in relation to the social relationships in the field as well as through repeated analysis of many aspects of our field sites. To facilitate this process, ethnographers must learn how to interact with the people in the field and how to take useful and reliable notes regarding the details of what happens in their research contexts. The field notes constitute a major part of the empirical data on which the conclusions of the research will be based.

The completed written ethnography both speaks and adds to established theoretical debates. Therefore, theory is important in ethnographic research for at least two reasons. First, theory has a key role in helping generate guiding questions for ethnographic investigation, allowing you to address larger questions about how culture works among diverse groups of people. Second, through applying theoretical tools to what you learn in the field you can better understand the social life in a certain research setting. It is through theory that the data gain wider meaning and relevance. Therefore, ethnographers must apply some theoretical concepts to their data at some point of the research.

Doing fieldwork

Fieldwork includes all activities that you need to carry out in order to collect your data (e.g. observations, interviews and site documents). Overall, fieldwork is a personal experience because all researchers are different and have varying interests and skills (Box 12.2).

Sometimes, the group of people that you want to study does not live or work in one geographic location. The idea of multi-sited fieldwork can be useful in business research, particularly when there is a goal to make cross-cultural comparisons between companies, businesses, customers, personnel or management groups, or activities in several countries. For example, the field site could consist of the finance units of multinational corporations, users of web services in different countries, or women-owned biotechnology companies in Europe. Multi-sited ethnography allows ethnographers to do research in more than one locale for the purpose of making comparisons between more local sub-cultures (Epstein et al., 2013).

—————————— BOX **12.2** ——————————

Guidelines for conducting ethnographic fieldwork

- Collect a variety of information from different perspectives and different sources.
- Use observation, open interviews, and site documentation, as well as audio-visual materials such as recordings and photographs.
- Write field notes that are descriptive and rich in detail.
- Represent participants in their own terms by using quotations and short stories. Capture participants' views of their own experiences in their own words.

Participant observation

Participant observation is a central data collection method in ethnographic research (see Chapter 8). In business research, the extent of participation can vary in between research projects. At the one end, the researcher makes shorter visits to the site (see Bruni et al., 2004; Eriksson et al., 2008). At the other end, the researcher shares the everyday life and activities of the people in the chosen setting. In business research, this could mean working in the organization studied, for instance. This would help in developing an 'insider's view', which means that you would experience and feel what it is like to be part of the group studied. Experiencing a site from the inside is what necessitates the participant part of observation. Simultaneously, however, there is always an observer side to this process. The challenge is to combine participation and observation in a way that enables understanding of the site as an insider while describing it to the outsiders (Wolcott, 2005).

The extent to which it is possible for a researcher to become a full participant in the culture they are studying will depend on the nature of the setting being observed. For example, Ram (1999) used his own ethnic background as one basis for choosing field sites (small companies) where he could become a full member of the group studied. Business researchers have also offered to work for the company that they have studied in order to gain an 'insider view' (see Watson, 1994). Being a participating member of the group studied develops a 'working knowledge' that enables a good understanding of the culture studied (Rosen, 1991: 16).

Whereas it would not be possible for a young business student to become the manager of a company and experience the site from this position, it may be possible for the researcher to work there as an assistant for a manager. In this way, they could then develop a partial insider perspective into managerial work. Actually, some ethnographers do not believe that understanding a culture necessarily requires becoming a full and active member of the group being studied. They claim that the ethnographer should try to be both an outsider and an insider, staying on in the margins of the group both socially and intellectually. Therefore, combining the outside and inside views is fruitful.

Ethnographic interviews

Besides observation, an ethnographic study can be centrally based on open-ended narrative, or life history interviews, which can also be called 'ethnographic interviews' (Heyl, 2007). Most often, however, ethnographers supplement what they learn through participant observation by interviewing people who can help them understand the setting or group they are researching. It can be useful to interview a variety of people at various points of an ethnographic research. In their ethnographic research on female entrepreneurship, Bruni et al. (2004) made several formal and informal interviews during their fieldwork with the people working in the companies chosen for the study.

Overall, interviews can be particularly helpful when choosing a site, after participant observation has been finished, or when the participants are going through changes that interest the researcher. While participant observation gives information on action and behaviour, interviews provide a chance to learn how people directly reflect on their own behaviour, circumstances, identities and events. This can be valuable in gaining an insider's perspective.

An important part of the interviews is to establish a rapport with the participant. The best way to do this is by being a good listener, which means to listen and hear much more than to talk and converse. Showing genuine interest towards the participant and doing what you can to make the other person socially comfortable are high priorities. When conducting the interview you should choose a setting where the participant can relax and talk openly. Be sure that the participant knows that the interview forms one part of your data and that they understand the overall implications of being interviewed (see Chapter 5).

Before starting to interview people, you should ask yourself what you want to learn from the interviews. Often, it is a good idea to make a list of all possible questions and then see which ones are most closely related to your research question. In order to let the participant talk from their own point of view, it is good to plan open-ended questions rather than structured ones. If the participant pauses during their talk or seems to be talking about irrelevant issues, wait awhile instead of immediately insisting on moving to the following question. This often leads to useful insights, even those that you would not have planned to ask.

Interviews can be taped with the participants' consent. Even if you are good at keeping notes, it is helpful to have an actual account of what was said and how. Taping allows you to transcribe interview data for closer analysis. If the participant does not want you to tape the interview, take enough time after the interview to write down more complete notes about what was said.

Site documents

A variety of site documents can be relevant to ethnographic research. These include: advertisements, work descriptions, annual reports, memos, correspondence, brochures, newsletters, websites, minutes of meetings, menus, and many other kinds of written items.

You can use site documents to learn about general issues which might affect the field site, or they can tell you how the participants of your study present themselves to other people. Site documents are helpful in placing the participants of your study in a wider context. You can also learn about what kinds of demands are placed upon the people in your site, or what kind of privileges they have. Site documents provide demographic information and documentation of historical events.

When considering whether a site document is relevant to your study, you can ask: What is written in this document and how? Why was this document produced? Who will read or use it, and how? What is not included in it, but could be? Privacy or copyright issues may apply to business-related site documents in particular; therefore, it is important to ask about this before they are included in your study. In business research, you should not use any documents that you do not have permission to use. If you are given permission to include information from the documents in your research report, you will need to cite the documents appropriately.

Field notes

Emerson, Fretz and Shaw (2011) give an extensive overview of all issues to be considered when making field notes. The general advice is that the field notes should be written either during the stay in the field or as soon as possible after leaving the field site. Even though you may not think so when observing, you are most likely to forget relevant details unless writing them down immediately. Writing down your field notes takes time. This is why you should make a plan about how to do this. For example, reserve enough time for writing down your notes every time you will leave the research site.

It is possible to distinguish between four main parts of field notes, which should be kept distinct from one another (Emerson et al., 2011). First, jottings are brief words or phrases written down at the field site. Usually recorded in a small notebook, jottings are intended to help you to remember things that you want to include when you write the more complete notes. While not all research situations are appropriate for writing jottings (e.g. having a conversation over coffee with the CEO), they do help when sitting down to write more complete notes afterwards.

Second, description means writing down everything you can remember about a specific event, for example, a board meeting, a training session, a one-to-one conversation at lunch. While it is useful to focus primarily on things which relate to your research question that you did or observed, some amount of more general description is also helpful. This might help with writing about the site later, but it may also help link related phenomena to one another.

Third, analysis is about what you learned in the setting about your research question and other related points. Are there any themes or patterns that you can identify that would help in answering your research question? How can you focus your observation on the next visit? Can you draw any preliminary connections or potential conclusions based on what you learned?

Fourth, reflection is about what you have thought, felt and learned when making observations. What was it like to conduct your research? Did you feel comfortable being at the site? Did you have any negative emotions during your fieldwork? In what ways did you connect with the participants, and in what ways did you not? Reflection is highly relevant in ethnographic research, but be careful to separate it from description and analysis. Finally, methods of writing the field notes are rather personal. Therefore, you can develop your own system of writing different types of notes. Whatever you do, remember to separate description from interpretation and judgement.

ANALYZING AND INTERPRETING ETHNOGRAPHIC DATA

In ethnographic research, analysis takes place throughout the research project and is tightly connected with interpretation. This means that, during your research process, you will continuously analyze, interpret and learn from your empirical data. In this respect, analysis involves both creative insight and careful attention to the purpose of your study. At some stage of your research process you stop collecting data and turn your attention more fully and systematically to the analysis. Then you will ask: What do my field data tell me? What have I learned in the field? What interesting and unique things can I say in order to answer my research question?

While there is no single way to approach the analysis of ethnographic data, the following points are useful to keep in mind. Start with reading through your field notes and other data. Do this several times. The first reading you can do quickly to get an overall picture of the data. However, as you proceed, it is useful to be much more thorough. Becoming familiar with the empirical data helps you to understand them. After some rounds of reading, start to make notes on the texts you are reading and pay attention to traces of patterns, connections, similarities, or contrastive points. Then write analytical memos of these.

Reduction of data is often the second step of the analysis. In ethnographic business research, you may have vast amounts of other data besides your field notes (e.g. hundreds of pages of documents). In this case you can, for instance, decide to use only certain parts of the documents (those that are closely connected to your research question), or to make summaries of them to make easier their use.

You can formalize the analysis further through coding, or by using a computer-assisted data analysis program like NVivo or Ethnograph (see Chapters 9 and 10). Coding is not a requirement, nor is the use of computer programs. Whether you use coding or not, look for specific and local meanings in your data. What terms, words and concepts do the participants use for various things? What can you, as a researcher, identify as patterns or themes, even if the participants do not? Are there alternative understandings for what you have found in your analysis?

When using respondent validation, you will explain your preliminary conclusions to your participants. Business people in particular are in a good position to share with you additional things, which can help to confirm or to problematize what you have found. Once you have findings and conclusions in mind, you may need to elaborate the preliminary research question of your study. Can you answer this particular question with what you have found? Would another research question be more appropriate and interesting? Working back and forth between the findings, conclusions, research questions and theoretical ideas is useful.

WRITING AND EVALUATION OF ETHNOGRAPHIC RESEARCH

The word ethnography literally means 'a portrait of a people', which reminds us that ethnography is about representing the field (van Maanen, 1995). Wolcott (2005), in turn, suggests that ethnography concerns both the processes of accomplishing the research and the research report itself, which is often written in the form of prose rather than in the form of a more traditional academic research report. He argues further that these two are so closely tied to each other that the research process deserves to be called ethnography only when the end product, the research report, follows the conventions of ethnographic representation, which means an emphasis on cultural interpretation.

Using the narrative form

Business-related ethnographic research often starts with presenting a problem or an issue in the guiding question. The researchers then proceed to explore this question or problem and analyze it in light of the fieldwork. Therefore, it is useful to clarify early on in the research report why the selected issue or problem is important and why it is worthy of investigation. Business-related ethnographic writing also puts a lot of emphasis on the implications of what you learned at the field site, which is useful for adding new insights into existing theory (Rosen, 1991).

Ethnographic writing includes a lot of detailed description presented in narrative form (Fetterman, 2010). Watson (1994), Rosen (2000) and De Rond (2008) are good examples of this. The purpose of description is to let the reader know what happened in the field, what it was like from the participants' point of view to be there, and what particular events or activities were interesting and worth exploring further. A detailed description and quotations are essential qualities of ethnographic accounts.

What is included by way of description will depend on what kind of research questions the researcher is trying to answer. Often, an entire activity or event will be reported in detail because it represents a typical or unique experience, or because it allows a very detailed micro-analysis (Kärreman and Alvesson, 2001). Even a comprehensive research report will have to leave aside much of the empirical data available. This is why you should be careful to keep the focus of your research in mind during the entire writing process.

Extensive description needs to be balanced by analysis and interpretation. An interesting and readable ethnographic research report provides sufficient description to allow the reader to understand the analysis, and sufficient analysis to allow the reader to understand the interpretation and explanation presented. Be sure that the points that you present as evidence are based upon your data. In order to understand your research, the reader needs to see the path from description, analysis and interpretation, to results and conclusions in the research report.

Situating yourself in the text

One of the major decisions that an ethnographer needs to make is how to situate themselves in the ethnographic text that forms the research report. Van Maanen (2011) discusses three modes of positioning in detail.

- In realist writing, the researcher is absent from the analysis and the text, the aim of which is to present realistically and objectively what happened in the field. Here, the researcher writes in passive mode without giving any personal accounts.
- In confessional writing, the ethnographer opts for a personal style, presenting emotional reactions, unexpected occurrences, and one's own expectations and experiences of the fieldwork.
- Impressionist writing involves the researcher offering tales in which they have participated in the field. Here, the overall story of the research report makes visible both the culture being studied and the researcher's way of knowing the culture.
- Since the ethnographic research process and the evidence presented engages the researcher intensively, it is best to use the first person form when writing the research report. Ethnographic writing is best described as evocative, descriptive and lively. It is academic writing, but it also requires creativity in rendering scenes, sights, smells, feelings, experiences and people as lifelike as possible. Help the reader to be in the field just as you were, and to feel and understand what it was like.

What counts as good ethnography is a highly contested question in many ways, with the key questions revolving around how to arrive at and write out interpretations. You will find different views about how to evaluate the quality of ethnographic research, depending on the philosophical and epistemological commitments of the research and the researcher in question (see Chapter 22). Hammersley (1992: 57–77) provides a thorough description of one possible set of criteria that can be used to evaluate ethnographic research, concluding that validity and relevance, as understood in any research, are central.

KEY POINTS OF THE CHAPTER

Ethnographic research has an interest in culture and cultural meanings with an emphasis on the 'emic' or 'the insider' view.

Ethnographies are based on fieldwork among the people whose culture is under study.

Ethnography focuses on interpretation, understanding and representation.

Methodological principles such as naturalism, understanding and induction draw on different philosophical backgrounds and, therefore, produce different types of ethnography.

Collect data from different perspectives and different sources, write field notes that are descriptive and rich in detail, and represent participants in their own terms by using quotations and short stories.

Write rich description followed by analysis and interpretation, and situate yourself in your writing. The narrative form of writing works well.

FURTHER READING

The collection of essays in Atkinson et al.'s (2007) *Handbook of Ethnography* provides a comprehensive and critical guide to ethnographic research.

LeCompte and Schensul's (2010) book on *Designing and Conducting Ethnographic Research* discusses key issues and processes of ethnographic research through accessible writing and a good number of examples.

EXERCISE 12.1

Mini ethnography

The purpose of this exercise is to learn the basics of ethnographic research from a small-scale ethnographic research project.

- Start by finding and reading an interesting ethnographic study published as a book or an article.
- Then use this study as an example and write a one-page plan of your own ethnographic study that you can conduct in a short time period.
- Carry out your study and write a short report of it.

- Ask a more experienced colleague or friend to read the report and give you feedback on the report.
- With the feedback, reflect on how you succeeded in your study.

EXERCISE 12.2

Evaluating ethnographies

The purpose of this exercise is to learn to evaluate ethnographic research.

1. Find two ethnographic studies published as theses, books, book chapters or articles, and read them.
2. With the help of this chapter and the one on research evaluation (Chapter 22), write an outline on how the two studied could and should be evaluated.
3. Evaluate both ethnographies with your outline and compare the evaluations.

Reflect on the following issues:

- were you able to use the same evaluation criteria for both studies?
- what problems did you have in the evaluation process?
- how did the evaluation process change your pre-assumptions concerning ethnographic research?

13

ACTION RESEARCH

This chapter will provide information on:

- the elements of action research
- how to do action research in business settings
- the differences between the various types of action research
- the roles of research objects and researcher in action research
- the data-gathering methods used
- ways to analyze data in action research.

WHAT IS ACTION RESEARCH?

Business research is very often related to practical questions and issues of organizations, marketing, financing, accounting, development and growth of business activities, and in general to research questions arising from these settings. Therefore, it is an often occurring phenomenon that researchers not only obtain their research questions from the practical, everyday life of businesses, but that they also collaborate, actively engage with and work within businesses in order to help them solve specific problems, develop some parts of business or organizational activities, give insight to strategic questions and make businesses work more efficiently. This sort of research, where close collaboration with the research object and its practical problem solving is part of the research process, is often termed action research. The term tells us about involvement and actions taken.

But what does action research mean as research design and as a method? Is it simply to walk in, fix the problem, describe the procedure in the research report, and call it an action research study?

Action research is most often described as being an inquiry with people, rather than research on people. This definition refers to the interactive research design and approach that consists of a group of research methodologies, rather than just one or two methods, which pursue action and research at the same time. Action research is thought to be especially suitable when the research question is related to describing an unfolding series of actions that are taking place over time in a certain group, organization or other community. Also, if the research question is related to understanding the process of change, development or improvement of some actual problem, then, in order to learn from it, action research is an appropriate application for research.

Think of a situation where a medium-sized business-to-business company is in the middle of a high growth period, acquiring new customers and expanding its activities from a national to an international level. This new opening up of markets and international business situations puts the company in need of recruitment of new personnel and, in general, in need for more attention for human resource development (HRD) and human resource management (HRM) activities. You are offered a position as a project assistant to the HRM manager in reorganizing and developing the HRD and HRM activities. As you are also at the same time planning your PhD thesis within this specific field, the position of working at the company would give you a brilliant opportunity to gather empirical data for your PhD work on HRD. But, if you accept the position, you will also be deeply involved in the HRD/HRM assistant work in the company, and you really wonder if you can combine the two.

It is important to understand that, in action research, there is no big difference between the researcher and the researched group/community/organization; they are not separate entities, even if they have clear differences. In action research, researchers are often seen as outside facilitators who bring in change to an organization, and who also promote reflection over the change, and finally do research on this specific case. Often, the differences between the researcher and management consultant diminish and even disappear, as academic research is geared towards achieving an understanding of the real-life problems related to business activities and producing change processes and solutions for these problems. The researcher is supposed, to some extent, to be involved in the activities on which they are doing the research. But is it always possible, and if so, do ethical concerns emerge, as Holgersson and Melin (2014) suggest? Action research can also put pressure on work practices (Holgersson and Melin, 2014), or the ways of communicating within an organization, for example.

Schein (1999) presents two classical roles or metaphors for this helping activity: one is the expert model as in the doctor–patient model, where patients go to a doctor and are given both the diagnosis and the prescription to cure the 'disease'. In that role, 'patients' remain somewhat distant from the 'doctor'. The other role is a more process-oriented consultation model where assistants facilitate the inquiry into one's own organization, work and work environment, and the issues and problems within it, and create and develop solutions jointly with the clients (Schein, 1995, 1999). The latter role or metaphor resembles more the idea of action research and the researcher as a 'helper' and facilitator.

In business research, action research can be classified in general as a collaborative approach to research that provides persons, organizations and businesses with the appropriate solutions or means to resolve specific problems autonomously. The degree of involvement of researchers varies, and there is not one way to define the right degree of involvement. Rather, the role of the researcher and the degree to which they get involved with the group/community/organization in question should be mutually negotiated, renegotiated during the process and also mutually agreed upon. This is also required by the general standards of research ethics (see Chapter 6). It is typical for action research that theoretical interests do not usually guide the research planning or design, when research questions are practical by nature. Sometimes, the theoretical interests are very closely related to the practical questions of a specific group/community/organization, but many times they are not.

The origins and key ideas of action research

Action research originates from social psychology, but also from anthropological and social anthropological community research, where researchers have actively been part of the community they have researched, provided them with new knowledge and enabled them to tackle problems of various kinds. As a specific research approach, action research was originally developed by several researchers. Most histories give credit to social psychologist Kurt Lewin (1890–1947), Elton Mayo (1880–1949) and especially to sociologist William Foote Whyte (1914–2000). Credit is given also to the Tavistock Institute and its work (Trist and Murray, 1993), and to the industrial democracy research tradition that has been especially prominent in Scandinavia (Greenwood and Levin, 1998).

Since its original development and use, the action research approach has been used and developed by researchers, among others, within the fields of community research, feminist research, pedagogical research and nursing studies (e.g. Reinharz, 1992; Laiho, 2010). The variety of labels used in action research, such as action inquiry, participatory inquiry, critical action research, industrial action research and participatory action research, also refer to the twofold aims in research: first, to the improvement of and finding solutions to some problems; second, of the involvement of researchers in that activity. Furthermore, the idea of reciprocal activity is important: the information produced in the process should be useful to a group of people, the organization or community in question. Action research in principle advocates for active participation and improvement of social situations and problems.

In this sense, action research also empowers individuals and groups of people. But what, in practice, does the participatory action mean in research?

Action research is not technically a research 'method'; rather, it should be understood and addressed as an approach to such research that requires involvement, a close relationship to the research object and participation as key starting points for research activities; and uses different methods in acquiring knowledge, in the research process and in problem solving. But what kinds of involvement and participation are usual for research in this approach? There are several models for describing how and in what ways the action research project and involvement should be carried on in research.

In his publications, Kurt Lewin developed a systematic model of research, which included several interconnected parts, such as interconnected cycles of planning, acting, observing and reflecting (writing up). Several models and forms of inquiry have been developed since Lewin's original idea, especially in the fields of organizational development and work life research, but most of them apply the cyclical four-step process of planning, taking action, evaluating the action leading to further planning, etc.

Coghlan et al. (2014) and Kemmis and McTaggart (2005) refer specifically to two points: when the people in the situation gain further understanding, reflect on, change and improve their own work situation (through jointly initiated research activities, for example); and when they are increasingly participating in the data collection, power sharing and learning processes in research, and gain empowerment in return. These aspects of action research also relate it to critical theory, even if critical theory and its assumptions are not necessarily present in action-oriented research.

DIFFERENT TYPES OF ACTION RESEARCH

Action research consists of several loosely-related approaches to research that share the above-mentioned key elements and principles, but which vary with the research settings, the grade of involvement and emphasis on a variety of aspects, such as learning, for example. Some differences are related to the degree of focus on problem solving, vis-à-vis focus on participation. There are also differences in the ways in which the local members of the group/community/organization of experts are involved in the research. In the following, some key types of action research are mentioned.

Participatory research, or participatory action research, is most often related to shared ownership of research projects, commitment to the social, political and economic development of the community, and orientation towards action (e.g. Kemmis and McTaggart, 2005; Burnes and Cooke, 2012). The issue of joint practices that are embedded in social interactions gears the research interest into open and shared communications and actual practices, instead of, for example, abstract levels of theorizing about these practices. Critical action research, or critical participatory action research, includes the previous aspects of participatory research and also the reflection of the language used in the participation and in research reflecting these activities.

Action learning is as closely related to a community-engaged learning activity as possible within the action research tradition. Action learning is often implemented in managerial settings in different organizations, and the idea is to bring people together to learn from each other's experiences. The aim to learn from each other includes relatively equal positions from where to discuss and open up one's own experiences; this can best take place only among peer equals. Action learning is based on the perceptions of the participants rather than on systematic data collection and analysis about the situation through other means (Kemmis and McTaggart, 2005; Burnes and Cooke, 2012).

While a soft systems approach and an industrial action research as specific types of action research are perhaps more closely related to the organizational features of industrial organizations, new varieties of action research have emerged that take larger, more complex problems into account.

Gummesson (2000) distinguishes four different types of action research for management. He calls them societal action science, management action science, real-time action science and retrospective action science. Gummesson's classification is not based on exclusive classes or empirical research, but more on classifying existing research traditions anew. As such, it does not offer a new classification in comparison with the earlier one presented, but it opens up action research as especially suitable for marketing research (e.g. Perry and Gummesson, 2004).

Another way of classifying the types of action research is according to how they differ from each other by their ways of looking at the importance and meaning of solutions: whether they are seen as technical or collaborative by nature; whether they are seen as more practical by nature; or whether the solutions have an emancipating role in the researched organization or among the persons or group of people researched.

The new diversity among action-oriented research also includes more political policy-oriented ethnographies, where the aim is often close to influencing issues such as legislation, community environment, politics, etc. Researchers doing participatory action research can use an activist-oriented applied anthropology (e.g. Cole, 2009). Thus, action research gets close to ethnography, and sometimes the distinction between the two is even rather artificial.

HOW TO DESIGN AN ACTION RESEARCH PROJECT
Gaining access

Let us go back to our example of you as a PhD student involved in work as an HRM project assistant. One of the features of action research is that it is a collaborative approach that provides the people/company/organization with the means to take systematic action themselves in order to resolve specific problems or develop some activity within the workplace/organization or group. In order to get there, the first step for you as a researcher is to get an idea of the field, to design the project as research in action through iterative activities and identify the research questions. For that purpose, both general and practical knowledge of the field and prior theoretical knowledge are needed.

Often, mere access is not enough; a more formal, written research contract is needed to gain recognition within the organization and among the group of people you will be working with. For that contract, information regarding the key stakeholders in organization, their expectations and possibly differing opinions should be recognized, as changes are not always wished for by all members of an organization. The roles in the research object in action research depend on a variety of things. Access is one of them: it is not always easy to get access to an organization. There are a growing number of action research projects being done and reported where practising managers themselves are undertaking the action research project in and on the context of their own organizations, practitioners who want to better understand and undertake their work (e.g. Williamson, Bellman and Webster, 2012), for example, when enrolled as participants in academic education programmes and MBAs. This has also evoked criticism towards action research. The question of who defines the problems in the organizations and companies to be investigated has been put forward, especially within accounting research, where there has been a longer tradition than within the marketing discipline in action research (e.g. McSweeney, 2000).

Framing the research question and action-oriented activities

It is important to note that the research question and the specific problems of the individual/company/organization are not necessarily the same. Quite often they are close enough to each other, but quite often these two diverge at some point in the research process. The question of who selects the topic and range for research is important, and very often the action researcher can have a steering group as a 'helping hand', both providing the inside knowledge and history of the organization and helping in planning, gathering the meetings, implementing and reflecting the project.

When you start to plan your project, you should have some pre-understanding of the company environment. Pre-understanding also refers to the knowledge that you as a researcher bring into the project. Is there a difference between action research and more grounded theory-inspired research? A need for a pre-understanding of theoretical issues and an active role in the research most likely direct your interest away from the possibility of adopting the grounded theory approach, as described in Chapter 15. Action research is specifically useful when researching process-related problems in organizations, such as learning and change. Williamson et al. (2012) stress the need for research to be in touch with the practice.

Implementing action research

When you develop the research plan, you should remember that, in action research, the whole research process is iterative: The planning is followed by acting, observing and reflecting, with a revised plan, acting, observation and reflection following again, most often in real time and not retrospectively. Many times, corrective and additional measures are needed as a consequence of the revisions. This process is often described as a spiral of self-reflection, leading to new cycles of planning, new actions taken, and reflecting again, etc. In reality, these stages often overlap and the process of research consists of overlapping activities, where one stage is not clear-cut from the next one. Even if the parts do become partly overlapped, the iterative nature of action research is an important part of the research project, as the change in the researched setting or the data-gathering process is impossible to finalize in a short period of time and with only a short interval of data gathering at the site. Therefore, the actual research process can take much longer than originally anticipated in the research design process.

A retrospective approach is possible, for example, when a real-time case is being written retrospectively, and used as an intervening learning tool in the organization. Action research, it is hoped, will lead eventually to 're-education' and changing patterns of thinking and action. This depends naturally on the participation of research subjects in identifying new courses of action. Action research is intended to contribute both to academic theory and to practical action, and the characteristics are most often defined in terms of outcomes and processes.

Coughlan and Coghlan (2002 distinguish the pre-step activity (1) (understanding the context and purpose) from six main steps (2), which are (a) to gather, (b) to feed back and (c) to analyze the data, (d) to plan, (e) to implement and (f) to evaluate the actions taken (Box 13.1), and finally a meta-step (3), which is the academic research – for example, the dissertation phase. The rationale for the pre-step comes from the empirical surroundings and the 'academic' reasoning for why it is important to study the phenomenon in question.

What about persons working in the company where you are about to develop new HRM standards and practices? How and to what extent should they become part of your research project? According to Kemmis and McTaggart (2005: 563), 'if practices are constituted in social interaction between people, changing practices is a social process'. Action research focuses on actual practices and processes, and in that sense the real material world, with specificities and practices that are rooted in specific situations, is present. Thus, in your action research, the HRM practices that need to be changed will necessarily involve the persons working in those departments, dealing with the tasks concerned in your research. Therefore, their informed consent is necessary for your research project.

DATA GATHERING AND ANALYSIS

As mentioned, action research is not technically a research 'method'; rather, it should be addressed as a systematic approach to such research that takes involvement, a close relationship to the research object, and participatory or even emancipating actions as key points of departure for the research. But what kinds of involvement and participation activities are usual for research in this approach?

Data are gathered in different ways, depending on the research context and research problem in question. Data-collection instruments thus represent a wide mixture of expert knowledge and the local information needed in the project. Methods and data used in action research range from surveys to observations and interviews, focus groups, action experiments and participant-written cases and narratives. Other materials can also be used, such as any kinds of operational statistics, sales reports, figures and numbers, policy documents, etc.

--- **BOX 13.1** ---

Six main steps for action research

1. Data gathering

- There are several ways of gathering the data in action research; most importantly, the data should be gathered through a variety of procedures and all gathering of data should be related to your research interests. Observations are natural data if your research project allows for this sort of data gathering, but other types of data are possible. Indeed, interviews seem to be very often the most typical form of data gathering in action research.

2. Data feedback

- As part of the action research project, data feedback for the analysis in the 'client' organization/group/community is often one crucial step for the researcher to take in the action research. Data can be gathered and reported by the researcher, but also by the researched group. Data feedback means allowing the researched group to be involved in the analysis to join the next step, that is, the data analysis and action planning and evaluation procedures.

3. Data analysis

- Typical, but perhaps not occurring very often in business studies, is where data analysis is done collectively with the researched group. The idea behind this collective analysis is to provide the researched community with 'seeds for development', and to use their expertise in the analysis, as they know their group/community/organization best. Some methods authors claim that clients' involvement for the analysis is critical for the success of the action research (Coghlan and Brannick, 2001; Coghlan et al., 2014).

4. Action planning

- The action plan follows on from the previous steps in action research and involves the key informants or core individuals from the 'client' organization. This is to ensure that the different steps for change, that is, actions, resistance, commitment, etc., are closely followed through with and that the action plan is developed for all the different dimensions needed.

5. Implementation

- A client group/community/organization implies that a practical plan be developed for action. The implementation plan can be very detailed, for example, a retraining programme, and implementation can take time.

6. Evaluation

- Evaluation most typically focuses on actions taken during the research process and implemented. Both the intentional (aimed and planned) and unintentional (sudden forms of resistance, conflicts, problems, etc.) consequences within the group/community/organization are analyzed by the researcher(s). Evaluation is often thought of as a key element for the learning process and the successful action research project in general. Depending on the nature of your project, evaluation can have several layers, from practical evaluation to theoretical aspects of evaluation.

It is typical for action research, that research materials are gathered through active involvement of the researched organization or group. Most often in action research, data gathering requires more resources than in other research settings. Why is this? As action research grew out of a need to learn more of the social systems while changing them, it also set the criteria of mutual understanding, and joint data gathering and problem solving with the researched community. Developing this sort of activity takes time and resources.

There are different, formal and informal openings to gather materials in organizations, and most of them involve the issue of informed consent. Social researchers follow the ethical principles of voluntary and informed consent. The question of consent becomes important in a new way when researchers enter the organization or business: to whom, how and to what extent do they relate their presence, role and aims? From whom do they ask for permission? The questions of ethical and unethical, informing the settings and one's own role in the research activity become important when a researcher enters the field and works in the 'natural settings'. Therefore, it is crucial that, for example, in the social and informal settings, where materials are available, such as over lunch or a beer after work hours, the informants are aware of both the gathering and the use of such materials, as well as being made aware of the gathering of observational materials in the meetings. Informed and voluntary consent should take place before gathering and using such materials, in order to follow the research ethics.

One of the challenges of action research in comparison with many other 'research methods' is that the data analysis is often done collaboratively with the organization, group of people or community involved. This is to ensure the closeness of results to the organization/group/community in question. At the same time, the analysis needs to fulfil the 'academic requirements', thus often including both language and tools not known to 'laypeople'. Therefore, it is important to add the transparency and translation of the analysis of the data to the aim of interventions planned and action planning. It can be argued that it is precisely here where action research has its power: when it remains 'close' to its research objects and is based on reciprocal activities, when done properly, it also can empower its participants, not just the science community.

Different types of inquiry are possible in action research. In addition to the 'pure inquiry' as classified by Schein (1999), other forms of inquiry also exist, such as 'exploratory diagnostic inquiry', where the logic of actions is explored, and 'confrontational inquiry', where the translation of researchers' ideas is done by the researchers for the participants, and dialogue is encouraged.

The data-gathering and analysis process inevitably needs to include an assessment of the quality of the action research project, in business studies especially, due to its closeness to a consulting project (Kemmis and McTaggart, 2005). One of the critiques towards action research sometimes put forward in business research implementations is related to this specific issue. Therefore, the issue of validity claims in research also needs to have more attention perhaps than in some other forms of qualitative research methods. Questions such as partiality and impartiality, and the validity of the narration given in the research need to be addressed explicitly if the aim in the research project is to give a valid representation of what has taken place in the organization/group/community that has been studied.

BOX 13.2

Getting your action research project through

The need to increase the validity of your action research project can benefit from focusing on the following issues:

- Explicitly state your position, your aims and your research interests for all audiences in your report.
- Explicitly give arguments for why the action research approach is needed in this particular problem solving (the value added from the action research approach to your research project).
- Explicate the goals of your project. This is important both for academic purposes and for the practical needs of the researched group/community/organization.

- Illustrate the possible points of inferences, including your own attributions and opinions, and the kind of dialogue this has evoked in the researched organization/group/community. This shows the knowledge level you have gained from interactions.
- Explicate the learning and/or change processes achieved during the different stages of your action research project in a detailed manner.
- Keep in mind the complexity of action research activities, such as the changing of an organization, and reflect the intended and unintended consequences to the project, if possible.

How to increase the validity of your research project

As has become apparent, the nature of problem solving varies a lot within action research, and no one single claim for validity alone can be put forward for the project (Box 13.2). However, as mentioned earlier, the 'closeness and interrelated nature of a research project and solving real-life problems', and slowly emerging research questions and results can cause more voiced claims for validity in action research than with other qualitative research projects.

There are several advocates for the close relationship between consultancy and research, while others argue that there are differences that need to be taken into account. Some even argue that 'action research is masqueraded consulting' with little connection to research. The aim of making the line between, for example, participatory action research and consulting more clear-cut is demanded, for example, within critical ethnography. Gummesson (2000) puts forward four points regarding differences between consultancy and an action research project:

1. Research requires theoretical justification, whereas consultancy requires empirical justification. Therefore, they cannot be the same.
2. Consultants who work with action research need to implement more rigorous inquiry and documentation. In that, they gain professionally, but research remains 'intact' in that process and cannot be 'harmed' by consultancy.
3. The difference between consultancy and action research lies in their ways of dealing with the process of the project. Whereas consultancy is linear, action research is cyclical, and requires more time.
4. Consultants work with a tighter time budget, and move to the next case after one is solved, whereas researchers might remain attached to their materials and revisit their case over time.

The closeness of actions to research and the interrelated nature of research and action make it impossible to draw a clear-cut line between the two. This puts perhaps more emphasis on the clarity of the conceptually-based arguments that you need to develop within your action research project. Action research has also been found to be an important empowerment tool within groups of people who are disadvantaged or do not have a voice for expressing their needs. Education research, as well as migration research and feminist research are all examples of where action research has been used actively and successfully.

How to proceed and finalize your project

How then do you proceed with your research project, given that you have access to your organization and consent to work with your project? In your project you should be able to focus on practices in a concrete and specific way, one that makes them visible for discussion and reflection and, thus, also visible for change in your target organization. It is quite usual that action research is a practically and collaboratively-oriented research activity, and that it engages people in exploring their own practices of communication, production, co-working and co-organizing their activities. You should, therefore, have built a trust relationship within the organization, have the informed consent of the people who are engaged in different HRM activities, and be involved in organizational settings in order to have sufficient knowledge and insight of the key activities that need to be developed further.

Thinking of your HRM PhD project and work as an assistant, it is probable that, by examining the previous ways of taking care of and organizing HRM activities, by knowing the key events and critically examining earlier activities, and by making a plan for development and change, it is possible to open up discussion on the ways for improving previous methods of dealing with HRM questions, developing new practices and introducing HRD activities. You can gather materials for your project and for the development action in the company by interviewing, observing and analyzing the existing documents, etc. You can also use focus group discussion in producing relevant questions. One leading question you would need to put forward for discussion could be of the type 'what kinds of problems do you face in HRM activities?' The variety of possible materials also suggests that there is no single way of doing action research and gathering research materials for it.

Your task, then, would be to gather information, analyze it and interpret the information you have gathered. The analysis will depend on the data-gathering methods you have used and the way you approach your action research project. For example, ways to analyze interview data from focus groups and ethnography are discussed in Chapters 14 and 12 respectively.

Business research questions are often based on 'real-life' cases, therefore, action research as a research mode is seen as a rather 'natural' choice for a research approach, especially when research has some relationship to activities, where new perspectives, developmental work, new practical tools being implemented, or the researchers' views of the business activities are needed. The roles of consultancy and researcher are thus not often very far from each other in business and management sciences, as many of the research questions originate from and have a close relationship to the 'real life of the business world'. Therefore, action research might be a good choice for those students who aim to work outside academia and do research work simultaneously. A mild word of caution is put forward in the following, though.

Action research is not by any means an 'easy' research approach, especially not in the sense that it will require close cooperation between the researcher and the group/community/organization of people as 'targets' of the research. In order to achieve trust within the group/community/organization in question, you must have confidence in your own knowledge, skills, aims and abilities as a researcher. Especially important are the social skills for understanding, analyzing and managing the often very complex social situations in the target organization, and the overall interactive nature of an action research project. As a researcher you should have enough knowledge of the 'target' organization to tackle the multitude of data and their layered nature that arises in the action research project and, more importantly, the 'action activities' that need to take place in the researched organization. Action research can lead, at its best, to a great insight of organizational life and, thus, produce the kind of research materials few researchers have the ability to achieve otherwise. At its worst, action research is a time-consuming and muddled process. Action research is especially situational by nature. The validation process in action research is a conscious and deliberate enactment of the research cycle. The report writing in action research needs to take all the above-mentioned features into account (Box 13.3).

Often, the processual nature of action research requires personal notes, diaries and follow-up of various processes in the research case. All of this material can be used when writing up the report.

One key element in action research is the way the empirical materials are communicated to the stakeholders. One way of doing this is to write a summary of the materials analyzed, which condenses the key characteristics, ranging from the problem statement to the results and to the solutions found. Sharing the results with the researched group/community/organization is part of the empowerment process that is so crucial in action research. The multi-voiced nature of reporting is important, that is, whose views and expressions are used, whose solution (if not jointly found) was supported, etc. The sharing can take place in different phases of the spiralling research process, and various methods can be used for this purpose. Such methods include the use of focus groups, where persons with similar interests discuss some parts of the findings (see Chapter 14 for more on focus groups). Also, informal meetings and group meetings can be used for this purpose.

--- **BOX 13.3** ---

How to write the action research project and how to communicate it to stakeholders

There are several possible ways of structuring the action research report (e.g. Kemmis and McTaggart, 2005). Often, the reporting adopts the following logic:

1. The expression of the purpose, aim and rationale of your research.
2. The description of the context, relating the project into a wider field, be that the surroundings, personnel questions, the company/organizational situation, etc.
3. Explication of the methodology and methods that you will use in the study. This follows the general logic of any PhD work.
4. Description of the story; and, depending on its complexity, this can extend to several chapters, for example, in a PhD thesis.
5. The self-reflection and learning processes, personal, but also extending to the organization/group examined.
6. Reflection of the story in light of the theory and experience. The reflection can extend to several chapters, depending on the role and position of theories in your PhD thesis.
7. Feedback to the larger research community.

WRITING AND EVALUATION OF ACTION RESEARCH

Most action research processes follow the spiral process, that is, the circularity described in Chapter 3. Often the ethnography and narrative forms are also used in writing the action research reports. However, the reporting in action research carries an extra duty, as it should include the participants and all stakeholders identified. The sharing of results with stakeholders is an integral part of the writing process, but you should also remember the integrity of PhD work if that is what you are working on.

One aspect of evaluating an action research project is that it is most often a unique situation where practical problem solving goes hand in hand with research. Therefore, the most usual evaluation criteria, such as generalization, might not be best suited. Some researchers readdress generalizations in action research as necessitating a process of reflective action. Greenwood and Levin (2005: 55) note that it is important to understand 'the contextual conditions under which the knowledge has been created'. Second, they list the transfer of the contextualized knowledge to another setting, where context might differ. Hence, generalization becomes an active process of reflexivity.

Practice and practical problem solving – knitting the research integrally to the problem solving – has always been close to the practice-oriented knowledge production of business research. Action research produces knowledge and actions that can be directly useful to a group/community/organization; and through those actions, research can empower people in many ways, especially by providing knowledge and raising their consciousness. Through actions, research is seen to make a difference to the practices and processes of individuals, groups and larger communities. In this, action research fulfils some of the principal ideas of critical theory research, where the practical element is often missing.

KEY POINTS OF THE CHAPTER

Action research is originally based on practical problem solving and systematizing that experience to research. The various forms of action research all have in common that they are highly interactive research approaches, doing research with people, rather than on people.

Action research uses a variety of research methods and methodologies, where involvement is suitable. Informed and voluntary consent, mutual trust and high ethical standards are required from the researcher when working closely with the researched group/community/organization.

Action research has varying connections to consultancy, but there are differences as well. An action research project seldom can be done within a short period of time, but it requires a length of time that is used for learning, co-learning and mutual reciprocal working before the research project is finalized.

Action research enables the researched group/community/organization to express their views during the research process as collaborators in the project.

Action research is a rewarding, but simultaneously often demanding, way of doing qualitative research if the research setting is dynamic or complex.

FURTHER READING

A good introduction to discussion concerning action research is the chapter by Greenwood and Levin (2005) in *The SAGE Handbook of Qualitative Research*; it presents several directions for action research.

Doing Action Research in Your Own Organization by Coghlan and Brannick (2014), 4th edn, brings a practical guide and instructions to action research in your work place, for example.

EXERCISE 13.1

Research design for action research

The purpose of this exercise is to teach you to think about two issues simultaneously in action research: your own research plan (research design) and a problem-solving scheme for the company/organization in question. With this exercise, you will learn to think about

(Continued)

the facets (academic and practical) of the same phenomenon that are in close and intimate contact in your research and work in the target organization/group/firm.

Write a research design and research plan for the PhD student's action research project described in this chapter. Take the following questions into account when writing your plan and try to answer them indirectly and/or directly while writing your research design:

- What kinds of tasks should the student need to describe first, and what steps should be taken in planning the project?
- What kinds of materials would need to be gathered for the action research project and how would the researcher be able to identify what kinds of problems the company possibly has in its HRM?
- Who would the researcher need to get involved as members for the steering group from the company?
- What type of HRM development plan would the researcher come up with during the research process?
- Who should the researcher contact within the company?

—————————————— EXERCISE 13.2 ——————————————

Learning to evaluate action research

This exercise takes you to the end part of your action research project. Earlier we stated that most action research follows the circularity of the research process described in Chapter 3 and reporting the action research thus carries an extra duty as it should include the stakeholders and the action process. Let's think of your project on HRM. What criteria would you use to evaluate the HRM project in the organization? Would you use the same criteria to evaluate your research project? Why?

14
FOCUS GROUP RESEARCH

This chapter will provide information on:

- What focus group research means
- How to organize and conduct focus groups
- How to analyze focus group data
- How to write and evaluate focus group studies.

WHAT IS FOCUS GROUP RESEARCH?

The term focus group derives from 'focused group discussion'. This means that a group of people is 'focused' on discussing a selected topic or an issue. Focus groups were used in the USA before and during World War II to study the reception of war propaganda broadcast on radio. Some of the key procedures of focus group research were refined in the 1950s by Robert Merton and his colleagues (Kamberelis and Dimitriadis, 2014). Since then, focus groups have been adapted into social science research and psychology as well as practical market and consumer research (Stewart and Shamdasani, 2014).

Focus groups are widely used in academic marketing research to study consumer behaviour, including attitudes, needs, perceptions, preferences and choices. In addition, focus groups have been adopted in business-to-business marketing research, which addresses topics such as industrial buying, development of competition, and business relationships and networks. Besides marketing, business researchers can use focus groups in all sub-fields of business research, varying from human resource management and workplace studies (Claes and Heymans, 2008) to accounting (Gammie, et al. 2003), and SME studies (Bøllingtoft, 2012). The aims of focus group research in business research include collecting empirical data on lay people's, experts' and managers' viewpoints, beliefs, experiences and, most importantly, on their spontaneous interaction (Edmunds, 2000). Focus groups work for all these purposes because of the interaction taking place among the participants.

Studying interaction provides an insight into how individuals are influenced by and draw on others' viewpoints in a group situation (Stewart and Shamdasani, 2014). Furthermore, focus groups allow researchers to explore why an issue is salient, as well as what is salient about it. In this way, the gap between what people say, considering their use of new products for example, and what they actually do can be better understood.

Finally, focus groups are valuable when you want to explore how viewpoints are socially constructed and communicated (Puchta and Potter, 2004). Thus, focus groups can illuminate the production of social and cultural understandings and narratives of everyday life. In social sciences, focus groups are also commonly used to empower participants and to initiate change by listening to their stories and analyzing their ways of understanding the world (Carey and Asbury, 2012).

A method or a data-collection technique?

A focus group researcher who is interested in interaction focuses on how people talk about a topic, not just what they say about it. This means that the researcher analyzes not only the content of the conversation, but also what the conversation situation is like in terms of emotions, tensions, interruptions, conflicts and body language (Stewart and Shamdasani, 2014). There can also be an interest in how people tell and retell different narratives or how they draw on and reproduce discourses in interaction (Puchta and Potter, 2004).

All the above-mentioned developments have strengthened the idea that focus group research is more like a method than just a data collection technique. An important aspect to keep in mind, however, is that focus group studies can be based on very different theoretical and epistemological orientations, although these differences are not commonly discussed in the more practically-oriented focus group methods books (Wilkinson, 2004).

In business research, focus groups can be used either as a method in its own right, or in combination with other methods (for different uses, see Box 14.1). In multi-method research, focus groups can be used to develop questions for survey questionnaires and structured interview guides, to help interpret survey findings and statistical data, and to provide an in-depth picture of a topic of interest after a survey has been conducted and analyzed. Focus groups can also be used to generate new research questions and new theoretical ideas for research.

—————————————————— BOX **14.1** ——————————————————

Three ways of using focus groups in research design

As the only method. Focus groups are the sole source of empirical data for the study, as in for instance, a study focusing on how the employees of a multinational company construct shared understandings of competence development at work.

As part of a multi-method qualitative research design. There are several sources of empirical data in the same study and one of them is focus groups. For example, a case study on a product development process of a new product could combine focus groups, personal interviews and documents.

As a supplement to a survey. Prior to a survey to identify new issues on a topic; or after a survey to expand and illuminate specific issues or to initiate change. For example, an action research project could use focus groups to empower citizens to consider themselves experts in initiating changes in their own neighbourhood.

KEY CHARACTERISTICS OF FOCUS GROUPS

A typical focus group consists of a group of about two to ten participants, a facilitator (a person who initiates and guides the interaction between the participants, often the researcher herself) and a topic or an issue that will be discussed. Focus group discussions are pursued in an informal atmosphere to encourage the group of people to express and share their viewpoints as freely as possible. A focus group event does not need to restrict itself to discussion only; it can include other kinds of tasks, such as drawing or painting, pictorial representations, drama and projective techniques (Edmunds, 2000).

You can easily find advice about when and how to use focus groups in consumer behaviour and practically-oriented market research. This advice works well for studying classic consumer marketing issues, such as attitudes, needs, perceptions and preferences concerning products and services and their marketing. When focusing on other than consumer marketing issues, you need to consider how focus group research suits the objectives and theoretical starting points of your research project (see Box 14.2 for examples of research questions that can be studied with focus groups). However, we suggest that you approach focus group research with an open and experimental mind and read different types of literature concerning them.

-- BOX 14.2 --

Research questions to be studied with focus groups

What are the attitudes, needs, experiences, perceptions, beliefs, priorities or choices of a group (of consumers, employees or managers for instance)? How do these evolve during group interaction, and why?

What is the variety of language practices (e.g. narratives, discourses and rhetoric) used by the participants? How are different language practices used?

How are group norms, values and cultural understandings constructed by the group? How do they evolve and change during group interaction?

What are the social processes taking place when the group produces a different kind of knowledge (e.g. common sense, taken-for-granted, sensitive, embarrassing or critical issues)?

There are several benefits to the business researchers and to the participants of focus group research. First, it can be empowering to the participants that they are treated as experts and allowed to work in close collaboration with the researcher during the focus group discussions. Second, in focus groups participants are not pressured to perform spontaneous reactions. They can take their time to digest the views and issues raised by other participants. Because there is time to consider one's responses, new points of view may arise, which would remain unsaid in personal interviews.

It is good to remember, however, that not all participants experience these benefits in a similar way. Focus groups can be suppressing for minorities and vulnerable groups with exceptional views or dramatic experiences (Carey and Asbury, 2012). They can also be intimidating for inarticulate or shy members. Some people may feel marginalized, intimidated, or just unwilling to talk in a group. Furthermore, focus group research is by nature open-ended and cannot be entirely predetermined, no matter how well the process is planned and implemented. This is why focus groups are not suitable for all research situations and all topic areas.

HOW TO ORGANIZE AND CONDUCT FOCUS GROUP RESEARCH

There is a major difference between 'a group interview' and 'a focus group discussion'. When facilitating focus groups, researchers encourage group interaction, which means that the participants talk to each other and answer each other's questions more than the facilitator's. Indeed, conversation and interaction among the participants is at the heart of modern focus group research (Puchta and Potter, 2004). Therefore, a focus group researcher should not be primarily interested in collecting individual opinions on a subject matter. Rather, they are interested in how people react to each other's questions, statements and points of view, how they build bridges between differing understandings, and how they construct shared conceptions during the discussion.

Ethical considerations for focus groups are similar to other social science research methods (see Chapter 6). When involving participants, the researcher needs to ensure that they give full information about the purpose of the study and the uses of participants' contributions. The facilitator needs to clarify with the participants that their contributions will be shared with the others in the group as well as with the facilitator. Participants must be encouraged to keep confidential what they hear during the session, and researchers need to secure everybody's anonymity in research reports.

Organizing focus groups

Organizing focus groups means that the participants are divided into small groups, which meet in one or several locations with the help of the facilitator. This is why you should do some serious planning. When considering all the necessary preparations for a focus group study, it can sometimes turn out that focus groups are neither practical nor affordable. Within the global business community, for instance, geographical distance and costs can be a hindrance to bringing together a focus group consisting of managers or employees of business units in different countries. For this purpose, you could consider using online focus groups (see Chapter 9).

Before starting to plan for a focus group study, you should think once more whether focus groups are the most appropriate way to find answers to your research questions. For instance, the groups might not pursue an active discussion if your topic is too sensitive (e.g. focused on personal or intimate issues), if the participant's cultural background does not support free exchange of viewpoints, or if the participants are competitors 'in the same market' (e.g. professionals, experts, managers, or entrepreneurs). Sometimes, it may be possible to define the topic of discussion in a way that avoids these risks; but if not, it might be better to choose some other way of collecting empirical data.

Before considering the details of the groups, you as a researcher should define the topic of discussion as clearly as possible and most preferably in writing. You need to carefully consider whether your topic is too wide or too narrow, and what would be the most suitable formulation for it. For example, your research question might be about how a collective understanding of an 'active organization member' is constructed in a group. What would be the topic of discussion in this case? Should it be stated as 'active orientation to work', 'being active in my work', or 'being an active member of an organization'? There are differences between these formulations in terms of whether they emphasize being active in any organization, or specifically in your own work organization. Although the differences may seem rather small, they can make a huge difference on how the participants start the discussion and how it continues.

What kinds of groups and how many?

The next phase is to decide on what kinds of groups you want to use and how many of them you will need. A usual piece of advice is that the participants in each group should have something in common for the discussion to proceed without major difficulties. The common feature may be an interest in an issue, or an experience, or it can be based on expertise, education, age or gender. Many researchers prefer a homogeneous group with the common threads being the issues for discussion. In this approach, it is believed that having too many different voices could detract from the overall purpose.

On the other hand, those advocating heterogeneous groups argue that one advantage of focus groups is that they can capture a range of opinions from people that are acknowledged to be different. Sometimes, even confrontational groups might be needed to inspire creative insights, opposite sides or a critique of an issue. These are effective with, for instance, controversial products or developments, which can range from red meat to cigarettes, and with issues of public debate such as the use of gene manipulation of food, the implementation of new reward systems at work, etc.

It is also important to consider whether focus group members know each other or whether they are complete strangers. The degree of familiarity unquestionably impacts group discussions. Many researchers prefer group members to be unfamiliar with one another in order to try to prevent acquaintances from influencing comments. In turn, when people know each other, the groups can be more 'naturally occurring' (e.g. people who work together or people who share a hobby). These allow the study of glimpses of interactions that come close to empirical data that could be collected by participant observation in an ethnographic study. An additional advantage is that people knowing each other can relate to familiar comments and to incidents in their shared daily lives. They may also ask each other about contradictions between what they believe and how they behave (e.g. 'How about when you bought a new car and paid a huge sum of money for it...?').

Participants for focus groups are selected based on research aims and on the expected contributions of the participants. You can also select participants randomly from a larger group that you assume to be able to give insight into the topic. For example, if someone wanted to know about consumer activists' views on the media, then purposive sampling (e.g. choosing participants from the register of a local consumer association) would be a good approach. If you were interested in lay people's views, you could choose the participants randomly from the telephone book. Convenience sampling, picking people the easiest and fastest way possible, can hardly be recommended for academic research.

Regardless of the selection method, focus groups are not used to provide statistically generalizable results applicable to a certain population. Instead, a useful measure of validity is transferability, which asks whether the results are presented in a way that allows other researchers to see whether your findings could apply to other contexts.

Each focus group can consist of about two to ten people, depending on the topic of discussion and the goals of the study. Most typically, groups are formed around four to eight people. Four participants should be enough for cross-fertilization of viewpoints, and eight is a manageable number of participants for most facilitators with at least some experience in moderating group interaction.

A smaller number of participants works best if the participants require an increased amount of individual attention from the facilitator (e.g. children and teenagers), if the participants need a lot of time to express themselves because they are not used to doing so in front of others, or if they are experts who have a lot to say about the topic. When deciding on the number of people in a group, you should remember that people sometimes do not come to the session although they have previously agreed to come. Therefore, you should invite more people than what the optimal number would be.

You can decide on the number of groups either in advance or during the research process. Iterative groups are purposely planned so that interpretations made with the first groups can be elaborated upon in subsequent groups. Furthermore, it is possible to add more groups later if necessary. As one focus group is not sufficient for most research purposes, two is considered a minimum. To obtain richer and more diverse empirical material, it might be necessary to conduct three or more groups. Most often business researchers organize just one meeting with each of the groups.

Timing and location of focus groups

Two hours is commonly taken as an optimal time frame for one focus group session. Whereas real-life discussions over dinner or at a bar are not limited in this way, you can also allow your focus groups to take a longer time. More time is particularly helpful when your project calls for the use of creative techniques such as brainstorming. In addition, sensitive topics may require lengthy warm-ups with the group. Three- to four-hour focus group discussions challenge both the facilitator's and the participant's energy; but, at the same time, the absence of time pressure can also be liberating. Whatever the time frame you choose, you should inform the participants about it beforehand.

Focus group discussions can take place in a number of locations. Neutral locations (e.g. rooms designed for focus group discussion) can be used, but some researchers suggest that it is in the natural settings that people negotiate the meanings that they live by.

Thus, focus groups should be conducted in workplaces, living rooms and shopping centres. These locations provide an excellent forum to study naturally occurring groups and to make observations while exploring discussions in their everyday context. For example, a group of business leaders could meet over lunch to discuss an issue provided by the researchers. Extra planning and coordination is required for these types of focus group. Provisions must be made for hosting and taping the sessions, for example.

Whatever the venue you choose, you need to be careful to match the nature of the participants and their expectations. Furthermore, the venue should be easily accessible to all. To guarantee that there are no practical problems, you should inspect the venue in advance.

Recruitment

Recruitment is the process of gathering the group together in the same place at the same time. This can be time consuming, especially if the topic under consideration has no immediate benefits or attractions to participants. People unknown to each other, but with specific interests, can be recruited by word of mouth as well as through social networks and key informants. Alternatively, you can use advertising or posters on noticeboards, e-mail lists, chat rooms or membership lists. One way is to find a contact that knows the target group. If one person is interested, then they may be able to recruit others or give their names at least. This type of recruiting is called the snowball technique. Focus group participants are often compensated in some way; the expenses of the participants can be paid for, child-care provided, small presents offered, and refreshments are often available throughout the session.

The researcher as a facilitator

In academic research, it is typical that the researcher themselves facilitates the discussions. In this way, one can ensure that the objectives will be met throughout the sessions as far as possible. It is also possible to have somebody else facilitate the groups, for example, a professional facilitator, who should then be briefed extremely well and given a detailed topic guide.

A topic guide, written in advance by the researcher, includes instructions on how focus groups will be facilitated: how the sessions are introduced, how the discussion is initiated and closed, what questions the facilitator asks and in what order. The topic guide also includes detailed instructions for the individual and group tasks if any are used. Ideally, focus group discussions are tape recorded and transcribed, or videotaped. In other cases, it is vital to consider in advance how notes are taken and by whom, and whether the group can be involved in recording key issues on a flip chart or notepads, for example.

The task of the facilitator is both a demanding and rewarding one. A good facilitator is first and foremost a good listener: empowering, emphatic, non-judgemental and adaptable. The age, gender and experience of the facilitator may be critical in some topic areas, but not in others. In highly sensitive topic areas, it may be necessary to match the facilitator to the group respondents. Developing a trust between the facilitator and the participants increases the likelihood of open, interactive dialogue. The participants may or may not expect the facilitator to be an expert in the topic of discussion. Whatever the case, the facilitator does not usually insert their opinions into the discussion (Krueger and Casey, 2009). However, there is an exception to this rule. Depending on the research questions, the facilitator may want to make interventions by asking provocative questions of the participants. The purpose of these is to tease out and compare a diverse range of meanings on the topic under discussion.

The main tasks of the facilitator include the explanation of the topic, the purpose and process of the discussion, helping people feel relaxed, listening to them, and facilitating interaction in the group. Empathy must be created with the members, relaxing them and getting a lively discussion under way. The facilitator keeps the session focused, but the degree of control depends upon the objectives of the research. If two or more facilitators are involved, then it is good to agree how much and what input each will give. For example, one facilitator may concentrate on facilitation and the other take notes and check the recording equipment during the meeting.

Conducting focus groups

It is good practice to remind the participants the day before the scheduled focus group session by telephone, e-mail or SMS. When starting the focus group discussion, the facilitator often asks each participant to introduce themselves briefly. Thereafter, the facilitator summarizes the topic and purpose of the discussion and starts with one or more warm-up questions to get interaction going among the participants. A good warm-up question varies according to the topic, although many groups can be started by asking each participant to talk about their day.

During the session, the facilitator keeps the conversation going by asking general, open-ended, conversational, and simply stated questions. Good questions use the language familiar to the participants. The facilitator also lets the group members know that it is fine to agree or disagree with the other participants. Furthermore, the facilitator ensures that everyone has a chance to express themselves, though without pressurizing any participants to speak when they are not willing to do so.

Focus group discussion can be designed to include tasks such as telling a story or drawing a picture. Furthermore, there is a range of more specific techniques and materials (see Box 14.3) that can be used to achieve particular goals with focus groups (Puchta and Potter, 2004; Krueger and Casey, 2009). These include the development of creative and imaginative visions for the future, elaboration of hard-to-grasp concepts, such as 'desire' or 'excitement', and construction of new ideas, frameworks and conceptions.

--- BOX **14.3** ---

Materials and techniques that can be used in focus group discussions

- Materials:

  o Product trials and demonstrations (e.g. prototypes of new products, packages).
  o Visual data, such as storyboards, photographs, advertisements, websites, magazines, drawings and paintings, etc.
  o Auditory data, such as interviews, radio programmes, music, etc.

- Techniques:

  o Brainstorming is a technique often used in a real-life business context to spontaneously produce a variety of (new) issues related to a topic.
  o Sentence completion is a type of word association where the facilitator presents the group with an incomplete sentence for completion.
  o Word sorting is a technique where the groups are presented with a number of words or sentences and asked to sort them into groups according to the attributes of a product, or brand, or a need they have.
  o Developing a campaign is a group activity that can be used to develop a product or service campaign around an issue such as 'youthfulness'.
  o Projective techniques include creating fantasies and analogies, imagining the future, and personification, for example.

When using specific materials and techniques, the competence of the facilitator is of crucial importance. They need to plan the assignments and their purpose in advance and give clear instructions at the beginning of the task. Some of the tasks can be performed individually, but most often they are performed as group work. Group work allows the observation of the communication that people use in everyday interaction, including jokes, anecdotes, gossip, teasing and arguing. In this sense, focus groups reach aspects of life that remain untapped in other types of research. When focusing on these types of aspect, it is recommended that there is an observer present in addition to the facilitator. As the role of the facilitator is to focus on moderating the group, the observer can concentrate on observing the details of how the group works.

Working either from a topic guide or more spontaneously, the facilitator usually moves the discussion from broad issues to more particular ones. They listen to the content of the discussion, but also pay attention to emotions, contradictions and tensions. The facilitator encourages the participants to share their viewpoints and challenge the views of other group members. Within a small number of respondents in particular, there can be a dominant person who may attempt to run the group or whose views colour those of the other members. Equally, there may be more withdrawn people or those who are indifferent to the topic and the group. The responsibility of the facilitator is to bring out the best of each participant without embarrassing anyone. This requires both authority and empathy.

When the time reserved for the session is almost up, the facilitator typically wraps up the session in one way or another. Most often, they summarize the discussion to make sure what the participants said. Finally, the facilitator provides a closing statement and thanks the participants for their time and effort in the group.

ANALYZING FOCUS GROUP DATA

Even with a satisfying focus group process, the success of your research is very much dependent on the analysis (Box 14.4). Analyzing focus groups can be much the same as analyzing any other qualitative data, with the exception or addition of a particular interest in interaction in the group. Therefore, it is possible to make any kind of qualitative analysis on focus group data, depending on whether the discussion was audio taped or videotaped (and transcribed), what the notes taken were like, and what kinds of other data are available (e.g. drawings or other visual data made by the participants, stories written or narrated by them).

BOX 14.4

What to analyze from focus group data

Aspects of interest that you can start your analysis with:

- Several participants repeated the issue, or made similar statements about it.
- Several participants silenced the issue, or made disagreeing statements about it.
- Participants in many groups repeated the issue, or made similar statements about it.
- Participants in just one group discussed the issue.
- When someone picked up the issue, a number of people in the group demonstrated either agreement or disagreement (verbally or non-verbally).
- The issue of agreement or disagreement had unusual importance to the participants.

Questions to proceed with:

- How intensely did the participants state their views about the issue?
- Did anyone change their point of view about the issue in a significant way?
- What clues do you have concerning the reasons for a change in the discussion?
- What was the context of the conversation when something interesting happened?
- What was the whole conversation like as a process?

Here again, the most important issues that you need to consider are: What is the method of analysis that will give answers to my research questions? How does my theoretical framework guide me in the analysis, or does it?

Familiarize yourself with the empirical data

In whatever format you used to collect your empirical data (e.g. audio tapes, video, notes, drawings, notepads, cards), it is most useful that you familiarize yourself with them and start making preliminary analyses as soon as possible after each discussion. There are several reasons for this. Soon after the discussion, you can still remember the details and make some additions to your notes and questions. Furthermore, soon after the session, you will still have a general feeling about the group, the reflection of which can help you work with the following groups. There is no need to wait until all groups have met to start the analysis.

When starting the analysis, it is good to read and listen to the group discussions several times. Explore what happened in each group. Sort the content in a way that makes good sense in relation to your research question. For example, you may find it useful to emphasize issues where substantial agreement exists in all groups and across different types of participants. Or your research question could guide you to identify distinctive and unusual points of view, perhaps because they may reveal an important minority perspective. Finally, interpret what you have described; explain the meanings you observe. Consider valid only those interpretations that you can support with the empirical data.

Qualitative content analysis and ethnographic analysis

Qualitative content analysis (see Box 14.5 and Chapter 10) is commonly used for drawing together and comparing focus group data. Qualitative content analysis is based on a systematic examination of the whole set of empirical data with the unit of analysis being the whole group, the group dynamics, the individual participants, or the participants' utterances (Barbour, 2008; Krueger and Casey, 2009; Stewart and Shamdasani, 2014). Qualitative content analysis may or may not be based on a coding scheme, but the purpose is to inspect the empirical data for recurrent instances, such as words, expressions, themes or discourses.

Wilkinson (2004: 182–94) suggests that there is a fundamental difference between qualitative content analysis and ethnographic analysis of focus group data. Ethnographic analysis is rarely systematic or comprehensive, but instead selective and limited. It aims to be contextual and represents the social world from the participants' perspectives rather than from the analyst's point of view. A particular challenge is to keep in mind the interactive nature of the data and to retain the sense of group discussion as a whole in the analysis.

———————— BOX **14.5** ————————

How to do qualitative content analysis of focus group data

Start with picking up viewpoints and statements that are either common or exceptional.

Continue with identifying and comparing information, groups or sub-groups, themes and patterns, and meaning.

You can also try to describe in a narrative stream what the participants as a whole said and did.

Finally, theorize about connections between points of view, themes and patterns of the discussion.

Wilkinson (2004: 188) prefers ethnomethodological or conversational analysis to be used for ethnographic analysis of focus groups. Conversation analysis (see e.g. Silverman, 2013) assumes that people build social context and meaning through interaction. Other methods of analyzing ethnographic data, such as observations, have also been suggested to suit focus group studies (Suter, 2000). Furthermore, narrative and discursive methods of analysis (Chapters 16 and 17) can be used to analyze focus group data.

WRITING AND EVALUATION OF FOCUS GROUP RESEARCH

Much of the discussion on writing deals with reporting practically-oriented focus group research to audiences comprising of company people, experts and decision makers. For these audiences, the written reports typically follow a structure based on the topic guide providing answers directly to the questions that were discussed in the groups. Although the advice given for reporting to practically-oriented audiences may help you prepare an interesting and easy-to-read report, academic research reports have other goals, too. There must be a relevant research question guiding the structure of the report, and the results of the research need to be contrasted with prior research.

Four structural alternatives

Focus group research can be reported with four different structural alternatives:

1. A thematic structure of a focus group research report is common when the study is based on content analysis. A thematic report uses a lot of quotations from the discussion; therefore, the researcher needs to make decisions on how to choose the most appropriate parts of the empirical data to put into the report.

2. An interaction structure communicates what happened in the groups. This can be reported separately for each group, or by giving examples of patterns of interaction in the whole focus group data.
3. A chronological structure describes the content of the interaction as it unfolded, beginning from the moment that the group started its discussions and finishing with the moment that the discussion stopped.
4. A narrative structure reports collective stories as they were constructed by the interacting groups in any order. A focus group report can follow the idea of ethnographic writing, as suggested by Wilkinson (2004). Here, the researcher would select specific incidents and episodes of group discussions to be reported in more detail.

A general piece of advice is that the report should provide a balanced and comprehensive view of the focus group study findings in relation to the purpose of the study, the theoretical framework used, and the research questions. Evaluation of focus group research varies according to the philosophical and theoretical background of the approach chosen. For instance, if the researcher has performed an ethnographic focus group study (Wilkinson, 2004), then it should be evaluated by the criteria set by ethnographic research.

KEY POINTS OF THE CHAPTER

'Focus group' refers to a group of people who are focused on discussing a selected topic or an issue. The difference between 'a group interview' and 'a focus group discussion' lies in how the facilitator encourages group interaction. This means that the participants talk to each other and answer each other's questions more than the facilitator's.

Focus groups generate rich and versatile empirical data. In academic business research, they can be much more than just a technique of data collection for practical consumer research. Besides the analysis of the content of focus group discussions, you can perform a detailed analysis of how ideas and experiences are constructed through social interaction in the group.

Organizing and conducting focus groups requires careful planning and good facilitating skills. Despite this, the successfulness of focus group research is dependent on the relevance of the research questions and on the quality of the analysis.

FURTHER READING

Stewart and Shamdasani's (2014) book on *Focus Groups* is a comprehensive description of the key issues involved.

Carey and Asbury's (2012) book on *Focus Group Research* provides a thorough introduction to creating and conducting focus group research projects with an emphasis on minorities and other vulnerable groups.

---------------------------------- EXERCISE **14.1** ----------------------------------

Conducting focus group research

The purpose of this exercise is to learn about how to conduct focus groups. You will learn about the roles and tasks of the people involved (the facilitator, participants and observers) and their interaction. The exercise can be performed with a class of students after they have read this chapter.

Start with choosing a topic to be discussed in a group. This can be somebody's own research topic, or a topic that is generally interesting to the students. Give the students the following roles:

- facilitator (one or two);
- participants (four to six usually works well);
- observers (the rest of the class observes the discussion).

Give the facilitators, participants and observers some privacy and time to plan how they can deal with their specific tasks. Remind the groups individually that:

- the facilitators need to plan how they want to start the discussion, how they can keep it going, how they can handle difficult situations, etc.;
- the participants need to decide in advance what kind of roles they want to play (e.g. a shy person or a dominant person; they should not tell these to the facilitators and the observers);
- the observers need to think in advance what they will be observing, how they will take notes, etc.

Arrange a space where the focus group discussion can be held (a quiet room with some chairs, perhaps a table...). Before giving the floor to the facilitators, decide on who will be the timekeeper.

When the discussion has been going for a period of time that was initially agreed upon, start reflecting on how the facilitators and the participants acted and how they experienced the situation. Then proceed to discuss what the observers have to say about:

- content (what was said or not said, and by whom) and form (e.g. formal, informal, vivid, enthusiastic, dull) of the conversation;
- interaction in the group (how people responded to each other, how they took turns, were emotions involved?);
- role and style of the facilitator (e.g. active, passive, supporting, empathetic, aggressive).

After the discussion, you can continue to work in small groups and summarize what went well with the group discussion and what could be improved. You can also have a discussion about which research questions could be generated on the basis of the group discussion.

EXERCISE 14.2

Observing interaction in a group

The purpose of this exercise is to learn about how to observe interaction in a group of people. It is most useful to do the exercise in pairs of students, or in a small group to enhance detailed discussion. The comparison of descriptions, analyses and conclusions by several students illustrates how we make interpretations on (at least to some extent) a different basis, and how we are able to justify them to others.

Choose a television discussion programme that has an interesting and relevant topic in terms of your research topic or your preliminary research question and videotape it. You can either choose a programme with a facilitator or a chair (most often a journalist), or one without any.

Prepare yourself to describe and analyze what happens during the programme when people discuss with each other. Think in advance how you will take notes of what you observe, and take time to watch the programme several times. Pay attention to issues such as:

- content and flow of the conversation (what is said or not said and by whom, how issues grow, follow each other, and diminish);
- interaction among the participants (how people are seated, how they respond to each other, what kind of vocabulary and language they use, how they argue, how they take turns, how they show emotions, sharing, tensions, disagreements, what their body language is);
- role and style of the facilitator (if there is any).

Prepare written notes about your description, analysis and conclusions, and try to relate these to your research topic and question. Present your notes to the other students and discuss similarities and differences in your descriptions, analysis, interpretations and conclusions.

15

GROUNDED THEORY RESEARCH

This chapter will provide information on:

- what grounded theory research means
- the role and content of grounded theory methodology
- ways of performing grounded theory research
- the key concepts used in the grounded theory approach
- the historical and contemporary developments of grounded theory methodology.

WHAT IS GROUNDED THEORY RESEARCH?

The grounded theory approach has wide use and applicability, and it has established its position within business studies. Grounded theory is mistakenly often used to refer to any possible approach that tries to develop theoretical ideas, or, more specifically, theoretical models, starting from the data. However, this 'layman's' conception of grounded theory as a rather pure version of 'inductive theory' – that the theory emerges by its own 'force' from the data, like tulip leaves emerge from bulbs in spring soil – is wrong and does not do justice to the grounded theory approach.

Grounded theory refers both to the method and the end result of the research process. Grounded theory methodology consists of a specific set of procedures for carving out the inbuilt middle-range theory from, and with the help of, the empirical data.

Middle-range theory refers to such theories that are delimited to specific aspects of social phenomena, instead of broad, macro-level theories that deal with abstract entities such as society or the economy. The specific procedures are used in order to develop theory during the research process, without commitments to specific kinds of data or specific theoretical interests. In this sense, the grounded theory approach is not a mere method or technique for qualitative data; rather, its application in research has more ambitions towards theory development than empirical analysis.

The idea of grounded theory has been targeted to criticism, partly because of its inductivist principle. Even if the contemporary form of grounded theory and the ways to use the method in business studies have travelled a long way from Glaser and Strauss (1967), the origins, orientation and early development of the grounded theory approach still have their presence. The early grounded theory methodology should be seen as embedded largely in the social science landscape of its origins, the period of the early 1960s. In the 1960s, the social sciences were dominated by the logico-deductive theory generation, analysis and method approach, and the idea of the grounded theory approach to a large extent reflects that time period, and those origins, even if new developments have taken place in its methodological part and assumptions concerning the new knowledge creation in research.

The founders of grounded theory approach, Barney Glaser and Anselm Strauss, in their book *The Discovery of Grounded Theory* (Glaser and Strauss, 1967), contrasted grounded theory with the logico-deductive approach, by arguing that, in principle, theory testing through hypothesis setting alone ignored the whole process of theory generation, and that variable-focused analysis was truly insensitive to the real-life problems. According to the grounded theory approach, 'theory evolves during actual research and it does this through continuous interplay between analysis and data collection' (Strauss and Corbin, 1988: 158).

Grounded theory research and theory building

Today, the use of grounded theory methodology has spread and found its way to the research methodology used, for example, in case studies and in various fields of social sciences, business research included (Timmermans and Tavory, 2007). In marketing research, grounded theory study of consumer responses to advertising (e.g. Johnson, 2014) has brought interesting results and increased an understanding of consumer market behaviour. Consumer experiences and consumer behaviour, as well as sub-fields such as tourist behaviour, are all fields for the grounded theory approach in business research, and especially in marketing research (e.g. Goulding, 2000; Black and Tagg, 2007; Wadham and Warren, 2014).

The grounded theory approach has also gained a foothold in organization studies and leadership studies and in strategic studies. And grounded theory is widely used in the study of technological changes and organizational changes

(Czarniawska-Joerges, 1988; Brown and Eisenhardt, 1997; O'Reilly, Paper and Marx, 2012; Kovalainen and Österberg-Högstedt, 2013; Parker and Guthrie, 2014). The wide use of grounded theory makes the list incomplete, so you should check within your discipline for the best examples.

Grounded theory methodology can be described as a highly developed idea consisting of a set of formally named and described procedures. These procedures are the key and the tools for producing a theory of social phenomena through the analysis of empirical data. How does grounded theory-based analysis of empirical materials 'produce' theory? We will come back to this later in the chapter; but briefly, the grounded theory methodology employs various approaches and logic in developing the theory: it uses both induction and deduction. In addition, verification in the theory development is regarded as important.

What most grounded theory application authors argue is that theory develops and evolves during the research process due to the constant overlap and interplay between the data collection and analysis phases (Glaser and Strauss, 1967; Corbin and Strauss, 1990; Charmaz, 1990, 2000, 2003; Strauss and Corbin, 1998). The informed reader may now ask whether this iterative process is not the standard ideal way for any qualitative research procedure and process, and especially so for some approaches more than others.

What is specific for the grounded theory approach in comparison with other qualitative methods and approaches is that the constant overlap and interplay between data collection and analysis phases is given specific procedural and rather formal form. A generation of new theory should emerge as a process of analysis, irrespective of the field where the method is applied. That this new theory should consist of a set of plausible relationships proposed among concepts and sets of concepts is the outcome of the method's application.

This 'outcome' of the grounded theory approach results in a substantial difference between the grounded theory approach and others, such as ethnographic methods, where the detailed description of materials and settings and the understanding of the research settings and empirical reality is often the key outcome of the research project, not the theory of some part of empirical reality.

In business research, it is easier to find examples of grounded theory applications from marketing and consumer studies than from leadership or accounting studies. The reason for this might be that the epistemic assumptions in those two latter fields are more dispersed and do not fit so well into grounded theory assumptions, compared with epistemic assumptions within marketing theory. This might be one explanation for the differences, but surely not the only one. We also need to take into account that the grounded theory approach has changed over the years and new formulations subscribe to different assumptions than earlier. In the following, we will take a look at both the original assumptions and the new developments.

The original studies and thinking about grounded theory were established using objectivist assumptions embedded in positivism, and this thinking is still present in the procedures and philosophy of grounded theory, even if much of the research done within grounded theory today is following constructivist assumptions (e.g. Charmaz, 2014).

The differences between the grounded theory approach and the narrative and discursive approaches to data, for example, differ not only in terms of dealing with and handling the data, but also even more profoundly, they continue to differ in their way of thinking about the role and position of theory in research, different ways for knowledge production and the possibilities and need for generalization on the basis of the research results. In the following, the basic ideas of grounded theory methodology and its usability and uses will be explored further, especially in relation to business research.

THE RATIONALE OF GROUNDED THEORY METHODOLOGY

Building any theory from case study materials has been the subject of a vast amount of methodology discussion, research, and even debate among the classics (Glaser and Strauss, 1967; Strauss, 1987; Eisenhardt, 1989; Strauss and Corbin, 1998) and among the contemporaries, mainly on the issue of how to combine data and theory, what is the role of interpretation in the process, when to use various methodological approaches and how to evaluate different approaches. Very often this discussion is related to the case study approach, which we presented in detail in Chapter 11. Case studies can be used for different aims, not only for providing descriptions or testing theories, but also for generating theories. In this theory generation, grounded theory methodology can be useful.

The grounded theory approach is developed for theorizing from the data through, and with the help of, a highly formalized and descriptive methodology. This is also the reason for critique: the emphasis on the formal coding process and ways to proceed with the data analysis has evoked a lot of criticism from many qualitative methods users. For some research settings and research questions, the formalized methodology might prove to be useful, whereas for others it might not. Besides the methods and their differences, it is also good to learn about how and in what ways they have been used in specific research settings. For this purpose, reading different kinds of publications is useful.

There are three different versions of grounded theory that are used in qualitative research. The different versions of grounded theory approach that exist and are used in research settings are, by and large, a consequence of work that draws research into different directions: the original ideas presented by Glaser and Strauss (1967) were developed and further elaborated in different ways and into different directions by, for example, Glaser (1992, 2002), Corbin and Strauss (1990), and Strauss and Corbin (1998), among others. Differences exist in both style and in the terminology used. Strauss (1990) developed the original method with a relatively complex process of systematic coding, which was not fully accepted by Glaser (1992).

The differences in relation to the method development have turned many researchers to the original book by Glaser and Strauss (1967). The third version of grounded theory is the constructivist version, mostly developed by Kathy Charmaz (2014, 2006). The latest tension in the method development is related to the constructionist version of grounded theory (Box 15.1).

We will take up some strands of method development discussion towards the end of this chapter; first, we will introduce the basic structure, key concepts and elements of grounded theory methodology and give examples of how grounded theory methodology has been used and implemented in business research settings. The presentation in this chapter relies both on the original ideas presented by Glaser and Strauss (1967) and later development by Strauss and Corbin (1998), and also takes up the remarks by Glaser (1992, 2002) if the differences are important to the actual data analysis procedure. It is in the later work by Strauss and Corbin (Corbin and Strauss, 1990; Strauss and Corbin, 1998) that the coding procedure gets extended into open coding, axial coding and selective coding, of which only the first one constitutes coding work as most often understood in qualitative research.

BOX 15.1

The relationship between reality and the grounded theory approach

When the grounded theory approach was developed by Barney Glaser and Anselm Strauss in the 1960s, it was first and foremost a reaction against the variable-centred hypothesis settings in research and against logico-deductive theorizing, not against the idea and role of truth – or theory – in research. Glaser and Strauss originally focus on two criticisms. According to them, logico-deductive theorizing, in general, strongly exaggerates the place of theory-testing in science, and it denies the possibilities for inductive reasoning in the formulation of theoretical ideas. They do not hold a naïve inductivist position, but note in their original book that 'the researcher does not approach reality as tabula rasa – (that she or he) must have a perspective to see relevant data and abstract significant categories from it' (Glaser and Strauss, 1967: 8).

These ideas are not unique in the debate over the ways in which knowledge and certainty concerning the knowledge and its position can be obtained in research. It is important to note that the so-called cultural turn and constructivism in the philosophy of sciences and social sciences had not gained position at that point in time when the original ideas of grounded theory were developed.

It can be noted that the original authors, Glaser (1992, 2002) and Strauss (1990, in Strauss and Corbin, 1998) differ later on, especially in their epistemological approaches. Developments and additions to the grounded theory approach, both in the direction of the realist methodology and in the direction of the constructivist approach (e.g. Charmaz, 2006, 2014), have been made.

KEY ELEMENTS AND PROCESSES

How does theory emerge from data analysis?

The grounded theory approach suggests that certain, relatively specific operations should be carried out when developing theory from data, much due to the complexity of the social phenomena studied. These operations, main elements and the key concepts will shortly be presented below. Again, Strauss (1990) and Strauss and Corbin (1998) have developed slightly differing presentations of the 'rules of thumb' than Glaser (1992). It is important to keep in mind that theory, that is, the aim, is not a universal law-like product, but more a result of a procedure where rules guide the search for meaning and understanding in the production of theory.

The key of the grounded theory analysis is understanding that it is not purely 'inductive theory', but involves various aspects of inquiry (induction, deduction, even verification). According to Strauss (1990, 1987), all three aspects are essential, but their roles vary: deduction without verification or qualification of a hypothesis or set of hypotheses is, according to him, truncated inquiry. Verification, for its part, cannot take place without deduction and experience with data that, for their part, generate insights, hypotheses or generative questions. These data-informed questions are then pursued further through data generation. In this sense, Glaser and Strauss (1967) implemented the abduction idea by Charles Pierce, whose concept of abduction put strong emphasis on the role of experience in the first phases of research practice. Later, discrepancies in the methods development appeared between the two original authors and their co-authors: Glaser (1992) has criticized the emphasis that Corbin and Strauss (1990; Strauss and Corbin, 1998) put on verification. According to Glaser (1992), the role of verification falls outside the original idea of grounded theory, which should be about the discovery of hypotheses or theory, not about verification.

Kathy Charmaz has taken up the idea of abduction anew in her version of constructionist grounded theory. According to Charmaz (2014), the grounded theory idea entails openness to all possible theoretical understandings. In order to develop tentative interpretations about the theoretical understandings, researcher needs to code the data and further, develop categories through codes. The basic principles of the closeness of the data thus remain the same in all three differing versions of grounded theory.

Grounded theory methodology in general requires a concept-indicator model of analysis, which in turn uses the method of constant comparison. What does this mean in practice in empirical research? Empirical indicators from the data, such as events or actions or activities that have been observed and written into documents or transcribed interviews, are compared with each other in the analysis process, with the aim of searching for similarities and differences between them. From this process of constant comparison, you as researcher will be able to identify underlying and emerging uniformities in the indicators and with these you are able to produce a coded category or concept. Then you will be able to compare these concepts with the empirical indicators and also with each other, in order to rephrase and possibly reformulate the definition of the concept and its properties. Each of these procedures requires systematic note making (see, e.g. Strauss and Corbin, 1998).

The theory generation takes place through the possible relationship between the concepts and sets of concepts, and the exploration of these tentative theories or theoretical propositions through additional or existing data. This is something you need to do during the process, and the investigation of the relationships among categories is usually known as theoretical coding. The process of theoretical coding is described in detail by Glaser (1978) and Strauss and Corbin (1998). Theory development thus takes place in immediate 'contact' with the data: the closeness of data is ever present in the grounded theory approach.

Theory development does not end with that, but testing of emergent theory is guided by theoretical sampling. Theoretical sampling means in practice that the sampling of additional activities or events is directed by the evolving theoretical constructs. Comparisons between the explanatory adequacy of the theoretical constructs and these additional empirical indicators go on until theoretical saturation is reached (Glaser and Strauss, 1967; Strauss, 1990). In this way, the resulting theory is considered to be conceptually dense, solid and grounded in the data. And this is the aim of grounded theory: to reach a core category that adequately explains the phenomenon under investigation.

The re-examination of data throughout the research project is the usual procedure in most qualitative research. However, few qualitative research methodologies direct the researcher to systematic connection building between categories that aim for theory building. Glaser and Strauss (1967) and also Strauss (1990) emphasize the complex nature of social phenomena. This is the reason why grounded theory methodology emphasizes the need for developing many concepts and systematically also their linkages in order to 'capture a great deal of the variation that characterizes the central phenomena studied' (Strauss, 1990: 7). In that sense, the grounded theory approach is an ambitious one when aiming for theory construction: the aim is not the thick description or the narrative interpretation of the materials. This aim for theory construction has also provoked criticism, which we will come back to later in the chapter.

Coding of data as an essential element of the analysis

The essential element for grounded theory methodology is the coding process of the data. Why is the coding so important? This is related to the more general questions of how and in what ways the researcher arrives at the interpretations made in the qualitative research, and how systematically these interpretations are being made. According to the grounded theory approach, a systematic way of working with the data and memo writing can give an explanation of what is done and how the conclusions are reached in the research. In this process, the coding of data is important. Strauss and Corbin (1998) are more explicit about the coding procedure, therefore becoming perhaps more popular in social sciences than the earlier version by Glaser and Strauss (1967).

The coding process in the grounded theory approach consists of three types of coding: open, axial and selective.

1. Open coding is the very first data classification and analysis process in the grounded theory approach. Open coding involves breaking down, analyzing, comparing and categorizing the data. Open coding is the product of an early analysis, and it actually describes what is taking place in the data (Strauss and Corbin, 1998). As the researcher you might wish to find key words, phrases or sentences during the open coding process. Open coding often starts with an initial line-by-line analysis. If you are a careful researcher, you end up having tens or even hundreds of codes that are not necessarily related to each other, but which provide an initial understanding of the materials. Coding the data in this way is the usual way of learning to know the data.

    This concerns all kinds of qualitative data. In open coding, all events, processes or incidences occurring are labelled and grouped together with the help of constant comparison, in order to formulate categories and properties. The next step, after the open coding procedure is done, is axial coding (see e.g. Strauss and Corbin, 1998: 23-7).

2. Axial coding helps you to move to a higher hierarchical level in abstraction in the data analysis. In axial coding, you might be interested in finding incidences or events that are related to each other in some, non-apparent way. Axial coding transfers the analysis away from description and towards linking codes together, in order to proceed with the explanatory categories, and working your way towards theory construction (e.g. Charmaz, 2014).

    Categories, brought forward through and with the help of axial coding, are higher order concepts that have wider explanatory power and combine all the earlier identified concepts in the materials (Strauss and Corbin, 1998). The constant comparative method tries to discover the latent patterns in the texts and in the expressions and words. The focus of grounded theory is on the conceptualization of latent patterns, and thus the concepts, and not as such on the accuracy of speech, or on the words and detailed wordings used as such in the interview text, as in conversation analysis, for example. Constant comparison is thus the key of the process, in revealing the latent patterns and their conceptualization. To begin with, first you compare one data set (e.g. one interview) with another data set (e.g. another interview).

3. Finally, selective coding integrates and refines your analysis towards a larger theoretical scheme. In selective coding you select one category that forms the basis for the theory, such as consumer preference theory.

    The original aim for theory building in the grounded theory approach has also meant that the level of abstraction had to rise higher during the process of analysis: the aim of the analysis and research process in general is from description to prescription. The process of abstraction means that theoretical concepts are integrated into a conceptually complex integrated theory (Strauss and Corbin, 1998). Glaser (1978) warns researchers from forcing the data into the theoretical codes; he refers to a range of possible coding 'families' or groups of codes that can be equally valid in the interpretation, as is often the case in qualitative research.

Even if Glaser and Strauss (1967) do not articulate for a coherent view of theory appraisal in their early book, several authors have later given valuable insights into the ways the theory appraisal should be understood in relation to an empiricist account of theory building. Grounded theory should, therefore, be regarded first and foremost as part of the realist tradition of methodology, and anti-realist perspectives are necessarily not fully compatible with the grounded theory approach, even if such developments have been taken forward lately in a very interesting way (e.g. Charmaz, 2014).

BASIC STEPS IN THE ANALYSIS

The previous part of the chapter has outlined the basic ideas and key concepts behind grounded theory thinking. What is seen as important in grounded theory is that it 'forces' you as the researcher to think in both analytical and conceptual ways; the aim is to move from description to prescription, as mentioned earlier. As the basic steps for grounded theory analysis are most often poorly described (due to their complexity) in research articles, our aim is to introduce them here at the most general level.

From reading the basic idea of the grounded theory approach above, you should by now have a relatively well-developed idea of the main aim of research based on the grounded theory approach. The research question is formulated as in any qualitative research: the research question can be in the form of a statement that identifies the phenomenon to be studied. It tells the readers of your research report about your own interest field and the focus of your study.

In developing and refining the research question, Glaser's views differ from those of Strauss (1990) and Strauss and Corbin (1998). In the following presentation, the original ideas by Glaser and Strauss (1967) and the later development by Strauss (1990) and Strauss and Corbin (1998) are taken up. Despite the later developments and directions taken in the method discussion, the processes described in this chapter can still be followed in research (e.g. Elharidy, Nicholson and Scapens, 2008; Joannidès and Berland, 2008).

In the grounded theory approach, Strauss and Corbin (1998) have emphasized the viewpoint that the researcher needs to consider three major issues before beginning the research inquiry. These issues are: choosing a problem and stating the research question; maintaining a balance between objectivity and sensitivity; and using the literature.

These 'rules' resemble most standard ideas for any research process start-up. That the researcher should maintain a balance between objectivity and sensitivity is a good rule as long as objectivity as defined by Strauss and Corbin (1998: 53) is relevant in your research project: 'objectivity enables the researcher to have confidence that his or her findings are a reasonable, impartial representation of the problem under investigation'. Even if it is useful in the grounded theory approach, this rule is not applicable to most forms of qualitative analysis that have discursive, narrative or postmodern elements, where the question of objectivity (as defined above) does not fit in. The latest constructivist developments in grounded theory do not subscribe to this rule either (e.g. Charmaz, 2014).

What about sensitivity, mentioned above? Sensitivity in qualitative research has, in the general sense, several meanings. In the grounded theory approach, sensitivity specifically means that you have insight into, and are able to give meaning to, the events in data. Immersion in the analysis of data leads to unexpected and rewarding 'aha' experiences, sudden alive notions concerning the data. This is the abductive element in the analysis. Both professional and personal experiences, such as having been a personnel manager and studying your own organization, can increase sensitivity, but can also block or misdirect interpretations.

According to the basic idea of grounded theory, once the area of research has been defined, the researcher should enter the research field relatively soon. Consequently, the literature is consulted as part of the iterative and continuing process of data collection, simultaneous analysis and emergent interpretation. Literature reading should not direct the empirical material gathering or analysis, but inform and enlighten the reader.

In the following, the procedure for discovering, verifying and formulating grounded theory in the research phase will be described, as that is the aim of the analysis. The collecting of data or organizing data is seen as the way to organize many ideas which emerge for the researcher during the analysis of data. In the grounded theory approach, concepts and terms are used that are specifically related to the way of doing the analysis. The most important ones are listed in Box 15.2. Detailed use of the terms can be found, for example, in Strauss (1990) and Strauss and Corbin (1998).

BOX **15.2**

Main procedures for grounded theory analysis according to Strauss

Strauss (1990: 23) has condensed the elements of the main procedures as follows:

1. the concept-indicator model, which directs the coding
2. data collection
3. coding
4. core categories
5. theoretical sampling
6. comparisons
7. theoretical saturation
8. integration of the theory
9. theoretical memos
10. theoretical sorting.

The most important activity in grounded theory methodology is the coding process, which consists of three types: open, axial and selective coding. Coding is the term for conceptualizing data. According to Strauss (1990: 20), coding includes raising questions and giving provisional answers (hypotheses) about categories and their relations. A code is the term for any possible product of this analysis.

From the data to the codes

Open coding, as mentioned above, is about uncovering, naming and developing concepts and categories by opening up the text (Box 15.3). In open coding, you break the data down into discrete parts, examine them closely and compare them for similarities and differences (e.g. Strauss and Corbin, 1998). You can do the open coding exercise through close micro-analysis of the texts, line by line or sometimes even word by word. The aim is to produce concepts (or categories) that seem to fit the data. It is important to remember that these concepts and their dimensions are, at this stage, entirely provisional. The open coding practice is a good way to learn to know your data, and most often it is done in any qualitative data analysis as a first step to get to know the data, often without labelling the procedure as 'open coding'.

─────────────── BOX **15.3** ───────────────

How to do open coding

There are several detailed guidelines and lengthy examples to be found in Strauss (1990) and in Strauss and Corbin (1998), for example. These guidelines can be put into general rules of thumb for open coding:

1. The first rule of thumb is to ask of the data a set of questions that relate them to your original research idea.
2. The second rule of thumb is to ask the question of what category we are talking about when a specific incident is found in the text.
3. A good guideline is also to analyze the data minutely. This produces microscopic analysis, which might not be needed for the whole of the data materials.
4. The fourth rule of thumb given by Strauss is the more general 'lean back and rethink' rule that is important for any qualitative analysis. In the grounded theory approach this is called theoretical memo writing.

Memo writing can be seen as a systematic way in which the researcher puts down theoretical questions, hypotheses and a summary of codes in order to keep track of ideas and codes. Again, memo writing is good practice for any qualitative researcher throughout the research process, but specifically during the data analysis. In some other qualitative methods, memo writing could be called a research diary.

Open coding offers a first idea of the data and it also verifies and saturates individual codes. Strauss (1990) remarks that the researcher should not become too attached to the initial codes achieved through open coding, as open coding can often produce hundreds of codes. From a general qualitative research point of view, open coding is about developing first the theoretical tools for indexing, classifying and explaining the data. That is not enough, though.

Open coding is followed by axial coding. Axial coding consists of intense analysis of one category at a time, and results in new and cumulative knowledge about categories and their relations. Axial coding also can take place during the end part of the open coding, when sub-categories are linked into categories. In the axial coding process, you put together the data in new ways. The aim of this exercise is to make explicit connections between categories and sub-categories, to be able to find a more developed or fuller picture of relationships or explanations that exist in relation to the data and the research question. Axial coding makes you think and rethink your data in new ways, and relates the results of the open coding in ways which are initially non-explicit.

As Strauss and Corbin (1998: 125) have stated, even if the text provides clues about how categories (from open coding) relate to each other, the actual linking takes place not descriptively, but rather at a conceptual level. There are two levels of analysis taking place: (a) the actual words used by the respondent (in the case of interview data are used) and (b) our conceptualization of these words, which is our interpretation of the events or of the incidents described in the text.

How do you do axial coding from the text materials? Generally, you should look for answers to questions such as why or how come, where, when, how and with what results, and in so doing, you are necessarily uncovering relationships among categories by conceptualizing the phenomenon.

The idea with axial coding is to facilitate the linking of sub-categories with their respective categories. Not all sub-categories can be easily categorized as causal conditions, contexts or consequences of category; in many cases, deterministic relationships between the phenomenon and causal conditions are not present in the data and, according to Barney Glaser, should neither be forced in the analysis (Glaser, 1992: 123). Strauss and Corbin (1998: 99) are of a different opinion concerning this linking process: while Glaser sees it as important to focus only on those categories that emerged from the observed situations, Strauss and Corbin see it as important to look at all data and fit them into categories.

Finally, selective coding is about integrating and refining the analysis, and from the major categories selecting one core category to form a larger theoretical scheme. A core category forms the focus around which all other categories are integrated.

According to Strauss and Corbin, selective coding also includes the validation of the systematic relationships between the central or the core category/ies and other categories. Some authors prefer to use the term 'categories' instead of 'concepts' (e.g. Charmaz, 2000, 2014); there is some inconsistency to be found among researchers using these two terms, so you should be aware of checking that you are using terms systematically throughout your research. Again, this applies to all research methods where terminology does not have full consistency.

Validation is done by generating hypothetical relationships between categories and using data from the field to test these hypotheses. Categories may be refined and reorganized in the completion of the theory. It is in this process where the data 'become' the theory. The move from description to conceptualization is helped by storyline memos (Strauss and Corbin, 1998).

We stressed the importance of memos earlier in this chapter. What is the role of memos in the grounded theory approach and, specifically, in relation to coding process? Memos have an important role in the analysis in helping to 'produce theory' from a number of categories through generating relationships and working towards more integrative frameworks. Memos are core in the theory-generating process, according to Glaser (1978); and as they have an important role, they should therefore be written and generated simultaneously with the data collection and analysis. In similar fashion, many qualitative research methods mention the importance of research diaries. In grounded theory, several instructions have been given concerning the use and writing up of memos, including advice such as 'memo writing is fun' and 'always give priority to memoing' (Miles and Huberman, 1994: 74). Memos help in relating ideas, theoretical thinking, relationships, etc. to the analysis process.

From coding to theory

The objective of selective coding is really to explicate the story by finding (identifying) a core category and linking the other categories to the core category. Again, how will you find these relations? Some researchers find it easier to use the so-called 'meta-theories' to help in carving out the core categories.

The concept identification process looks at the concepts (and, furthermore, the most dominant ones among them and their underlying properties and processes) in order to proceed to theoretical statements (or theory building). Even if the procedure can be given formal structure, it rests on your intuition. According to Strauss and Corbin (1998: 275), grounded theory is 'a general methodology, a way of thinking about and conceptualizing data … applicable to quantitative as well as qualitative studies'.

Coding as such, therefore, does not 'save' grounded theory analysis; this is because the core category analysis, which leads to theory development or theoretical statements, is the most crucial outcome of the analysis. In fact, one of the criticisms directed towards the grounded theory approach has been its emphasis on 'identifying codes', without explaining how the codes are related to each other (e.g. Goulding, 1998, 2000) and even to theory that emerges in the process. According to Goulding (1998), only when the theory has substance, or when no new findings arise from data, should the researcher review the work in the field and relate the theory to it through the integration of ideas.

As you can easily notice from this short introduction to the grounded theory approach, this complexity in the analysis processes and the overlap between the coding procedures, interpretation and theory building makes the process of analysis and writing clearly an effort for many: the normative rules for building up the analysis seem to give a positivist staple on the whole grounded theory approach (Charmaz, 2014). Yet, the coding procedure has some resemblance to other coding procedures described earlier in the book. As Bryman and Burgess (1995) note on the usability of a grounded theory approach, in spite of the frequency of citations of grounded theory among researchers, it is questionable whether it is employed by researchers in its entirety. That the research methods immerse with other methods and that parts of the various methods are used elsewhere is understandable, as methods and their theoretical underpinnings also evolve and are actively developed.

GROUNDED THEORY APPROACH REVISITED

Above, we have gone through the basic elements of grounded theory in order to give an insight into the process and procedure of grounded theory in its most used format. The different versions and recent developments have given a new flavour and new directions to grounded theory methodology, but these have, at the same time, evolved and changed the original ideas developed by Glaser and Strauss (1967). Some researchers focus on two versions of grounded theory methodology. Strauss and Corbin (1998) took a path differing from the original idea, and Glaser (1992) in his book responded to that.

The delineations between Glaser and Strauss and Strauss and Corbin are visible in their respective books. The differences could perhaps be boiled down mostly to differences in understanding the issue of constant comparisons, theoretical memoing and sorting, as well as the role and importance of verification. All the distinct differences stem from the evolvement of two different approaches with clearly differing underlying epistemologies and properties related to them. After this discrepancy, new developments towards constructivist approaches in grounded theory have even evolved (Charmaz, 2014).

What about the role of the researcher in the research process? The linguistic or cultural turn has, in general, brought forward the discussion of the role and position of the researcher, the ways for interpretations, and the different possibilities for theory construction and development. The most recent discussion has concerned the ways and possibilities for 'constructivist grounded theory', where the position of researcher and interpretation of the data are very different to the original idea of the grounded theory approach.

It is also in this respect that we see the differences between the later development by Glaser (2002) and Strauss and Corbin (1998) evolve. There are various types of comparative analysis which cannot be classified as a grounded theory approach. Typical for them is that parts of the grounded theory approach are used for classification or organization of data but theory generation is left out from research settings.

According to Glaser (2002), categories, which are concepts, come from the 'monotony' and detailed work of the constant comparative method; as described above, these concepts are linked with sensitive and theoretical sampling and are constantly fitted to the data. Glaser's view concerning the role of the researcher is very clear: he sees the researcher's personal preferences as problematic, as they bias the interpretations of the data and, therefore, they should be treated as variables to consider. But as Glaser (2002) remarks, the constant comparative process will reveal these, what he calls, researcher biases. Strauss and Corbin (1998) think differently about the role of the researcher: the researcher is actively part of the process and their interests and input should be an integral part of the analysis. For Glaser, the researcher is objective, for Strauss and Corbin, the researcher is subjective.

The epistemic discussion of the nature of knowledge and knowledge production is at the core of some of the shifts and changes in the ways grounded theory approach is being adopted and used. The original idea of grounded theory by Glaser and Strauss was not to conflate it into a set of rigid rules to be followed, but it is increasingly used as a mixed-method among others: instead of adopting the intellectual ground of approach, the adoption goes into direction and areas where most 'clear rules' prevail. This development is also criticized in the methods books focusing solely on the grounded theory approach (e.g. Goulding, 2002; Charmaz, 2014).

Critique and renewal of grounded theory

Several slightly differing and even partly alternative versions of the grounded theory approach concerning, for example, an emphasis on data processing, have been developed over the years. There are other issues as well that have led to reconsidering the place of the grounded theory approach among the interpretative qualitative methods. Goulding (1998: 55) calls these 'methodological slurring', which centres largely on methodological transgressions. The later additions include such unsuitable suggestions as 'rigid rules', 'visual diagram' and 'sample size of 12 should be the minimum' (Goulding, 1998: 55). Even if methodological discussion goes further, a number of misconceptions have remained regarding its applicability and its relation to positivist practices.

The critics of grounded theory have been many, starting from Glaser (1992) himself, who has criticized the way the grounded theory approach has developed towards a technical direction. Another form of criticism against the grounded theory approach is targeted towards its commitment to realism, which was mentioned earlier. When committed to the realist tradition, the approach blinds itself from possible limitations. The idea that materials and data are already theory laden is not acceptable in the traditional grounded theory approach, even if it is part of the present qualitative tradition to a larger and larger extent.

Marketing and consumer studies have adopted the grounded theory approach as closely related to the field of consumer research. The origins of the grounded theory approach in the study of behaviour seem to give the approach more suitability for those areas where the understanding of the nature of consumption experiences is important (e.g. Goulding, 1998). Still, the complexity of the method itself, as briefly described here as well, does not make it an easily adoptable methodological choice.

Another field where grounded theory has been well suited is organizational theory (Locke, 2001) where the grounded theory approach can, according to Locke:

1. capture the complexity of contexts;
2. link with practices and, thus, organizational actions;
3. enable theoretical work in new areas of organizational life;
4. put life into well-established fields as an alternative view.

Grounded theory methodology is largely adapted in educational and information systems research. Good examples of adoption and adaptations of the methodology can be found, for example, in Thornberg et al. (2013), Thornberg (2012) and Dunne (2011). The computer-assisted qualitative data analysis programs such as NVivo owe much to the grounded theory approach in their presumptions of a certain style of analysis. Computer-aided analysis of qualitative data will be discussed in detail in Chapter 9.

Methodological development is also taking place. This constructivist direction, sketched out by Charmaz (2000, 2014), among others, has been rejected by Glaser (2002). Charmaz has described the subjectivity and ambiguity of constructivist grounded theory in her own research and argues that they also permeate the objectivist approaches of grounded theory (Charmaz, 2006: 149). Charmaz's research and theorizing on grounded theory has brought forward the constructivist and interpretative views and has drawn a line between these and the positivist and objectivist grounded theory approach. The contemporary view on grounded theory is that it is not one method, but many: it is a family of methods, as different forms exist and are used today under the umbrella title of grounded theory. In business research, the grounded theory approach to research continues to gather recognition within the broad qualitative paradigm.

WRITING AND EVALUATION OF GROUNDED THEORY RESEARCH

A grounded theory-based research project usually evolves with a tentative literature base to begin with. The field data and the development of codes and categories receive a lot of attention in the research project and, thus, also guide writing in both accuracy in claims-making and conceptual thinking. Depending on which direction you take in your project, you might need to take both aspects into account in your own writing. However, even narrative accounts and narrative writing go along with the grounded theory approach; even aesthetic principles can apply to the ways of writing, and a multitude of voices is possible in grounded theory reports (Charmaz, 2014). Reflexivity and aesthetic merits, as well as the narrative's substantive contribution, are all important for grounded theory-based research reports.

What about evaluation of grounded theory research reports? Should all details in coding processes be the crucial criteria, or are there other criteria that have importance in evaluation? The original evaluation criteria by Glaser and Strauss (1967) and later by Glaser (1978) for assessing grounded theory studies included fit, workability, relevance and modifiability. They meant, by and large, that theory must be suitable and fit to the empirical world it analyzes. Workability included the aspect of understanding and explanation, and modifiability allowed for changes of the theory to take place. Charmaz (2006: 527) brings forward additional criteria for evaluation, that is, saturation of categories, and asks what saturation means. Charmaz also rejects the idea of saturation and offers explicit criteria for grounded theory research, namely credibility, originality, resonance and usefulness.

Credibility consists of several aspects: the researcher's own familiarity with the research topic and setting, sufficient data for claims that are made in the research, and systematic analysis development between categories and observations. Originality refers to the categories developed in the analysis: Are they new, do they have significance, do they challenge, refine and change the current ideas and concepts? Resonance refers to the researcher's ability to draw novel meanings and analytic interpretations. Finally, usefulness refers to the practical aspects of the usefulness of the research results (Charmaz, 2014). All these together have an analytic impact, which, together with evocative writing, can make well-grounded arguments for the case.

KEY POINTS OF THE CHAPTER

The key steps in the grounded theory approach relate to theory building through close working with empirical data. The data are coded through three types of coding: open coding, axial coding and selective coding.

Open coding is the very first data classification through which data get categorized for axial coding (i.e. the second classification), where non-apparent relations in the data and moving from description to explanatory categories are of interest. Selective coding integrates and refines the analysis to the theoretical level.

Presently, the grounded theory approach is being developed by several methods authors in the direction of constructivism, which was not originally the idea of the founders of the method.

The grounded theory research method is much used in business research. Methods do develop over time; bits and pieces of them are being used variably. You should be aware of the background assumptions of any method you will use in your own research.

FURTHER READING

The books by both Goulding (2002) and Locke (2001) give good coverage of the recent use of grounded theory in some specific fields of management research.

Charmaz's (2006 and 2014) book *Constructing Grounded Theory. A Practical Guide through Qualitative Analysis* gives good coverage of the new aspects of the constructivist grounded theory approach and many valuable examples from her own and other social scientists' research.

EXERCISE 15.1

Initial stage of grounded theory analysis

The purpose of this exercise is to learn the first steps of grounded theory analysis. With this exercise you will learn what minutely analyzed material in the open coding phase can consist of.

If you have your own interview materials transcribed, you could try a simple exercise based on grounded theory.

1. Start by reading the materials through and looking at specific (or any) incidents in the text.
2. Analyze the data minutely, line by line, in order to find out the incidents.
3. Ask the question, of what category are we talking about in the case of specific incidents?
4. Write down the categories you can think of.

EXERCISE 15.2

Developing the analysis further. This exercise relates to Exercise 1

After the open coding for Exercise 1, you can work further with the materials, and move on to axial coding, by trying to find new connections between the categories you have found in the materials. You can also try selective coding which would then be about selecting one core category for theory development. You could tentatively try to make a plan for these different forms of coding.

16
NARRATIVE RESEARCH

This chapter provides information on:

- what is specific about narrative research
- what the key concepts and understandings of narrative research are
- how to collect and analyze narrative data
- how to write and evaluate narrative research

WHAT IS NARRATIVE RESEARCH?

Narrative research is an umbrella term for research, which acknowledges the power of storytelling. Narrative theorists such as Polkinghorne (1988) and Bruner (1986) have suggested that 'story' is the oldest form of influence in human history and this is why storytelling is one of the primary forms of communication among human beings. Compared to non-narrative texts, stories are richer and thicker and thus, more compelling and memorable. They also give us context. The theory also holds that narrative is a means by which we organize, explain and understand our life and social relations. In this respect, stories and narratives concern human action and experience.

The background of the narrative paradigm and theory lie in philosophy, literary and communication studies and languages (Bal, 2009). Many social scientists (e.g. Riessman, 1993; Clandinin and Connelly, 2000; Elliott, 2005), have worked extensively to develop narrative methodologies and methods, which acknowledge the value of oral and written stories in constructing our understanding about reality.

Social scientists' interest in stories cover the analysis of individual, group, organizational and cultural narratives, and the use of narrative inquiry as a methodological approach to explore any kind of empirical data.

The narrative research approach has also gained an interest among business researchers, especially organization and management theorists (see e.g. Czarniawska, 1997, 1998, 1999; Gabriel, 2000; Boje, 2001). Czarniawska (1998: 13–14) outlines four alternative ways of doing narrative research within organization studies. The same uses can be extended to concern other areas of business research, too. Thus, it can be said that narrative business research has at least four different forms:

1. writing narratives for research purposes such as ethnographies, case stories, career stories. For an example, see De Rond (2008);
2. collecting and analyzing stories told by people (e.g. employees, consumers, entrepreneurs, consultants, business educators). For an example, see Gabriel (2000);
3. conceptualizing aspects of life (e.g. organizing, consuming, managing, entrepreneuring) as story making, and business research as story reading. For an example, see Starkey and Crane (2003);
4. making disciplinary reflection that takes the form of literary critique, for instance, analyzing the plot of strategic management theory, or the characters and drama in HRM theory. For an example, see Hagan and Cohen (2014).

Boje (2001), in turn, distinguishes between four specific trends in organizational storytelling research:

● First, researchers use stories to describe and measure some other phenomena, such as organizational culture or strategic decision making.
● Second, researchers study stories in their performance context, asking 'what is the role of stories in specific organizations?'
● Third, researchers use stories as practical tools (e.g. as part of an action research project) to enhance strategic management, organizational development, coaching, and marketing and sales.
● Fourth, researchers use and interpret stories in a way that allows for marginalized and suppressed voices to tell their stories as counter-narratives for the more conventional ones.

A number of large companies are actually using stories as management communication vehicles (see e.g. Denning, 2004; Brown et al., 2005). Here, stories and storytelling processes are considered management tools, used by management in order to enact change or to boost the performance of the company. The telling of stories is used to achieve a practical outcome or change in an individual, a small group of people, or an organization. Although the idea of using stories and narratives to implement organizational change or other outcomes is appealing, Boje (2001) urges researchers to ask whether this really works. Is it possible that the company management or anybody else can intentionally craft a story to change the whole organization?

There is a lot of methodological diversity in narrative research, which can be difficult for a novice business researcher to deal with. For instance, there is a considerable difference between realist, constructionist, postmodern and post-structural approaches to narrative research (Bold, 2011). Furthermore, many researchers find it difficult to formulate the practical implications of their narrative research findings. This is why you should always consider what kind of narrative research you are aiming to do, and whether practical implications are important in your study (see Box 16.1 for examples of research questions that are suitable for narrative research).

BOX 16.1

Examples of research questions suitable for narrative research

- How do stories relate to how business issues (e.g. teams, organizations, markets, change projects, business training) evolve over time?
- What is the social context of business-related stories?
- How do organization members and groups, consumers, or other business-related actors:

  - o construct different types of stories
  - o use various storytelling methods or techniques
  - o experience stories
  - o use stories as resources to make sense of their work and their life
  - o choose which stories to connect to.

KEY CONCEPTS AND UNDERSTANDINGS OF NARRATIVE RESEARCH

'Story' and 'narrative' are among the core concepts of narrative research. In everyday language, but also in some of the narrative research approaches, these terms are used interchangeably without any difference. However, narrative researchers usually find it useful to make a distinction between them.

A story

To put it simply, 'a story' is a piece of fiction that narrates a chain of related events or happenings that involve certain characters. Some stories are more private and some are widely shared in a culture. The story of Adam and Eve would be an example of a story shared in the Christian culture. Your own life story would be an example of a private story, which you might not want to talk about to any audience other than your closest friends. The story usually includes the entire sequence of events, from the very beginning until the end. It can be either fictional or factual, and it is often chronological.

A narrative

'A narrative' is the textual actualization of a story at a specific time, in a specific context and to a specific audience. It has a defined structure and a coherent plot. Organization theorist Yiannis Gabriel (2000: 239) defines 'narrative' as having 'plots and characters, generating emotion in narrator and audience, through a poetic elaboration of symbolic material'. A narrative may also have a specific point of view to the story. This means that 'narrative' is a story that is told in a specific way by one or more narrators. For instance, the narrator(s) can tell the story from one character's or several characters' points of view, or without a straightforward chronological order. For example, the story of Adam and Eve could be used to construct a narrative that is told either from Adam's or Eve's point of view, both drawing on a gender perspective to the story.

Narratives and discourses

In her textbook on narrative research, Jane Elliott (2005) refers to the work of Hinchman and Hinchman (1997), who describe narratives as 'discourses with a clear sequential order that connect events in a meaningful way for a definite audience and thus offer insights about the world and/or people's experiences of it'. Relying on this, Elliott outlines how narratives are different from other discourses by three elements. First, narratives are temporal: they have a beginning, a middle and an end. Second, narratives are meaningful. One central way in which they convey meaning is by ordering events into a temporal sequence, which leads to a conclusion. This is why narratives have a causal dimension. Third, they are social, as they are produced for specific audiences.

Grand narratives

One way to understand what a narrative is, is to specify between different onto-logical levels of narratives (Somers, 1994). Accordingly, there are meta-narratives (or grand narratives), which are globally shared cultural beliefs ordering, explaining and producing abstract social knowledge. A meta-narrative concerns a grand, all-encompassing story of the historical development of the world and it is charac-terized by 'universal truth'. The majority of meta-narratives are rather optimistic and they provide a framework upon which individual or small group experiences and thoughts can be organized.

Personal narratives

While meta-narratives ignore the heterogeneity and variety of human experience, ordinary people's mundane, personal stories focus exactly on that. Instead of the global and abstract aspects of human life represented by grand and meta-narratives, they focus on local contexts and on the diversity and emotionality of human experience. A personal narrative is a recollection of events and emotions as experienced by an individual in the course of their own life (Riessman, 1993). The personal narrative can cover the whole life of the individual or focus on certain periods, episodes or issues.

The narrative approach also offers the researchers a chance to think and write about themselves, to include their own personal narratives into the study. Carolyn Ellis (2004), who combines ethnography and narrative research in her own studies, argues that all researchers have personal experiences invested in their memories, which are worthy of sharing with readers. Her methodology book on autoethnography (Ellis, 2004) and Clandinin and Connelly's (2000) textbook on narrative inquiry provide excellent examples of how their own experiences are weaved into their research and how the narrative approach enables one to reflect on this.

Collective stories

A third level of narrative, in between meta-narratives and personal narratives, deals with various types of collective story co-produced by communities of people (Rappaport, 1995; Richardson, 1995). In the context of business research, organizational narratives (Czarniawska, 1998; Boje, 2001) shared by the members of a specific organization provide good examples of these, as well as narratives produced by professional communities (e.g. Brown and Duguid, 1991; Orr, 1996).

HOW TO COLLECT AND ANALYZE NARRATIVE DATA

Empirical data used for narrative research can take various forms, and not all data are originally in narrative form. However, all of the following data are useful for doing business-related narrative research, and all others except the first and last category can be written either by the researcher or by the participants:

- Narrative interviews and conversations. These can be done individually or in groups and they are usually transcribed into texts. They involve the co-authoring of the narrative, because the relationship between the researcher(s) and participant(s) creates one of the contexts in which meaning is constructed.
- Oral histories, chronicles, biographies, and family stories. The purpose is to have the participant(s) recollect their past experiences, and this is why they involve memory work, which can be assisted by the researcher.

- Journals and autobiographical writing. Journals are day-to-day records of practices and reflections on those practices, weaving together the private and the professional. Autobiographical writing moves to the wider life context in which the individual reflects on the tension between self and others.
- Letters. These are written to a specific 'other' with the expectation of a response.
- Field notes and other stories from the field. These may be written in more or less detail with more or less descriptive content.
- Photographs, memory boxes and personal artefacts. Each item marks a particular time, place or event around which a story is told.

Narrative interviewing

In contrast to other types of intensive and open interview, narrative interviewing concerns the production of stories. This refers to paying attention to the little stories that people tell spontaneously in interview situations, but also to the role of the interviewer as an activator of narrative production (Elliott, 2005: 28–35), or as a co-constructor of narratives (Ellis, 2004). A narrative interview is open in two different ways: there are no prior hypotheses or propositions to be 'tested', and the participant is encouraged to talk openly. This means that the participant is allowed to tell their story from their own point of view and with their own words and ways of expression without a predefined list of interview questions, or any structured interview agenda. A narrative interview can also be conversational, in which case the interviewer can also decide to tell their own story about the topic at hand.

A narrative interview most often assumes that 'narrative expression' reflects both conscious concerns and relatively unconscious cultural, societal and individual processes. The focus may be on the particularity of individual experience and emotions in unique historical and societal locations and processes, or on the retelling of cultur-ally and socially shared grand narratives. Undertaking a narrative interview may sound quite easy, but in practice it may require some unlearning. This is particularly true for the business researcher who is used to performing structured or semi-structured inter-views, which enhance short and precise answers and suppress any story-like material. Learning to distinguish a narrative-pointed question from a content-oriented, factual and information-collecting question – both of which are common in qualitative business research – and letting the participant speak in an uninterrupted way demands hard work.

A narrative-pointed question is open-ended and it can cover either a longer period of time or focus on a specific event. For example, when studying the work of female managers, you could ask the research participant to tell you about her work his-tory as a manager. This question would cover the whole period of time that she has worked as a manager. Alternatively, you could start with a question pointing at a more specific event and ask her to tell you about 'what happened in your work when you were employed by the company in which you work today?' Then you could continue by asking further questions: 'are there any other things you remember happening?', 'does it make you think of anything else that has happened?', 'are you thinking about something else that happened?' As you can see, it is important to pose the questions without defining the content of what the storying should be about and to let the participant decide.

In a narrative interview, the rules of everyday communication are often followed, but moderated by either a positive form of active listening or active story sharing. When practising positive forms of active listening, you allow the participant to talk freely, but also to take pauses as much as they need in order to think through or recall the events or experiences being described. In any kind of interview, much of the communication is non-verbal; therefore, it is essential that you also practice the non-verbal expression of active listening. This can be done by an attentive listening posture, a degree of eye contact, and non-verbal sounds like 'hmm', which indicate that you are listening.

Narrative analysis

The methods and techniques of making narrative inquiry offer a lot of choice for the researcher (see e.g. Holstein and Gubrium, 2011; Cortazzi, 2014). In a similar way to any qualitative research, the purpose and goals of your study, as well as your research questions, should guide you when making the decision about what type of analysis is appropriate in your study. Furthermore, just as in any research, you often need to adapt and refine the specific methods and techniques to suit the goals of your own study.

Based on a dichotomy presented by Bruner (1986), Polkinghorne (1995) makes a useful distinction between analysis of narratives and narrative analysis (see Box 16.2). Analysis of narratives means that the researcher collects stories that are told by people, and then uses some techniques to analyze their plots, narrative structures, or story types. Here, the focus is on narrative as a form of representation.

When performing 'narrative analysis', the researcher organizes and interprets empirical data that describe some more or less consistent events, happenings and actions in a way that they construct one or more narratives that will be interpreted and discussed. This involves a lot of narrative writing throughout the research process. The focus is on 'narrative' as a mode of analysis.

There are also other categorizations that help in comprehending the differences of exploring narrative data. Mishler (1995) – see also Elliott (2005: 38) – makes a distinction based on the central functions of language, including meaning, structure and interactional context. Meaning refers to the content of the narrative (what happened, to whom, where and how?); structure refers to how the narrative was put together (what are its structural elements, the type of plot?); and interactional context refers to the interactive and contextual nature of narratives.

Riessman (2002) adds one more category, that is, performance, which means that the interest extends beyond talk into how narrative is performed by the narrator alone, or as a dialogue between the researcher and the participant through the combination of spoken language and body talk (gestures, movements, facial expression, etc.). Separating these categories does not mean that they could not be used in the same study. On the contrary, many narrative studies employ several of these methods of analysis (Box 16.3).

BOX 16.2

Two basic types of analysis in narrative research (Polkinghorne, 1995)

Analysis of narratives: focus is on 'narrative' as a form of representation. You collect stories that are told by people and use some specific methods to analyze their plots, narrative structures or story types.

Narrative analysis: focus is on 'narrative' as a mode of analysis. You organize and interpret empirical data describing events, happenings, and actions in a way that allows you to construct one or more narratives.

BOX 16.3

Four alternatives for the focus of analysis

Meaning: focus on content (e.g. issues, themes, patterns) of the narrative: what is told.

Structure: focus on narrative devices, as well as structural and linguistic elements: how the story is told.

Interactional context: focus on co-production through dialogue in context: how somebody tells the story to another person in a specific context.

Performance: focus on telling of stories through words, gestures, silences, tracings and images: how the story is told in order to achieve a specific outcome.

Analysis of meaning

When focusing on meaning and content of the narrative, you aim to answer the question of 'what is told'. Thematic or pattern analysis is a commonly used technique for organizing empirical data, also in narrative studies (Riessman, 1993, 2004). For this purpose, a theme can be defined as a concept, trend, idea or distinction that emerges from the empirical data. In narrative research, thematic analysis has at least two different meanings. First, you can examine any empirical data for themes (working across interviews, for example) and then develop a storyline to integrate themes into meaningful stories. Here, the narratives are clearly constructed by the researcher and their construction is a central part of the analysis. Another alternative is to examine the narratives as they are told or written by other actors in order to find patterns of themes. For instance, you could study a set of written autobiographies, or life stories told by managers in an interview situation, and explore if there are some common themes or patterns in them.

Analysis of structure

The structural analysis of narratives focuses on 'how the story is told': what narrative devices are used, and what are the structural and linguistic elements of the narrative. Compared to thematic analysis, there is more emphasis on language and its constitutive power. As argued by Riessman (1993), structural analysis forces you to make an analysis extending outside the content of the narrative. A common framework used in performing a structural analysis of narratives draws on the work of Labov and Waletzky (1967).

In this framework, the analysis that you make moves towards a reduction of a narrative structure in order to be able to answer the question 'what is the point of this story?' (Mishler, 1986: 236). This type of analysis is rather formal and predefined (see Box 16.4), and its emphasis lies in generalizability. Here, your goal can be to categorize narratives according to their elements or plots and to claim that there are some categories of stories which can be found in all similar contexts. For example, you could suggest that all organizations have 'success stories' and that these include the same types of structural elements or plots across organizations. Literary theories also provide many other ways in which you can implement structural narrative analysis. A common way of analyzing narratives is to explore their genres, for example, tragedy, comedy, romance and satire or irony.

BOX 16.4

A general framework for structural analysis of narratives (Labov and Waletzky, 1967; see also Riessman (1993: 18) and Elliott (2005: 8-9)

Abstract: summarizes the events or incidents of the story.

Orientation: describes the setting, time, place and characters.

Complicating action: offers an evaluative commentary on what actually happened.

Evaluation: tells what the events mean to the narrator.

Resolution: describes how it all ended.

Coda: returns the perspective to the present.

Analysis of interactional context

Focusing on the interactional context of narrative research emphasizes the co-constructed and co-narrated nature of narratives (Elliott, 2005). There are two important issues involved. First, narratives are not produced in a vacuum; rather, they are shaped by the social and cultural context in which the narrator lives. Therefore, the purpose of your analysis is to make sense of both the narrative and its social and cultural context.

Second, narratives are most often produced in interactive situations in which there is a teller and a listener, that is, somebody tells the story to another person. Therefore, your interest should lie in how the narrative is co-produced in a dialogue between the teller and the listener. When focusing on interaction that takes place in the interview situation, you can investigate narratives from a conversation analysis perspective, for instance (Riessman, 2002). This means you would focus on the sequential location of narratives in everyday conversation.

Analysis of performance

In addition to being interactive, narratives are also performative in a wider meaning. People tell stories to each other in order to accomplish something: to answer a question, to complain, to inform, to alert, to tease, to explain, to justify and so on. Furthermore, people tell their stories through words, gestures, silences, tracings and images. Here, you as a researcher are both the co-producer and the interpreter of the performance, which often has some contradictory elements.

WRITING AND EVALUATION OF NARRATIVE RESEARCH

Narrative writing is a craft that is essential for all narrative researchers, and particularly so when narrative is used as a mode of inquiry in research. In this case, you need to process your research materials into some kind of narrative form. When analyzing a set of stories as they exist, that is, as produced by others, it depends on your choice of writing as to how much narrative writing skill is needed.

Developing a descriptive whole with a plot and characters

The most basic form of a written narrative requires you to organize the events and details of the empirical data into a clear and descriptive whole: a story that makes sense to the reader. Outlining a narrative with an interesting beginning, eventful middle and a conclusive end, a plot, and some characters helps the reader understand your point and make sense of it. This applies both to the narratives that you construct as part of your analysis and to the final research report, which is a narrative covering your whole research process. As in social scientific narrative research, it also makes sense to write the whole research report in narrative form in narrative business research (Box 16.5).

A fully developed narrative most often involves one main idea, which is told from a specific point of view. In a narrative research report, it makes sense that you as a researcher are one of the characters and that your writing style is reflexive, at least in a way that you reflect on your own identity, your 'self' as part of the research process (Elliott, 2005: 153). This does not mean that other forms of reflexivity would not be important in narrative research. These include reflexivity in relation to your research questions, collection of empirical data and their analysis, and your results and conclusions.

BOX 16.5

Some criteria for quality in a narrative research report

A narrative research report has a beginning, a middle and an end; a scene, events and a plot; and some characters.

The plot, indicating the purpose of the research, develops throughout the research report.

The researcher is present in the research report through their voice and signature.

The report balances between the voice of the researcher and that of others.

The narrative also leaves room for silences, or stories not told, and the possible meaning of these for the study.

The report allows the reader to see and experience the path from empirical data to the final research report.

Voice and signature

For many narrative researchers it is important that the researcher is present in the research text. You can achieve this by writing with a clear and personal voice and developing your own signature to your writing. This means writing in the first person and in a way that is recognizable as your own and distinct from other writer's signatures. This can also mean that you reflect on your own experiences concerning the issue being studied and the research process (Ellis, 2004). Clandinin and Connelly (2000) deal with the issue of the researcher's presence in narrative inquiry through the metaphor of voice, and use the concept of multiple 'I's. Attention is drawn to which 'I' the researcher is using at any one time: the 'I' who speaks as researcher, individual man or woman, participant, narrative critic, theory builder, and so on.

Chronological or non-chronological?

Whereas the traditional narrative format is based on telling the story in a logical and most often chronological order, a narrative research report can also be constructed in a non-chronological order. For a novice business researcher it is easier to tell the story in a chronological order and not jump from one event to another, or suddenly change scene. However, there are effective variations to this rule and you can experiment with these as you gain more experience in narrative writing. One writing strategy is to start in the middle of things and then use flashbacks to fill in the background information. You can also make different choices concerning the degree of traditional social science, or business research analysis, and various forms of fictive writing. Therefore, you can use different types of creative writing strategy to make your narrative research non-conventional and more interesting to the non-traditional reader (Richardson, 1994).

What is specific about narrative writing compared to many other scientific texts is that a narrative research report needs to be told with passion and excitement: with a taste of life and emotion (Ellis, 2004). Like good description, narratives need to have a rich texture of details so that the reader can live along (e.g. see, hear, smell, touch, move) with the events, characters and things that are being written about. The reader should be able to experience the story, not simply read it. Dialogue, for example, adds to the quality of the narrative, and so do descriptions of the scene and the characters.

Although your narrative should be rich in texture, it is often better to be suggestive rather than exhaustive. This is because you should leave some room for the reader's imagination. Giving too many details overwhelms the reader's imagination and slows down the pace of the narrative. The use of pacing usually increases the quality of narrative writing. It is also advisable to use varied vocabulary for two reasons. First, you need to keep the interest of the reader throughout the narrative; second, you want to show a good command of language related to your research topic.

One version of truth

The purpose of narrative research is not to produce one definite truth about something that is 'out there', but to offer one version of it, told by somebody from a specific point of view. In narrative research, facts are interpreted; therefore, it is always possible to narrate the same events in a different way. This is why the evaluation criteria of positivist and postpositivist research cannot be used.

Arguing that the validation of narrative research cannot be reduced to certain technical procedures, Riessman (1993) suggests four criteria to evaluate narrative studies: persuasiveness (is the interpretation reasonable and convincing?); correspondence (allowing the participants of the study to check the interpretations); coherence (to show that an interpretation is more than ad hoc); and pragmatic use (whether the study has use as a basis for other researchers' work).

As became evident earlier in this chapter, narrative research approaches have been taken into practical use by consultants and business managers (e.g. Denning, 2004). This should also provide an increased positive ground to make managerial implications on the basis of more academic narrative research. However, it is good to keep in mind that a professional academic researcher does not jump into radical recommendations too early, or too eagerly. As in any other research, you need to ground your recommendations thoroughly into your research results.

KEY POINTS OF THE CHAPTER

Narrative research is based on the ideas of narrative knowing and storytelling as basic human activities. Compared to non-narrative texts, stories are richer and thicker, more compelling, easily memorable, and they give us context.

There are several ways of performing narrative research. Both stories told by people and non-narrative texts can be used as data. In the first case, you perform 'analysis of narratives' and in the second case you perform 'narrative analysis'.

In relation to your research questions, you can choose from a great number of specific modes of analysis in narrative research. Analysis typically focuses on meaning, structure, interactional context or performance.

The purpose of narrative writing is not to produce one objective truth about what is being studied, but to offer one version of it, told by the researcher from a specific point of view. This has an effect on how narrative research should be evaluated.

FURTHER READING

Bold's (2011) book *Using Narrative in Research* is an easy-to-read introductory text for students not familiar with narrative methodology.

Czarniawska's (2004) *Narratives in Social Science Research* gives detailed guidelines on how to perform narrative research and also provides some case studies.

───────────── EXERCISE **16.1** ─────────────

Analysis of narratives

The purpose of this exercise is to learn to analyze stories that are told by people, that is, narrative as a mode of representation.

Ask your fellow students to tell you (or you can write these together in a classroom setting) a story of something interesting or intriguing that has happened to them when they worked in business companies or some other organizations.

(Continued)

Analyze these stories according to their meaning and content, and according to their structure (for structural analysis, you can use the scheme provided by Labov and Waletzky, 1967).

Discuss and compare the stories and the analyses that you made. For instance, see where their similarities and differences lie. If you have a number of stories, you can consider how to group them together into a simple typology (e.g. hero stories and victim stories).

EXERCISE 16.2

Narrative analysis

The objective of this exercise is to learn to construct a narrative on the basis of a non-narrative text. In particular, the exercise teaches you what it takes to produce a consistent, narrative whole and to rehearse narrative writing.

- Start with sharing and discussing your common experiences as business students (or something else that you have in common) with your fellow students. Make detailed notes about what you talked about: What are your experiences? How and why have they changed? etc.
- Second, construct a narrative of your collective experiences on the basis of your notes (you can also write the narrative collectively). Before starting to write, consider the following points: Who are the characters? What is the scene and the setting? What is the main plot of the narrative? Also, make a decision on what is the point of view of the narrative. For example, do you want to write a success story or a story of continuous ambivalence towards business research, or something else. When writing, try to include as much detail as you can.
- Third, when you have finished writing, ask a fellow student to read the narrative and give you some feedback on it. If you wrote the narrative collectively, then you can, for example, read it aloud and then discuss and evaluate it. Pay attention to the general quality of narrative writing and its persuasiveness, coherence and pragmatic use.

It may be useful to consult some textbooks on narrative and fictional writing before starting (also see Chapter 21), and also use their help in discussing and evaluating the narrative.

EXERCISE 16.3

Narrative writing

You can easily rehearse narrative writing by writing about your own experiences. With this exercise, you will learn to construct a story with a plot around a specific experience.

- Start by making a list of your experiences that might be interesting to other people. These might include the excitement of starting in a new job, the joy of becoming friends with a new person, or the disappointment of being rejected with a conference paper submission.

- Choose one experience from the list above and choose your writing strategy; spontaneous writing without pre-planning or a more planned approach.
- If you chose spontaneous writing, give yourself a time limit (e.g. 20 minutes) and write a story about your experience.
- If you chose a more planned approach, first make a rough sketch about your experience (e.g. a mind map) and then give yourself a time limit (e.g. 20 minutes) to write the story.
- When you have finished, ask your friends or family members to read the story or read it aloud to them.
- Ask for feedback: was the story understandable, interesting, touching, exciting, entertaining?
- How would you revise it on the basis of the feedback?

17
DISCOURSE THEORETICAL RESEARCH

This chapter will provide information on:

- discourse theory and discourse analysis
- the different forms for discourse analysis
- how various forms of discourse analysis can be performed
- what does not count as discourse analysis
- how discourse analytic research can be written and evaluated.

DISCOURSE THEORY AND DISCOURSE ANALYSIS

Think about how two notably distinct discourses can be used to discuss consumers in Western societies, describing them either as 'hedonists' or 'utilitarians'. The former discourse describes the pleasures of being a consumer and a shopper, and the latter discourse describes the utility and rationality in consumption. The chosen discourse delivers us the vocabulary, expressions, and also the style needed to communicate about these two groups of consumers. In this way, discourses can give indications of how you think and talk about something. Discourses also produce and circulate cultural meanings attached to these understandings. As a theoretical and methodological concept, 'discourse' also has a more specific meaning.

In research settings, discourse analysis is an important research methodology within qualitative studies, which focuses on the cultural meanings attached to people, artefacts, events and experiences. Cultural meanings are mediated through language practices, and discourse analysis provides a means to study these practices and their consequences. Therefore, discourse analysis is not the study of language per se (as in linguistics), but it focuses on social action that is mediated through language. More precisely, according to discourse theory, the meanings cannot be disentangled from the language. In addition to the difference between the study of language and the study of discourse, it is also good to keep in mind the difference between discourse analysis and conversation analysis. While both study written or spoken texts, conversation analysis focuses on the study of talk in interaction and discourse analysis explores meanings that are produced and mediated textually.

Discourse analysis draws on discourse theory, which is a broad and complex inter-disciplinary field ranging from linguistics and anthropology to sociological theories and critical studies. For these fields, the philosophical and practical starting points are quite far apart from each other. This is why there is much controversy in terms of method and theory, as well as the nature of discourse and its relation to cognition and social structure, for instance (e.g. Wetherell, Taylor and Yates, 2001a; Wetherell and Edley, 2008).

We are not able to give a general description of the whole coverage of discourse theoretical research and its varieties in this chapter. You can find excellent overviews of the variety of discourse theoretical approaches and respective methods of analysis in Wetherell et al. (2001a, 2001b). In this chapter, we will focus on discourse as a cluster or formation of ideas, images and practices that provides ways of talking about a particular topic.

The origins of discourse theoretical research lie in classic rhetorical theory and its successors. Modern discourse analysis derives partly from the formalist and structuralist work of Vladimir Propp (1968) on the morphology of Russian folktales. Since then, discourse theoretical research has been based on the ordinary language philosophy movement (Potter, 2001). The conception of 'language-as-social' also brought up the relevance of the social and historical context of discourse. Understanding language as social action (Goffman, 1981; see also Kress, 2001) has led to the study of discourse as knowledge production and the politics of discourses, implying that discourses are always intertwined with some form of power relations (Foucault, 1980; Hall, 1997: 6).

Discursive research in business

Along with the social constructionist world view (Berger and Luckmann, 1967), an increasing number of researchers are doing discursive studies on issues that are relevant in the context of business research.

In business research, the terms 'discourse' and 'discourse analysis' are used invariably to mean somewhat different things. What is common in the use of these terms is the presumption about the relevance of language practices in constructing the social world. However, there are still two different ways of approaching this from a philosophical point of view. First, there is discourse analytic research which claims that there is no other reality 'behind' language, that is, there is no need to make a distinction between 'talk' and 'action'. Second, there is research which assumes that there is another reality behind talk, although talk and action are interrelated. Around ten years ago, the Academy of Management Review published an interesting dialogue concerning the differences between constructivist or social constructionist (the first type of research) and realist (the second type of research) conceptions of discourse; see Lock and Willmott (2006) and Phillips, Lawrence and Hardy (2006). Since then, discourse analytical research has also grown in business studies in the US.

BOX 17.1

Three types of discourse analytic research

Foucauldian discourse theory and analysis

Social psychological discourse analysis

Critical discourse analysis (CDA)

In addition, business researchers often rely on a conceptual and methodological division between macro- and micro-level discourse analyses (Alvesson and Kärreman, 2000, 2011; see also Boje, 1991). Macro-level analyses connect discourses to their societal and historical contexts, as well as describe and critique the discursive worlds that people inhabit. Micro-level analyses, in turn, entail very detailed studies of social interaction, which can sometimes come rather close to conversation analysis. Whereas macro-analyses do not study language from the point of view of linguistics, micro-analyses have connections to linguistics in their focus on how language is actually used by human actors in everyday interactive situations.

Definitions of discourse and discourse analysis can be diverse depending on the epistemological stance of the researcher. There are mainly three types of discourse analytic research that are increasingly used in business research: Foucauldian, social psychological and critical (Box 17.1). Even if the different forms of discourse analytic research are not always separable from each other, there are features in each that differentiate them. Of these, Foucauldian discourse analysis – not a method but theory – is rather challenging for a novice business researcher, whereas the two other types of discourse analysis – having been influenced by Foucauldian debates – are more accessible. In the following sections, we will describe the starting points and key concepts of each, and give some examples of how they can be used in business research.

FOUCAULDIAN DISCOURSE THEORY AND ANALYSIS

Since the 1980s and early 1990s, organization theorists in particular (e.g. Burrell, 1988; Knights and Willmott, 1989; Knights and Morgan, 1991; Deetz, 1992; Clegg, 1994) have turned to the ideas of the French sociologist and social critic Michel Foucault. Foucault's writings have been used to study organizational power–knowledge relations, surveillance, and the historical specificities of discourses on management and organization; for examples, see Fleming (2014) and the list of articles in the 'Further reading' section at the end of this chapter.

One of Foucault's major publications, a book titled *Archaeology of Knowledge* (Foucault, 1972), outlines a basic theoretical idea of discourse on which he built his later research on the genealogy of power. In contrast to some other discursive approaches, Foucault's concept of discourse does not include micro-analysis of language practices (Foucault, 1980; Hall, 2001). Therefore, it is often based on an analysis of a variety of documentary and historical data. Personal interviews are not so commonly used as in other versions of discourse analysis.

The concept of discourse

As an example, a study by Knights and Morgan (1991), focusing on the strategic management discourse, does not provide a detailed analysis of the language in use within the field of strategic management. Instead, it addresses the content, form and power of strategic management knowledge. For Foucauldian researchers, a discourse consists of groups of related statements that cohere to produce meanings and effects (Box 17.2). In other words, a discourse is the way an issue or a topic is 'spoken of'; furthermore, a discourse produces the 'truth' about objects that they speak of (Carabine, 2001: 268). In the field of business, discourses produce objects such as 'team organizations', 'networks', 'accounting systems' and 'globalization'.

The production of 'truth' through discourse

Foucault's main interest was focused on how the production of 'truth' about some topic, issue, artefact or idea is governed and legitimized by the discourses that people produce and reuse. Foucault argued that production of knowledge about something can never be separated from institutionalized discourses, which always have power.

An understanding that people must conform to the conditions specified in a statement before they can become the speaker of that statement is particularly relevant to Foucault's discourse theory. In other words, institutionalized discourses prevail over human agency; therefore, meaning does not originate in the person who is speaking. Instead, meaning is governed by the rules of discourses themselves. Foucault used archaeology and genealogy as his methods of discourse analysis.

As his concept of knowledge refers to a wide range of issues, including ideas, theories, everyday assumptions, language, routines and practices, Foucault argued in favour of rather general research inquiries. In business research, these have included more general formulations of research tasks such as 'Rereading HRM practices from a Foucauldian power-knowledge perspective' (Townley, 1993), reception of Foucault's ideas in the field of organization studies (Curtis, 2014) and more specific questions such as 'how "quality" and "standards" become discursive objects' (Xu, 2000).

BOX 17.2

Foucauldian concept of discourse

A discourse consists of groups of related statements, which cohere to produce meanings and effects.

A discourse is the way an issue or a topic is 'spoken of'.

A discourse produces the 'truth' about objects that it speaks of.

In Foucauldian terms, knowledge is not conceived as an intentional outcome of individual effort, but rather as an effect of everyday action and interaction. The social construction of knowledge is an ongoing activity and the collective stocks of knowledge appear as institutions (such as language), theories, organizations, archives, texts, and as practices and artefacts. Together, they constitute a historical base for any person to have knowledge about something. Most of the time, these actors use the knowledge devices at hand and do not produce new ones. However, if routine interaction and interpretation are disturbed, people do construct new knowledge (and new discourses) through processes of social interaction.

Performing Foucauldian discourse analysis

One major problem with the Foucauldian discourse theoretical approach has been the question of how to perform empirical research with various research questions and in different research settings. The works by Foucault himself do not give much advice on this because Foucault does not explicate his own research processes and methods. The key reason for this is that Foucauldian discourse analysis is not actually 'empirical' but philosophical, which in this case means that discourse theory cannot be detached from discourse analysis. Although the techniques offered by the more language-oriented approaches to discourse analysis have been used in some research that Foucault inspired, they do not always serve well to address the interests of this type of discourse research.

Carabine (2001) provides one example of research that is inspired by Foucault in her study focusing on how lone motherhood was 'spoken of' in Britain in the early 1990s. You, as a business researcher, could use her framework to study, for instance, how internationalization of small companies was spoken of in the EU during 2000–2005. Following what Carabine advises, you could start by reading all of your textual data and investigating what is the image of the internationalization of small companies that is being produced in these texts. What do these texts tell us about internationalization of small companies? It would be of help if you would consider how internationalization of small companies is related to growth and success, venture capital, ownership and innovation, for example. Some of the ways that internationalization of small companies could be spoken of might include: a necessity for economic welfare; a problem if internationalization happens too little or too slowly; or a homogeneous process that all small companies should go through in a similar way. You might also find a counter-discourse challenging the relevance of internationalization within the small-company context. The steps described here would serve as the beginning of the analysis, which could then move on to analyzing the power effects of this discourse or the relationship of this discourse with other discourses, for instance.

Social psychological discourse analysis

The second version of discourse analysis used in business research comes from constructionist psychology and social psychology (Gergen, 1985, 1992, 1995). It is mostly concerned with how identities as versions of self are constructed as factual and real, and how people position themselves in relation to other people, groups, ideas and objects. It also focuses on explicating how particular contexts are brought into being and rendered meaningful through people's engagement with each other. Here, you would be interested in how people use different and often conflicting discourses to understand the world around them, or to achieve goals.

Key concepts

This version of discourse analysis draws on the work of psychologists and social psychologists such as Jonathan Potter and Margareth Wetherell (Potter and

Wetherell, 1987, 1994, 1995; Potter, 1996a, 1996b, 1997, 1998), and it sometimes comes close to conversation analysis and rhetoric analysis. As one example, Brown and Coupland (2005: 1052) 'investigate graduate trainees' accounts of their experiences as organizational newcomers, and silence emerged during the course of the project as a subject of particular interest'. These authors use the concept of 'interpretative repertoire' to study what terms and metaphors are used by the trainees to characterize and evaluate actions and events linked to the theme of 'silence' in their interview data. Another example focuses on how rhetoric is connected to deliberate manipulation of institutional logics and change. Suddaby and Greenwood's (2005) study explores the arguments and language that are used to connect competing conceptions of a new organizational form to the nature and role of two professions: lawyers and accountants. Critical perspective is developed in Wodak (1996) and Wodak and Mayer (2001).

Social psychological discourse analysis suggests that social interaction is performative and persuasive; it is negotiation about how we should understand the world and ourselves (Potter and Wetherell, 1987; Wetherell and Potter, 1988; Potter, 2012). This means that social interaction aims at creating consensus, mitigating blame and justifying power relations. The task of discourse analysis is to unravel the form and functions of particular discursive constructions, and to indicate how they arise from various language practices and how they are used by actors in particular social contexts. Researchers adopting this approach often focus on the conduct of conversational interaction in institutional or mundane settings, and on the study of ideology and social critique.

Interpretative repertoires

A central concept that you can use to describe discursive resources that speakers share and draw upon in their accounts is 'interpretative repertoires' (Potter and Wetherell, 1987; Stokoe and Edwards, 2009). Interpretative repertoires are coherent and systematic ways of talking about things, and they may be organized around one or more central metaphors. They are historically developed and make up an important part of the common sense of a culture. However, they may also be specific to a certain institutional domain, such as 'the business enterprise'.

The idea of an interpretative repertoire is intended to clarify that there are language-related resources available that can be used in a range of different settings to do particular tasks. These resources are flexible in ways that allow an actor to draw on and rework them selectively according to the setting and the situation at hand. It is the attempt to accommodate to the local use (by various actors) that distinguishes interpretative repertoires from the more Foucauldian notion of discourses (Parker, 1992). When exploring interpretative repertoires, you should keep in mind that speakers and writers most often draw on a number of different repertoires.

Ideological dilemmas and subject positions

Edley (2001) adds two other central concepts to what he labels 'discursive psychology'. These are 'ideological dilemmas' and 'subject positions'. Ideological dilemmas refer to the beliefs, values and practices of a given society or culture: to their 'common sense' or 'way of life'. 'Subject positions' refer to how ideology constructs discursive spaces or identities into which people are drawn when they communicate. These concepts are relevant in your analysis because they explicate how discourses and the social construction of selves are connected. In other words, whatever we speak or think will be in terms of the language that is provided for us by history.

Performing social psychological discourse analysis

Wetherell and Potter (1988: 177) write that there cannot be any distinctive rules or recipes on how to perform discourse analysis, because analysis involves the development of interpretative schemes that may be changed, or even abandoned, during the research process (Box 17.3). Therefore, you always need to figure out for yourself the way of analysis that is most appropriate for your own study.

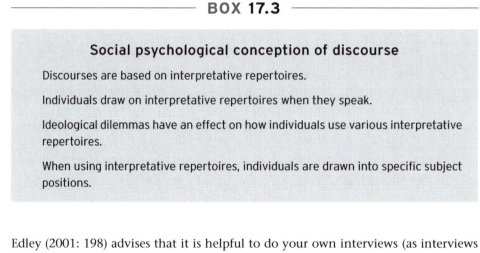

——————————————— BOX **17.3** ———————————————

Social psychological conception of discourse

Discourses are based on interpretative repertoires.

Individuals draw on interpretative repertoires when they speak.

Ideological dilemmas have an effect on how individuals use various interpretative repertoires.

When using interpretative repertoires, individuals are drawn into specific subject positions.

Edley (2001: 198) advises that it is helpful to do your own interviews (as interviews are often used for studying interpretative repertoires) and to become familiar with them. By reading the interviews over and over again, you start to find patterns across different people's talk, images, metaphors and figures of speech that keep coming up. You can also develop your own coding system to make this easier. Exercise 1 at the end of this chapter gives you one alternative to start practising social psychological discourse analysis.

Overall, a good way to learn how to do discourse analysis is to read discursive research made by other researchers and then try to build your own application of these. It can be said, however, that studying interpretative repertoires implies a very close engagement with textual data in a way that illuminates their significance and meaning.

A typical goal of your analysis could be to show how established discursive devices are used to manage human interaction. In doing this type of analysis, you would need to show what the discursive features are and what they do, how they are used, and what they are used for. To be able to do this, you must move iteratively back and forth between the more general and the more specific features of the text that you are studying. Therefore, when doing discourse analysis, be prepared to perform several rounds of analysis and interpretation.

CRITICAL DISCOURSE ANALYSIS

The third version of discourse analysis used in business research is called CDA. There are several versions of CDA, but many business researchers draw on the specific version of CDA developed by the British media researcher Norman Fairclough and colleague (Fairclough, 1992; Fairclough and Wodak, 1997; Fleming, 2014). Their version of CDA focuses on analyzing real instances of social interaction by combining linguistic analysis and ideological critique.

In a similar way to the other versions of CDA, the version developed by Fairclough and colleague builds on the critical research in social sciences (see Chapter 18), which sees social life both as constrained by social structures and an active process that produces change. The article by Munir and Phillips (2005) provides an excellent example of this. The authors examine the institutionalization of a new technology and the actions of an institutional entrepreneur by asking 'how Kodak managed to transform photography from a highly specialized activity to one that became an integral part of everyday life' (Munir and Phillips, 2005: 1665). Using CDA as a method, the authors provide new insights into two issues. First, they show how institutional fields evolve; second, they illustrate how institutional entrepreneurs use discursive strategies to embody their interests in the resulting institutions.

What is critical about critical discourse analysis?

What does the term 'critical' mean in the context of critical discourse analysis (CDA)? Critical studies are discussed in more detail in the next chapter, but as an overall idea just as with any other type of discourse analysis, CDA (Box 17.4) is based on a belief of discourse as both socially constitutive and socially conditioned. However, the aim of CDA is 'to address the issues of social power by elites, institutions or groups that result in social inequality, including political, cultural, class, ethnic, racial and gender inequality' (van Dijk, 1995: 249; also, Poutanen, 2013, 2016). CDA focuses on the ways social and political domination are reproduced in written texts and the spoken language of individuals and institutions. This means that CDA's locus of critique is on social structure and the relationship between language, discourse and speech. Overall, performing CDA is a moral project, as it impinges on uncovering the ways and forms of power relations and ideologies.

Much of the discursive business research that calls itself 'critical' draws on post-modernist, language-oriented, and socially constructed positions in one way or another (e.g. Chia and King, 2002). Fairclough (2001) opposes this orientation of discourse analysis where objects, structures and entities are seen as emergent products of processes. Instead, he advocates for the analysis of discursive and non-discursive objects. The current use of CDA in business research puts more emphasis on the critical realist ontology than on postmodernism (Fairclough, 2005; Curtis, 2014).

BOX 17.4

The concept of discourse in CDA

Discourses as representations of social life.

Differently positioned actors represent life as different discourses.

Discourses are networked together to form social order: the order of discourse.

Performing critical discourse analysis

How does CDA differ from other types of discourse analyses? What makes it 'critical'? CDA became known as a research method in the late 1980s, followed by programmatic development by Fairclough, van Dijk and others (e.g. Fairclough, 1989; van Dijk, 1998, 2001). The aim within CDA is 'to address the issues of social power by elites, institutions or groups that result in social inequality, including political, cultural, class, ethnic, racial and gender inequality' (van Dijk, 1995: 249). More specifically, CDA states that discourse is socially constitutive and socially conditioned. 'The critical approach is distinctive in its view of a) the relationship between language and society; and b) the relationship between analysis and the practices analysed' (Wodak, 1997: 173).

Specific to CDA is that language is viewed as a form of social practice and, therefore, focus is given to the ways in which social and political domination are reproduced in texts and talk produced by individuals and institutions. In Critical Discourse Analysis, Fairclough (1992: 2) introduces a three-dimensional framework for studying discourse. The first dimension in the CDA analysis is discourse-as-text, which puts the focus on the linguistic features and organization of concrete actions of discourse. The systematic analysis in this dimension should be focusing on choices of words, patterns in vocabulary (wording, metaphor), grammar (modality), cohesion of the text and text structure. Two good examples of this dimension analysis are the use of passive verbs in news reporting or official texts such as annual reports that can distance the political decision makers or those making strategic decisions in the company.

The second dimension is 'discourse-as-discursive-practice'. Here, discourse is seen as something that is produced, consumed, and circulated in society. Analysis of discourse as discursive practice directs attention to speech acts, coherence and inter-textuality, all of which situate talk and text into its context. Context in CDA is very important and should be analyzed carefully, as it reveals two contextual features that Fairclough distinguishes from each other. The first is 'manifest intertextuality', that is, discourse representation: how quotations are selected and contextualized. The second feature is 'constitutive intertextuality' (also 'interdiscursivity'), which refers to how heterogeneous elements in the different texts are interrelated.

The third dimension is 'discourse-as-social-practice'. By this Fairclough refers to the ideological effects and hegemonic processes in which discourse is a feature. What does hegemony mean? Hegemony refers to power that is achieved through constructing alliances among groups through consent, so that 'the articulation and rearticulation of orders of discourse is correspondingly one stake in the hegemonic struggle' (Fairclough, 1992: 93). Hence, power and dominance are present and are targets for CDA.

The concept of hegemony suggests that CDA is not an 'easy' or straightforward method to be applied by a novice business researcher. CDA's locus of critique is in the social structure and in the relationship between language, discourse and speech.

Performing CDA, therefore, is a moral project, as it impinges on uncovering the ways and forms of power relations and ideologies. On a methodological level, CDA is not a one-dimensional practice either. Discourse as an integral element of social processes and social events is crucial, but complex. As Fairclough has said, the objective of discourse analysis is not simply to analyze discourses per se, but the researcher should be capable of performing 'analysis of the relations between discourse and non-discoursal elements of the social' (Fairclough, 2005: 924).

In his book, Fairclough (2005) has discussed how organizational change could be studied by using CDA; he outlines four issues that are central here: emergence, hegemony, recontextualization, and operationalization. Emergence relates to the processes of new discourses emerging and their constitution as new articulations of elements of existing (old) discourses. New discourses emerge through 'reweaving' – connections between old discourses and relations of a variety of processes taking place. Emerging new discourses can contribute to organizational change, for example, as in the case of the marketization of public services.

Hegemony, in turn, refers to the articulation of discourses, which are often organized around the dominant discourse, help in maintaining the status quo in organizations, and often resist change very effectively. Recontextualization refers to processes of particularly emergent hegemonic discourses across structural boundaries (e.g. between organizations) and scalar boundaries (from local to national to inter-national). The flow of discourses between organizations, internally and globally, is related to the social relations and social struggles in the organizations and their networks.

Finally, operationalization refers to making practical-level operationalization of such discourses, their enactment in new ways, their materialization as objects of the physical world, the networks of social practices included.

Organizational discourse research has also been associated with postmodernist, language-oriented and socially constructed positions (Chia and King, 2002), but several other directions exist as well. However, Fairclough (2005) opposes this orientation where objects, structures and entities are seen as emergent products of processes, and advocated for the analysis of discoursal and non-discoursal objects. The use of CDA in business research puts more emphasis on critical realist ontology than on postmodernism and other extreme versions of social constructionism (Fairclough, 2005).

WHAT DOES NOT COUNT AS DISCOURSE ANALYSIS?

While it is difficult to give general advice on how to perform different types of discourse analysis, it may be easier to say what does not count as discourse analysis. Antaki et al. (2003) argue that discourse analysis can easily be misunderstood in a way that you are not actually doing any kind of analysis on your data. Although the article by Antaki et al. (2003) is more based on the practices of social psychological discourse analysis, it is an extremely useful read for any researcher attempting to do discourse analysis. Furthermore, many of the issues dealt with in the article also apply to any form of qualitative analysis.

According to Antaki et al. (2003), you are not doing discourse analysis if you summarize, take sides, parade quotes, make circular identification of discourses and mental constructs, make a false survey, or spot features of talk or text that are already well known (Box 17.5). These six forms of non-analysis are typical to novice researchers in particular.

--- BOX **17.5** ---

Six forms of non-analysis as identified by Antaki et al. (2003)

1. Underanalysis through summary
2. Underanalysis through taking sides
3. Underanalysis through overquotation or through isolated quotation
4. The circular identification of discourses and mental constructs
5. False survey
6. Analysis that consists of simply spotting features.

First, any business researcher is familiar with doing some kind of theme analysis as part of their qualitative research projects. Antaki et al. (2003) remind us that summarizing themes according to what is said or written in a text does not, as yet, involve any analysis of the discourse that is being used. On the contrary, summarizing empirical data through themes loses the detail of the original text. A summary is always shorter and tidier than the original text, and the themes are usually phrased in your words, not the words of the participants of your study. Overall, a summary will lose information and meaning, and add none.

Second, position taking does not count as analysis of the data. Position taking means that you offer the readers your own moral, political, or personal stance towards what the participants of your study are saying. Whether you can take sides in your study or not is a highly debatable issue among qualitative researchers. Whatever you think about the politics of research, Antaki et al. (2003) do not call it 'analysis'.

Third, a very different type of non-analysis occurs when you compile an exhaustive list of (long) quotations cut out of the empirical data and think that these will speak for themselves. Extensive quotation, by using extracts from one or many interviews or from other texts at the same time, and saying little about the content and meanings of the quotations, is not discourse analysis – nor is it any other type of qualitative analysis. Furthermore, making any kind of critical comments on what is being said or written does not count as analysis.

Fourth, Antaki et al. (2003) write that compiling quotations from many texts into a profile can be part of discourse analysis. In this case you would investigate whether the participants use shared discursive resources. You could, for example, present a profile of quotes in order to show how different speakers draw upon a specific repertoire, ideology or discourse. Profiling fits the requirements of discourse analysis because there is an analytic extra. However, you should not leave these quotations to speak for themselves without giving any interpretation of them. Furthermore, interpretation does not mean that you should say something about the speaker's cognitive or mental processes, that is, 'don't get into their heads'. Finally, good analysis does not just treat talk and text as the expression of views, thoughts and opinions; it shows their purpose in that discourse.

Fifth, a very common danger for business researchers is the tendency to generalize from your own empirical data to the world at large. This happens often when you discover that the participants commonly use certain discourses or ways of speaking. In this case, you easily start treating your findings as if they were true of all members of the category of people that the participants of your study belong to.

Sixth, discourse researchers have already identified and labelled a variety of conversational and rhetorical procedures that are common to many texts. When you are doing discourse analysis, you should know such work (i.e. through prior research of your study) and be able to relate it to your own findings. It is important to remember, though, that simply the recognition of the common conversational and rhetorical procedures is not analysis as yet. Instead, a proper analysis illustrates how these procedures are used to manage interaction in your own study. In other words, you need to show, for instance, what the procedure does, how it is used and for what purpose, and how it is handled sequentially.

WRITING AND EVALUATING DISCURSIVE RESEARCH

In academic business journals, you will find a variety of examples about how discursive research can be reported. The way of reporting depends, among other things, on what kind of discourse the theoretical and methodological approach has been taken. One major difference lies in whether the researcher uses extracts of talk and text under study. Within the language-oriented approaches, it is necessary to use quotations and extracts in order to show in detail how discursive resources are used or how they operate.

When using extracts, it is more typical to separate the theoretical and the empirical parts of the study, although these can also be intertwined in the research report. When relying on the Foucauldian approach, the use of extracts from empirical data is not a necessity because the conceptualization of 'discourse' is not language based and the research questions are more general than in the other approaches.

However, even here the researcher needs to show the reader what the discourses under study are like, by using words and concepts from that discourse for instance. This can be done by using longer or shorter quotations from the texts under study.

Reflexive and non-reflexive ways of reporting

Margaret Wetherell (2001: 396–7) makes a basic distinction between two ways of reporting discursive research: reflexive and non-reflexive. Reflexivity implies that the researcher acknowledges the theories, values, experiences and politics which guide their research and makes these explicit in the research report. It also means that the researcher pays attention to how they themselves rely on scientific conventions and use various discourses in reporting their research. As a result, the researcher may decide to use other genres of writing besides the traditional scientific one, namely stories, poems or dialogue.

Reflexivity can also refer to an interest in how the researcher and the participants together construct the reality in an interactive situation (e.g. in doing interviews). Non-reflexivity in discursive research does not necessarily mean that the researcher would deny the interpretative nature of the research. The researcher may have taken a pragmatic or practical stance according to which it is not necessary to keep reminding the reader of the constructionist nature of research. The researcher may decide that it is enough to clarify the epistemological and theoretical starting points of the study and, thereafter, keep the focus on the issues that are being studied.

Combining general and specific criteria in evaluation

The evaluation of discursive research also depends to a certain extent on the specific approach adopted. The constructionist and non-conventional (particularly

Foucauldian) nature of discursive research does not make it relevant to use the criteria of positivist or postpositivist research, such as reliability, validity and replicability. Stephen Taylor (2001: 320–4) provides a useful discussion on the criteria that can be used in discursive research that is situated and contingent. He suggests that the general principles of good practice in academic research can be applied to discursive research side by side with the more specific evaluation criteria of qualitative research and discursive research in particular.

As with all academic research, discursive studies should also be linked to prior research. The research report should also be coherent and rigorous; it should present enough detail in analysis and it should explicate the research process. What comes to qualitative research in general, and discursive research in particular, is that there are four different criteria that can be used: fruitfulness, quality of interpretation, quality of transcription and usefulness. The quality of transcription is particularly relevant in discursive research that uses interviews as empirical sources, because an inadequate transcription can obscure the events and the interactions and change the meanings of the discursive resources (Taylor, 2001: 323).

Feeding knowledge back to society

A final theme concerning the value of discursive research to society, which is critically important in business research, is its applicability. The critical question is how new knowledge produced by discursive studies can be put to use outside academia. Bloor (1997) suggests that there are two main routes through which research results can be applied: by influencing policy makers and by influencing practitioners. Many business researchers rely on the latter, attempting to influence the management, experts or employees of business organizations.

Taylor (2001: 325–8) also elaborates on two different ways of feeding knowledge back into the society that discursive researchers can adopt. The first involves making direct recommendations about change and the other involves the production of critique towards current practices. Making direct recommendations is by no means new to the community of business researchers. On the contrary, many business researchers consider this a central feature of all business research.

Within discursive business research, a recommendation might concern the introduction or strengthening of a new discourse (on customer orientation, for instance) that would enhance a change of concrete practices concerning customer service. As discursive research can be in itself oriented towards a critique of current affairs, it should not be difficult to give critical feedback to policy makers or practitioners. Business-related critical feedback might concern, for example, the dominant discourse on female entrepreneurship that homogenizes all women into the same category of small, service sector businesses that do not innovate or grow.

KEY POINTS OF THE CHAPTER

Discourse analytic research focuses on the meanings of artefacts, events and experiences. There are several discourse theoretical approaches, but language as a social practice is relevant in all of them. Because of the strong theoretical underpinnings, discourse analysis is not an easy choice for a novice business researcher.

Discourse analysis can be performed differently depending on your discourse theoretical starting points and the concept of discourse that you use. Foucauldian, social psychological and critical discourse analysis are commonly used in business research. They are performed differently because of differing general objectives and goals.

You can choose to write about a discursive study in a reflexive or non-reflexive way. Reflexivity implies that you make explicit in your writing what guides your research, as well as pay attention to the scientific conventions and discourses that you draw on when reporting your research.

A combination of general and specific evaluation criteria can be used in evaluating discursive research. In business research in particular, it is beneficial to think about how you can feed the results of your study back to the business life.

FURTHER READING

The two books *Discourse Theory and Practice: A Reader* (Wetherell et al., 2001a), and *Discourse as Data: A Guide for Analysts* (Wetherell et al., 2001b) provide a thorough introduction to the various discourse theoretical approaches and methods of analysis.

Hardy et al.'s (2004) *Handbook of Organizational Discourse* relates discourse analysis to the organizational and business research setting.

A good number of academic articles deal with discursive research in strategic management (Knights and Willmott, 1991), HRM (Zanoni and Janssens, 2003; Harley and Hardy, 2004), mergers and acquisitions (Vaara and Tienari, 2002; Riad, 2005), entrepreneurship (Ahl, 2002; Perren and Jennings, 2005; Munir and Phillips, 2005) and accounting (Miller and O'Leary, 1986; see also Grant and Hardy, 2004).

EXERCISE 17.1

Social psychological discourse analysis

The purpose of this exercise is to learn how to perform one version of discourse analysis in a systematic way. You can do the exercise alone, with a fellow student or in class. It is more useful if you have somebody that you can discuss it with.

You can choose either interviews or other texts, and use either one or many texts.

Start by reading the interviews several times to get an overall picture of what is said and how. After you are familiar with the interview texts, read them through once more and try to answer the following questions:

What kind of similar and different meanings can you identify from the text? What kind of conflicting meanings and tensions are there? For example, 'I appreciate the expertise of our employees, but their work needs to be monitored very closely'.

What kind of vocabularies and interpretative repertoires do the interviewees draw on when they describe various things? For example, do they use 'individualistic' or 'collective action' repertoires?

EXERCISE 17.2

Subject positions in the discourse analysis

The purpose of this exercise is to learn how to analyze subject positions on discourse. You can do the exercise alone, with a fellow student or in class. It is more useful if you have somebody that you can discuss it with.

You can choose either interviews or other texts, and use either one or many texts.

Start by reading the texts several times to get an overall picture of what is said and how. After you are familiar with the texts, read them through once more and try to answer the following questions:

From which subject positions do the actors speak, for example, from a leader's, an employee's or an expert's subject position? (Note that all actors can have several subject positions.)

What types of identity do the actors construct for themselves and for others? For example, what types of roles, responsibilities, power and opportunities do they allow for different actors?

Finally, write separate sections on both questions of this exercise, and discuss them with fellow students. Think about how you could proceed with the analysis. How you could avoid the six forms of non-analysis described by Antaki et al. (2003).

EXERCISE 17.3

Learning from discourse analysis done by other researchers

The purpose of this exercise is to learn how research made by others can help you in designing your own research methodologically and methodically. This exercise is also more useful if you can discuss it with somebody.

Start by choosing either Foucauldian analysis or CDA. Think about which one is more interesting in terms of your own research topic.

(Continued)

Next, search for two academic research articles that illustrate how the author has performed discourse analysis. You can choose articles from the list provided in recommended reading or search for others that will better suit your learning goals.

Read the articles several times and try to figure out how the author has done their study. Answer the following questions:

- What is the research question of the study?
- What is the theoretical background of the study?
- What kind of empirical data are used?
- How are the empirical data analyzed?
- What are the main findings and conclusions?

Discuss each of the questions and try to evaluate the study. Also, explore how you could adapt the approach used with your research topic.

18
CRITICAL RESEARCH

This chapter will provide information on:

- what critical research means
- the many directions of critical research
- how to conduct critical research
- how the analysis is organized and reported in the critical research
- how to evaluate the quality of critical research.

WHAT IS CRITICAL RESEARCH?

Can all research that is related to business activities, management or business-related questions, but not adopting a managerial point of view, be labelled as critical research? What are the characteristics of critical research? In what ways do they differ from the characteristics usually related to business research or social sciences research in general? Is it possible to do critical research in the discipline of business, or is it really a contradiction in terms?

After reading through this chapter, you should be able to answer these questions. You should also be able to separate the different directions of critical research. As critical research is not a method in the mechanical sense of the word, but more a research philosophical approach, we will not offer 'how-to-apply steps' to critical research in your research in this chapter. Instead, we will discuss the emergent field of critical research based on critical theory and thinking, and its key elements that are applicable in business studies.

The research tradition of critical research is rooted in social philosophy and social sciences history; therefore, the tradition and history of critical research will be discussed briefly. The roots of the development of critical research are important in understanding the various developments in critical research. The possibilities for critical research in business studies will be reflected towards the end of the chapter.

Possibilities for critical research

Research can and should challenge previous knowledge through argumentation and empirical research theoretically, methodologically and through new research questions. This does not yet make research 'critical research' in the methodological sense. Many research reports and articles that call themselves critical do not follow the logic of critical theory, or critical research, which forms the basis for methodological thinking. So, what is critical research then? Instead of focusing solely on method and its applicability, this chapter also explores some key issues that need to be taken into account with critical research analysis in business research.

The introduction of a critical approach into business and management as a disciplinary field and the creation of space for critical management studies has received much attention over the last two decades (e.g. Reed, 2005; Al-Amoudi and Willmott, 2011; Tourish, 2013). There has been growth both in the number of publications and interest towards critical management studies (CMS). This interest has emerged as a potentially valuable empirical way of understanding how and why business firms, multinational companies, organizations or units within corporations operate the way they do. *The Oxford Handbook of Critical Management Studies* (Alvesson, Bridgman and Willmott, 2009) addresses a variety of topics under the umbrella of critical management studies, including the methodologies (Duberley and Johnson, 2009).

Simply 'being critical in research settings' is not enough to call your research methodologically critical research. There are specific methodical and methodological directions that are worthy of being called 'critical' in the sense that they include elements of attachment to social reality in ways which are crucial for the theoretical ideas of critical research. Such methods are, for example, critical discourse analysis, which is discussed in more detail in Chapter 17. Also, the critical hermeneutic approach, which, for example, often uses qualitative content analysis, is often thought to be the same as critical research. Hermeneutics emphasizes the social and historical context of text production.

Even at a quick glance, critical research has much to offer for business research. Many business operations are not well explained from the processes taking place within the business, thus requiring 'an outside view' of the processes and activities taking place in the business. Critical research can offer one such view, as an example from marketing shows: citizens are often called consumers, and weight to citizen's consumer rights is given high priority in public. Using critical research might be interesting in exploring what possible problems are related to conflating citizenship rights with consumer rights, for example.

All research can be considered to be critical to some extent in the general sense of research logic. You should include an analytical inspection of previous research in your research scrutiny and weight previous results received against the new ones. This inspection procedure most often is critical by style and nature. In this scrutiny, you will give a description of what and how the analysis has previously been done, which methods and data have been used, and what outcomes and results have been received in earlier studies.

In addition, you should also show the possible gaps in the previous knowledge achieved, making niches and possibilities for new knowledge visible. This paves the way for arguing for the need for new knowledge. Through this type of argument building, your own research idea and research setting are strengthened. This type of critical research scrutiny should be an integral part of all research designs, but it does not constitute the sufficient idea of critical research in social sciences.

Why is that? As a method, critical research stems from critical theory and critical realist traditions. This type of critical scrutiny, as described above, often focuses on the validity and relevance of research findings. If the goal of research is to produce knowledge, then criticism in this context should be concerned with the question of whether that goal has been achieved. More generally, critique should thus focus specifically on the knowledge claims in terms of their contribution to a body of research knowledge (Hammersley, 2005: 184; see also Poutanen, 2007).

THE MANY DIRECTIONS OF CRITICAL RESEARCH

The key point to understanding the role of critical research in business studies is that critical research takes distance to the managerial and business perspectives as the starting point for the research. This often means that the viewpoints and perspectives of business management or those of companies are thus not taken for granted as starting points in research settings.

As already mentioned, the adoption of a viewpoint that deviates from managerial perspectives does not alone create a sufficient basis or criteria for research to be called critical by its methodological choices. Much of management and business research studies deal with other than formal company/management/business-related viewpoints and research questions. Research projects related to employees, production, marketing issues or merger acquisitions do not sign up for any formal managerial or corporate policy viewpoints or ideas, but do not follow the logic or ideas of critical research either. A lot of emphasis in critical research is put on 'alternative' or 'new' ways of doing research, in comparison with mainstream management and business research (e.g. Suddaby, Hardy and Hui, 2011).

How does the relation between 'reality' and 'theory' get defined in critical research? As in all social sciences, critical research in business studies can also be characterized as a mixture of explanatory research and philosophical approaches.

It might be helpful to think of the relationship between the 'real' world (data) and theory (i.e. research framework) in the following way: critical research, following the tradition of critical theory, in general acknowledges the structures and mechanisms existing in the world. These are seen as existing beyond the constructivist idea, as permanent elements, existing in society and emergent and knowledgeable to the researcher. In other words, critical research does not fully sign up for the ideas of the social constructionist approach. It acknowledges the existence of several understandings of the world, but emphasizes the existing structures and mechanisms related to these permanent structures beyond constructionist ideas.

To take up an example of a critical research project in management studies, the researcher within the critical research tradition might be interested in analyzing from which social strata or social class the recruitment of managerial elite takes place. The researcher acknowledges the existence of societal structures, social classes, strata and professions, and their permanence, presence and mediation in different ways in the individuals' and groups' lives and activities and even in the decisions made in companies. Yet, the researcher would not think theories describing these societal and economic structures and circumstances as separate, unchanging, objective and unrelated from each other, as a researcher in positivist tradition would do. Neither would the researcher subscribe to the idea that societal positions and different strata would be socially constructed at the individual level and, thus, fully elusive or co-constructed in the making. Thus, the researcher would support the idea of existing societal structures, ranging from societal enclaves to professions, and the mechanisms in these, that carry in themselves and mediate the issues and ideas related to the societal classes, strata, profession and recruitment of elites through and with the help of those mechanisms. The researcher would be more interested in analyzing the development and change of the managerial elite, instead of analyzing the individual meanings, discourses or narratives concerning the elite's individual experiences, unless those become part of the elite construction. The common themes for critical research in general may, for example, be the integration of theory and practice in research, and the adoption of normative and practical aims in research settings instead of merely descriptive or explanatory settings. These themes apply to critical research in business studies as well as to critical research in management studies.

Critical research consists of a broad field of enquiries and it has close connections with the philosophy of the social sciences. It is mostly for this reason that the method of critical research is connected to specific traditions within the social sciences and philosophy. There are several directions that have been developed under the umbrella of critical research.

Critical research in business research

Critical perspectives have increasingly been applied to the research of organizations, management and firms, and their different functions, such as accounting and marketing, during the last decade. This is not only because of the ethical problems related to financing, organizational behaviour or politics implemented and found in business practices and procedures. Critical perspectives are not one but many, but at least they have in common the point that they distinguish from more functionalist, managerially driven research settings.

Critical analysis has been a widely used method in the analysis of media. The areas of film studies and cultural studies provide examples; but also closer to business studies, media studies analyzing business CEOs' presentations, advertisements and other forms of business communication are widely performed. Common to critical research (irrespective of the direction) is the motivation to transform existing practices. In business research, this means signing for transformation of economic practices.

Research methods in critical research should not in the first place be understood solely as tools for data management or a mechanical device for the research process to proceed to outcomes. For practical reasons, methods are often thought of as tools, even mechanical tools, that enable us to 'do analysis'. However, methods should be logically seen as one part of the ongoing discussion of the possible ways of analysis in the social sciences. This view is shared within those qualitative methods approaches, where the connection between a specific theoretical framework and empirical data is seen as intertwined. This view is especially prevalent in critical research.

In practice, the data-gathering process and data analysis are often done simultaneously, and as closely related to each other as possible. Theoretical viewpoints are merged in the analysis, or they guide the data analysis in a close-knit fashion. This is also the most usual approach in critical research, irrespective of its orientation within critical thinking and connections to critical theory.

Critical thinking in management studies has close links with the postmodern turn in social sciences, perhaps more so than in other social sciences (e.g. Fineman et al., 2005; Al-Amoudi and Willmott, 2011; also Poutanen and Kovalainen, 2015), and less close relations to critical realism (Sayer, 2013; Tourish, 2013).

HISTORY OF CRITICAL RESEARCH

Critical research in the form of critical realism, as it is often discussed, is an open and evolving paradigm that includes many different perspectives and criticisms. Critical research in management and business research has traditionally included two aspects. The first aspect can be termed the common sense criticism aspect, which we have outlined previously. The second aspect could be termed the critical theory aspect and the third the critical realism aspect. Critical realism is a 'younger' concept than critical theory, is defined by its special relation to the philosophy of the social sciences and, increasingly, gaining a foothold in the social sciences and economics. It is important to distinguish these two meanings from each other, as they are attached to different kinds of epistemological commitments. In empirical research, these differences play a minor role in the application of critical perspective.

The first aspect, 'common sense criticism', relates any critical inspection and analysis of empirical data and theoretical views. No clear or unifying rules can be attributed to 'common sense criticism'. The idea that relates the common sense criticism to critical research is the idea of emancipation. Emancipation is related to the German social philosopher Jürgen Habermas and his philosophy.

To be able to understand the difficulties in the making of the 'critical', one needs to look at the history of critical research that stems from social philosophy and social theory. Let us turn now to the second and third aspects mentioned above: both the 'critical theory aspect' and the 'critical realism aspect' are linked with critical theory and its development.

Originally, critical theory had strong connections to Habermas's social theory, while common sense criticism is taking place in everyday life research with no specific relation to critical theory. To add to the confusion, critical realism as a theory is based on slightly more different theoretical ideas than critical theory. Yet all these terms are used in management and business research variably, and often even intermixed without much prior knowledge of the differences. Common for much business research in critical tradition is that the need for action research is eminent (such as 'repair something', 'make things work better', or 'change people's ways of thinking'). But not all action research is critical. Some conceptual clarification is thus needed. In the following, we briefly illustrate these different views in order to give insight into the growing field of critical research in business studies.

Differences between the four Cs: critical theory, critical thinking, critical realism and critical management studies

It is worthwhile for the researcher in business to understand the difference between critical theory and critical thinking. Critical self-reflection does not necessarily take place from the critical theory perspective. Critical theory focuses upon the close connections between politics, values and knowledge. How should we understand politics, values and knowledge and their close connections in business research? And how do we make these aspects visible?

Critical theory stems from the theoretical approach of the Frankfurt School of social philosophers, who rejected objectivity in its traditional sense. Critical theory brought forward the critique of positivism and nurtured a critical approach to social analysis that would detect existing social problems and promote social transformation:

according to critical theory, aiming to explain the causes of oppression will result in practical efforts to eliminate it (Poutanen and Kovalainen, 2009). Common to both critical research and to postmodern research is the combination of social theory and philosophy with disciplinary theories.

Critical realism provides the key response to the 'crisis of positivism', with its answer differing from postmodernist theory and its relativism problem. Critical realism has gained a foothold in economics, where the Cambridge Critical Realist Group has been influential in the methodological discussion within economics (Lawson, 1997), and also latterly within the social sciences, where the actor/structure discussion has risen anew. Critical realism contains both a philosophical aspect and a social scientific aspect. The critical realist perspective in social sciences emphasizes that both social structures and agencies exist in society but that they are different phenomena with different characteristics (Danermark et al., 2002; Poutanen and Kovalainen, 2009).

Sometimes, the term 'critical theory' is used for putting together 'any approach drawing inspiration from the substantive critical traditions of, for example, feminism, Marxism, ethnography and symbolism, post-structuralism, hermeneutics, postmodernism and environmentalism' (Burton, 2001: 726). It is clear that conflating such a wide spectrum and variety of traditions together is unhelpful for any research project claiming to be critical and seeking methodological orientations of critical research.

Despite the sometimes unclear background, critical research in management and business studies has elicited new perspectives on conventional organizations and businesses and mainstream management and business theories.

In management studies, critical management studies have developed to include a variety of dimensions and a diversity of critical approaches (Al-Amoudi and Willmott, 2011; Bhaskar, 1997). The imminent problem with that proposal is that the idea of critique as a method and its epistemic grounds becomes unclear and it may be difficult to find a common denominator for 'critical approaches' ranging from deconstructionist reading of texts to social movements with a standpoint.

The growth of the post-structural and postmodern perspectives in research has also increased the diversity within critical research in management and business research. Thus, differences exist in defining what constitutes 'critical' in business research. Not all forms of critical research follow the traditional critical theory argumentation, nor are they attached to the same epistemological claims within critical realism (e.g. Lawson, 1997; Parker, 2002; Poutanen, 2007).

Therefore, connections between critical theory as it has been described in social sciences and critical business research are dynamic and not fully defined. Critical research in business studies, like all other research, needs to develop the appropriate research designs and methodological tools to succeed in its goals. Already now it has opened up new insights into business studies, both from the practical point of view (as in accounting) and from the theoretical point of view (as in marketing).

THE KEY CONCEPTS IN CRITICAL RESEARCH

Critical research is about theory, method, research philosophy and analysis of specific problems occurring at the same time. Therefore, it is easier to discuss the principal aspects of choosing the methods for critical research. Morrow and Brown (1994: 24) have suggested some methodological principles for critical theory research; see Box 18.1. These principles open up vast possibilities for critical research in terms of applicable methods. However, when the underpinning philosophical arguments are strong, you as the researcher need to be careful when choosing the methods, as not all methods are equally valid for critical research. For that purpose, it is extremely helpful to read more about the historical roots and about the dichotomy between realism and relativism (Box 18.2).

BOX 18.1

Methodological principles for critical research

Social analysis always has an interpretative (hermeneutic) dimension.

Meaning and language (hence discourses) are the forms of reality construction that both reveal and conceal the experiences of subjects.

Structures may be species specific or historically constituted.

Social and cultural structures constrain human action.

Meaning and structures are produced and reproduced across space and time.

There are no individual methods available or signed for critical research alone.

BOX 18.2

Cornerstones of critical research

1. The emphasis on the social construction of reality and a focus on the issues of power and ideology are most often present in critical research. The social construction is not relativist, but an elaborated version of the context-dependent idea of ontology, which is emphasized more than epistemology.
2. The centrality of language has created the basis for the main tenets in critical theory.
3. As central as language is, there is also the question of to whom critical theory and research is addressed. This question refers to the political nature of critical theory.

These three points are the classical key issues in critical research in all social sciences, and in business research. These can be used as checkpoints when you are thinking whether the report has a critical research angle or not.

Calhoun (1996: 35) suggests that critical theory generates critique in three different ways:

- in engagement with the contemporary social world;
- in engagement with the historical and cultural conditions of the intellectual activity;
- in engagement with the re-examination of categories and frameworks used in research.

It is possible to implement these aspects in your own research, even to evaluate your own work towards the standard of the measure. The implementation clearly refers to theoretical work, but also to empirical studies. Within business research, the question of research methodology has become an issue: methodological pluralism is not necessarily highly visible in critical business research.

WHAT METHODS DOES CRITICAL RESEARCH USE?

Critical research in business, or in any other discipline, does not subscribe to any specific methods, analysis procedures or data-gathering techniques subscribed to critical research only. Using ethnographic methods to conduct a critical study in organizations or of a particular phenomenon in organizations is, however, quite usual, and even a mainstream choice today. It is useful, therefore, to make one distinction here: critical research in business studies seldom follows the full logic and ideas of critical realism. The reasons for this will be discussed later in this chapter.

In the general spirit of critical research, Alvesson and Deetz (2000: 17) have defined the tasks of critical management studies as follows. The tasks include insight, critique and transformative redefinitions. What do these tasks mean in terms of a practical research project? The first one, the insight task in the research, shows how committed you are to the basic ideas of critical research. These basic ideas include the hermeneutic, interpretative and ethnographic goals of local understandings that are closely connected and related to the people and situations under scrutiny.

The second task, the critique task, shows your commitment to 'analytical aspects of critical traditions, which recognize the possibility of domination' (Alvesson and Deetz, 2000: 17).

Finally, the transformative redefinition task includes the role of social action and pragmatic perspective in distributing knowledge: the idea that something can be changed through the knowledge obtained in your research.

The tasks defined by Alvesson and Deetz (2000) do not fall far from Calhoun's (1996) view on critical research described earlier. Critical researchers interact with their research subjects and use methods in pretty much a similar manner as other researchers in business studies. The specific feature of critical research lies in the multitude of perspectives adopted and used in the approach. This does not mean that all perspectives would be opened up in one research project. This multitude of perspectives also differentiates you as a critical researcher from an action research-oriented person, of which you can find examples in Chapter 13.

Critical management research, in a similar manner to critical theory, can be defined as being methodologically reflexive. Methodological reflectivity includes the questioning of what is known about the world and in what ways (e.g. Parker, 2002).

While the tradition of critical management studies has expanded into organization studies, HRD, accounting, marketing and other fields of business studies, the concept of critical management studies has become an umbrella term for a range of critiques in management and business studies. Therefore, it is not useful to point out specific methodological devices for critical management studies and critical research, as variety is vast and the method closely entangled with the research question and the theoretical framework.

The centrality of language, importance of interpretation and self-reflexivity, as well as the idea that relationships between concept and object and between signifier and signified are never stable, and often mediated through and by social relations within structures, should be present in all critical analysis (Johnson and Duberley, 2000: 132; Bessant, 2012). This idea is extended to the use of concepts in research, in the spirit of Foucault's analysis (see Chapter 17), where, for example, leadership is understood as a discursive concept that arises at all levels of organizing.

How to analyze empirical material from the critical research point of view

It is worthwhile to note that critical research in business studies differs from the critical incident analysis or critical incident technique. Critical research in business research always includes theoretical as well as emancipatory elements. Critical incident analysis includes tracking down such situations where purposes or intents of the act are clear and where the consequences of these purposes or intents are 'sufficiently definitive to leave little doubt concerning its effects' (Flanagan, 1954: 327). This specific technique will be discussed in detail below.

The descriptions given above on the key themes open up possibilities for a wide variety of data collection, such as interviews, documents, observations, and analysis techniques, such as ethnographic interpretation, action research, deconstruction and historical reconstruction (Harvey, 1990: 196). The challenge for any researcher who, for example, is doing ethnography in the spirit of critical theory or critical research is to find the ways to link the detailed analysis of ethnography to internal and external social relations, that is, the wider societal and social structures and power relations. Harvey (1990) gives three ways to find a way to link the detailed analysis of ethnography to wider societal and social structures and power relations, which takes it in the critical direction; see Box 18.3.

BOX 18.3

Linkages between ethnographic analysis and societal structures

1. Consider the subject group of your research in a wider context.
2. Focus on wider structural relations and examine the ways in which the social processes that are evident in the subject group are mediated by structural relations.
3. Integrate the ethnography you are writing into deconstruction of social structures; 'ethnographic techniques are thus used to elaborate an understanding that goes beyond surface appearance and thereby specifies the nature of the essential relationship of the structure under analysis' (Harvey, 1990: 12, 2002).

Critical marketing research has had relatively little impact in marketing as a disciplinary field, even if it is seen as important in opening up new avenues of enquiry (Tadajewski, 2010). All business disciplinary fields, such as accounting, finances, international business, HRM, organization studies and marketing, deal with historically embedded and culturally and socially constructed institutions, practices and processes. These embedded institutions, their practices and processes can be analyzed from a critical perspective within all subject areas in business research, even if in a variety of ways, for example, as in Modell (2009) and Bryer (2014). See Box 18.4.

BOX 18.4

What is the core aim of critical research?

1. The overall aim in critical research is to make a difference to the mainstream. This does not say very much about the content alone.
2. The key point is the classical view stemming from hermeneutics: researched 'facts' cannot be extracted from the values of the researched and those of the researcher/s and scientific community.
3. Therefore, none of the processes, ranging from research plan to data collection or knowledge creation in the research processes, is assumed to be objective and neutral, but dependent on the values and interests of both parties.
4. The notion of social is specific. Social is always seen as dependent on intentional human actions. Human actions are seen as embedded in social positions and social relations.

WRITING AND EVALUATION OF CRITICAL RESEARCH

The previous parts of this chapter have shown how interwoven the philosophy of science ideas are with critical research. Principles of critical research stem from the philosophical tradition and have taken many turns (Box 18.5). Implementation of a critical research perspective assumes some prior knowledge of critical research and some prior knowledge of the theoretical critique that exists in research.

BOX 18.5

The historical and theoretical connections of critical theory

Critical theory has strong roots in European philosophy, and in that within the Frankfurt School within European philosophy. The more developed critical research in management and business studies has followed the traditions of critical research in social sciences, which originates from the so-called Frankfurt School (Fay, 1987; Habermas, 1977).

The Frankfurt School was influential in the social sciences from the 1930s onwards, and then diverged from the positivist preferences in 1930s German philosophical circles, where the diversion was called by its members 'the critical theory of society'. The key ideas in the critical school thinking have been specifically in the analysis of structural relationships of power, control and discrimination, mediated through language on the one hand, and in the understanding of the activity of the knowing subject on the other. This approach has been most important in critical realism thinking, in critical economics, but also to some extent in critical business studies and in critical management studies (e.g. Alvesson and Deetz, 2000).

Critical realism offers a set of criteria for evaluating claims about reality and methodology. To explain events and processes, critical realism offers ways to analyze structures and mechanisms which might be especially relevant in business life analysis. Although still relatively rare, there are wide possibilities for critical realist accounts in business studies.

Is 'critical discourse analysis' part of the critical research tradition? It is possible to say 'yes' and 'no'. Critical discourse analysis is discussed in Chapter 17. Critical discourse analysis shares some of the ideas stemming from and influenced by the Frankfurt School, but it signifies more the ideas and thoughts developed within classical rhetoric and sociolinguistics.

The materials used in the critical discourse analysis often include interviews and observations. It is the researcher's task to use different tools and techniques for critical reflection and action. In that work, critical discourse analysis is useful; see Box 18.6.

BOX 18.6

The guideline for doing critical research

- Adoption of ethnography as a research method or approach does not alone make the research critical research.
- The practical way for doing critical research is simply the tight-knitting of empirical materials-gathering and methods used for that with the more philosophical and theoretical aspects of critical research, briefly described above.

Ackroyd (2002) applied critical analysis when analyzing managers' work and organizational change. He was able to show that, while the structural conditions may be important in determining what choices the managers make in their activities, in reality, 'managers enact their circumstances rather than simply adapt to them' (Ackroyd, 2002: 70). Martin and Wilson (2014) used critical realism to reflect upon issues concerning discovery processes and opportunity development. Ramologlou (2013) used critical analysis in meta-theoretical research aiming at the identification of factors that may be hindering entrepreneurship research from cognizance of realist (and realistic) insights (see also Blackburn and Kovalainen, 2009). What is common for both examples is that, to a large extent, they follow theoretical notions of critical research and aim to influence theory development.

Critical research traditions do not sign the claims of universal truth, but they are discursively situated and implicated in relations of power (Kinceloe and McLaren, 2005). The evaluation criteria for critical research depend upon the direction the research project is taking. For those following a critical ethnography more closely, the epistemological principles apply that hold for critical research in general.

KEY POINTS OF THE CHAPTER

Critical research is not a 'method' in the technical sense of the word, and being critical in research does not mean that research could be labelled as following critical research.

Critical research is a multi-dimensional field, where theoretical approaches and philosophical underpinnings are related to each other in a specific way.

Critical management studies govern a wide variety of fields that are not directly related to critical research traditions in social sciences, but relate to several other traditions.

If you are interested in doing critical research in management and business studies, then you should also become acquainted with the social science tradition and contemporary research.

FURTHER READING

Danermark et al.'s (2002) *Explaining Society. Critical Realism in the Social Sciences* gives a balanced overview of critical realism, including critical theory and research. Poutanen's (2016) chapter on critical perspectives in entrepreneurship research in the *Edward Elgar Handbook of Entrepreneurship Research* opens up, among other things, the process view in critical research.

─────────────── **EXERCISE 18.1** ───────────────

Planning critical research study

The aim of this exercise is to help you to think about your research topic from a wider societal perspective. The exercise is most useful when discussed together in class.

1. Think about your research topic and the issues involved and relate these to a current societal or economy-related question, such as globalization or inequality in social life.
2. Write down your arguments concerning why and how your research topic relates to the wider societal or economic question that you chose.
3. Consider what would be the relevance of this type of wider perspective in your research and how could you perform it in practice?

19

FEMINIST RESEARCH

This chapter will provide information on:

- gender and feminist research
- what relevance feminist research has for business research
- how gender is analyzed in business research
- whether feminist research is assigned to some specific research methods.

WHAT IS FEMINIST RESEARCH?

It is possible nowadays to find the term 'feminist' in the subject index in most research methods books in social sciences. But is it possible to find the term 'feminist research' from the subject index of an ordinary textbook in business research? Most often it is not, or perhaps with just one or two references only. Still, we can find feminist research in business research. This chapter will valorize the multi-disciplinary field of feminist qualitative research in business research and discuss its methodologies and methods.

Feminist research has several directions and methodologies at play. In business studies the tradition of feminist research stems from the critique of leadership, and of an organization's way of organizing work. Through that literature the usages of femininities and masculinities have become well known (Acker, 1990, 1992, 2000; Calás and Smircich, 1996; Letherby, 2003) in business research. The issues of low numbers of women in managerial positions and the male image of managerial positions have been under critical scrutiny in management studies for a long time, since from the 1970s. As a research topic, the questions about feminism and marketing surfaced later, bringing up issues on gender as an important category in marketing segmentation, consumption and marketing practices (e.g. Bristor and Fischer, 1993; Catterall, Maclaran and Stevens, 1997), and also gender stereotypes regarding media, advertising and assumed consumption patterns. Much of this discussion has been on the theoretical issues and critique of existing theoretical frameworks. Less attention has been given to the specificities and dimension of feminist research methods (e.g. West and Zimmerman, 1987).

--------------------------------- BOX **19.1** ---------------------------------

Some key questions for feminist research in business studies

What about gender? Can we think that an interview done by a woman would be essentially different to that of one committed by a man? What about research topics? Are they specific to feminist research and, if so, how can they be defined and separated from other research topics, in order to be called feminist ones?

How does feminist research – if it has political intentions – go with business research?

These questions are among the most common questions when feminist research is discussed within business research, as 'business' and 'firm' are often seen as masculine projects and antonyms to issues related to feminist interests, which are often seen as synonymous with the feminist movement, equality, social change, shared values, social criticism and the question of women in society in general. Also, the idea of feminist research in layman's thinking is related to biological (not social) sex, and thus refers to individual men and women, instead of societal or social categories.

Feminist research often has an interest in making visible those systematic relations that can be sexist, racist, heterosexist and other forms of domination and subordination (Alsop, Fitzsimons and Lennon, 2002; Meehan, 2004). In the following we will discuss the key issues related to feminist methodologies and the challenges they put forward in business research and the methods used in business research. The intertwining of the feminist approach and business research can thus introduce new perspectives, but it may also leave some issues out from research settings. As in any research project, multi-dimensional and multi-disciplinary frameworks are often very demanding to handle.

Different disciplines tend to use and advocate for a particular range of analysis techniques or methods, but there is no existing carved and fixed relationship between specific methods or research techniques and particular methodologies, even if there are close and logical relationships that are established. Feminist methodology consists of several methodologies, as there are different fields of science advocating for different sets of rules for producing knowledge, ranging from psychology to anthropology to economics. In the following, we will restrict our description to feminist qualitative research; even then, this is a highly diversified field, being closely connected to several intellectual and disciplinary discourses and domains. We acknowledge the existence of feminist quantitative analysis, where issues such as gender-responsive budgeting, economic analyses of gender-specific programmes and inequalities of the global economies, labour markets and economies in general bring forward issues of crucial value from a gender point of view.

Feminist research and qualitative research methods

No single feminist method can be pointed out as the primary feminist research method, as research settings are often at the intersections of different disciplinary fields and fields such as postmodernism, postcolonialism and feminism. Still, methodological choices can be political choices in the sense of directing the ways for and types of knowledge that are to be produced in research. Methodological choices can also be based on adding knowledge or challenging previous understandings with new or alternative ways of gathering data and analyzing them (e.g. Kvasny, Trauth and Morgan, 2009; Zelizer, 2011). These ways for knowledge production usually mean choosing qualitative research methods.

Feminist research is usually defined as a multi-disciplinary area, and it can be said that feminist research can and has been done within business research. There are many interesting cross-cutting areas where gender, business research and feminist theories meet. There are also highly influential texts that have put forward interesting analyses within business research sub-disciplinary fields. We will point out some connections later in this chapter.

At the most general starting point, feminist research contains a commitment to non-exploitative relations between the researcher and their subjects (Oakley, 1981); but again, it might get difficult to define and reflect upon the nature of the relationship between interviewee and interviewer in a business research context: research about women as managers, business-owners or as consumers is not necessarily feminist by its orientation, but can simply look at women or men as variables. Almost as often the issues of race, class and gender and their complex relationships are left out of business research contexts, simply because they do not 'fit in' with the mainstream theoretical literature in business research.

Even if there is no single universal or stable definition of what feminist research is, there are some common features that distinguish it from other social analyses of gender, for example. It can be said that feminist knowledge is grounded on experiences of gendered social life. The notions of gender, its position and relation to other fields of social life are often taken up in feminist-inspired research in business research or feminist business research.

Methodologically, feminist qualitative research overlaps with other qualitative approaches and ways of analysis. One specific distinguishing feature for the feminist approach, however, is the critique of the taken-for-granted maleness of various issues, which within the business research range, for example, from leadership to questions of economic power, the 'glass ceiling', ownership structure and maleness of management (e.g. Hart, Holli and Kovalainen, 2009; Kovalainen and Hart, 2014). The same critique goes with the assumed femaleness of issues in business. Feminist critiques of these conventional assumptions of business research and management research challenge and share critiques originally coming from other directions, such as postmodernism. Personal involvement, the questioning of theoretical praxis and the multi-discipline nature of feminism are issues often asked for from feminist research in business research (e.g. Lorber, 2000; Nathanson, 2014). In the following, the possibilities and forms of feminist research in business research are described and discussed.

BUSINESS RESEARCH AND GENDER

Most classic management and business research textbooks and research articles have failed to take gender into account when the classical questions of leadership, management and personnel, persons and personalities in workplaces, firms, businesses and organizations are being discussed, researched, analyzed and reported. Gender may be mentioned as a reference to sex, the biological category of women and men, when the empirically-oriented research questions of the overwhelming majority of men in managerial positions or salary differences come up, very often in relation to power positions in firms or the number of women/men in specific positions in corporations.

Even contemporary literature on management, organizations and businesses rarely discusses the issues of gender in other than quantitative (minority–majority, glass ceiling) terms. Why is that? The idea of personhood in the domain of business research is strongly related to individuals and individualist notions: the social and societal aspects of personhood, and its construction, are not seen as relevant. Identity politics in managerial work intersects with individuals that are gendered, and its gendered effects (Poutanen and Kovalainen, 2013).

Much of the business research has maintained the idea of individuals doing the trick in business: the individual and personhood are important in business activities, business start-ups, mergers and acquisitions, and the stereotype of this agency has been (and still to a large extent is) male (Poutanen and Kovalainen, 2014). If business research emphasizes, in general, the role and importance of personhood and personality, why is it so that personhood or personality in businesses seems to be so strongly attached to men and the male personality as the natural business person? The majority of business managers at the top level are still predominantly men (Kotiranta et al., 2010).

What other things can gender possibly mean in business research? Women-in-management research seldom focuses on those theoretical grounds that lie outside business research, thus leaving untouched the issue of gender as a theoretical construction. In the following, we will briefly open up these questions.

Even if gender is included in organizational analysis, it is sometimes represented apart from organizational lives, structures, or processes, as if those working and living in organizations have identities but no gender. However, gendered individuals are key factors in the organizational processes, being inter-individual, structural and symbolic by nature and also the core of organizational life, as shown by Rosabeth Moss Kanter (1977) in her classic book *Men and Women of the Corporation*.

Still, gender comparisons have had a long history in business and management literature, especially in leadership and organization studies. Maccoby and Jacklin's (1974) book *Psychology of Sex Differences* became a classic in emphasizing that no differences exist among men and women in their psychological make-up. In organization and management studies, this result was quickly diffused into research. Most of the research on women's leadership in the 1970s and 1980s asked why women were less likely than men to become leaders and managers. This rhetoric was used in business research mainly to gain equality between men and women, and research methods were about comparing men and women along various dimensions, either emphasizing similarities or differences, depending on the theoretical approach of the researcher in question.

In organization and management analyses, gender has most often been used in its ahistorical 'difference dimension': the research has concentrated on analyzing and debating whether differences exist between women and men in organizations, and the implications of these results. Management and business theories have not included gender as a conceptual and theoretical category (Kovalainen, 1995). Helms Mills and Mills (2000) explore key problems of discrimination and organizational change with a fluid set of rules with different meanings and gendered outcomes. Gender studies also continue to intersect, especially with organizational issues. Still, gender studies, when included in business or management theory books, are often in a special section, not included in 'mainstream' theories (e.g. Aaltio and Kovalainen, 2003).

GENDER IN RESEARCH

We start here with the question of gender in relation to feminist research and business research, and give first the basic definition of gender. Whereas gender is often understood as categories of sex, that is, categories of women and men, and thus as a quantifiable variable, it also and more importantly has wider cultural, societal and social meanings that differ from the dichotomy of women/men, as mentioned earlier.

Gender refers not only to women and men, but more widely also to the culture and society where women and men live and work and become socialized and are part of the larger groups. Gender also refers to the socially constructed ideas of, and thoughts about, gender in culture and in society, where gender is to a large extent about labelling and categorizing women and men, femininity and masculinity, and also about changing ideas of women and men, femininity and masculinity. In this way, business activities and people who work there also become labelled.

Thinking of gender in relation to business research issues, gender is thus a construct that relates also to an individual's intimacy, education, job (female-dominated jobs, male-dominated jobs), career (the concept of a glass ceiling, the 'dual-career' couples) and career developments. Gender relates to cultural business images ranging from advertising, which uses and plays with gender roles in many ways, and to targeting products and services, to customers, and to issues of hierarchy and power, where gendered posts and positions become clearly visible (a share of women among CEOs, boards, holders of presidencies, the career development of women, the images and cultural stereotypes of the 'efficient manager', etc.). Gender is interestingly and differently present in issues that deal with men and women in organizations: even work–life balance is most often related to women's careers than to men in companies' personnel policies.

Gender thus has many roles and meanings. It is present in many ways in the culture, and thus also in businesses, companies and corporations, manifesting itself both as women and men, in different numbers. It is also in the organizational culture, in organizational teams, and in groups and ways of organizing the practices of work and the hierarchies of organizations. Questions concerning the value of individuals become manifest in organizational life through career promotions, size of offices, informal groups and formal and informal decision-making bodies, and are measured differently in the case of men and women.

In society in general, but specifically in business life, gender relations are closely related to power relations. The complexity of gender as a concept thus stretches beyond the dichotomy of women and men as countable and opposite categories of 'women' and 'men'. Gender, indeed, labels and defines much of the activities in business and management, but as a theoretical construction it has not been seen as integral for business research and management research. This is very much due to the fact that the applied nature of management and business research is to a large extent pragmatically and user-oriented; thus, research questions are often defined through practical, problem-related issues and emerging up-to-date questions in business life. Theoretical and culturally laden conceptions of gender fit this mode of research poorly.

Gender is thus not merely a biological category of women and men, but it is actively done, produced and reproduced in everyday life situations in business and organizations, as well as in other aspects of social life. The general image of 'manager' and 'boss' is still much closer to the male stereotype than female (Kovalainen, 1995; Aaltio-Marjosola and Kovalainen, 2001). We also easily become prisoners of these culturally prevailing stereotypes: a woman as a manager or a boss can be seen as a deviation, and we tend to reproduce that deviation in many ways. For example, we raise women up as managers, thus putting them under a double burden where they have to succeed both as women and as managers. Also women hire and fire people, make bad strategic decisions and can be nasty bosses. However, instead of taken as individuals, women are often seen to represent their whole gender. One example of this 'tokenism' is the normative expectation for behaviour for the minority groups, such as for women in management. The results of several studies suggest that having a gender type associated with the job increases normative pressure to conform to typical gender roles (Lorber and Farrell, 1991). Gender role expectations are not in favour of women in the corporate world.

WAYS FOR ANALYZING GENDER IN BUSINESS RESEARCH

These ways of theoretically constructing gender put new challenges on empirical research as well. What do we analyze when we observe organizational settings where women and men are working? Do we make simple notes on age, the number of each sex, or do we note that cultural patterns, gender codes, gendered patterns of behaviour and clothing emerge? Gender is present in many ways in the most dominant fields in business research, like organization and work-related research fields, consumer fields and areas related to power, hierarchy and careers, but is often silenced as a research topic. What do we analyze when we choose women as our interest group and interview their business start-ups and business activities?

Feminist theories are not 'only' about women's issues; more importantly, feminist theories can be used as conceptual lenses to create a more inclusive field of organization studies, as Calás and Smircich (1996) have stated. In business research, gender has often been displayed by a proportion of men and women in different positions. More recently, gender has been analyzed through processes and practices, as in organizing gender in hierarchies (Poutanen and Kovalainen, 2013). One example of the 'number reporting' type of research is the reports whereby research aims at showing the gendered minority positions, and thereby arguing for the need for balancing acts for equality. Therefore, numerical data in argumentation strategy are used in order to make the case convincing, as in the following section.

Women's studies, gender research and feminist research, which all differ from each other with the emphasis on gender, women or feminism, have tried to impact on many of the basic conceptual categories used in organizational studies and business research. The underlying idea is that changes in the theoretical constructs not only allow gender into the original theoretical premises, but gender as a theoretical construction is itself actively processed and embedded into the theoretical starting points in research (Aaltio-Marjosola and Kovalainen, 2001: 29). What are such concepts?

Examples could be taken from the fields of management and leadership studies, where research has shown that leadership, understood as 'management of meaning', is not without gender either (Box 19.2).

Literature and research on women in management did concentrate for a long time on two major areas of study:

1. reasons for the low number of women in higher managerial positions; and/or
2. assumed or perceived differences between female and male persons in managerial positions.

These two fields have resulted in emphasis on quantitative research methods when the quantities of women and men are being analyzed.

Importantly, these types of analysis have brought forward individual charac-teristics, opinions, attitudes and knowledge on women in management positions, but in general have been unable to change the theoretical assumptions or break the theoretical glass ceiling within those fields of research. This is often because of the lack of reflexivity in research: why and what is being studied, in what ways and with what kinds of epistemic assumptions.

BOX 19.2

Strategies in knowledge production: convincing with numbers

According to international comparisons, the share of women managers (in managerial and administrative jobs) varies widely: from 46% in the USA, to less than 10% in Japan. There is, however, a wide difference in women's shares between private companies and public organizations. For example, the percentage of women officials and managers in the US private sector was (only) 36.4% in 2002, compared with 46% of all women officers and managers. The average percentage of women in the highest decision-mak-ing body (board) of the 50 biggest publicly quoted companies was 10% in 2004.

Also in the USA, women's share in corporate boardrooms remains relatively low in spite of the high share of women managers (46%) in general. Women held only 15% of all Fortune 500 board seats. The US figures seem high when compared with the Japanese ones. In Japan, the share of women managers has remained very low, 1–2%. According to a 1997 survey, women held only 82 out of about 45,000 major executive positions (0.2%). In addition, two-thirds of those positions were held by women who were related to the founder of the company. According to the same survey, Japanese women hold only 0.2% of all corporate board seats in publicly held companies.

While an average of 10% of the members of the highest decision-making body (board members) were women in the biggest publicly quoted European compa-nies in 2004, the position as a board president is very seldom open for women.

There are no women presidents on the boards of the 50 biggest publicly quoted companies in 14 European countries out of 30 countries. Why are women missing, despite the equal and majority numbers in business education? (Kovalainen, Vanhala and Melárt, 2007)

There are different ways of analyzing gender in business research, ranging from gender differences to gendering processes, questions in marketing and consumption, as well as in management education. Research literature on management has, however, many times failed to acknowledge that managers, for example, have historically been predominantly men (e.g. Calás and Smircich, 1996). From the gender division between women and men in work and organizational positions, many assumptions of the impact and issue of femininity and masculinity are being made in research. The cultural and ideological stereotypes that fashion 'masculine' and 'feminine' attributes in strongly dualistic and exclusionary terms have proved very resistant to facts, shown for example by rigorous meta-analytic research, according to which there are more similarities and commonalities than differences between leadership styles of individual men and women (Eagly and Johnson, 1990; Eagly, Johannesen-Schmidt and van Engen, 2003).

Would women as researchers treat traditional fields of business research, such as research on strategy, international business activities, new business formation or innovation and knowledge management, or indeed, questions of accounting, in a different manner than men? Is feminist research attached to the gender of the researcher, to the gender of those researched, or the ways the traditional topics are being approached? Examples might open up different views into gender research or feminist research in business research. However, it is a rather simplified idea to relate the gender of the researcher into ways of selecting methodological or theoretical approaches used in the research. When method is seen as an integral part of the research process, through the methodological choices the researcher makes, questions of an epistemic nature of the knowledge produced become important. The question of the relationship between knowledge claims and methodologies will be briefly discussed in the following.

KEY METHODS OF QUALITATIVE FEMINIST RESEARCH

Above, we have given definitions to gender and explained in what ways 'gender' means more than 'women/men' or 'sex' categories, and taken up examples from business research. What about feminist research? Defined at the most general level, feminist research consists of a variety of approaches, where the common issue has been the critique towards ways of producing scientific knowledge as objective, value free and neutral. Many researchers other than feminists also underwrite this view today.

Feminist research does not necessarily agree upon specific methods or research approaches, but it can be stated that at the heart of much feminist research in social sciences there is the goal to take action and bring change in the condition of women in some way with the help of research (Box 19.3). Thus, the political element is very closely related to feminist research and research influenced by feminist intentions (e.g. Reinharz, 1992: 251; Ramazanoglu and Holland, 2002; Naples, 2003).

BOX 19.3

Some characteristics of feminist research

The following key characteristics for knowledge production are used in feminist research. As general rules of thumb, they are also applicable to business research.

1. Feminist methodology is not distinguished by female researchers doing research on women, but it concerns both men and women.
2. There are no research techniques that are distinctively feminist, but some methods and techniques are used more by feminist researchers.
3. There is no unitary ontological or epistemological position that is distinctively feminist, and several positions exist.
4. Feminist methodologies exist and they are distinctive to the extent that they are shaped by feminist theories, politics and ethics.

We could add to this list a question that Sara Ahmed (2000) has put forward in asking what gets counted and recognized as feminist research or gender research? What kinds of characteristics are needed from research or work to be classified as feminist by its theoretical and/or methodological approach?

It is often stated in standard methodology textbooks that the choice of epistemology is hardly an individual decision made by individual researchers. This is very true: a novice researcher should not think of choosing the 'best' or most 'suitable' epistemology, unless familiar with the philosophy of sciences, as different epistemologies suggest and even dictate different rules for establishing the knowledge base. For feminist research, the domain of knowledge claims and their basis is an important and relevant question, as the aim of the research is more often also to create a new research field and analyze and understand questions seldom put forward in mainstream research settings.

Different epistemological assumptions require different kinds of understandings of what knowledge is and how it is gained, and with what certainty we can talk about reality and the relationship between theory and empirical materials. Most often, the feminist approach in research has been related to postmodern perspectives. Epistemologically, this means most often signing for assumptions of several realities that are knowable only through the language and culture, and rejection of one truth only. Feminist research, however, can be related to empiricist and realist epistemologies as well, especially in economics and psychology (Poutanen, 2007).

In what ways does feminist research sign up with different research methods? Feminist researchers have for a long time put emphasis on a number of issues in research settings that display the place and role of gender in social sciences. For example, the asymmetry in power relations in interview situations between the interviewer and interviewed that may be based on gender, race and social class (Maynard and Purvis, 1994; Marchand and Runyan, 2014) is one classic example of the factors often forgotten even today in business research, even if intersectionality has become an interesting new topic in organization studies.

Even if a researcher monitors their position in the interview situation, the monitoring and reflection do not always extend to the questions, and the possible impacts, of gender. And if gender is taken up in the research discussion, it is most often dealing with the genders of the interviewer and interviewed, not the subject matter as such. The gendered issues of sexuality, its existence and presence, the use and abuse of sexuality in organizations, and sexualized power, are often neglected even in those areas of business research that relate to HRM, managing people and work within teams and groups in organizations, even if they should have high relevance.

Often, the definitions on which we base an analysis of sameness and of difference may also be problematic in research settings (Stanley and Wise, 1990: 23). Many feminist researchers emphasize that women and men have different experiences, which cannot be conflated into the same experience and called 'human' (Ramazanoglu and Holland, 2002; Naples, 2003). This argument has been taken further, when the differences between women as a group, and differences between men as a group, are seen as important starting points for research. No single unitary positions exist from where women's (or men's) experiences would be seen as similar: women executive officers and women secretaries might share cultural values, but they are positioned differently in the office and in the organizational hierarchy, they use different kinds of power and are also both in an asymmetrical situation in relation to each other.

Feminist postmodernism refers to the rejection of unitary single-truth claims in research. With postmodern rejection of stable positions, it does not sign for social criticism and social change, the twin aims related to some feminist theories and research. The importance of context in terms of the researchers and the researched, is acknowledged in feminist research. There is variety in approaches within feminist research that is also visible in business research. Feminist empiricism argues that data and information about women's issues and experiences are usually missing or of lesser importance in current theories. This is counteracted through the production of more accurate information and the interpretation of social settings, such as organizations (Wilson, 2001; Alsop et al., 2002). The postfeminist research carries intersectionality within its presuppositions (e.g. Negra, 2009).

HOW TO WRITE AND EVALUATE FEMINIST ANALYSIS

Earlier, we took up the question of whether gender makes a difference in interview situations. Is there a feminist or a gendered way of researching? We wish to develop the answers to these questions further by taking up some possibilities for feminist analysis which are crucial for writing and evaluating the research. Debates in feminist methodology about conducting ethical and reflexive research by highlighting a research context have taken up several problematic issues, for example, how to safeguard anonymity, confidentiality and reciprocal trust which can be developed during fieldwork (e.g. Mauthner, 2000).

The feminist analysis can focus on discursive, institutional, relational and structural materials and questions in business research, as in any social science study. Differences in the levels of analysis will have an effect on the materials chosen for the research: for structural or institutional materials you may wish to analyze documents and organizational structures; and, for example, if you are interested in analyzing the power structures in customer–salesperson dialogue or management–personnel dialogue, you may focus on discursive practices and processes taking place in those discussions. As in any qualitative research, you should remember that the research question also focuses on the level of analysis and the possible materials used for solving the research question.

You should choose your research method with regard to what kind of data are appropriate for your project and what kinds of knowledge claims are possible with the data you have. Much of the research within feminist tradition has advocated face-to-face interviews and focus groups (Chapters 8 and 14) as feminist methods that are often used, as they both – as research methods – give voice to those aspects of respondents' experiences often otherwise forgotten in research settings. Also, action research (Chapter 13) has been used as a research method to enable the empowerment of women in a research situation and including them as participants in research activities. Ethical questions of privacy, consent and confidentiality are also important in feminist research (see Chapter 6). The direction you choose will give information on the ways of proceeding with the research project, but there are aspects that might be seen as joint evaluation criteria. These may include multiple positions and identities and acknowledgement of differences in research processes. Irrespective of the approach feminist research takes, the questions of voice and reflexivity are important to take into account.

In their classical work within management and business research, Marta Calás and Linda Smircich (1996) divide the feminist approaches within the field of organization studies into a variety of categories, ranging from a liberal feminist approach to a socialist feminist approach. Even though their approaches vary, they share some common features at the general level of analysis. According to Calás and Smircich (1996), feminist discourse in general closely relates to its local and political contexts: for example, postcolonial and third-world paradigms. Again, the elements of social change are related to theoretical and research-related interests.

Another reason for ignoring gender in organization theory and research lies in the difficulty of immersing many theoretical approaches into organizational analyses. Gender can easily be represented as gendered bodies and individuals, even if the gender analysis covers other aspects of work life and organizational theories. This perspective can even be called 'body-counting', which means that differences between the sexes are found and used for argumentation for greater equality, for example, but the emergence of differences itself is not interpreted. The perspective of 'doing gender' in organizations becomes understood when we sensitively explore how organizations and management construct gender. For that purpose, various discourse analysis and critical research approaches are possible.

Examples may expand upon our ideas of what it means to understand gender as an analytical category. Let us take an example from a field close to business research, that of economics. Mainstream neoclassical economics treats domestic work (household tasks, cooking, cleaning, caring – all done primarily by women) as invisible, non-existing work, which falls outside of production and the exchange economy. This treatment of domestic work implies that it does not exist in the formal national productivity measurements (such as gross national product), as it does not have a measurable market value.

This idea renders child-raising, caring, nurturing, loving, cleaning, and cooking as non-productive and invisible. Feminist economists, however, have been able to offer us a picture of who does what in one 'production' unit at home by calculating the worth of domestic work, and who does it, and how much time women and men spend on it. They have also been able to estimate the worth of domestic work, in comparison with national productivity measures (Ferber and Nelson, 1993), thus revealing the distortion of counting only formal production in formal organizations in measures of productivity (Acker, 2000: 202–3). This feminist analysis of domestic work also changes the theoretical premises and basic conceptual definitions within neoclassical economics: what it means when we research productivity, which elements are included and excluded, and how the idea of productivity is constructed.

Feminist research is often seen as differing from 'mainstream' research through the difference in ontological and epistemological questions. It can be stated, as mentioned earlier in Box 19.3, that there is not a single, unitary aspect of feminism; therefore, several approaches are possible. Even if there are many method choices available, the quest for specific analysis criteria related to feminist theories, politics and ethics exists, as mentioned earlier.

One example of organization theories from a social constructionist perspective, in which identities are defined and redefined through their relationships with others, is that we become socially constructed through work groups, teams and interactions in changing and constant relationships. Gender gets 'done' not solely through or within these interactions. Although the stereotypical image of a secretary is female and that of a police officer is male, the analyses of how gender becomes easily defined as female and male requires a detailed description and discussion of the interactions, processes, and practices of 'doing' the gender. What are the visible and invisible processes and practices of how gender 'gets done' in the work processes and in the expectations and practices in organizations? The occupation of 'secretary' becomes gendered in the processes and practices prevailing in the work place, as discussed by Rosemary Pringle (1988). Indeed, nurses and airhostesses have similarly become defined as female, and their femininity might become one 'asset' for empowerment in the organization through complex gendered social relationships, whereas femininities, professionalism, and culturally stereotypical attitudes become a mixed web of the professional image (Hochschild, 1983; Gherardi, 1995; Poutanen and Kovalainen, 2016).

The specific challenge to feminist research is the question of reflexivity. All qualitative research can be reflexive, but in the feminist approach the idea of attending systematically to the context of knowledge construction, at every step of the research process, is often seen as important, as you can establish your position and perspective through the procedure. This is important when research aims, for example, to incorporate social criticism and social change, as in feminist consumer studies (Fischer and Bristor, 1994; Catterall et al., 1997).

What about research questions arising from actual political agendas? Most often, research starts not from women's own experiences, but from a more theoretically or politically laden question, such as race, class and gender. Dawn Metcalfe and Afanassieva (2005), in their article 'The woman question? Gender and management in the Russian Federation', started with the aim to examine the social and economic changes that have shaped women's work identity in the USSR and Russian Federation. The authors unravel the complexities of the 'woman question' in the Soviet discourse and explore the individual subjectivities of managing gender and managing transition from a feminist point of view with the help of interview material from female professionals and female managers (Dawn Metcalfe and Afanassieva, 2005).

These are all varieties of examples on how and in what ways the data are used and produced, and still these examples could be labelled as feminist research with hugely varying settings, research questions and, thus, data and methods used. Whether you will use the terms 'data collection', 'data production' or 'postmodern reiteration' will depend how much you think about the underlying realities and ways of getting and obtaining the knowledge. While many feminist researchers use the words 'data production', there is considerable variation here with the terms and their usage (e.g. Maynard and Purvis, 1994; Olesen, 2005; Skeggs and Wood, 2012). In addition, the performative aspects and the 'doing gender' points of view raise the importance of language and discourse in any analysis of gender and businesses, gender and organizations and corporations.

Postmodern research in particular has offered feminism ways to deal with issues of method, where counting the numbers of men and women still exist. Postmodern thinking has questioned the connections between knowledge, rationality and reality, and by challenging these connections it has provided new possibilities for research to tackle, with subjugated voices, stories about experiences, personal notions and memories. This, in turn, is related to the questioning of binary thinking and deconstruction of oppositional categories of men and women. The deconstruction has been very influential in feminist thinking (e.g. Haraway, 1989, 1991), but also closely connected to Foucauldian analysis of power relations within the binaries, and modes of resistance through non-oppositional categories in socially constructed discourses (Butler, 1990; Braidotti, 1991; Chinn, 2010).

This way of thinking has also promoted a strong and lively rereading of qualitative methods books and their methodological procedures: texts are thus not seen as records of experiences in ethnography, for example, but could be impressionist tales as well (van Maanen, 2011), or poems which are composites of real events and utterances that the researcher or participant has experienced and observed. These notions also relate to the issues of representation (e.g. Evans, 2000; Segal, 2010). Feminist methods are thus not one, but many, and can open up interesting avenues for business research.

As for business research and management research, perhaps the most important 'novelty' that feminist research and gender studies have been able to bring forward has been in the ways the 'mainstream' knowledge has been challenged through empirical research, and new ways of thinking through deconstruction of categorical thinking.

Questions such as managers as men, masculinities and maleness of knowledge producers, and among researchers within business research, are important; organizational structures as stable institutions, identities of managers, construction of product images, advertisement, company and corporation images as gendered images are also all questions that can be opened up and challenged by feminist research and gender studies within business and management research, but also from other disciplinary fields, such as cultural studies and sociology.

KEY POINTS OF THE CHAPTER

There are several ways to do feminist research. The commitment to non-exploitative relations between researcher and subject is characteristic of feminist research, as it should be common in all qualitative research.

In business research, feminist research has been able to open up new research questions and directions for the analysis of business activities, the economy as a gendered phenomenon, and the positions of women and men.

Feminist qualitative research has close connections to most qualitative research methods, and methods applied in business research range from ethnography to discourse analysis and critical research.

FURTHER READING

A good and concise overview into qualitative research from the feminist point of view is given by Olesen (2005) in the *Handbook of Qualitative Research*. For those interested in identities, *The SAGE Handbook of Identities* (2010), edited by M. Wetherell and C. Talpade Mohanty includes, among others, L. Segal's article on Genders, and S. Chinn's article From Identity Politics to Queer Theory.

EXERCISE 19.1

Gender in women's journals and economic journals

The purpose of this exercise is to learn to do gender analysis on any existing materials. With this exercise, you will learn that gender is displayed in many ways in the presentation of everyday life, as well as in the economy.

Pick two papers, one representing a women's magazine and the other an economic daily or weekly newspaper or journal. Look at the advertisements and/or journal articles and try to analyze the following points.

1. What kind of images do these articles/ads mediate of women and men?
2. What kinds of gender stereotypes (stereotypical male and female roles) can you find from the texts in that publication and from the pictures used in that publication?
3. Try to deconstruct the elements of masculinity and femininity in the journals. What kinds of gender-stereotyped images do they give of men and women?
4. Can you find any deviations in the text and/or in the pictures of the stereotypical images?

EXERCISE 19.2

Gendering management

The aim of this exercise is to find out about gender roles and their presentation in a management context.

Find an article in the same journals about a female manager or a female boss, or alternatively about a male manager or a male boss. Often, these articles are feature articles concentrating on this person specifically, but sometimes also discussing the company development at the same time. Read the article through carefully and answer the following questions:

1. How is gender represented/constructed in the text you have chosen to analyze?
2. What are the text's assumptions regarding gender?
3. What kinds of characteristics and/or tasks, etc. are attributed to members of each gender?
4. What are the images of women/men in the text?

20
VISUAL RESEARCH

This chapter provides information on:

- what is visual research?
- ways of using visual materials
- the key concepts in visual research
- how to analyze visual data
- how to write about and evaluate visual data and visual research.

WHAT IS VISUAL RESEARCH?

The most usual and common way to understand 'data', 'analysis' and 'results' in any qualitative research in business studies is through textual materials. The interviews become transcribed into texts, and figures, numbers and signs in qualitative research refer to the analyses most often loaded with interpretations. Ethnographic memos of space become textual materials. Indeed, ethnographies most often 'translate the visual into words' (Pink, 2007: 119).

Increasingly, the visual materials have become part of the research, as data and as cultural representations, and visuality as an approach has become a framework to be used in business studies. Organizations and businesses use images, logos, videos and design, to display and to communicate, to make a distinction and stand out. For that reason visual materials have become one of the hot topics of business research. But how do you understand and analyze the visual materials in business research? This chapter will introduce and explore the use of visual materials, images and technologies in business studies.

Visual materials refer to data that are not in the traditional written or spoken form. Visual materials include pictures, hypermedia, videos, motion pictures, www-pictures, pictures and paintings available in books, advertisements, CD-ROMs, digitalized form, either two- or three-dimensional, etc. Visual material can be constructed of other types of artefacts such as packages, visual images of advertisements and so on. They also include – apart from existing data – new data and new types of data gathered within the project: videos, hypermedia, pictures, illustrations and images.

Visual methods are as varied as verbal ones. Visual research can and often does involve the use of other methods and methodologies, such as ethnography, discourse analysis, narrative analysis and semiotics, to mention a few. Visual and verbal methods are thus often complementary, not oppositional. Visual research is often representational by approach, multiplying layered representations of experience. Visual research can also be realist by approach (such as using photographs as sources of knowledge within text, as information sources or videos as documentary material), but also, and increasingly so, reflexive and culturally laden by approach, such as using hypermedia as representation, and referential relations between signs as in semiotics (Hall, 1997).

To give you a quick example of the relevance of visual materials, think about how photographs articulate and give possibilities for a multitude of interpretations in research settings. Therefore, the old saying, 'one photo is worth a thousand words' holds very much true in qualitative research. In cultural history and art history research, pictures and images, drawings and paintings have been key research material (Hall, 1997; Pink, 2007). Pictures give both historical and present testimony to micro-history and local habits, clothing, housing, and other similar issues. They also mediate the cultural images, meanings and open up re-interpretations to several issues. In business studies and even in social sciences – apart from cultural studies – however, visual materials are not so common in research and their systematic use, in particular, has remained rather limited.

With the growth of ethnography and widening uses of ethnographic materials, such as ethnography as fiction and emphasis on subjectivity in the production of knowledge, the use of visual materials such as photography, art, video and hypermedia, have become more common. The visual materials should thus not only be understood as realist 'data' but also increasingly they are understood as cultural texts and representations of layered and laden knowledge and meanings. The multitude of research on advertisements is a good example of the many and diverse uses of both visual materials and visual methods in the analysis.

WAYS OF USING VISUAL MATERIALS

Visual materials can be used in research in several ways, depending on the research question and the theoretical frame of reference adopted. The ways of using visual materials in research and the methods available for visual analysis range from content analysis to cultural analysis and semiotic analysis as well as their different versions. The differences and overlapping between different methods relate to the differences in understanding the images and the visual material in research. Visual materials can be analyzed independently but also in relation to language and in interaction with theories. Ways of using visual materials in research range from cultural studies and media studies to visual anthropology, to visual semiotics and to ethnomethodology. These different genres of research where visual materials have differing but equally powerful roles would all require separate descriptions. This chapter gives an overview of the varieties and a general idea of the uses of visual materials and ways for visual analysis.

Even if there are various ways of doing analysis on visual materials, there are usually two primary perspectives for understanding the use of the visual materials in qualitative research projects. This division is based on different research philosophies, and is useful for understanding the variety in the uses of visual materials. The division also follows the earlier sketched idea that the method of analysis is dependent on the research question and its commitments.

First, visual materials such as 'reflections and records of reality' can be used as documentary evidence. The analysis aims to extract this type of documentary information. In this orientation visual materials are gathered and analyzed as facts or records, in much the same way as interviews, documents, and other types of qualitative data can be taken as factual evidence. As one example of this, you can use content analysis to investigate pictures. This is the way that some conversation analysts, for instance, use video materials in their research (Erickson, 2011; Luff and Heath, 2012). The classification can take place with the help of the research question, for example, with relatively traditional picture analysis that focuses on rather neutral classifications that express the state-of-the-art as it is. Such classifications can tell about the persons and their positions in the visual material, the number of them, and any other classifying categories. Moving from analyzing pictures separately, some visual methodologists, such as Banks (2001) argue that the photograph's content may trigger the exploration of relationships between visual objects and possible narratives. There are different ways of organizing and systematizing this type of analysis, ranging from simple classificatory devices to cultural and intertextual analysis and to software programmes for those qualitative researchers who want to analyze video, auditory, and still image data.

A second, more usual way for using visual material in qualitative research is to understand and use it as a construction and a way of constructing meanings and understandings, including processes of construction, as in ethnomethodology. This more reflexive approach to visual materials seeks to develop and use the full and layered potential of the visual materials in qualitative research. Visual materials can be used in research to analyze the cultural meanings and layers, and the subjective and reflexive readings of culture. This type of research is often called 'cultural studies' or, more precisely, 'visually-oriented cultural studies'. As an example, semiotics and, more specifically, semiotically inspired consumer studies use photographs, art and videos for this purpose. Here, it is relevant to understand the social and cultural settings of visual materials and to study how the analysis of visual images in semiotics and in structuralism takes place, for example. For an overview of current work to show the wide range of contemporary research that uses video materials, see for example, Pink (2007) and Erickson (2011).

In practice the difference in the ways to use visual materials is not straightforward, nor rigid. Thus the boundary in the ways to use visual materials is blurred and changing rapidly. For that reason, the recipe book approach to using the visual materials in the business research is not possible, as 'there can be no blueprint for how to do fieldwork' (McGuigan, 1997: 32). The research questions and research design are the key elements in thinking how and in what ways the visual materials can be used.

THE USE OF VISUAL MATERIALS IN BUSINESS RESEARCH

In anthropology, in media studies and in cultural studies, photographs and pictures of social settings and cultures have been an important part of the research, either as part of the culture described or as research materials in their own right. Similarly, the use of new visual methodology, such as visual ethnographies in the analysis of business cultures, and the analysis of media images and pictures in advertisements, as well as visual images in job advertisements and annual reports, for example, could have a new role in business research. The analysis of visual materials can provide a new way of looking at the economy, business life, working life and consumer cultures (for the visual analysis of working life, see, e.g. Felstead, Jewson and Walters, 2004).

Studying the visual environment of the corporate headquarters, or the symbolic meanings produced by the new designs of consumer products are just some examples of how visual materials can offer fresh and exciting perspectives to business research. An equally interesting new field for business research is the analysis of spaces and places which embody cultural and shared values and assumptions, commercial values and industrial tacit knowledge. Here, interesting and new connections and interdisciplinary research emerge. In visual research, methodologies and theories are easily interwoven and may guide the research in particular ways. Researchers should therefore be knowledgeable of the ways in which to incorporate visual materials and methods into an established methodology of business studies.

Business researchers can use visual materials in a number of ways, which should be determined in relation to the research objectives and questions. For example, you can use visual materials as your main data or as supportive data, which leads to a different type of analysis. Using visual materials as additional data or as materials for culturally-oriented business research is a new field worth exploring in research.

Also software packages specifically designed for the transcription, management and analysis of video materials have been developed and used in research.

Examples of such analysis can be found in numerous articles (e.g. in Erickson, 2011). Dempster and Woods (2011) analyze the visual material concerning the economic crisis of 2009 with the help of such software. The authors describe several styles of transcription used in the process of making sense of the visual data and the selection and coding of analytically interesting segments of the media files in their data. They worked with coded video materials and media data to develop a coherent narrative. The narrative in the ways media constructed the economic crisis was one of their points of interest, and for that purpose, the software package was one possible way to organize the video material. In their paper, Dempster and Woods (2011) describe their collaborative process, as facilitated by the software, and how that affected the analysis of the data. Finally, the authors describe the results of their analysis in terms of the multi-layered narrative of the data, and discuss the limitations of using the software in the analysis.

The visual materials do not require the use of media software. Business corporate offices and headquarter designs can be analyzed through photographs and pictures. How you analyze that material depends on your research question, but such visual material can tell you about the nature of the business activities and indicate a high or low degree of bureaucracy, for instance. As an example, Larsen and Schultz's (1992) famous study of a Danish bureaucracy addresses the various ways in which material artefacts, such as office furnishings, reflect clearly the asymmetrical organizational power relations. Similarly, Ewenstein and Whyte (2009) analyze through visual data how buildings' visual representations are used, and how these are meaningful to different stakeholders, eliciting their distinct contributions. Hancock and Tyler (2000), Linstead and Höpfl (2000), and Thompson, Warhurst and Callaghan (2000) have analyzed images and visual materials in differing contexts when showing how the management of both environmental and embodied aesthetics can be understood to operate as a mechanism of employee control.

The application of visual methods in marketing and consumer research was investigated by Shin Rohani et al. (2014). The number of publications using and taking advantage of the visual materials and analyses has increased and the approaches most often applied have been factual and less constructionist by orientation. New approaches through video, the Internet and neuroscience imaging have however widened the application arena within marketing and consumer research (Dubois, Rucker and Galinsky, 2012; Shin Rohani et al., 2014).

ANALYZING VISUAL MATERIALS

The question of how to make sense of visual materials is closely linked with the question of how to analyze visual materials. It has been argued widely that meaning-making of the visual is not the same as meaning-making of the language (Monaco, 2009; Davison et al., 2012). The analysis of visual data can be a complicated matter, and figuring out how to relate visual and textual analysis can be even more difficult, if you do not have that type of frame of reference in your research project to begin with.

Factual, cultural and constructionist analyses

In a similar way to texts, visual data are commonly treated and analyzed as a direct representation of reality. Therefore, visual data are considered as testimonial, true and objective materials. Visual content analysis usually takes this approach by isolating frames or images or sequences of scenes (Bell, 2001) and then classifies the materials according to specified dimensions, which can in turn be treated as variables that should be mutually exclusive and exhaustive. However, photographs or paintings, for instance, represent both truth and construction of truth at the same time. Let's take an example of how difficult it is visually to distinguish these two: J.M.W. Turner's painting *A disaster at sea* (c. 1835, Tate Gallery, London) relates to a historically accurate event, a wreck of a ship at the French coast near Boulogne in 1833. Yet, the haziness of colours of white, gold and umber and the shadowy figures are constructed in such a way that the shipwreck is not the sole interpretation for the viewer. The cultural layers can be interpreted from paintings as well as from any visual materials.

With photographs, the examples may be closer to everyday experiences and thus easier to understand: they give true evidence of a specific situation, but at the same time they construct reality through the choices that the photographer made when deciding when to take the picture, who to include in it, etc. In addition, photographs as well as paintings are also complexly coded cultural artefacts. Therefore, visual materials can always be analyzed from both viewpoints, both qualitatively and quantitatively (e.g. Harper, 2005; Pink, 2007).

Historically, visual materials have provided a lot of visual information to support the realist idea of traditional ethnography. In this tradition, photographs were considered facts that constituted the truth and gave materials for different kinds of analysis. This is one way that visual materials are still used. New ways of using visual materials are emerging in business research as well: video recordings provide interaction in everyday settings in organizations, and give access to finer details of talk, discussion and bodily gestures, in comparison with devices such as written research notes or interview taping. Analysis of video recordings can even include detailed examination of specific fragments of materials, if that is suitable for your research question.

One way of looking at the materials, in order to learn about them, is to look at the ways the interaction in the conversation, for example, takes place: what is being said, by whom, and in what way.

Besides relying on the positivist and realist epistemologies, you can also analyze visual materials from the point of view of how images in materials produce meanings and subjective imaginings and also shared cultural images among groups of people and communities. On the other hand, there are no specific or rigid rules for the analysis of visual materials. Most researchers develop ad hoc solutions for the purpose of their own study (e.g. Heath and Hindmarsh, 2002: 111; Belova, 2006; Pauwels, 2010).

The uses and ways to deal with visual materials are plenty. Panayiotou (2010) analyzes the visual narratives of several popular films to explore how masculinity is constructed in the cinematic workplace, focusing on the representations of managers and the interplay between the practice of management and the practice of gender. Meier Sörensen (2014) takes the visual artefacts and interprets them through the theoretical understanding of marginal positions. For the analysis of the art, Meier Sörensen offers a method of aesthetic 'juxtaposition' of the visual artefacts. The analysis of the visual and social artefacts in business can consist of materials gathered by participants themselves, as in Brown, Costley and Varey (2010). The variety of materials may also give researchers more possibilities in their interpretations (Shin Rohani, Aung and Rohani, 2014).

The constructive understanding of visual materials can imply, for example, classification through visual readings and relational readings (Keats, 2009; van Leeuwen and Jewitt, 2001). Relational readings can refer both to intratextual and to intertextual readings. Alternatively the classification of the visual material can take place through close reading. Close reading means the cultural interpretation and analysis of the visual material, its reorganization and interpretation through references and intertextualities. The analysis and close reading can concern the composition of the pictures, for example (Swan, 2010).

For video analysis, there is systematic observation software available that can be used to organize and systematize large video corpora, assist in case selection, and facilitate comparability and cross referencing (see, e.g. Snell, 2011). While this software has conventionally been used to produce quantitative results that can be subjected to statistical analyses, it can also assist in complementary qualitative analyses. Even culturally inspired research can use visual materials as 'ordinary' data. This way of using visual materials is often about incorporating a visual dimension into an 'already established methodology based on a "scientific" approach' (Pink, 2007: 5).

In all these studies, visual materials are not used as supportive materials but as the main materials of research in several and very differing ways. The aim with the examples is to show that there is not just one way of using visual materials in research, but plenty. What is common for all of these examples is that the materials, methods and theories used in the studies are intertwined. In business research, the study of visual images is most often related to cultural studies, the use of artefacts as mediating devices in organizations, and to semiotics and aesthetics, but also to critical research. In general, visual culture represents conventions of the social world, such as social hierarchies and organizational positions: the office space and furniture of the

CEO are most often bigger and the room more often has a view, in comparison with the secretary's office space, furniture and working station. In addition to the realist approach, one can also go much further in interpreting and analyzing the picture, product designs and images as cultural constructions and cultural images, as done in some of the more recent examples taken up here.

Analysis in visual anthropology, semiotics and cultural studies

Visual anthropology takes the visual as with complex reflections and treats it in the analysis in a similar complex way: thus the real and the construction tend to be taken into account. What is crucial for the visual anthropological analysis is the contextual information. This can be done through direct analysis, which means the examination of the content of the visual image. The indirect analysis relates the visual image to other types of knowledge and uses the image as a vehicle (Collier, 2001). Several ways of 'looking' at the visual images have been presented, note making, detailing and returning to larger contextualized interpretations are outlined for working with visual images in anthropology. Yet, the steps to be taken relate to the research question.

Cultural studies introduce closely linked questions about the ways the viewer looks and analyzes. The reflective part of the visual analysis becomes important, in addition to context: the aim is not – as often in visual anthropology – the contextualized and detailed narrative but reflexive subject position, the context of viewing, the context of production, and then the conventions become of interest (Lister and Wells, 2001).

Semiotics, 'science of signs', looks at the visual materials through 'hidden cultural meanings' and cultural layering of meanings, that is, by analyzing the representational (denotative) and symbolic (connotative) meanings in the images. One version of semiotics is social semiotics. The various ways of looking at these elements require cultural knowledge and specific interest in using cultural repertoires in visual analysis (van Leeuwen and Jewitt, 2001).

WRITING THE VISUAL MATERIALS INTO RESEARCH

There are many ways of writing pictures and visual images into your research text (Mason, 2005; Mannay, 2010). How to use and dissect the visual imagery into the textual form, and how to use visuals in the research settings, depends on your research question and research design. Rose suggests three ways of using and analyzing photographs and pictures as key visual elements (Rose, 2012: 298).

In photo-documentation, photographs are planned as part of the research design (see Chapter 3), and they are analyzed through a particular visual phenomenon.

Photo-documentation is not widely used in business studies, and in writing, the careful documentation needs to be tied into reflexive discussion, otherwise it risks using photographs that are simply used as illustrations. In photo-elicitation, research participants are asked to take photographs, which are then discussed in an interview with the researcher. Involvement of active picture taking and discussing them into the research settings adds an additional layer to the interviews by and through the discussion of the photographs, but requires good planning and involves not only consent of the participants but also careful documentation of the instructions given (Rose, 2012: 308).

Writing of the photo-elicitation is often introduced as critical visual methodology and critical visual writing (Croghan et al., 2008). In photo-essays, a series of photographs is put together, in order to analyze the situation in question, for example. Photo-essays carry the tradition of the visual anthropology of making films (Banks, 2001), and as such photo-essays are not method, rather a way to open up research findings to a wider audience (Pauwels, 2010).

These three ways of using and writing about photographs cover only a small amount of visual materials and their analysis and have no reference to the theoretical bases of the analysis. Semiology, discourse analysis, feminist theory and cultural studies are prescribed to specific ways of analyzing the visual materials. Here, detailed knowledge of the method is crucial, but usage of visual materials relates first and foremost to the choice of whether the visual materials are used as primary data for research or as observations or visual products (Rose, 2012). Pauwels proposes that working towards a more visual discourse in research implies visual literacy and cultural competence along with the skill to translate scientific insights to verbal–visual constructs (Pauwels, 2010: 561).

KEY POINTS OF THE CHAPTER

This chapter has proposed ways of dealing with visual materials in business research.

The visual materials can be treated in different ways: from factual orientation to cultural semiotic and constructionist orientation. Choosing your method depends on the research question you wish to answer.

The use of the visual materials in the analysis can range from content analysis with variable approach to cultural close reading, interpretation of contextual matters and semiotic analysis.

FURTHER READING

Rose, G. (2012) *Visual Methodologies. An Introduction to Researching with Visual Materials*. SAGE: London. Rose's book introduces widely the different possibilities and limitations you may face with visual data materials and their use in the research.

--- **EXERCISE 20.1** ---

Choose an advertisement from a magazine

Look at the ad and try to analyze the various elements in the picture. Keep track of the ways you do the classification of the elements in the picture. Do you look for factual issues or culturally signified meanings?

--- **EXERCISE 20.2** ---

Choose an advertisement from a magazine. Alternatively you can look at the video clip of a TV ad

Look at the ad and try to find various types of conventions from the visual image or picture. Conventions are codes that are often a time-bound, socially agreed way of doing something. Conventions are often understood as carriers of traditions. What types of conventions can you spot in the picture or in the video?

PART IV

WRITING, EVALUATING AND PUBLISHING

21
WRITING PROCESS

This chapter provides information on:

- What is specific about qualitative research writing
- How to structure a qualitative research report
- How to find your own writing style
- How to develop your skills in qualitative writing
- How to write about qualitative business research to different audiences.

WHAT IS QUALITATIVE RESEARCH WRITING?

The question of qualitative research writing has been discussed by many qualitative researchers during the past decades (e.g. Richardson, 1990, 1995; van Maanen, 1995, 2011; Richardson and Adams St Pierre, 2005; Wolcott, 2009). Although there is no single answer to the question of how we should represent and write qualitative research, there are some common issues that we find relevant.

Scientific writing and qualitative writing

A central issue for many qualitative researchers is that qualitative writing differs from what we call scientific writing, which is closely related to the positivist research tradition. Whereas scientific writing aims to be objective by using impersonal pronouns and the passive voice, qualitative writers allow themselves to be present in their writing.

It is also common in qualitative research that the authors reflect on their writing process and choice of style in their research report. In addition, qualitative writers rely on vivid description, storytelling, and metaphorical language to carry meaning and hold their readers' attention. Overall, besides being interpreters of cultural meanings, qualitative researchers and writers tend to acknowledge their position as active producers of those meanings (Glesne, 2010; Eriksson, Henttonen and Meriläinen, 2012).

Think like a novelist

One way to understand the specific nature of qualitative writing is to start thinking like a novelist, that is, someone who creates a setting in which to place the characters and events that produce a plot (Ellis, 2004; Marvasti, 2011). You can think about your research process as a story: it started in some place; the data were collected at some locality and with some people; and the research text started with some context. It can be argued that, in order to perform a credible qualitative study, you as a researcher need to construct the setting in your writing and help the readers to enter this setting where the data once lived. This is why you should not remain an outsider of this story, but be present in your text as one of the characters.

Choose your intended audience

Despite all that is written above, there is no one proper way to write about qualitative research in the social sciences or in business research. Among other things, the success of your writing depends on how well your writing mode and style speaks to the readers. This is why good writing is rarely produced without attention to the audience (Richardson, 1990).

There are at least two types of audience in any kind of research: real and intended. The real audience is anyone who reads your research texts, and the intended audience is the target group that you have in mind when planning your writing. Business students and researchers have many potential audiences: the other researchers in the same field of study; instructors, supervisors and examiners; business practitioners; and the business media.

Because qualitative research allows you to choose between several writing strategies, styles, rhetorical modes and researcher roles, it is crucially important that you consider in advance what your intended audience will be (Richardson, 1990; Marvasti, 2011). Many of us have several ways of writing that we can choose from, or at least we can develop alternative ways of writing that will suit our audiences.

Deciding on your intended audience before you start to write makes the process of writing easier because it simplifies the detailed decisions about style and rhetoric, for example. Writing with a specific audience in mind gives you more in terms of unity of purpose and style and, in this way, involves your reader more directly with your arguments. This is why it is always easier to write with a real audience in mind. If you do not have a particular intended audience in mind or if you think that your research is for everybody, your writing easily becomes too general.

Writing to academic audiences, business practitioners and the business media

There is a difference between writing to the academic research audience and writing to business practitioners. One basic difference is that whereas the academic audience is interested in how theory is involved and linked to your research, business practitioners rarely show any interest in this issue. Business practitioners are interested in your results and their practical implications, not on how you came up with the results. Therefore, writing to business practitioners most often leaves out aspects of the research process and descriptions of the choices that you made along the way.

Writing to the media, particularly to business media, is yet another area requiring specialized competence and writing skills. The media is most often interested in 'the news', that is, what new, exciting, and surprising things you can say about some business-related issue. In the same way as the practitioners, the media is rarely interested in the specifics of your research process, nor your theoretical and methodological choices.

THE STRUCTURE OF THE QUALITATIVE RESEARCH REPORT

Many qualitative researchers begin to write a research report with crafting an outline, including a table of contents. When writing these, it is necessary to make some decisions about the structure of the research report. It is common to make a distinction between the macro- and micro-structure of a research report. The macro-structure refers to how the main sections or chapters are organized in the report, and the micro-structure indicates what the more detailed structural choices are.

In the same way as any good research report, qualitative writing deals with the following tasks: introducing the purpose of the research, critically reviewing and referring to the literature; describing the methods used, analyses made, and discoveries achieved, as well as providing discussion and conclusions about the topic studied (Marvasti, 2011).

However, what is specific about qualitative research reports is that the outcomes of these tasks are not necessarily presented within the conventional macro-structure of scientific research consisting of introduction, methods, analysis and discussion.

Indeed, many qualitative researchers think that the conventional macro-structure cannot convey their message in the best possible way. A qualitative research report can be more like a novel, in that there is a theme (topic, problem, research questions, and arguments) that forms a plot, which ties all the chapters and sections of your report together.

Whatever the structure that you choose, each part of your research report should benefit the whole. Do not include any part that does not provide relevant content considering the whole. Ultimately, the choice between a conventional macro-structure or some other kind of macro-structure depends on the context in which you are working, your personal preference, your writing skills, and your target audience (Wolcott, 2009).

When writing a business research thesis or a journal article, it is relevant to consider whether the audience (e.g. your instructors and examiners; journal editors and reviewers) is receptive or hostile to a change in traditional structure. Sometimes, you can even convince a hostile audience to accept an alternative structure if it is skilfully crafted.

Introducing your research

Whatever the macro-structure you choose to have, you must title your research report, write some kind of introductory part, link your research to the relevant literature at some point, describe your methodology, present your empirical analysis and findings, discuss them and give some conclusions. In titling their work, qualitative researchers often use imagination and creativity. It is quite typical to combine a vivid phrase or a question followed by a more descriptive sub-title. Try to select a title for your work that will encourage the readers to want to read it and let them know in advance what it is about. Sometimes, using a quote from your interviews or field notes can be a clever way to generate interest. Nevertheless, the title of your work should somehow reflect the idea or the content of your study, and be 'readable' throughout different cultures, audiences and even age groups.

The introduction is where you give your intended audience reasons to read your research text. Therefore, you should be able to convince the reader that your research is important and relevant to them. A common way of doing this is to situate your argument into an ongoing discussion in the media and in the business world, but most importantly, in the research literature. When introducing your research, you usually position your research within the prior research done by other researchers on the same topic, and within a specific theoretical approach (see Chapter 4).

Wolcott (2009) argues, however, that the conventional organization of the literature in one separate section in the beginning of your research report is unhelpful to most qualitative researchers. He argues that, instead, you should draw on the literature as and when you need it and not consider it a 'big chunk'.

Qualitative research is supposed to be sensitive to the empirical materials; therefore, the literature often emerges as relevant in response to your empirical data and the analysis that you make. This is why the literature cannot be completely identified or written about before doing the analysis and identifying your main findings and conclusions.

Describing methodology and methods

A description of your methodology and methods should give a detailed account of the research process: what was done; how and why. This is most often done in a separate section outlining the methodological approach and the specific methods used, the collection of empirical materials and their analysis, and the problems or issues that were raised during the study. Whatever your choice of structure, you should discuss your research design in a way that the reader can evaluate. Even if what you have done at some point was very intuitive or just guesswork, let the reader know it anyway.

Presenting analysis

Because qualitative research is sensitive to empirical data, their presentation takes a lot of time and effort and also considerable space in the final research report. One central issue concerning the structure of your research report is to decide how you want to present your empirical analysis and your findings. While there is no one answer to this, you need to consider which way of presenting is suitable to your research design and research questions, and which way of presenting would appeal to your audience.

Chenail (1995) distinguishes between alternative ways in which the analysis of qualitative materials can be presented in a research report. Each of the presentation modes can incorporate references to the literature throughout the analysis.

'The quantitative-informed presentation' follows the strategies commonly found in quantitative business studies. Here, empirical materials are arranged along clusters, categories, themes or frequencies.

In 'The theory-guided presentation', writing about empirical materials is governed by the theory or theories used in the study. For example, the examples are arranged to illustrate theoretical categories and concepts.

In 'The natural presentation', empirical materials are written about in a way that resembles the issue and topic being studied. For instance, if you are studying how consumers discuss food consumption and collect your materials with focus groups, present this as a dialogue among the participants.

'The narrative presentation' relies on storytelling, which can take a chronological form or not. Here, empirical materials are arranged around a plot that will guide the analysis. 'A simple to complex' type of presentation means that you start with giving the simplest empirical example you have and continue in a way that the complexity increases example by example. By doing this, you provide the reader with a better chance of following your analysis.

- In 'The first to last' type of presentation you write about the empirical materials as a chronicle, showing your own personal journey in performing the analysis.
- 'The most important to least important' mode presents the most central findings first and less central discoveries last.
- In 'The dramatic presentation' you order the empirical materials in a way that you start with minor findings and save the most central discoveries until last.

Discussing the results

In this section you are expected to discuss various aspects of your research results in comparison with the results that other researchers have presented earlier. Discussion need not be a separate section at the end of your research report. You can discuss your findings throughout all the sections which deal with analysis and your own findings.

Discussion ends with conclusions, which can be a separate section. In your conclusion, you should return to the key themes and issues developed at the beginning of your report. The conclusion summarizes how the research you have presented has addressed the conceptual frame you put forth in your introduction or elsewhere. A conclusions section can be as short as a few paragraphs or as long as several pages; the length will depend on the complexity of your focus and results.

The conclusion often includes a discussion of any new insights the research can contribute to the broader literature. Additionally, any limitations of your research should be stated, as well as the suggestions that you would have for future research. Any practice applications or policy implications of your work should also be included in the conclusions section. Your references section should contain a full citation for each and every work you referred to, paraphrased, or quoted in your paper.

QUALITATIVE WRITING STYLES

All writers develop their own style, be it planned and rehearsed or not. When doing qualitative research, you can, and you should, read about and experiment with different writing styles in order to develop an understanding of how they can be used and developed. Thus, it is relevant to consider what styles you (and your supervisor) are willing to adopt and how your role changes within them.

Three roles of a qualitative researcher

Glesne (2010) describes three roles for a qualitative researcher, (i.e. artist, translator or interpreter, and transformer) which can be applied side by side in the same research report, or separately throughout the study. The artist experiments with different writing styles and rhetorical modes and can even move on to writing fiction and poetry (for an example, see Ellis, 2010). In a translator or interpreter role, the qualitative writer attempts to understand the research participant's world, and translates this into text (for an example, see Orr, 1996). A transformer, in turn, is a catalytic educator whose aim is to help the readers to acquire new insights and perspectives on human aspects of life (for an example, see De Rond, 2008). The two latter roles are clearly more common in qualitative business studies than the first one.

Rhetorical modes

When developing your writing style, you can also experiment with various rhetorical modes: expository, descriptive, narrative and persuasive. Instead of focusing on one style only, it is more useful to develop your writing style to include several rhetorical modes. It is quite typical that several rhetorical modes are combined in qualitative business research reports. Furthermore, different rhetorical modes can be used for different audiences.

The aim of expository writing is to inform, explain, describe or define the subject to the reader. Therefore, we use expository writing to report facts, to define terms or to give instructions. Because expository writing is concerned with presenting facts to the audience, it should be objective and unbiased. This type of writing is typical in sciences and in informative journalistic writing (e.g. news, documentary articles). When reporting qualitative research, you can use expository writing when presenting some factual information, such as the business context or the background of the company studied. Also, expository writing suits when writing for business people.

Descriptive writing paints a picture of a subject through the use of vivid imagery and specific detail. Descriptive writing tries to convey a particular impression of a person, place, or thing, using strong 'word pictures'. It is a great way to convey emotion and attitude and may stand alone or be incorporated in other forms of writing. Vivid descriptions can be great tools for persuasion and they often add interest to introductions or conclusions.

Narrative writing is used to tell a story about the research and its topic. Most often, narration presents a series of events in order to inform the audience. Narrative writing is often combined with descriptive writing (e.g. when describing a setting and characters) and expository writing (e.g. when providing exact information about events or background).

Persuasive writing is used to convince the audience to believe or agree with the writer's argument or interpretation. Much of the academic writing is done in the persuasive mode. Persuasive writing relies primarily on logic and specific supporting examples, but it often incorporates expository, descriptive and narrative modes.

The writer's voice

All the above issues are relevant in learning to know what our 'voice' as a qualitative writer is like. The writer's 'voice' (Wolcott, 2009) is a literary term commonly used to describe a person's writing style. The voice is not predetermined and unchangeable, but it is continuously shaped by:

- conventions of the context (e.g. the conventions of business research and your own disciplinary background);
- your assumptions about the intended and real audiences (e.g. fellow students, other researchers, supervisors and examiners, business people, general audience);
- your choice of role or position (e.g. artist, translator or interpreter, transformer);
- your choice of rhetorical modes (e.g. expository, descriptive, narrative and persuasive);
- your choice of specific words and the way in which those words are arranged in sentences and paragraphs to create meaning (e.g. richness of the vocabulary, length of sentences, logic of paragraphs).

DEVELOPING SKILLS FOR QUALITATIVE WRITING

You can find plenty of advice on how to develop your writing skills in the literature (see e.g. Woods, 2006; Wolcott, 2009; Sword, 2012), but it is not possible to review all this in our book. Instead, we will turn your attention to some of the critical aspects that we find particularly relevant and difficult for business students.

Begin early

When writing qualitative research reports (thesis, article) you cannot begin too early. Although you have loads of other projects and courses as well as other things going on, you should not wait until days or weeks have passed and think that writing a qualitative thesis is something that you can do efficiently and without much intellectual effort. You should not wait to begin your writing until you have read 'enough' on your topic. This will never happen. Instead, read about your topic and start writing at the same time.

In the process of reading and writing you will discover that, on the one hand, you know more than you think and, on the other hand, you will also find out what you do not know. In a similar way, you should not wait to begin writing until you have collected and analyzed all your empirical materials. It is important to begin writing about your empirical materials early on, because qualitative writing is a form of inquiry. As you write, you will also explore and refine your perspective, thoughts and ideas.

Develop your arguments

In one way or another, most qualitative research reports rely on one or several arguments and offer justified knowledge about them. Describing and linking your arguments together very clearly in your research report is often considered vitally important in the field of business studies. There are three basic ways of justifying knowledge in a research report: by your own argument; by citing or quoting other researchers; and by empirical evidence from your own study. Crafting a strong theoretical argument can be achieved by several means:

- writing strong introduction and conclusion sections for your research report;
- carefully situating your arguments within the research literature and prior empirical research;
- integrating theoretical arguments with empirical analysis and conclusions.

Get distance and edit your writing

Editing and rewriting are fundamental to writing well in any research context. Therefore, the entire manuscript should be reworked for cohesion, accuracy and consistency (Woods, 2006). Qualitative writers seldom have problems writing enough words; instead, they write too many words (Wolcott, 2009). This is why you will probably need to condense your text as you edit it. In addition to this, you should pay attention to issues such as (see also Sword, 2012):

- poorly developed argumentation (e.g. you have too many arguments, or your arguments are vague or self-evident);
- unnecessary, overused, or redundant words and phrases (e.g. very, rather, quite, however, thus, hence, therefore);
- long and complex sentences;
- bad expression (e.g. clichés and truisms);
- passive voice (e.g. 'the research was carried out in France' instead of 'I carried out the research in France');
- consistency (e.g. the use of terms, numbering, and references in the same way throughout the report).

Finally, leaving your writing aside for a while enables you to distance yourself from it. This, in turn, helps you to see your own writing from the outside, almost as if it were written by somebody else. Reserving some time in your research project to distance yourself from your own writing helps you to identify overused phrases and patterns, spot discrepancies, and strengthen your interpretations and conclusions.

While distancing yourself is a useful practice, getting somebody else to read and comment on your text is even better. This person does not need to be a researcher, and it is often even better if they are not. Therefore, it is particularly helpful if you can ask your friends or family members to perform this reading and commenting task for you. Because they are not experts in research, there is a possibility that they do not take for granted what you say and how you present it, but ask for clarification and elaboration to make your text more understandable.

KEY POINTS OF THE CHAPTER

Writing is a central activity in all qualitative research. Qualitative writing differs from traditional scientific writing, although there is no one best way of doing it. Qualitative writing often resembles writing a novel, but you still need to develop your own writing style through experimentation and rehearsal.

There are many potential audiences for qualitative writing within the field of business research; it is helpful to experiment with these and learn to take your audience into account in order to get your message through.

The structure of a qualitative business research report can vary a lot, but it can also follow the traditional macro-structure of empirical research. Whatever the structure, you must introduce your research, describe your theoretical and methodological approach, and present analysis, results and conclusions in your report.

FURTHER READING

Harry Wolcott's (2009) *Writing Up Qualitative Research* is an easy-to-read book, focusing on the practical issues of qualitative writing.

Helen Sword's (2012) book *Stylish Academic Writing* is a refreshing, practical and easy-to-read guide that you can use for developing your research writing skills.

――――――――――――――― EXERCISE **21.1** ―――――――――――――――

Writing for different audiences

The purpose of this exercise is to learn to write to the potential audiences of business research. With this exercise, you will learn to pay attention to the expectations of more academic and practically-oriented audiences in particular.

Think about the key results of your research project. Write a one-page summary about them to three different types of audience, considering carefully the interests of each of them and how you will get your message through to them:

- your supervisor;
- one of your research participants, or a business person that you know;
- a business journal or magazine (name the one that you choose).

Make a comparison of the three texts and analyze how the content and style are different. If they are not different, perform the exercise again.

EXERCISE 21.2

Persuading others with your writing

The objective of this exercise is to experiment with a writing style that is different from traditional scientific writing. Furthermore, the exercise provides an opportunity to learn how to write a good story, which is an essential skill in qualitative research writing.

- Think about your research process as a story and write this story down on paper. Pay attention that your story is built around a plot, a specific context, and characters. Also, make a decision about how personal you would like the story to be and how much you will write about yourself in the story.
- Give your story to a fellow student and ask them to read it. Even better if you have both written a story about your research processes and you can exchange them.
- After reading the story, discuss it and see how well the reader can understand the plot and the main points of your story, and how well they can relate to the story. You can discuss questions such as 'How does the plot evolve?', 'What is the main message of this story', 'Does the story feel familiar to the reader who has gone through their own research process?', 'Is the story honest, trustworthy and reliable?'

EVALUATION

This chapter provides information on:

- What is specific about evaluating qualitative business research
- How the classical evaluation criteria can be used
- How the evaluation criteria developed for different types of qualitative research can be used.

KEY ASPECTS OF QUALITATIVE BUSINESS RESEARCH EVALUATION

One of the challenges confronting you as a qualitative researcher is how to assure the readers of your research about its scientific nature, its quality and its trustworthiness. Adopting explicit evaluation criteria increases the transparency of your research and provides you with the means to highlight the strengths and limitations of your research. However, we want to emphasize that you should not evaluate your research only at the end of your project, but do so continuously during the whole research process. Any evaluation criteria that are applied just at the end of the study cannot guide your research in a direction that ensures good quality. This is why we have also discussed research evaluation in each of the chapters in Part III of the book, highlighting what is specific for each qualitative research approach in terms of research evaluation.

Evaluation criteria that are developed for assessing quantitative research do not necessarily fit qualitative research projects. Trying to assess qualitative research with the help of evaluation criteria adopted from quantitative research, and vice versa, can lead to poor-quality research. This is why you should think carefully about which evaluation criteria are compatible with your research approach and the aims of your study.

Novice business researchers often confuse the basic logics of qualitative and quantitative research in their studies. Good examples of such confusion are provided by the questions that the teachers of qualitative methods regularly get from their students. Students ask, for instance: 'How many interviews do I need to do to get my thesis accepted?' Here, the logic of quantitative acceptability enters into qualitative research. For a supervisor, it is rather tempting to answer: 'Well, you might need some five more, to be on the safe side'. This should not mean that the number of five interviews would be decisive. More preferably, the answer should be that: 'Regarding your research question and your aims to focus on diversity, you might need to collect more empirical data'.

In this chapter, we provide a summary of the often-used logics of qualitative business research evaluation. Several concepts that are used to evaluate qualitative research originate from quantitative research, and they have only been partially adapted to fit qualitative methodology. It is important to remember, however, that the terminology of evaluation – even if the same words as in quantitative research might be used – has a different connotation and meaning when used in qualitative research settings. Therefore, going back to our student's problem of the number of interviews or cases, it is not the number of interviews as such that counts. Instead, it is the materials obtained from interviews, the quality of the interviews and the logic through which the decisions to choose specific interviewees or cases that are more decisive in doing good-quality research are made.

As we have seen in this book, qualitative research approaches are numerous, and so are evaluation practices. We have discussed some details of these in Chapters 11–20 in Part III, which cover a wide range of qualitative approaches ranging from case and focus group research into discursively, politically and culturally-oriented research. The first two approaches mentioned are often built around practical problem solving, whereas the others are more tightly knit with theoretical and methodological discussions within social sciences. With differing underlying philosophies, principles and practices, it is understandable that various qualitative research approaches cannot share any unified evaluation criteria.

We suggest that it is helpful to distinguish between three different ways of using evaluation and assessment criteria in qualitative business research:

- Adopting the classic criteria of good quality research, which originally stems from quantitative research.
- Adopting alternative but common criteria for qualitative research.
- Abandoning the idea of common evaluation criteria for qualitative research approaches.

In the following, we will discuss each of these strategies in more detail.

ADOPTING THE CLASSIC CRITERIA OF GOOD-QUALITY RESEARCH

The three concepts of reliability, validity and generalizability provide a basic framework for the evaluation of research in social sciences as well as in business research; for an overview, see for example, Patton (2014).

Reliability

Reliability is one of the classic evaluation criteria commonly used in quantitative research. Reliability tells you the extent to which a measure, procedure or instrument yields the same result on repeated trials. Therefore, the question of reliability is related to the establishment of a degree of consistency in research in the sense that another researcher can replicate your study and come up with similar findings. Qualitative researchers and methods books are divided in their opinion of whether the accuracy of interview and observation accounts, for instance, can be evaluated with the classic criteria of reliability and validity in research.

Validity

Validity is another classic evaluation criterion. It refers to the extent to which conclusions drawn in research give an accurate description or explanation of what happened. In principle, to be able to say that research findings are valid is to say that they are true and certain (Schwandt, 2001). True, here, means that your findings accurately represent the phenomenon referred to and that they are backed by evidence (i.e. they are certain).

Again, qualitative researchers and methods books are strongly diversified in their opinion about whether validity is an adequate evaluation criterion in qualitative research. In qualitative research, the term 'validity' is used in a rather differently defined meaning: the aim is to provide research with a guarantee that the report or description is correct. This is done through analytic induction and reflexivity.

Common procedures for establishing validity for research are analytic induction, triangulation and member check. Glaser and Strauss (1967: 102) developed the use of analytic induction within the grounded theory approach. They suggested that analytic induction should combine the analysis of the data after the coding process with the process when the data are integrated with theory. This partly has led to grounded theory being understood as 'inductive theory'. Strauss (1987: 12) later redefined their position in the following way: '... it is important to understand that various kinds of experience are central to all these modes of activity – induction, deduction and verification – that enter into inquiry'.

Triangulation is the process of using multiple perspectives to refine and clarify the findings of your research. Triangulation has many alternative forms that can be used either separately or in combination (Guba and Lincoln, 2005; Lincoln, Lynham and Guba, 2011); see Box 22.1. When using triangulation as a basis for evaluation, we can ask: Did the researcher use one or more types of triangulation? How and with what effects? As some forms of triangulation may be quite resource consuming (e.g. using several researchers or different types of empirical data), the researcher might use only one type of triangulation in their study. The challenge in triangulation is the possibility of ending up with controversial, paradoxical, and even conflicting research results. However, these may also be a source for new and exciting angles, ideas and research questions.

BOX 22.1

Forms of triangulation

Triangulation of methodologies: combining qualitative and quantitative materials in the same study.

Triangulation of methods: several methods and techniques of analysis are used to validate findings.

Triangulation of data: evidence from multiple empirical sources is used to cross-check information.

Triangulation of theories: several theories are used in explaining, understanding and interpreting the case.

Triangulation of researchers: several researchers investigate the empirical materials and cross-check their interpretations and conclusions.

It is good to remember that triangulation draws on the idea that there is one version of reality that can be approached from different angles and viewpoints, and using these different views adds to the overall understanding of the researched field. However, even if the reality does not produce similar ways of analyzing, gathering materials or using methods, triangulation offers a way forward in identifying the different ways the materials can be seen and analyzed (Flick, 2002). The suitability of any kind of triangulation for the elaboration of interpretations and meanings can, of course, be seriously questioned, and triangulation as such is not applicable to all methods presented in this book.

Member check is yet another way to increase the quality of your study. It is a procedure by which you feed the interpretations that you make as a researcher back to the participants of your study. In practice, this means that you let the participants check your interpretations of what they did and what they told you. Although this seems quite easy and simple, profound questions of knowledge production, sharing the similar notions of meanings, compromising with the vocabulary and expressions that you use in your research, and establishing the possible 'truth' are all problematic from an epistemological point of view. However, instead of checking the compatibility of your interpretations with theirs, you can also conceptualize member check as a process of establishing a dialogue between you and the participants of your study.

Generalizability

Generalizability deals with issues of whether the research results can be extended in one way or another into a wider context. In quantitative research, generalizability deals with representative samples. In qualitative research, it implies a well-grounded and well-argued selection of research cases, or people.

To point out the differences in quantitative and qualitative research logic, Yin (2014) makes a distinction between 'statistical generalization' and 'analytic generalization'. In analytic generalization, empirical results of the case study are compared with a previously developed theory. If two or more cases support the same theory, then replication may be claimed.

As evaluation criteria, validity is supported by realist and critical realist approaches, which rely on rigorously defined qualitative methodologies (Denzin and Lincoln, 2005; Lincoln et al., 2011). Validity as a concept, is less suited to the various forms of relativism.

ADOPTING ALTERNATIVE BUT COMMON EVALUATION CRITERIA

Several problems with the use of classic evaluation criteria in qualitative research have generated novel ways for evaluating it (Creswell, 2012; Patton, 2014). If your research relies on relativist ontology (suggesting that there are multiple realities), and subjectivist epistemology (emphasizing that the researcher and the participant jointly create understandings), we advise you to replace the traditional notions of validity, reliability and generalizability with the evaluation criteria that are developed to better accommodate these philosophical starting points in research.

In their seminal work, Lincoln and Guba (1985) substituted reliability and validity with the parallel concept of 'trustworthiness' containing four aspects: credibility, transferability, dependability and confirmability as ways to assess qualitative research that do not rely on the realist or critical realist conceptions of the social world. Particularly in constructivist research, trustworthiness is the 'goodness' criteria for research. General descriptions of these are the following:

- Dependability. This is concerned with your responsibility for offering information to the reader, that the process of research has been logical, traceable and documented. All these activities establish the trustworthiness of research.
- Transferability. This is concerned with your responsibility to show the degree of similarity between your research, or parts of it, and other research, in order to establish some form of connection between your research and previous results. The idea of transferability is not about replication, but more of whether some sort of similarity could be found in other research contexts.
- Credibility. The key questions to ask from your research when evaluating its credibility are: Do you have familiarity with the topic and whether the data are sufficient to merit your claims? Have you made strong logical links between observations and your categories? Can any other researcher, on the basis of your materials, come relatively close to your interpretations or agree with your claims?
- Conformability. This refers to the idea that the data and interpretations of an inquiry are not just imagination. Conformability is about linking findings and interpretations to the data in ways that can be easily understood by others.
- In addition, the concepts of coherence and consistency, as well as plausibility and usefulness, often replace the concepts of validity and reliability in qualitative research.

Still, we can argue (with classical terms) that validity and reliability of qualitative research depend on epistemological judgements for how the study is developed and argued through. The trustworthiness criteria taken up earlier and also the issues of authenticity are important in establishing the recognition of qualitative research, even in those areas of business studies where quantitative research is in a mainstream form.

ABANDONING THE IDEA OF COMMON EVALUATION CRITERIA FOR QUALITATIVE RESEARCH

Qualitative research aims to capture the multiplicity and complexity of social life, and this aspect is inherently present in the research questions and in the ways they are studied. The unique characteristics of different situations, social actions, processes and interactions in qualitative research put forward a varying mix of pressures for considering how successfully a research project or a publication has filled its task and purpose.

The philosophical debates on how the social world can be represented have led some researchers to suggest that the more traditional forms of research assessment could be abandoned. Within post-structural and cultural studies in particular, the importance of locality, textual reading of materials, discourse analysis and feminist analysis methods are considered strategic devices and resources for understanding. On this basis, it has been argued that no traditional forms of assessment, or none of the evaluation criteria described in the previous two sections, could be used in research. Instead, researchers should be encouraged to plurality and indeterminacy in evaluating their studies.

In this spirit, multi-voiced, multi-focused, self-reflexive as well as literary and artistic accounts are replacing the postpositivist, global criteria for research evaluation (e.g. Richardson and Adams St Pierre, 2005).

The argument goes that each research project and publication should be evaluated and assessed from a position of its own, instead of using any universal criteria for assessment. This refers to the philosophical position where researchers are part of the knowledge production and reproduction, and therefore no universal and stable criteria for assessing the goodness or badness of the research project should be possible. However, even if all common evaluation criteria would be abandoned, it is still possible for other researchers to evaluate your research project later on from any point of view they see fit.

KEY POINTS OF THE CHAPTER

Evaluation of qualitative research should take place during the whole research process, not only at the end of it. It should be performed with an acknowledgement of the philosophical and methodological background of the study in question.

Novice business researchers often confuse qualitative and quantitative research logics when trying to evaluate qualitative research projects. This confusion can easily lead to poor performance in evaluating activities; therefore, it can also lead to poor quality research.

When your study is based on the realist or critical realist philosophy of research, you can use the classic evaluation criteria (reliability, validity, generalizability).

When doing constructionist qualitative research, you can use the criteria that have been developed to assess the 'goodness' or 'trustworthiness' of qualitative research (e.g. conformability, credibility, dependability and transferability).

When taking a post-structuralist or cultural starting point, there are no general criteria that you can use in all studies. Instead, you will need to come up with criteria that are context specific and locally suitable.

FURTHER READING

Chapter 10 in Creswell's (2012) *Qualitative Inquiry and Research Design. Choosing among Five Traditions* gives an overview of the debate over quality standards in qualitative research and discusses the specific criteria that can be used in biographical, phenomenological, grounded theory, ethnographic and case study research.

Chapter 9 of Patton's (2014) *Qualitative Research and Evaluation Methods* illustrates various ways that qualitative research can be evaluated with traditional scientific criteria, with social construction and constructivist criteria, artistic and evocative criteria and critical change criteria.

Lincoln and Guba's (1985) classic book *Naturalist Inquiry* offers detailed discussion on the differences between positivist and postpositivist research logics and grounds for using evaluation criteria that are designed for assessing the trustworthiness of qualitative research.

EXERCISE 22.1

Using various criteria to evaluate research

The objective of this exercise is to learn how to use different criteria for research evaluation. Furthermore, you will learn to match the evaluation criteria to the qualitative approach that you use.

- Choose two research articles from scholarly business research journals that use different qualitative research approaches (e.g. one article based on case study research and another on narrative research). It helps if the articles deal with issues that are familiar to you, or methodologies about which you have prior knowledge.
- Read through both articles and specify to yourself what the qualitative approach and methods used are (these are not always very clearly described).
- Take the first article, read it through again and consider how it could be evaluated from its own starting points. With the help of this book and other literature, make a list of evaluation criteria that you can use.
- When you think that the list is complete, perform the evaluation and write down a short summary of it.
- Do the same with the other article.
- When you have finished the evaluation of the two articles, think through once more how they differed from each other and what kind of effect this had on the evaluation you did.

It is very useful to do this exercise together with your fellow students in a way that two or more students evaluate the same articles. By comparing the evaluations you did and the criteria you chose, you will also learn to justify your own views about these.

23

PUBLISHING

This chapter provides information on:

- What is specific about publishing in qualitative business research
- Where to publish qualitative business research
- Publishing research books, book chapters and scholarly journal articles
- Publishing for practitioners.

WHAT IS PUBLISHING?

New knowledge produced by business research is valuable for other researchers working in the same field of study, but also for society at large including business practitioners, policy makers and the general public. In the case of business research, published research can also be very relevant for the business community. This is why every researcher should think about how to disseminate their research results for others to read. In addition to face-to-face communication at seminars, conferences and informal discussions, written communication is an effective means of disseminating research to a variety of different audiences.

Business researchers commonly publish their research in books and journal articles, but also in conference papers, working papers as well as theses and dissertations. The scholarly outlets reach other researchers, but they are not the most effective in disseminating research to practitioners, decision makers and the general public. One reason for this is that researchers, practitioners and decision makers work within different social and cultural contexts with an emphasis on differing interests and values. Social and cultural contexts have an influence on what kind of research evidence and publication formats are considered relevant and useful by different audiences.

Within business research, there has been much debate concerning the possibility of making research results more accessible to practitioners (Bansal et al., 2012; Bartunek and Rynes, 2014). While some researchers argue that the bridge between theory and practice in business studies is difficult to overcome, others emphasize the necessity of doing so. Some researchers argue that specific qualitative research approaches (e.g. case studies, action research) are more favourable than others in making business research more accessible to practitioners. Although bridging the gap between theory and practice requires many decisions throughout the study we think that publishing is one of the key issues in the process.

Whatever strategies and outlets are used for publishing, the purpose is to make research findings available to other people – researchers and wider audiences. Furthermore, if the audience finds some piece of research interesting, it may have an impact on how the members of that audience think and act in the future. From a societal point of view, it is preferable that research has an impact, not only on future research, but also on wider spheres of life.

Besides the usefulness of making research results publicly available to others, publishing can also serve other purposes, particularly for the researcher in question. Publishing the results of your research can advance your career prospects, especially if your future job requires you to be able to perform or manage research projects, or if your tasks would include buying, interpreting or evaluating research results presented by others. These types of tasks are common in many business-related professions and performing them well may require some basic knowledge about publishing. Furthermore, disseminating the results of your research in easily accessible formats to wider audiences outside the academic community could even provide you with a new job in a company or some other organization.

Also, if you think that you might want to continue your studies towards a doctorate and also work in academia then publishing is important for you. University students can even be required to publish something in order to complete their degrees, especially a doctoral degree. If you are a doctoral student at a business school, you will publish the results of your doctoral research in some written form. Although your research must be explained in your doctoral thesis, which might not be read by many people, you may also want to publish your doctoral research as a book that can reach a wider audience. Alternatively, you can publish your research in one or more journal articles. These could be targeted for scholarly audiences, but also for business practitioners and decision makers.

In some countries, a finished doctoral thesis may already contain a number of published journal articles and a separate introduction chapter, which ties them together. If this is the case in your country, we advise you to familiarize yourself with the guidelines of your university besides reading this chapter. Although we provide a general introduction to the process of publishing scholarly journal articles, you will need more specific guidance on how to make a publication plan according to the guidelines given by your university and discipline.

HOW TO PUBLISH QUALITATIVE BUSINESS RESEARCH

Choosing where to publish your research can be an important decision, especially if you plan to work at a university, or if you look for a research-related career elsewhere. Besides your own interests and plans, the choice of the publication outlet can be influenced by the research traditions, conventions and norms of the academic community of which you are a member. For instance, some academic communities may value books and book chapters over journal articles and vice versa. Also, some academic communities might appreciate conference and working papers, but others would not. Our advice is to discuss your publication plans with colleagues, peers and supervisors in order to develop a publication strategy that suits your research project, career aspirations, and other plans.

Conference papers

Novice business researchers often start publishing their research as conference papers. In addition to the written form (e.g. a full paper or an extended abstract), conference papers are most often presented orally at the conference. Many conferences accept papers and presentations on the basis of abstracts, but some require the submission of a full paper prior to acceptance. Some conferences, but not all, publish abstracts or full papers in printed or digital conference proceedings. In addition to offering publishing opportunities, conferences are excellent venues for meeting research colleagues from around the world. Presenting your research and networking with other researchers at conferences can provide valuable feedback for your research and help you find opportunities for collaboration and co-authored publishing. When choosing an appropriate conference for your research, it is helpful to ask colleagues and supervisors about the conferences they attend in addition to browsing the conference websites.

Books and book chapters

Many business researchers publish their research in books and book chapters published by academic publishing houses. Doctoral students might be able to publish their dissertation as a book. In some countries, the doctoral dissertation can be published as a book in the university series without any revision. However, it is also possible to revise the dissertation into a book, which is then targeted for a wider audience than academic researchers, possibly including business practitioners and decision makers. In addition, you could also write a monograph, which is separate from the doctoral dissertation, but based on the same data. Or you can contribute a chapter to a book edited by someone else.

Choosing an appropriate publisher for a book follows the same basic principles as with all publication outlets. The most important aspect is to identify a publisher that is relevant to your research field. Many academic publishers are interested in business-related books, but they may have some differences in how they emphasize research-related issues or some other aspects, for instance, concerning practitioner audiences. This is why it is good to carefully consider the intended audience of your book before choosing a publisher to contact. Professional book publishers have good web pages where you can get a lot of information on how to make a book proposal and how the process proceeds thereafter.

Scholarly journal articles

Scholarly journals are periodicals that follow a specific process called 'peer review' when deciding which articles they will publish. Publishing your research work in scholarly journals is one of the main modes of scientific communication and an effi-cient way of disseminating research results to other academic researchers. Business research journals cover a wide scope of topical areas and research perspectives with differing emphases on methodological, theoretical and other scholarly aspects.

When you want to publish your research in scholarly journals, how do you find a journal that could be interested in publishing your research? If you have one or more co-authors, some of them might have experience in choosing relevant journals. If you are a student or a novice business researcher writing a solo-authored article, your super-visors and senior colleagues probably have experience of the journals in their subject areas and they could help you to choose an appropriate journal. In addition, we advise you to visit the websites of the scholarly journals in your research field, and espe-cially those that have published the key research that you refer to in your own paper. Then find out how these journals describe their interest areas and target audiences and whether they seem to match your paper. Scholarly journals often wish to have an ongoing discussion about some topical areas or some more specific questions. When your research fits these, the journal might be a good place for your article. Also, check early on that the journal wants to target the same audience that you wish to reach.

There are also other important issues when choosing a scholarly journal in which to publish. First, the publishing processes of journals can differ to some extent. While most scholarly journals use a double-blind peer review process, about which we will explain further on, some might use other types of evaluation, for example, that done by the editor. Second, scholarly journals are ranked in various evaluation systems paying attention to such issues as the citations that the journal gets (i.e. Impact Factors), or to a combination of several criteria that are used to assess the scientific quality of the journal. Your senior colleagues and your library will be able to help in getting more information about these.

Depending on your career aspirations in the academic world, journal rankings might be relevant for you when choosing the journals that you target with your research. Universities and business schools have started to pay increasing attention to where their research is published, favouring their researchers to publish in scholarly journals that use the double-blind review process and have good rankings in various evaluation systems.

For you as the author of the article, other issues such as the speed of getting feedback from the journal, the time gap between acceptance and publication, copyright and open access policies could also be very relevant. You can find many answers from the journal web pages, but sometimes you will have to ask your questions directly from the journal. You might also want to assess if the publisher, editor and the members of the editorial board are respected researchers in your field.

When you have chosen where to publish, you need to take care that your manuscript fits with the requirements of the publisher. The publishing process can be somewhat easier the earlier you can decide on the journal that you wish to submit to. If you identify the appropriate journal at the beginning of the article-writing process, it is easier to take into account a full range of contextual and technical aspects that will increase the match between your manuscript and the journal. In addition to their focus on certain topical areas, all journals have some specific technical requirements for the manuscripts. These can be found from the author guidelines published on the journal website. Technical requirements may focus on the structure, layout and length of the manuscript as well as on the details for submitting the manuscript through the website. It is a commonly accepted norm that the same article manuscript should not be submitted to more than one journal at the same time.

The peer review process

Scholarly journals typically receive a lot of submissions and only some of those will be published after a peer review process. Besides journal articles the peer review process is often used for conference papers as well as books and book chapters.

The purpose of the peer review process is to improve the quality of published research in a way that it can make an impact on other researchers' work. When submitting a manuscript to a scholarly journal, the editor makes the first evaluation considering the following points: Does the manuscript present original research that has not been published elsewhere? Is the research interesting enough to the readers of this specific journal? Does the manuscript communicate the main points and the results of the research in a well-written format?

The editor may reject the manuscript immediately if it is not ready for peer review, or if it does not fit the profile of the journal. However, if the editor finds it worthwhile, the manuscript will be sent out to two or three other researchers in the same field of research asking for their expert evaluation. The peer review process is most often double-blind, which means that the reviewers do not know whose work they are reviewing, and the authors do not know who is reviewing their work.

In business research journals, the peer review process often takes several weeks or even months. When the editor receives the reviews back, a decision will be made whether the manuscript is accepted or rejected. You may also be requested to make minor or major changes to the manuscript and resubmit it to the same journal and the same reviewers. It rarely happens that a peer reviewed scholarly article will be accepted without any revision at all. Also, the probability of being rejected is high. If your manuscript is rejected straight away, or after one or more rounds of revision, you can then choose another journal to submit to and start the process again from the beginning.

Publishing for practitioners

As we mentioned at the beginning of this chapter, disseminating your research results to the practitioners in your research field, and more widely to the general public, can be very relevant in business studies. Many business researchers are well aware that business practitioners and policy makers need to be able to understand their research in order to apply it in their own settings. Thus, it is common that business researchers consider it relevant to publish both for their academic community and to practitioners working in their field of interest.

Addressing both academic and practitioner audiences in a single publication is difficult. Therefore, business researchers interested in communicating with practitioners need to have a double agenda in publishing. In addition to publishing scholarly articles for other researchers in academic journals, they also search for opportunities to produce publications that are relevant, interesting and useful for the practitioners working in their field.

Often the process of producing easy to understand practitioner-oriented publications requires that the researcher has a chance of talking with the practitioners for the purpose of testing ideas and the formats for their written communication. Interacting with practitioners in your field and writing to them in easily accessible formats can actually improve your understanding of your own research and in this way be directly beneficial for research also. Your ability to communicate with wider audiences can also be vitally important if you need funding for your research. Particularly in business research, but also elsewhere, funding bodies and companies that sponsor research have become increasingly interested in the practical relevance and impact of research projects that they give funding to.

How do academic and practitioner journals differ from each other? In the same way as academic journals are targeted at a specific scholarly community, practitioner journals are targeted at a specific professional market, most often managers in different positions. Compared to academic journals, practitioner journals put more emphasis on the ability of the author to write about practical implications rather than present theoretically and methodologically sound research. In practitioner journals, the editor often selects articles for publication without the peer review process typically used in scholarly journals.

While practitioner journals resemble academic journals in that the articles are often research-related and the authors can be researchers, professional and trade magazines are another category of useful practitioner-oriented outlets. While practitioner journals publish articles written by researchers, professional and trade magazines typically publish articles written by journalists who may have interviewed researchers. In addition, professional and trade magazines may have specific spots in the journal (e.g. a researchers' corner) in which they publish short articles that are written by researchers. Yet another difference is that business-related practitioner journals are often published by higher education institutions whereas professional and trade magazines are published by professional associations and other similar organizations.

Publishing in both practitioner journals and professional and trade magazines is worth considering by business researchers who wish to disseminate their research results to wider audiences and have an impact on society and business. But what should you write for a practitioner journal? Focusing on the needs of the practitioners is very important from the start of the writing process. First of all, you should think about how business practitioners can benefit from your research? For instance, can you write of an improved way of innovating or can you propose a new way of measuring some aspect of business performance?

Often, the most difficult part is to remember throughout the writing process that what makes a good academic article is not the same as what makes a good practitioner article. The content of your previous academic papers can indeed offer value to the practitioners, but you cannot present it in the same form that you used in your writing to the academic audience. This is why you will need to have a different mindset when writing an academic article compared to when you are writing a practitioner article. Link the article to the real world wherever possible, using relevant examples preferably with high profile companies. Article and word lengths for practitioner journals are shorter than for academic journals; practitioners are busy people, whose professional reading time must be carefully focused but lively.

KEY POINTS OF THE CHAPTER

Disseminating your research to various audiences through publishing is an important part of the research process.

Publishing can affect your career aspirations, especially if you plan to work in a research institution (e.g. university).

There is plenty of choice for business researchers when choosing research outlets (e.g. conference papers, books and book chapters, journal articles).

Making an effort to choose an appropriate publication outlet for a piece of research and preparing the manuscript according to the publisher's specifications increases your chances of getting published.

FURTHER READING

Writing for Peer Reviewed Journals by Thomson and Kamler (2013) is an accessible book about publishing that uses a lot of examples from different disciplines, mostly from the humanities and social sciences.

Writing for Academic Journals by Murray (2013) discusses all aspects of publishing in detail and provides a lot of advice for authors. The third edition of the book contains good discussion on how to use social media in publishing.

EXERCISE 23.1

Preparing a publication plan

The goal of this exercise is to help you plan your publications. Write a short abstract of the research that you are doing or plan to do in the near future. How would you want to publish this research? Consider various options (e.g. conference paper, book or book chapters, scholarly journals and practitioner journals) and write a short publication plan indicating what types of publications you could produce and what would be the main point in each of those.

EXERCISE 23.2

Taking action

The purpose of this exercise is to help you to take action according to your plan. First read your plan and then search for appropriate publishing outlets. If you plan to publish a book or book chapters, how can you do that? Which publishers would be interested in your manuscript? What kinds of instructions do they give to potential authors on their website? How do they describe the publication process? If you plan to publish articles, which journals would be relevant? What kinds of instructions do they give on their website for potential authors?

24
BREAKING THE BOUNDARIES

WHAT IS QUALITATIVE BUSINESS RESEARCH?

We hope that our book has illustrated that qualitative research is not a fixed and stable entity without history and context, but more like a living and transforming process. This is exactly why it is so difficult to define a set of specific features that would be shared by all researchers. By making their own studies and shaping qualitative methods for their own use, each qualitative researcher is an active participant in the process of redefining the answer to the question 'what is qualitative research?'

As a result, there is no definite consensus over the 'right' or 'best' ways of doing qualitative research. Depending on the method, some methods and their use have more conventions, application rules and also longer traditions of use than others.

The varieties of use of qualitative methods do not mean that there would not be any stability or consensus over what counts as good quality in qualitative research. We have tried our best to show you that, although qualitative research is an emerging and changing field, there is also some agreement on how we can perform qualitative research that produces grounded new knowledge and interesting new approaches in research. Chapters 1–6 in Part I, Chapters 7–10 in Part II and Chapters 21–24 in Part IV discuss issues that are shared by many qualitative researchers.

At the same time, we hope that reading through the chapters of this book has made it clear that you always have a multitude of alternatives when choosing how to perform qualitative inquiry in research. As our descriptions of various approaches and methods in Chapters 11–20 in Part III illustrate, the complexity and sophistication of some qualitative approaches and methods is also a matter that you need to take into account.

The place of theory in qualitative business research

Throughout the book, we have discussed the question of what is the role and place of theory in qualitative research. Although theory and theoretical concepts are key issues in most qualitative research in one way or another, differences in the specific ways of using and defining theory illustrate once more the differing, and even controversial, nature of various qualitative research approaches.

In case study research, for instance, some researchers prefer to study 'the case' with sophisticated predefined theoretical frameworks or models and search for supporting evidence for these. Other researchers prefer to explore 'the case' without a predefined theoretical framework, concentrating on how the actors of that case understand it. Thereafter, they seek to understand their view of the case by contrasting this with a variety of theoretical concepts and ideas. Consequently, the outcomes of these two research strategies most probably differ considerably. Similar examples can be found in each of the method approaches presented in this book. The same method used in different studies can result in different outcomes, as method does not require similarity in the research design. The research setting and research question, embedded in research design, are crucial for the overall design of the study and the outcome of it.

CIRCULARITY OF THE RESEARCH PROCESS

We have argued throughout the book that whatever theoretical or methodological position you may have, the key to success in your research project is not only dependent on the method and how you use it. What will guarantee good results is your insightfulness, sensitivity and ability to formulate and reformulate your research questions, and to refine the methodological and theoretical frameworks of your study throughout the research process.

The reformulation of research questions does not take place only once, at the beginning of your research, but most often several times during the whole research process. In a similar way, you may need to readjust and rewrite your theoretical and methodological positioning during the research process.

The circularity of the research process takes place in most successful qualitative research processes, and also in business research. Although doing qualitative business research is exciting and inspiring, it takes a lot of hard work. Besides the work that you need to put in when designing, performing and reformulating the different phases of your study, you also need to justify your decisions concerning the choice of methodologies and methods. An acceptable justification always draws on academic convention, but it should also be strongly based on the purpose, objectives and research questions of your own study.

The interconnected nature of data and analysis

In most business research methods books, data collection and data analysis are presented and discussed separately. A good question is how do we make a difference between the data collection and the data analysis? In qualitative research, the distinction between data collection and data analysis is not at all clear-cut, but these two are intertwined and closely related to each other. In practice, the researcher, while being in the process of gathering data, as in doing the interviews, quite often already starts to create and develop categories, and begins to organize and classify interview material, etc. This often happens even before all the intended and planned data for the research are gathered. The need to understand and analyze the issues taking place in the researched case or materials makes the processes of data gathering and analyzing closely related.

This merging of data collection and analysis becomes a whole that begins in the data-gathering stage and does not end until the writing is complete. While this might be the practice, it is also important to understand the detailed, systematic and organized ways for data analysis in different approaches. Equally important is to remember that the qualitative research process differs from the quantitative research process specifically in the research procedure and the ways the empirical data and knowledge are related to the theoretical knowledge.

Using methods to perform analysis

It is typical of qualitative research that methods are considered both as practical tools, that is, that they are techniques for performing the analysis, and as frameworks for engaging with the analysis of data. Even if we can disentangle the data collection and analysis from each other, they are always closely related.

There are many ways to proceed when analyzing qualitative data in business research. Despite the vast growth in the use of qualitative methods in business studies, there is still relatively little information about how to conduct qualitative data analysis in a detailed manner. Our book aims to provide help in terms of which methods to choose, based on what criteria the different methods should be chosen, and how to proceed after the method of analysis has been chosen.

Each chapter of the book gives you an overview both of the ideas and possibilities of the method in question and sheds light on the techniques and representational styles of the method. For some methods, historical and theory development are given in order to make the method and its roots known to business students.

COMBINING QUALITATIVE AND QUANTITATIVE RESEARCH

Many methods books give advice on how to combine qualitative and quantitative research in the same study (e.g. Tashakkori and Teddlie, 2010; Creswell, 2014). This is often useful and sometimes necessary. However, because of the differing philosophical origins, combining qualitative and quantitative research is far more challenging than performing either one of them separately. This is why we suggest it is better first to learn and perform them separately, and only thereafter try to combine them in the same study. Although combining qualitative and quantitative research can produce good-quality research with novel perspectives, we do not recommend that a novice business researcher take such a road during the very first research project. However, if you have more experience in doing empirical research, then you can also benefit from the advantages of combining qualitative and quantitative research. Qualitative research can provide more detailed insight and develop new aspects for quantitative research, and vice versa. Quantitative research can provide a general overview and grounded information on the relationship between various issues of matters that you can then explore in more detail with qualitative research. However, you still need to be aware of the differences in the logic of different methodologies, their requirements and restrictions, and also of the problems of trying to combine them.

LEARNING CONTINUES...

Learning to use a variety of research methods is a life-long challenge for every researcher. In this book, we have not been able to explore the full range of all qualitative research approaches that are available to you. Instead, we have concentrated on those that, according to our experiences as teachers and researchers, have a good potential in producing innovative and interesting business research. Compared to the first edition of our book, we have added one more wide approach of qualitative research into Part IV, the visual research approach, which has increasingly drawn the attention of business researchers during the past decades.

Considering the approaches and methods that we describe in our text, this book can only help you to get started with your learning process, and you will need to consult more research literature on specific methods after you have chosen the approaches and methods that you prefer to use. Finally, we hope that you have enjoyed learning about the various approaches of qualitative business research that we have discussed and that our book has inspired you to try out some of these in your own research project.

GLOSSARY

Abduction, abductive   Concept partly developed by Charles Sanders Peirce (1839–1941), who defined it as a process of forming an explanatory hypothesis. In social sciences the concept means the logic of reasoning: abductive reasoning starts from facts (examination of data), and then comes forward – through several plausible explanations or interpretations – to a most plausible one.

Action research   The variety of labels used, such as action inquiry, participatory inquiry, participatory action research, refer to the aims of change, improvement and involvement through research. The process is both educative and empowering. Methods used in action research vary from observations to interviews, action experiments and participant-written cases and narratives. See Chapter 13.

Analysis of narratives   The researcher collects stories that are told by people and uses various techniques to analyze their plots, narrative structures, or story types. The focus is on narrative as a form of representation. See Chapter 16.

Anonymity   Keeping the identity of the participant hidden. Anonymity is the most usual way to treat informants in social science research. Different variations in the degree of anonymity exist.

Autoethnography   A form of writing that unites ethnographic and autobiographical materials, and aims at keeping the author present in the text. Relates the life experiences, viewpoints and beliefs of the author to the issues studied.

Axial coding   Method of coding data in grounded theory that identifies incidents that are related to each other. Brings the data back together after the initial line-by-line coding. See Chapter 15.

Biographical research   Also known as life-history method. A focus on individual's experiences. Materials can be obtained from interviews and individual (naturalistic) documents such as letters, diaries, personal documentation. The key idea in the biographical method or life-history method is that an individual's subjective experience is best understood through personally produced documents.

CAQDAS Computer-assisted qualitative data analysis software. Software planned and used for qualitative research, especially for coding and analyzing textual data. See Chapter 9.

Case study A mostly qualitative research approach which studies one or several cases (people, organizations, processes) holistically and in their social, economic and cultural contexts. In business research, there are key differences between extensive and intensive case studies. See Chapter 11.

Code, coding Organizing and categorizing qualitative data by labelling a piece of text with symbols, descriptive words or category names. A researcher can use ready-made coding schemes based on theory or they can develop a coding scheme of their own. Coding that proceeds in stages is a key phase in grounded theory research. See Chapters 10 and 15.

Concept Bearer of meanings, abstract ideas. Concepts relate to each other and form theories.

Confidentiality The principle that participant information and data in research are kept secret and not revealed without their owner's consent.

Conformability This is one of the four ways to add trustworthiness to qualitative research; it is about linking findings and interpretations to the data in ways that can be easily understood by others. See Chapter 22.

Constant comparison, constant comparative method Exploration of similarities and differences across incidents in the data. See Chapter 15.

Constructionism Broad theoretical framework that sees the world and what we know of it, such as facts, descriptions, etc., to be constructed through various discourses and contingent rhetoric. Language is seen as a set of social practices that constructs reality. There are different forms and traditions in constructionist thinking that differ in their views of reality.

Constructivism Focuses on the individual; concerns how individuals construct and make sense of their world.

Content analysis One form of textual analysis. Content analysis is used for comparing and contrasting text (speech, documents, cultural artefacts, films, advertisements, etc.) to test hypotheses. Qualitative content analysis, or ethnographic content analysis, is less used in business research in comparison with quantitative content analysis (advertisement and media research, etc.). See Chapter 10.

Context   The interrelated conditions in which something exists or occurs. The term has different meanings in various qualitative approaches. In case studies, for instance, the context includes the circumstances and conditions (e.g. economic, political, social, historical and institutional) that surround the event, process or person that we have defined as 'the case'. In discourse analysis, context refers to the parts of a discourse that surround a word or passage and produce its meaning.

Conversation analysis   Specific form of textual analysis. The analysis focuses on the structures of talk, in order to find out how social interaction is produced by the speakers. Conversation analysis requires detailed analysis of precise transcripts of the speech acts. In conversation analysis, as in most textual analyses, language has a central and active role.

Credibility   Relates to the ways of showing that the work is trustworthy: logical links between observations and categories that others can, on the basis of the claims, come to relatively similar interpretations or agree with the claims. See Chapter 22.

Critical incident analysis (and critical incident method)   A research technique for structured interviews. The critical incident method involves asking respondents to describe critical incidents that are related or connected to the issues that are important to the interviewed person, organization or any other field of activity in the focus of research. The critical incident method can be employed both in qualitative and in quantitative research.

Critical realism   Based on realist epistemology, emphasizes the structures of the social world and is concerned with the identification of these structures. See Chapter 18.

Critical research   Generic term that is used to mark research that challenges mainstream knowledge claims. A theoretically and methodologically diverse field and most often has theoretical, political and ideological underpinnings. See Chapter 18.

Critical theory   Complex and multi-disciplinary theory that seeks to explain and analyze the ways in which existing consciousness perpetuates existing societies. Relates to the Frankfurt School and its main philosophers: Horkheimer (1895–1973), Adorno (1903–1969), Marcuse (1898–1979), and contemporaries like Jürgen Habermas. See Chapter 18.

Cross-case analysis   Comparison of cases with the aim of finding similarities and differences between them. See Chapter 11.

Deduction, deductive   Form of reasoning in which conclusions are formulated about particulars from general or universal premises.

Dependability Relates to the ways of showing that the work is trustworthy; process of research showing it has been logical, traceable and documented. See Chapter 22.

Digital data, digital research Also called e-research and online research. Refers to data and research activities that rely on communication that is mediated through digital technologies. See Chapter 9.

Discourse A system of meaning that enables interpreting and understanding a particular object, or set of objects.

Discourse analysis Refers to both theory and method. As theory: a theory of language and communication and of knowledge construction through and with the help of language. As method: discourse analysis consists of a broad field of methods with specific procedures and belongs to the textual analysis; it can also be called an interdisciplinary approach used in many approaches, ranging from conversation analysis and ethnomethodology to post-structuralism. See Chapter 17.

Electronic research See digital data, digital research.

Emic Indigenous or internal account of the language or social situation under study. In empirical research, often refers to local language, concepts and expressions used by the participants of the study in describing their understandings, points of view and experiences. See Chapter 12.

Empiricism Refers to the idea that knowledge of the world is gained through experience and senses; in social sciences, emphasizes empirical hypothesis testing. One form of positivism, subject to critique from interpretivism. In qualitative methodology, grounded theory uses observations in systematic theory building and, thus, partly leans on empiricism.

Epistemology, epistemological The study of the nature and limits of knowledge and justification. Varieties of epistemologies close to qualitative research range from empiricism and constructionism to feminist epistemologies. See Chapter 2.

Ethnography A form of qualitative research focused on describing the culture of a group of people; the discovery and comprehensive description of the culture of a group of people; it's a form of qualitative research focused on describing the culture of a group of people. See Chapter 12.

Etic External account of the language or social situation under study. In empirical research, refers to the use of theoretical and other concepts chosen by the researcher when analyzing and understanding the issues under study. See Chapter 12.

Extensive case study Several cases are studied, and most often compared with each other, to produce an analytically generalizable idea about how an issue related to them can be understood and explained. See Chapter 11.

Facilitation Helping a group of people come to conclusions, done by a facilitator. In group discussions (e.g. focus groups), this role is called a moderator. See Chapter 14.

Feminist research An approach that gathers together a wide range of ideas, where the main emphasis is on gender bias and the gendered nature of research, concepts, theories and science structures, ranging from traditional epistemology to empirical research. See Chapter 19.

Field study, field research Generic term of all forms of social science research where direct, first-hand observation and data gathering take place in naturally occurring situations. Critique is directed, first, towards the idea of naturalistic fieldwork or data gathering in places that are displaced from familiar settings, and second, towards the idea of 'field as entity, or single site', where some phenomena occur in their natural settings. Critique against 'field approach' in qualitative research points out the various ways that the ideas of 'field' have changed: field is no longer a naturally occurring location or one single entity.

Fieldwork Descriptive term for the collection of various types of data, particularly in ethnographic research. Often requires living or working among a group of people for the purpose of learning about their culture through observation. Observation data are typically written down as field notes. See Chapter 12.

Focus group A method of collecting qualitative data through discussion and interaction. A group of individuals is drawn together by a researcher, or a moderator, to discuss their personal experiences or viewpoints on a particular topic or issue. See Chapter 14.

Framework A basic conceptual structure for the research. Framework usually consists of sets of assumptions, concepts, values, and practices that constitute a way of viewing reality and/or the research focus in research.

Generalization A broad statement or belief based on a limited number of facts, examples, or statistics. For instance, theories are generalizations, which imply that an idea has general application.

Grounded theory A qualitative approach, often used in a non-specific way, referring to any approach which tries to develop theoretical ideas from the data. See Chapter 15.

Hermeneutics   Theory and method of interpreting meaningful human action, and emphasizes the need to understand the activities and actions from the perspective of the agency.

Holism, holistic   The idea that social life cannot be reduced to the activities of individuals, thus opposing methodological individualism. According to holism, any social activity must be analyzed at the level of social 'wholes' (school classes, groups, etc.), not at the individual level. Sometimes used, slightly mistakenly, as a synonym for contextualism. Foucault's archaeology is often given as an example of a holistic approach.

Induction, inductive   Reasoning from the observed cases is widened to general claims about the issue under inspection. Induction runs from particular to the general, for example, from empirical materials to theory.

Inductive analysis   Often related to qualitative analysis; typically, qualitative analysis combines both inductive and deductive logics in the analysis.

Informed consent   Key principle in social research; agreeing or disagreeing to participate in a study after being informed of its purpose, procedures, risks, benefits, alternative procedures, and limits of confidentiality. See Chapter 6.

Intensive case study   One or few cases are studied holistically and intensively in their proper contexts. The purpose is to produce a thick description or a narrative description that provides an understanding of the unique nature and workings of the case. See Chapter 11.

Language   A central concept for qualitative research. According to the radical version, language shapes what we see and how we see it, and the things shaped by language constitute the reality that we study. In moderate version, language and interpretations mediate reality and our awareness of it.

Member check   Also called member or respondent validation; allowing the participants of the study to give feedback on the analysis, findings and conclusions of the study.

Method   A theoretically informed way, or technique, for collecting and analyzing empirical data.

Methodology   A set of theories of how research proceeds. Methodology includes the methods, procedures, and techniques that are used to collect and analyze empirical data.

Narrative analysis   The researcher organizes and interprets empirical data describing events, happenings and actions, and constructs a narrative that they will interpret and discuss as part of their research. The focus is on narrative as a mode of analysis. See Chapter 16.

Narrative research   The study (and the construction) of narratives or stories, which are meaningful to people in one way or another. See Chapter 16.

Objectivism   Multiple meanings, most often thought of in the sense of ontological realism, that there is an independently existing world of objective reality which can be discovered through research.

Objectivity   Often understood in two ways, either referring to the process of research, where uniform consensus can be met through a set of procedures, or referring to impartiality and absence of self-interest.

Observation   A method of collecting data by human, mechanical, or electronic means. The researcher may or may not have contact or communication with the people whose actions are being recorded. See Chapters 7, 8 and 12.

Online research   See digital data, digital research.

Ontology, ontological   Relates to the existence of knowledge about the world. It deals with the ideas research has about the existence of and relationship between people, society and the world in general. Ontological assumptions embrace all theories and methodological positions. See Chapter 2.

Paradigm   Conceptual framework of beliefs within which scientific theories are constructed and within which scientific practices take place. In social sciences, paradigm often refers to general perspective. Kuhn (1922–1996) used the word in two meanings in his book *The Structure of Scientific Revolutions* (1962). First referring to cognitive framework within one field, such as radio astronomers, and second referring to a cross-disciplinary matrix of beliefs, values and methods. The term is often used in a loose way. See Chapter 2.

Participatory action research   One modification of action research. Changing the situation or environment of the researched context is seen as important; researchers actively involved in changing the world. See Chapter 13.

Phenomenology   Philosophy developed by E. Husserl (1859–1938). Influential in the birth of social constructionism. Has influenced the form of qualitative research in which the researcher attempts to understand how one or more individuals experience a phenomenon through 'reductions'.

Positivism   Methodological and philosophical approach that basically assumes a world that exists independent of our ways of getting to know it, and the only legitimate way of acquiring knowledge of it is through empirical research. Several versions of positivism exist.

Postempiricism   Argues that evidence is not necessarily needed for judging the truth or falsity of claims, as data are seen as not detachable from theory and meanings are seen as closely related to facts.

Postmodernism   An approach that stresses the uncertainty of knowledge and organization, the multiple ways of seeing the world and the disintegration of an authentic individual self in acquiring knowledge of it. See also post-structuralism and postpositivism.

Postpositivism   Used often in two meanings. Referring to 'non-positivism', any other way of acquiring knowledge of the world other than positivist or logical positivist way. In a more strict sense, postpositivism also refers to logical empiricism, and a synonym for postempiricism.

Post-structuralism   A loose collection of theoretical positions, which developed from structuralist theories of language.

Realism, realist   An ontological position, which assumes that the world has a nature which is knowable irrespective of the knowing subject. The world may be either empirical reality or reality that is beyond our knowledge, depending on the ontological assumptions.

Reflexivity   In opposition to the idea of the objectivity and neutrality of knowledge, qualitative research proposes the idea of reflexivity. In qualitative research, reflexivity refers to the researcher's continuous and systematic attention to the process and context of knowledge construction. Paying attention to how the researcher's background and position affect, for instance, what they choose to study and from which perspective, what methods they judge adequate, what findings they consider appropriate, and how they frame and communicate the conclusions of their study.

Relativism   An ontological position, where reality is determined by the language or concepts. Relativism challenges the idea that universal claims about the world can be made or universal entities exist.

Reliability   The extent to which a measure, procedure, or instrument yields a consistent result on repeated trials. See Chapter 22.

Replication logic   The idea that the more times a research finding is shown to be true with different sets of people, the more confidence we can place in the finding and in generalizing beyond the original participants. See Chapter 11.

Selective coding   Relates to the theory building method in grounded theory that aims to choose one category to be the core category, and relating all other categories to that category. See Chapter 15.

Semiotics   Analysis of signs and approach where hidden or culturally laden meanings are to be analyzed.

Sensitizing concepts   Concepts, ideas and questions that serve as the starting point for data collection and analysis, particularly in inductive qualitative research. They inform a researcher where to look and what to look for, as well as give some idea of what they can expect to find. Sensitizing concepts often evolve during the research project. See Chapter 11.

Thematic analysis   A form of analysis which has the theme or category as its unit of analysis, and which looks across data from many different sources to identify themes (it is similar in this way to content analysis). See Chapter 10.

Theory   An explanation or an explanatory system that discusses how a phenomenon operates and why it operates as it does; a generalization or set of generalizations used systematically to explain some phenomenon.

Thick description   The precise definition of thick description of data is related to the ways through which information of the research object is being produced. Thick description was introduced by Clifford Geertz (1973). Most often in qualitative research, thick descriptions are the rich, detailed accounts of the culture, its social settings, events and individuals. These create the contextual setting for the interpretation, and help readers to understand the interpretations made.

Transcription   Transforming speech (e.g. interviews) into typewritten text. The accuracy of transcription varies according to the purpose for which the typewritten text is used.

Transferability   Relates to the ways of showing that the work is trustworthy: shows a degree of similarity between different pieces of research. Establishes some form of connection between the research and previous results. See Chapter 22.

Triangulation   Triangulation can be defined as a procedure that is used for validation of the research results. The original concept of triangulation was defined by Webb et al. (1966) to achieve greater confidence in research findings. The original use of triangulation is based on the idea that there are different types of data that can confirm the research results. Triangulation is currently used to refer to the uses of multiple observers, theoretical perspectives, sources of data, and methodologies. See Chapter 22.

Trustworthiness criteria Four criteria to be used as equivalents for conventional criteria of validity and reliability in qualitative research. Credibility, transferability, dependability and confirmability are discussed in Chapter 22.

Validity The degree to which a study reflects or assesses the specific concept that the researcher is attempting to measure. See Chapter 22.

Visual data, visual analysis Visual data and analysis is based on pictures, hypermedia, videos, motion pictures, www-pictures, pictures and paintings available on the Internet, books, advertisements, CD-ROMs, etc. See Chapter 20.

REFERENCES

Aaltio, I. and Kovalainen, A. (2003) 'Using gender in exploring organizations, management and change'. In B. Czarniawska and G. Sevón (eds), *Northern Lights. Nordic Organization Theory Book*. Stockholm: Liber. pp. 175–201.

Aaltio-Marjosola, I. and Kovalainen, A. (2001) 'Personality'. In E. Wilson (ed.), *Organisational Behaviour Reassessed. The Impact of Gender*. London: SAGE. pp. 17–36.

Abrams, B. (2001) *Observational Research Handbook: Understanding How Consumers Live with Your Product*. Illinois: NTC Business Books.

Acker, J. (1990) 'Hierarchies, jobs and bodies: a theory of gendered organizations'. *Gender and Society*, 4(2): 139–58.

Acker, J. (1992) 'Gendering organizational theory'. In A.J. Mills and P. Tancred (eds), *Gendering Organizational Analysis*. Newbury Park: SAGE. pp. 248–60.

Acker, J. (2000) 'Revisiting class: thinking from gender, race and organizations'. *Social Politics*, 7(2): 192–214.

Ackroyd, S. (2002) *The Organization of Business: Applying Organizational Theory to Contemporary Change*. Oxford: Oxford University Press.

Adams, T.E., Jones, S.H. and Ellis, C. (2014) *Autoethnography*. Oxford: Oxford University Press.

Ahl, H. (2002) *The Making of the Female Entrepreneur: A Discourse Analysis of Research Texts on Women's Entrepreneurship*. Doctoral Dissertation, JIBS Dissertation Series No. 015, Jönköping International Business School.

Ahmed, S. (2000) 'Whose counting?'. *Feminist Theory*, 1(1): 97–104.

Al-Amoudi, I. and Willmott, H. (2011) 'Where constructionism and critical realism converge: interrogating the domain of epistemological relativism'. *Organization Studies*, 32(1): 27–46.

Alsop, R., Fitzsimons, A. and Lennon, K. (2002) *Theorizing Gender*. Cambridge: Polity Press.

Alvesson, M. and Deetz, S. (2000) *Doing Critical Management Research*. London: SAGE.

Alvesson, M. and Kärreman, D. (2000) 'Varieties of discourse: on the study of organizations through discourse analysis'. *Human Relations*, 53(9): 1125–49.

Alvesson, M. and Kärreman, D. (2011) 'Organizational discourse analysis – well done or too rare? A reply to our critics'. *Human Relations*, 64(9): 1193–202.

Alvesson, M. and Willmott, H. (2003) Introduction. In M. Alvesson, and H. Willmott (eds), *Studying Management Critically*. London: SAGE.

Alvesson, M., Bridgman, T. and Willmott, H. (2009) 'Introduction'. In M. Alvesson, T. Bridgman and H. Willmott (eds), *The Oxford Handbook of Critical Management Studies*. Oxford: Oxford University Press.

Alvesson, M., Hardy, C. and Harley, B. (2008) 'Reflecting on reflexivity: reflexive textual practices in organization and management theory'. *Journal of Management Studies*, 45(3): 480–501.

American Psychological Association (2010) Ethical Principles for Psychologists and Code of Conduct. APA: Washington. www.apa.org/ethics/homepage.html

American Sociological Association (2008) Code of Ethics. Washington: ASA. www.asanet.org/page.ww?section=Ethics&name=Ethics

Antaki, C., Billig, M., Edwards, D. and Potter, J. (2003) 'Discourse analysis means doing analysis: a critique of six analytic shortcomings'. *Discourse Analysis Online*, 1(1). http://extra.shu.ac.uk/daol/articles/v1/n1/a1/antaki2002002-t.html

Arnould, E.J. (1998) 'Ethical Concerns in Participant Observation/Ethnography'. In Joseph W. Alba & J. Wesley Hutchinson (eds), NA – Advances in Consumer Research Vol. 25. Provo, UT: Association for Consumer Research, pp. 72–4.

Arnould, E. and Wallendorf, M. (1994) 'Market-oriented ethnography: interpretation building and marketing strategy formulation'. *Journal of Marketing Research*, 31(4): 484–504.

Atkinson, P. and Coffey, A. (1997) 'Analysing documentary realities'. In D. Silverman (ed.), *Qualitative Research. Theory, Method and Practice*. London: SAGE.

Atkinson, P., Coffey, A., Delamont, S., Lofland, J. and Lofland, L. (eds) (2007) *Handbook of Ethnography*. London: SAGE.

Bal, M. (2009) *Narratology: Introduction to the Theory of Narrative*. Toronto: University of Toronto Press.

Banks, M. (2001) *Visual Methods in Social Research*. Thousand Oaks, CA: SAGE.

Bansal, P., Bertels, S., Ewart, T., MacConnachie, P. and O'Brien, J. (2012) 'Bridging the research–practice gap'. *The Academy of Management Perspectives*, 26(1): 73–92.

Barbour, R. (2008) *Doing Focus Groups*. London: SAGE.

Bartunek, J.M. and Rynes, S.L. (2014) 'Academics and practitioners are alike and unlike the paradoxes of academic–practitioner relationships'. *Journal of Management*, 40(5): 1181–201.

Bazeley, P. and Jackson, K. (eds) (2013) *Qualitative Data Analysis with NVivo*. London: SAGE.

Belk, R., Fischer, E. and Kozinets, R.V. (2013) *Qualitative Consumer and Marketing Research*. London: SAGE.

Bell, P. (2001) 'Content analysis of visual images'. In T. van Leeuwen and C. Jewitt, (eds), *Handbook of Visual Analysis*. London: SAGE.

Belova, O. (2006) 'Speaking for themselves? Problematising the production of meaning in visual artefacts'. *Culture and Organization*, 12(1): 37–49.

Berger, P. and Luckmann, T. (1967) *The Social Construction of Reality*. New York, NY: Anchor.

Bessant, K.C. (2012) 'The interactional community: emergent fields of collective agency'. *Sociological Inquiry*, 82(4): 628–45.

Bhaskar, R. (1997) *A Realist Theory of Science*. London: Verso.

Billig, M., Condor, S., Edwards, D., Gane, M., Middleton, D. and Radley, A. (1988) *Ideological Dilemmas: A Social Psychology of Everyday Thinking*. London: SAGE.

Black, I. and Tagg, S. (2007) 'A grounded theory of doctors' information search behaviour: implications for information provision, pharmaceutical market entry and development'. *Journal of Marketing Management*, 23(3–4, April): 347–66.

Blackburn, R. and Kovalainen, A. (2009) Researching Small Firms: Past, present, future trends. *International Journal of Management Reviews*. 11(2): 127–48.

Blaikie, N. (1993) *Approaches to Social Enquiry*. Cambridge: Polity Press.

Bloor, M. (1997) 'Techniques of validation in qualitative research: a critical commentary'. In G. Miller and R. Dingwall (eds), *Context and Method in Qualitative Research*. London: SAGE. pp. 37–50.

Blumer, H. (1969) *Symbolic Interactionism: Perspective and Method*. Englewood Cliffs, NJ: Prentice-Hall.

Boje, D.M. (1991) 'Organizations as storytelling networks: a study of story performance in an office-supply firm'. *Administrative Science Quarterly*, 36(1): 106–26.

Boje, D.M. (2001) *Narrative Methods for Organizational and Communication Research*. London: SAGE.

Bold, C. (2011) *Using Narrative in Research*. London: SAGE.

Bøllingtoft, A. (2012) 'The bottom-up business incubator: leverage to networking and cooperation practices in a self-generated, entrepreneurial-enabled environment'. *Technovation*, 32(5): 304–15.

Bradford, T.W. and Sherry, J.F., Jr (2013) 'Orchestrating rituals through retailers: an examination of gift registry'. *Journal of Retailing*, 89(2): 158–75.

Braidotti, R. (1991) *Patterns of Dissonance. A Study of Women in Contemporary Philosophy*. Oxford: Polity Press.

Brewer, J.D. (2000) *Ethnography*. Buckingham: Open University Press.

Brewerton, P. and Millward, L. (2009) *Organizational Research Methods*. London: SAGE.

Brinkmann, S. and Kvale, S. (2014) *InterViews. Learning the Craft of Qualitative Research Interviewing*. London: SAGE.

Bristor, J.M. and Fischer, E. (1993) 'Feminist thought: implications for consumer research'. *Journal of Consumer Research*, 19(March): 518–36.

Brown, A. and Coupland, C. (2005) 'Sounds of silence: graduate trainees, hegemony and resistance'. *Organization Studies*, 26(7): 1049–69.

Brown, C., Costley, C.L. and Varey, R. (2010) 'Capturing their dream: video diaries and minority consumers'. *Consumption, Markets and Culture*, 13(4): 419–36.

Brown, J.S. and Duguid, P. (1991) 'Organizational learning and communities-of-practice: toward a unified view of working, learning, and innovation'. *Organization Science*, 2(1): 40–57.

Brown, J.S., Denning, S., Groh, K. and Prusak, L. (2005) *Storytelling in Organizations: Why Storytelling Is Transforming 21st Century Organizations and Management*. Burlington, MA: Elsevier Butterworth-Heinemann.

Brown, S.L. and Eisenhardt, K.M. (1997) 'The art of continuous change: linking complexity theory and time-paced evolution in relentlessly shifting organizations'. *Administrative Science Quarterly*, 42: 1–34.

Bruner, J. (1986) *Actual Minds, Possible Worlds*. Cambridge, MA: Harvard University Press.

Bruni, A., Gherardi, S. and Poggio, B. (2004) 'Doing gender, doing entrepreneurship: an ethnographic account of intertwined practices'. *Gender, Work and Organization*, 11(4): 406–29.

Bryer, A.R. (2014) 'Participation in budgeting: a critical anthropological approach'. *Accounting, Organizations and Society*, 39(7): 511–30.

Bryman, A. (ed.) (2013) *Doing Research in Organizations*. London: Routledge.

Bryman, A. and Burgess, R.G. (1995) *Analyzing Qualitative Data*. London: Routledge.

Burnes, B. and Cooke, B. (2012) 'Review article: the past, present and future of organization development: taking the long view'. *Human Relations*, 65(11): 1395–429.

Burr, V. (1995) *An Introduction to Social Constructionism*. London: Routledge.

Burrell, G. (1988) 'Modernism, post modernism and organizational analysis 2: the contribution of Michel Foucault'. *Organization Studies*, 9(2): 221–35.

Burrell, G. and Morgan, G. (1979) *Sociological Paradigms and Organizational Analysis*. London: Heinemann.

Burton, D. (2001) 'Critical marketing theory: the blueprint?' *European Journal of Marketing*, 35(5–6): 722–46.

Butler, J. (1990) *Gender Trouble: Feminism and the Subversion of Identity*. New York and London: Routledge.

Calás, M.B. and Smircich, L. (1996) 'From "the woman's" point of view: feminist approaches to organization studies'. In S. Clegg, C. Hardy and W. Nord (eds), *Handbook of Organisation Studies*. London: SAGE.

Calhoun, C. (1996) *Critical Social Theory*. Oxford: Blackwell.

Carabine, J. (2001) 'Unmarried motherhood 1830–1990: a genealogical analysis'. In M. Wetherell, S. Taylor and S. Yates (eds), *Discourse as Data: A Guide for Analysts*. London: SAGE. pp. 267–310.

Carey, M.A. and Asbury, J.E. (2012) *Focus Group Research*. Left Coast Press.

Castagno, A.E. (2012) 'What makes critical ethnography "critical"'. In S.L. Lapan, M.T. Quartaroli and F.J. Riemer (eds), *Qualitative Research: An Introduction to Methods and Designs*. San Francisco, CA: Jossey-Bass. pp. 373–90.

Catterall, M., Maclaran, P. and Stevens, L. (1997) 'Marketing and feminism: a bibliography and suggestions for further research'. *Marketing Intelligence & Planning*, 15(7): 369–76.

Charmaz, K. (1990) 'Discovering chronic illness: using grounded theory'. *Social Science and Medicine*, 30(11): 1161–72.

Charmaz, K. (2000) 'Constructivist and objectivist grounded theory'. In N.K. Denzin and Y.S. Lincoln (eds), *Handbook of Qualitative Research*. Thousand Oaks, CA: SAGE. pp. 509–35.

Charmaz, K. (2003) 'Grounded theory'. In M. Lewis-Beck, A. Bryman, and T. Liao (eds), *The SAGE Encyclopedia of Social Science Research Methods*. Thousand Oaks, CA: SAGE. pp. 440–4.

Charmaz, K. (2005) 'Grounded theory in the 21st century: applications for advancing social justice studies'. In N.K. Denzin and Y.S. Lincoln (eds), *Handbook of Qualitative Research*. Thousand Oaks, CA: SAGE. pp. 507–35.

Charmaz, K. (2006) *Constructing Grounded Theory. A Practical Guide Through Qualitative Analysis*. London: SAGE.

Charmaz, K. (2014) *Constructing Grounded Theory*, 2nd edn. London: SAGE.

Chenail, R. (1995) *Presenting Qualitative Data. The Qualitative Report*, 2(3). http://www.nova.edu/ssss/QR/QR2–3/presenting.html

Chia, R. and King, I. (2002) 'The language of organization theory'. In R. Westwood and S. Linstead (eds), *The Language of Organization*. London: SAGE.

Chinn, S. (2010) 'From identity politics to queer theory'. In M. Wetherell and C. Talpade Mohanty (eds), *The SAGE Handbook of Identities*. London: SAGE.

Claes, R. and Heymans, M. (2008) 'HR professionals' views on work motivation and retention of older workers: a focus group study'. *Career Development International*, 13(2): 95–111.

Clandinin, J. and Connelly, M. (2000) *Narrative Inquiry: Experience and Story in Qualitative Research*. San Francisco, CA: Jossey Bass.

Clegg, S. (1994) 'Power relations and the constitution of the resistant subject'. In J. Jermier, W. Nord and D. Knights (eds), *Resistance and Power in Organizations*. London: Routledge.

Clegg, S.R. and Rhodes, C. (2006) 'Introduction'. In S.R. Clegg and C. Rhodes (eds), *Management Ethics: Contemporary Contexts*. Abingdon, Oxon: Routledge.

Coffey, A. and Atkinson, P. (1996) *Making Sense of Qualitative Data*. London: SAGE.

Coghlan, D. and Brannick, T. (2001) *Doing Action Research in Your Own Organization*. London: SAGE.

Coghlan, D., Shani, R., Roth, J. and Sloyan, R.M. (2014) 'Executive development through insider action research: voices of insider action researchers'. *Journal of Management Development*, 33(10): 991–1003.

Cole, S.A. (2009) 'A cautionary tale about cautionary tales about intervention'. *Organization*, 16(1): 121–41.

Collier, M. (2001) 'Approaches to analysis in visual anthropology'. In T. van Leeuwen and C. Jewitt (eds), *Handbook of Visual Analysis*. London: SAGE.

Collins, J. and Hussey, R. (2003) *Business Research. A Practical Guide for Undergraduate and Postgraduate Students*. New York: Palgrave Macmillan.

Contu, A. and Willmott, H. (2005) 'You spin me round: the realist turn in organization and management studies'. *Journal of Management Studies*, 42(8): 1645–62.

Corbin, J. and Strauss, A. (1990) 'Grounded theory research: procedures, canons and evaluative criteria'. *Qualitative Sociology*, 13(1): 3–21.

Cortazzi, M. (2014) *Narrative Analysis*. London: Routledge.

Coughlan, P. and Coghlan, D. (2002) 'Action research for operations management'. *International Journal of Operations & Production Management*, 22(2): 220–40.

Creswell, J.W. (2012) *Qualitative Inquiry and Research Design*, 3rd edn. Thousand Oaks, CA: SAGE.

Creswell, J. (2014) *Research Design. Qualitative, Quantitative and Mixed Methods Approaches*. London: SAGE.

Croghan, R., Griffin, C., Hunter, J. and Phoenix, A. (2008) Young people's constructions of self: notes on the use and analysis of the photo-elicitation method. *International Journal of Social Research Methodology*, 11(1): 1–12.

Curtis, R. (2014) 'Foucault beyond Fairclough: from transcendental to immanent critique in organization studies'. *Organization Studies*, 35(12): 1–12.

Czarniawska, B. (1997) *Narrating the Organization. Dramas of Institutional Identity*. Chicago: The University of Chicago Press.

Czarniawska, B. (1998) *A Narrative Approach in Organization Studies*. Thousand Oaks, CA: SAGE.

Czarniawska, B. (1999) *Writing Management. Organization Theory as a Literary Genre*. Oxford: Oxford University Press.

Czarniawska, B. (2004) *Narratives in Social Science Research*. London: SAGE.

Czarniawska-Joerges, B. (1988) *Ideological Control in Nonideological Organizations*. New York: Praeger.

Danermark, B., Ekström, M., Jakobsen, L. and Karlsson, J.C. (2002) *Explaining Society. Critical Realism in the Social Sciences*. London: Routledge.

David, M. (ed.) (2006) *Case Study Research* (Four-Volume Set, SAGE Benchmarks in Social Research Methods Series). Thousand Oaks, CA: SAGE.

Davison, J., Steyaert, C., Marti, L. and Michels, C. (2012) 'Multiplicity and reflexivity in organizational research'. *Qualitative Research in Organizations and Management: An International Journal*, 7(1): 34–53.

Dawn Metcalfe, B. and Afanassieva, M. (2005) 'The woman question? Gender and management in the Russian Federation'. *Women in Management Review*, 20(6): 429–45.

Deegan, M. (2007) 'The Chicago School of Ethnography'. In S. Delamont, J. Lofland, L.H. Lofland, A. Coffey and P. Atkinson (eds), *Handbook of Ethnography*. Thousand Oaks: SAGE. pp. 11–25.

Deetz, S. (1992) *Democracy in an Age of Corporate Colonization: Developments in Communication and the Politics of Everyday Life*. Albany, NY: State University of New York.

Delbridge, R. (2014) 'Promising futures: CMS, post-disciplinarity, and the new public social science'. *Journal of Management Studies*, 51(1): 95–117.

Dempster, P.G. and Woods, D.K. (2011) *The Economic Crisis Through the Eyes of Transana*. Forum Qualitative Sozialforschung / Forum: Qualitative Social Research, 12(1), Art. 16, http://nbn-resolving.de/urn:nbn:de:0114-fqs1101169. Retrieved 10.8.2014.

Denning, S. (2001) *Squirrel Inc. A Fable of Leadership Through Storytelling*. Jossey-Bass.

Denning, S. (2004) *The Springboard: How Storytelling Ignites Action in Knowledge Era Organizations*. Boston: Butterworth-Heinemann.

Denzin, N.K. and Lincoln, Y.S. (2005) 'Introduction'. In N.K. Denzin and Y.S. Lincoln (eds), *The SAGE Handbook of Qualitative Research*. London: SAGE. pp. 1–32.

De Rond, M. (2008) *The Last Amateurs. To Hell and Back with the Cambridge Boat Race Crew*. London: Icon Books.

De Rond, M. (2012) *There is an I in Team: What Elite Athletes and Coaches Really Know about High Performance*. Boston: Harvard Business Press.

Derrida, J. (1978) *Writing and Difference*. London: Routledge.

De Vaus, D. (2001) *Research Design in Social Research*. London: SAGE.

DeWalt, K. and DeWalt, B. (2010) *Participant Observation: A Guide for Fieldworkers*. Walnut Creek, CA: Altamira Press.

Dey, I. (1999) *Grounding Grounded Theory: Guidelines for Qualitative Inquiry*. San Diego: Academic Press.

Dolowitz, D., Buckler, S. and Sweeney, F. (2008) *Researching Online*. Palgrave MacMillan.

Duberley, J. and Johnson, P. (2009) 'Critical management methodology'. In M. Alvesson, T. Bridgman and H. Willmott (eds), *The Oxford Handbook of Critical Management Studies*. Oxford: Oxford University Press.

Dubois, A. and Gadde, L.-E. (2002) 'Systematic combining: an abductive approach to case research'. *Journal of Business Research*, 55(7): 553–60.

Dubois, D., Rucker, D.D. and Galinsky, A.D. (2012) Supersize me: product size as a signal of status'. *Journal of Consumer Research*, 38(6): 1047–62.

Dunne, C. (2011) 'The place of the literature review in grounded theory research'. *International Journal of Social Research Methodology*, 14(2): 111–24.

Dyer, W., Jr and Wilkins, A. (1991) 'Better stories, not better constructs, to generate better theory: a rejoinder to Eisenhardt'. *Academy of Management Review*, 16(3): 613–19.

Eagly, A.H., Johannesen-Schmidt, M.C. and van Engen, M.L. (2003) 'Transformational, transactional and Laissez-faire leadership styles: A meta-analysis comparing women and men'. *Psychological Bulletin*, 129(4): 569–91.

Eagly, A.H. and Johnson, B.T. (1990) 'Gender and leadership style: A meta-analysis'. *Psychological Bulletin*, 108(2): 233–56.

Eberle, T.S. and Maeder, C. (2011) 'Organizational ethnography'. In D. Silverman, (ed.), *Qualitative Research*. London: SAGE. pp. 53–73.

Edley, N. (2001) 'Analysing masculinity: interpretative repertoires, ideological dilemmas and subject positions'. In M. Wetherell, S. Taylor and S.J. Yates (eds), *Discourse as Data: A Guide to Analysis*. London: SAGE. pp. 189–228.

Edmunds, H. (2000) *Focus Group Research Handbook*. New York: McGraw Hill.

Eisenhardt, K. (1989) 'Building theories from case study research'. *Academy of Management Review*, 14(4): 532–50.

Eisenhardt, K. (1991) 'Better stories and better constructs: the case for rigor and comparative logic'. *Academy of Management Review*, 16(3): 620–27.

Elharidy, A.M., Nicholson, B. and Scapens, R.W. (2008) 'Using grounded theory in interpretive management accounting research'. *Qualitative Research in Accounting & Management*, 5(2): 139–55.

Elliott, J. (1988) 'Educational research and outsider–insider relations'. *Qualitative Studies in Education*, 1(2): 155–66.

Elliott, J. (2005) *Using Narrative in Social Research. Qualitative and Quantitative Approaches*. London: SAGE.

Elliott, R. and Jankel-Elliot, N. (2003) 'Using ethnography in strategic consumer research'. *Qualitative Market Research. An International Journal*, 6(4): 215–23.

Ellis, C. (2004) *The Ethnographic I: A Methodological Novel About Autoethnography*. Walnut Creek, CA: AltaMira Press.

Ellis, C. (2010) *Final Negotiations: A Story of Love, and Chronic Illness*. 2nd edn. Philadelphia: Temple University Press.

Emerson, R., Fretz, R. and Shaw, L. (2011) *Writing Ethnographic Field Notes*. 2nd edn. Chicago; London: The University of Chicago Press.

Epstein, D., Fahey, J. and Kenway, J. (2013) 'Multi-sited global ethnography and travel: gendered journeys in three registers'. *International Journal of Qualitative Studies in Education*, 26(4): 470–88.

Erickson, F. (2011) 'Uses of video in social research: a brief history'. *International Journal of Social Research Methodology*, 14(3): 179–89.

Eriksson, P., Henttonen, E. and Meriläinen, S. (2008) 'Managerial work and gender – Ethnography of cooperative relationships in small software companies'. *Scandinavian Journal of Management*, 24(4): 354–63.

Eriksson, P., Henttonen, E. and Meriläinen, S. (2012) 'Ethnographic field notes and reflexivity'. In L. Nandoo (ed.), *An Ethnography of Global Landscapes and Corridors*. Intech. pp. 10–22. Open access at the Intech Open website.

Eriksson, P. and Kovalainen, A. (2008) *Qualitative Methods in Business Research*. London: SAGE.

Eriksson, P. and Kovalainen, A. (2010) 'Case study research in business and management'. In A.J. Mills, G. Durepos and E. Wiebe (eds), *Encyclopedia of Case Study Research*. London: SAGE. pp. 93–6.

Eriksson, P. and Rajamäki, Heidi (2010) 'Biotechnology Marketing. Insider and Outsider Views'. *Journal of Commercial Biotechnology*, 16(2): 98–108.

Eriksson, P. and Räsänen, K. (1998/2012) 'The bitter and the sweet: evolving constellations of product mix management in a confectionery company'. *European Journal of Marketing*, 32(3–4): 279–304.

European Parliament (2006) *The Charter of the Fundamental Rights of the European Union*. www.europarl.europa.eu/charter/default_en.htm [21.10.2006].

Evans, P. (2000) 'Boundary oscillations: epistemological and genre transformation during the "method" of thesis writing'. *International Journal of Social Research Methodology*, 3(4): 267–86.

Ewenstein, B. and Whyte, J. (2009) 'Knowledge practices in design: the role of visual representations as "Epistemic Objects"'. *Organization Studies*, 30(1): 7–30.

Fairclough, N. (1989) *Language and Power*. London: Longman.

Fairclough, N. (1992) *Discourse and Social Change*. Cambridge: Polity Press.

Fairclough, N. (2001) *Language and Power*. Harlow: Longman.

Fairclough, N. (2005) 'Discourse analysis in organization studies: the case for critical realism'. *Organization Studies*, 26(6): 915–39.

Fairclough, N. and Wodak, R. (1997) 'Critical discourse analysis'. In T.A. Van Dijk (ed.), *Discourse as Social Interaction*. London: SAGE. pp. 258–84.

Farquhar, J.D. (2012) *Case Study Research for Business*. London: SAGE.

Fay, B. (1987) *Critical Social Science*. Ithaca, NY: Cornell University Press.

Feldman, M., Bell, J. and Berger, M. (2003) *Gaining Access: A Practical and Theoretical Guide for Qualitative Researchers*. Walnut Creek, CA: AltaMira Press.

Felstead, A., Jewson, N. and Walters, S. (2004) 'Images, interviews and interpretations: making connections in visual research'. In C. Pole (ed.), *Seeing is Believing? Approaches to Visual Research*. Oxford: Elsevier Science. pp. 105–21.

Ferber, M. and Nelson, J. (eds) (1993) *Beyond Economic Man: Feminist Theory and Economics*. Chicago: University of Chicago Press.

Fern, E. (2001) *Advanced Focus Group Research*. Thousand Oaks, CA: SAGE.

Fetterman, D. (2010) *Ethnography*, 3rd edn. Thousand Oaks, CA: SAGE.

Fielding, N.G., Lee, R.M. and Blank, G. (eds) (2008) *The SAGE Handbook of Online Research Methods*. London: SAGE.

Fineman, S., Gabriel, Y. and Sims, D. (2005) *Organizing and Organizations*. London: SAGE.

Fischer, E. and Bristor, J. (1994) 'A feminist poststructuralist analysis of marketing relationships'. *International Journal of Research in Marketing*, 11(4): 17–31.

Flanagan, J.C. (1954) 'The critical incident technique'. *Psychological Bulletin*, 50(4): 327–58.

Fleming, P. (2014) 'Review article: when "life itself" goes to work: reviewing shifts in organizational life through the lens of biopower'. *Human Relations*, 67(7 July): 875–901.

Fletcher, L. (2002) '"In the company of men": a reflexive tale of cultural organizing in a small organization'. *Gender, Work and Organization*, 9(4): 398–418.

Flick, U. (2002) *An Introduction to Qualitative Research*. London: SAGE.

Flick, U. (2007) *Designing Qualitative Research*. London: SAGE.

Fontana, A. and Frey, J. (2000) 'The interview: from structured questions to negotiated text'. In N.K. Denzin and Y.S. Lincoln (eds), *Handbook of Qualitative Research*, 2nd edn. London: SAGE.

Foucault, M. (1972) *The Archaeology of Knowledge*. London: Tavistock.

Foucault, M. (1980) 'Two Lectures'. In C. Gordon (ed.), *Power/Knowledge: Selected Interviews*. New York: Pantheon.

Fox-Wolfgramm, S. (1997) 'Towards developing a methodology for doing qualitative research: the dynamic-comparative case study method'. *Scandinavian Journal of Management*, 13(4): 439–55.

Fuchs, C. (2013) *Social Media: A Critical Introduction*. London: SAGE.

Gabriel, Y. (2000) *Storytelling in Organizations: Facts, Fictions, and Fantasies*. London: Oxford University Press.

Gammie, E., Paver, B., Gammie, B. and Duncan, F. (2003) 'Gender differences in accounting education: an undergraduate exploration'. *Accounting Education*, 12(2): 177–96.

Geertz, C. (1973) *The Interpretation of Cultures*. New York: Basic Books.

Gergen, K. (1985) 'The social constructionist movement in modern psychology'. *American Psychologist*, 40(3): 266–75.

Gergen, K. (1992) 'Organization theory in the postmodern era'. In M. Reed and M. Hughes (eds), *Rethinking Organization: New Directions in Organizational Theory and Analysis*. London: SAGE. pp. 207–26.

Gergen, K. (1995) 'Relational theory and the discourse of power'. In D.-M. Hosking, H.P. Dachler and K.J. Gergen (eds), *Management and Organization: Relational Alternatives to Individualism*. Aldershot, UK: Avebury. pp. 29–50.

Gherardi, S. (1995) *Gender, Symbolism and Organizational Cultures*. London: SAGE.

Gibbert, M. (2004) 'Crafting strategy imaginatively: lessons learnt from Siemens'. *European Management Journal*, 22(6): 669–85.

Girod, S. (2005) 'The human resource management practice of retail branding: an ethnography within Oxfam Trading Division'. *International Journal of Retail & Distribution Management*, 33(7): 514–30.

Glaser, B. (1978) *Theoretical Sensitivity*. Mill Valley, CA: Sociology Press.

Glaser, B. (1992) *Basics of Grounded Theory Analysis: Emergence Versus Forcing*. Mill Valley, CA: Sociology Press.

Glaser, B. and Strauss, A. (1967) *The Discovery of Grounded Theory: Strategies for Qualitative Research*. Chicago, IL: Aldine Publishing Co.

Glaser, B.G. (2002) 'Constructivist grounded theory?' *Forum Qualitative Sozial- forschung/Forum: Qualitative Social Research* (online journal), 3(3, September). www. qualitative-research.net/fqs-eng.htm [12.10.2005].

Glesne, C. (2010) *Becoming Qualitative Researchers: An Introduction*, 4th edn. Boston: Pearson.

Goffman, E. (1981) *Forms of Talk*. Oxford: Basil Blackwell.

Goulding, C. (1998) 'Grounded theory: the missing methodology of the interpretivist agenda'. *Qualitative Market Research*, 1(1): 50–7.

Goulding, C. (2000) 'Grounded theory and consumer behavior'. *Advances in Consumer Research*, 27(September): 261–6.

Goulding, C. (2002) *Grounded Theory: A Practical Guide for Management, Business and Market Researchers.* London: SAGE.

Grant, D. and Hardy, C. (2004) 'Struggles with organizational discourse', *Organization Studies*, 25(1): 5–14.

Greenwood, D. and Levin, M. (1998) *Introduction to Action Research.* Thousand Oaks, CA: SAGE.

Greenwood, D. and Levin, M. (2005) 'Reform of the social sciences and of universities through action research'. In N.K. Denzin and Y.S. Lincoln (eds), *The SAGE Handbook of Qualitative Research.* Thousand Oaks, CA: SAGE. pp. 43–65.

Guba, E.G. and Lincoln, Y.S. (1994) *Competing Paradigms in Qualitative Research.* In K. Denzin and Y.S. Lincoln (eds), *Handbook of Qualitative Research.* Thousand Oaks, CA: SAGE. pp. 105–17.

Guba, E. and Lincoln, Y. (2005) 'Paradigmatic controversies, contradictions and emerging confluences'. In N.K. Denzin and Y.S. Lincoln (eds), *The SAGE Handbook of Qualitative Research.* Thousand Oaks, CA: SAGE. pp. 191–216.

Gubrium, J. and Holstein, A. (2001) 'From the individual interview to the interview society'. In J.F. Gubrium and J.A. Holstein (eds), *Handbook of Interview Research: Context and Method.* London: SAGE.

Gummesson, E. (2000) *Qualitative Methods in Management.* Thousand Oaks, CA: SAGE.

Habermas, J. (1977) *Theory and Practice.* London: Heinemann.

Hagan, T.L. and Cohen, S.M. (2014) 'A literary analysis of global female identity, health, and equity'. *Advances in Nursing Science*, 37(3): 235–48.

Hall, S. (1997) *Representation: Cultural Representations and Signifying Practices.* London: SAGE.

Hall, S. (2001) 'Foucault: power, knowledge and discourse'. In M. Wetherell, S. Taylor and S. Yates (eds), (2001) *Discourse Theory and Practice: A Reader.* London: SAGE.

Hamilton, R. and Bowers, B. (2006) 'Internet recruitment and e-mail interviews in qualitative studies'. *Qualitative Health Research*, 16(6): 821–35.

Hammersley, M. (1992) *What's Wrong with Ethnography?* London: Routledge.

Hammersley, M. (2005) 'Should social science be critical?' *Philosophy of Social Sciences*, 35(2): 175–95.

Hammersley, M. and Atkinson, P. (2007) *Ethnography. Principles in Practice*, 3rd edn. London: Routledge.

Hancock, P. and Tyler, M. (2000) '"The look of love": gender and the organization of aesthetics'. In J. Hassard, R. Holliday and H. Willmott (eds), *Body and Organization.* London: SAGE. pp. 108–29.

Haraway, D. (1989) *Primate Visions: Gender, Race, and Nature in the World of Modern Science.* London: Routledge.

Haraway, D. (1991) *Simians, Cyborgs, and Women: The Reinvention of Nature.* London: Routledge.

Harley, B. and Hardy, C. (2004) 'Firing blanks? An analysis of discursive struggle in HRM'. *Journal of Management Studies*, 41(3): 377–400.

Harper, D. (2005) 'What's new visually?'. In N.K. Denzin and Y.S. Lincoln (eds), *The SAGE Handbook of Qualitative Research*, 3rd edn. London: SAGE.

Hart, L., Holli, A.M. and Kovalainen, A. (2009) 'Gender and Power in Politics and Business in Finland'. In K. Niskanen and A. Nyberg (eds.) Kön och makt i Norden. Del I. *TemaNord* 2009:569. Kopenhagen: Nordiska Ministerrådet, 65–130.

Harvey, D. (1990) *Critical Social Research*. London: Unwin Hyman.

Harvey, D. (2002) 'Agency and community: a critical realist paradigm'. *Journal for the Theory of Social Behaviour*, 32(2): 163–94.

Hassard, J. and Parker, M. (1993) (eds) *Postmodernism and Organizations*. London: SAGE.

Heath, C. and Hindmarsh, J. (2002) 'Analysing interaction: video, ethnography and situated conduct'. In T. May (ed.), *Qualitative Research in Action*. London: SAGE.

Heider, D. and Massanari, A.L. (eds) (2012) *Digital Ethics: Research and Practice*. New York: Peter Lang.

Helms Mills, J. and Mills, A. (2000) 'Rules, sense making, formative contexts, and discourse in the gendering of organizational culture'. In N.M. Ashkanasy, C.P.M. Wilderom and M.F. Peterson (eds), *The Handbook of Organizational Culture and Climate*. Thousand Oaks, CA: SAGE.

Hewson, C. and Laurent, D. (2012) *Research Design and Tools for Internet Research*. SAGE Internet Research Methods, 1. London: SAGE.

Heyl, B. (2007) 'Ethnographic interviewing'. In P. Atkinson, A. Coffey, S. Delamont, J. Lofland and L.H. Lofland (2007) *Handbook of Ethnography*. SAGE. pp. 369–83.

Hillebrand, B., Kok, R. and Biemans, W. (2001) 'Theory-testing using case studies: a comment on Johnston, Leach and Liu'. *Industrial Marketing Management*, 30(8): 651–7.

Hinchman, L. and Hinchman, S. (1997) *Memory, Identity, Community. The Idea of Narrative in the Human Sciences*. New York: SUNY Press.

Hine, C. (2005) *Virtual Methods: Issues in Social Research on the Internet*. Oxford: Berg.

Hine, C. (2010) *Virtual Ethnography*. London: SAGE.

Hine, C. (ed.) (2012) *Virtual Research Methods*. SAGE Benchmarks in Social Research Methods. London: SAGE.

Hochschild, A. (1983) *The Managed Heart: The Commercialization of Human Feeling*. Berkeley, CA: University of California Press.

Holgersson, S. and Melin, U. (2014) 'Pragmatic dilemmas in action research: doing action research with or without the approval of top management?' *Systemic Practice and Action Research*, 27(1): 1–17.

Holstein, J. and Gubrium, J. (2004) 'The active interview'. In D. Silverman (ed.), *Qualitative Research: Theory, Method and Practice*. London: SAGE. pp. 140–61.

Holstein, J.A. and Gubrium, J.F. (eds) (2011) *Varieties of Narrative Analysis*. Thousand Oaks: SAGE.

Humphrey, C. and Scapens, R. (1996) 'Methodological themes. Theories and case studies of organizational accounting practices: limitation or liberation?' *Accounting, Auditing and Accountability*, 9(4): 86–106.

Hytti, U. (2003) 'Stories of entrepreneurs: narrative construction of identities'. *Publications of the Turku School of Economics and Business Administration, Series A-1.* Turku: Turku School of Economics and Business Administration.

ISA Code of Ethics (2006) www.ucm.es/info/isa/about/isa_code_of_ethics.htm.

Jameson, D. (2000) 'Telling the investment story: a narrative analysis of shareholder reports'. *Journal of Business Communication*, 37(1): 7–38.

Jesson, J. (2011) *Doing Your Literature Review: Traditional and Systematic Techniques.* London: SAGE.

Joannidès, V. and Berland, N. (2008) 'Reactions to reading "Remaining consistent with method? An analysis of grounded theory research in accounting"'. *Qualitative Research in Accounting & Management*, 5(3): 253–61.

Johnson, J.S. (2014) 'Qualitative sales research: an exposition of grounded theory'. *Journal of Personal Selling & Sales Management*, 35(1): 1–12.

Johnson, P. and Duberley, J. (2000) *Understanding Management Research. An Introduction to Epistemology.* London: SAGE.

Johnston, W., Leach, M. and Liu, A. (2000) 'Using case studies for theory testing in business-to-business research: the development of a more rigorous case study methodology'. *Advances in Business Marketing and Purchasing*, 9: 215–41.

Jännäri, J. and Kovalainen, A. (2015) 'The research methods used in "doing gender" literature'. *International Journal of Gender and Entrepreneurship*, 6(1): 1–21.

Kamberelis, G. and Dimitriadis, G. (2014) 'Focus group research: retrospect'. In P. Leavy (ed.), *The Oxford Handbook of Qualitative Research*, Oxford: Oxford University Press 315–39.

Kärreman, D. and Alvesson, M. (2001) 'Making newsmakers: conversational identity at work'. *Organization Studies*, 22(1): 59–89.

Katila, S. and Eriksson, P. (2013) 'He is a firm, strong-minded and empowering leader, but is she? Gendered positioning of female and male CEOs'. *Gender, Work & Organization*, 20(1): 71–84.

Keats, P.A. (2009) 'Multiple text analysis in narrative research: visual, written, and spoken stories of experience'. *Qualitative Research*, 9(2): 181–95.

Kelle, U. (2000) 'Computer assisted analysis: coding and indexing'. In M. Bauer and G. Gaskell (eds), *Qualitative Researching with Text, Image and Sound.* London: SAGE. pp. 282–98.

Kemmis, S. and McTaggart, R. (2005) 'Participatory action research'. In N.K. Denzin and Y.S. Lincoln (eds), *The SAGE Handbook of Qualitative Research.* Thousand Oaks, CA: SAGE. pp. 559–603.

Kinceloe, J. and McLaren, P. (2005) 'Rethinking critical theory and qualitative research'. In K. Denzin and Y.S. Lincoln (eds), *The SAGE Handbook of Qualitative Research.* Thousand Oaks, CA: SAGE. pp. 303–42.

Kivits, J. (2005) 'Online interviewing and the research relationship'. In C. Hine (ed.), *Virtual Methods: Issues in Social Research on the Internet.* Oxford: Berg.

Knights, D. and Morgan, G. (1991) 'Corporate strategy, organizations and subjectivity: a critique'. *Organization Studies*, 12(2): 251–73.

Knights, D. and Willmott, H. (1989) 'Power and subjectivity at work: from degradation to subjugation in social relations'. *Sociology*, 23(4): 535–58.

Kornberger, M., Justesen, L. and Mouritsen, J. (2011) '"When you make manager, we put a big mountain in front of you": An ethnography of managers in a Big 4 Accounting Firm'. *Accounting, Organizations and Society*, 36(8): 514–33.

Kotiranta, A., Kovalainen, A. and Rouvinen, P. (2010) *Female Leadership and Company Profitability*. In A. de Bruin, C.G. Brush, E. Gatewood, and C. Henry, (eds), *Women Entrepreneurs and the Global Environment for Growth: A Research Perspective*. Edward Elgar Publishing Ltd. pp. 57–72.

Kovalainen, A. (1995) *At the Margins of the Economy. Women's Self-Employment in Finland 1960–1990*. Ashgate: Avebury.

Kovalainen, A. (2016) Qualitative research in entrepreneurship. In R. Blackburn, J. Heinonen, D. de Clercq (eds) Edward Elgar Handbook in Entrepreneurship Research. London: Edward Elgar Publishing Ltd

Kovalainen, A., Vanhala, S. and Melárt, L. (2007) *Women and Economic Decision Making in Private Firms*. Informal Ministerial EU Meeting. Published Background Paper. Ministry of Social Affairs. Finland.

Kovalainen, A. and Österberg-Högstedt, J. (2013) 'Entrepreneurship within social and health care – a question of identity, gender and professionalism'. *International Journal of Gender and Entrepreneurship*, 5(1): 17–35.

Kovalainen, A. and Hart, L. (2014) Role of Self-regulation in Listed Companies Recruiting Women into Top Positions and Boards in Finland. In M. DeVos & Culliford P. (eds) (2014) *Gender Quota for the Board*. Intersentia, Cambridge: Intersentia. pp. 109–22.

Kozinets, R.V. (2010) *Netnography: Doing Ethnographic Research Online*. SAGE.

Kress, G. (2001) 'From Saussure to critical sociolinguistics: the turn towards a social view of language'. In M. Wetherell, S. Taylor and S. Yates (2001) *Discourse Theory and Practice: A Reader*. London: SAGE. pp. 29–38.

Krippendorff, K. (2012) *Content analysis: An Introduction to Its Methodology*. London: SAGE.

Krueger, R. and Casey, M. (2009) *Focus Groups: A Practical Guide for Applied Research*. 4th edn. Thousand Oaks, CA: SAGE.

Kuhn, T.S. (1970) *The Structure of Scientific Revolutions*, 2nd edn. Chicago, IL: University of Chicago Press.

Kuhn, T.S. (1977) *Essential Tension: Selected Studies in Scientific Tradition and Change*. Chicago, IL: Chicago University Press.

Kvasny, L., Trauth, E.M. and Morgan, A. (2009) 'Power relations in IT education and work: the intersectionality of gender, race and class', *Journal of Information, Communication and Ethics in Society*, 7(2/3): 96–118.

Labov, W. and Waletzky, J. (1967) 'Narrative analysis'. In J. Helm (ed.), *Essays on the Verbal and Visual Arts*. Seattle, WA: University of Washington Press.

Laiho, A. (2010) 'Academisation of nursing education in the Nordic Countries'. *Higher Education*, 60(6): 641–56.

Larsen, J. and Schultz, M. (1992) 'Artifacts in a bureaucratic monastery'. In P. Gagliardi (ed.), *Symbols and Artifacts: Views of the Corporate Landscape*. Berlin: Walter de Gruyter. pp. 281–302.

Laukkanen, M. and Eriksson, P. (2013) 'New designs and software for cognitive causal mapping'. *Qualitative Research in Organizations and Management*, 8(2): 122–47.

Lawson, T. (1997) *Economics and Reality*. London and New York: Routledge.

LeCompte, M.D. and Schensul, J.J. (2010) *Designing and Conducting Ethnographic Research*. USA: Rowman Altamira.

Letherby, G. (2003) *Feminist Research in Theory and in Practice*. Buckingham: Open University Press.

Lincoln, Y.S. and Guba, E.G. (1985) *Naturalistic Inquiry*. Thousand Oaks, CA: SAGE.

Lincoln, Y.S., Lynham, S.A. and Guba, E.G. (2011) 'Paradigmatic controversies, contradictions, and emerging confluences, revisited'. In N. Denzin and Y.S. Lincoln (eds), *The SAGE Handbook of Qualitative Research*, 4: 97–128.

Linstead, S.A. and Höpfl, H.J. (eds) (2000) *Aesthetics of Organisation*. London: SAGE.

Lister, M. and Wells, L. (2001) 'Seeing beyond belief: cultural studies as an approach to analyzing the visual'. In T. van Leeuwen and C. Jewitt (eds), *Handbook of Visual Analysis*. London: SAGE.

Lock, J. and Willmott, H. (2006) 'Institutional theory, language, and discourse analysis: a comment on Phillips, Lawrence and Hardy. Dialogue'. *Academy of Management Review*, 31(2): 477–88.

Locke, K. (2001) *Grounded Theory in Management Research*. London: SAGE.

Lokman, M. (2006) 'E-mail interviewing in qualitative research: a methodological discussion'. *Journal of the American Society for Information Science & Technology*, 57(10): 284.

Longino, H.E. (2002) *The Fate of Knowledge*. Princeton: Princeton University Press.

Lorber, J. (2000) 'Using gender to undo gender'. *Feminist Theory*, 1(1): 79–95.

Lorber, J. and Farrell, S.A. (1991) *The Social Construction of Gender*. Newbury Park, London; New Delhi: SAGE. pp. 61–91.

Luff, P. and Heath, C. (2012) 'Some "technical challenges" of video analysis: social actions, objects, material realities and the problems of perspective'. *Qualitative Research*, 12(3): 255–79.

Mannay, D. (2010) 'Making the familiar strange: can visual research methods render the familiar setting more perceptible?'. *Qualitative Research*, 10(1): 91–111.

Marchand, M.H. and Runyan, A.S. (2014) 'Introduction'. In M.H. Marchand and A.S. Runyan (eds), *Gender and Global Restructuring*. London: Routledge.

Mariampolski, H. (2006) *Ethnography for Marketers: A Guide to Consumer Immersion*. London: SAGE.

Martin, L. and Wilson, N. (2014) 'Opportunity, discovery and creativity: a critical realist perspective'. *International Small Business Journal*.

Marvasti, A. (2011) 'Three aspects of writing qualitative research: practice, genre, and audience'. In D. Silverman (ed.), *Qualitative Research*, 3rd ed. London: SAGE. pp. 383–96.

Mason, P. (2005) 'Visual data in applied qualitative research: lessons from experience'. *Qualitative Research*, 5(3): 325–46.

Mauthner, M. (2000) 'Snippets and silences: ethics and reflexivity in narratives of sistering'. *International Journal of Social Research Methodology*, 3(4): 287–306.

Maynard, M. and Purvis, J. (eds) (1994) *Researching Women's Lives from a Feminist Perspective*. London: Taylor and Francis.

Maccoby, E.E. and Jacklin, C.N. (1974) *The Psychology of Sex Differences*. Stanford: Stanford University Press.

McGuigan, J. (1997) 'Introduction'. In J. McGuigan (ed.), *Cultural Methodologies*. SAGE: London. pp. 1–11.

McSweeney, B. (2000) '"Action research", mission impossible?'. *Accounting Forum*, 24(4): 379–90.

Meehan, J. (2004) 'Feminism, critical theory, and power'. *Philosophy & Social Criticism*, 30(3): 375–82.

Meier Sörensen, B. (2014) 'Changing the memory of suffering: an organizational aesthetics of the dark side'. *Organization Studies*, 35(2): 279–302.

Miles, M.B. and Huberman, A.M. (1994) *Qualitative Data Analysis*. Thousand Oaks, CA: SAGE.

Miller, P. and O'Leary, T. (1986) 'Accounting and the construction of the governable person'. *Accounting, Organizations and Society*, 12(3): 235–65.

Mishler, E. (1986) *Research Interviewing: Context and Narrative*. Cambridge, MA: Harvard University Press.

Mishler, E. (1995) 'Models of narrative analysis: a typology'. *Journal of Narrative & Life History*, 5(2): 87–123.

Modell, S. (2009) 'In defence of triangulation: a critical realist approach to mixed methods research in management accounting'. *Management Accounting Research*, 20: 3: 208–21.

Monaco, J. (2009) *How to Read a Film: Movies, Media, Multimedia*. Routledge: London.

Moore, F. (2011) 'Holistic ethnography: studying the impact of multiple national identities on post-acquisition organizations'. *Journal of International Business Studies*, 42(5): 654–71.

Morrow, R. and Brown, D. (1994) *Critical Theory and Methodology*. Thousand Oaks, CA: SAGE.

Moss Kanter, R. (1977) *Men and Women of the Corporation*. New York, NY: Basic Books.

Munir, K. and Phillips, N. (2005) 'The birth of the "Kodak Moment": institutional entrepreneurship and the adoption of new technologies'. *Organization Studies*, 26(11): 1665–87.

Murray, R. (2013) *Writing for Academic Journals*. 3rd edn. Open University Press. Berkshire: McGraw-Hill Education.

Naples, N. (2003) *Feminism and Method: Ethnography, Discourse Analysis and Activist Research*. New York, NY: Routledge.

Nathanson, E. (2014) 'Dressed for economic distress'. In D. Negra and Y. Tasker (eds), *Gendering the Recession*. Durham and London: Duke University Press.

Negra, D. (2009) *What a Girl Wants? Fantasizing the Reclamation of Self in Postfeminism*. New York: Routledge.

Oakley, A. (1981) 'Interviewing women: a contradiction in terms'. In H. Roberts (ed.), *Doing Feminist Research*. London: Routledge.

Olesen, V. (2005) 'Early millennium feminist qualitative research'. In N.K. Denzin and Y.S. Lincoln (eds), *Handbook of Qualitative Research*. London: SAGE.

O'Reilly, K., Paper, D. and Marx, S. (2012) 'Demystifying grounded theory for business research'. *Organizational Research Methods*, 15(2): 247–62.

Panayiotou, A. (2010) '"Macho" managers and organizational heroes: competing masculinities in popular films'. *Organization*, 17(6): 659–83.

Parker, I. (1992) *Discourse Dynamics: Critical Analysis for Social and Individual Psychology*. London: Routledge.

Parker, L.D. and Guthrie, J. (2014) 'Addressing directions in interdisciplinary accounting research'. *Accounting, Auditing & Accountability Journal*, 27(8): 1218–26.

Parker, M. (2002) *Against Management*. London: SAGE.

Patton, M. (2014) *Qualitative Research and Evaluation Methods*. Newbury Park, CA: SAGE.

Paulus, T., Lester, J. and Dempster, P. (2013) *Digital Tools for Qualitative Research*. London: SAGE.

Pauwels, L. (2010) 'Visual sociology reframed: an analytical synthesis and discussion of visual methods in social and cultural research'. *Sociological Methods & Research*, 38(4): 545–81.

Peräkylä, A. (2005) 'Analyzing talk and text'. In N.K. Denzin and Y.S. Lincoln (eds), *The SAGE Handbook of Qualitative Research*, 3rd edn. London: SAGE. pp. 869–886.

Perren, L. and Jennings, P. (2005) 'Government discourses of entrepreneurship: issues of legitimation, subjugation, and power'. *Entrepreneurship Theory and Practice*, 29(2): 173–84.

Perry, C. and Gummesson, E. (2004) 'Action research in marketing'. *European Journal of Marketing*, 38(3–4): 310–20.

Pettigrew, A. (1985) *ICI – The Awakening Giant*. Oxford: Basil Blackwell.

Phillips, N., Lawrence, T. and Hardy, C. (2006) 'Discussing "discourse and institutions": a reply to Lok and Willmott. Dialogue'. *Academy of Management Review*, 31(2): 477–88.

Pillow, W.S. and Mayo, C. (2011) 'Feminist ethnography'. In S.N. Hesse-Biber (ed.), *Handbook of Feminist Research: Theory and Praxis*. Thousand Oaks: SAGE. pp. 187–2005.

Pink, S. (2007) *Doing Visual Ethnography*. SAGE: London.

Poland, B. (2001) 'Transcription quality'. In J. Gubrium and J. Holstein (eds), *Handbook of Interview Research: Context and Method*. London: SAGE. pp. 628–650.

Polkinghorne, D. (1995) 'Narrative configuration in qualitative analysis'. *Qualitative Studies in Education*, 8(1): 5–23.

Polkinghorne, D.E. (1988) *Narrative Knowing and the Human Sciences*. Albany, NY: State University of New York Press.

Potter, J. (1996a) *An Analysis of Thinking and Research About Qualitative Methods*. Mahwah, NJ: LEA.

Potter, J. (1996b) *Representing Reality: Discourse, Rhetoric and Social Construction*. London: SAGE.

Potter, J. (1997) 'Discourse analysis as a way of analysing naturally occurring talk'. In D. Silverman (ed.), *Qualitative Research: Theory, Method and Practice*. London: SAGE. pp. 144–60.

Potter, J. (1998) 'Qualitative and discourse analysis'. In A.S. Bellack and M. Hersen (eds), *Comprehensive Clinical Psychology, Volume 3*. Oxford: Pergamon.

Potter, J. (2001) 'Wittgenstein and Austin'. In M. Wetherell, S. Taylor and S. Yates (eds), *Discourse Theory and Practice: A Reader*. London: SAGE. pp. 39–46.

Potter, J. (2012) 'Discourse analysis and discursive psychology'. In H. Cooper (Editor-in-Chief), *APA Handbook of Research Methods in Psychology: Volume 2. Quantitative, Qualitative, Neuropsychological, and Biological*. Washington: American Psychological Association Press. pp. 111–30

Potter, J. and Wetherell, M. (1987) *Discourse and Social Psychology: Beyond Attitudes and Behaviour*. London: SAGE.

Potter, J. and Wetherell, M. (1994) 'Analyzing discourse'. In A. Bryman and B. Burgess (eds), *Analyzing Qualitative Data*. London: Routledge.

Potter, J. and Wetherell, M. (1995) 'Discourse analysis'. In J. Smith, R. Harré and R. van Langenhove (eds), *Rethinking Methods in Psychology*. London: SAGE.

Poutanen, S. (2007) 'Critical realism and post-structuralist feminism – the difficult path to mutual understanding'. *Journal of Critical Realism*, 6(1): 28–52.

Poutanen, S. and Kovalainen, A. (2009) 'Critical theory'. In A. J. Mills, G. Durepos and E. Wiebe (eds), *Encyclopedia of Case Study Research*. SAGE: London. pp. 259–64.

Poutanen, S. and Kovalainen, A. (2013) 'Gendering invention process in an industrial plant – revisiting tokenism, gender and innovation'. *International Journal of Gender and Entrepreneurship*, 5(3): 257–74.

Poutanen, S. and Kovalainen, A. (2014) 'What is new in the "New Economy"?'. In J. Gruhlich and B. Riegraf (eds), *Gender and Transnational Spaces. Feminist Perspectives on New Inclusions and Exclusions (Geschlecht und Transnationale Räume. Feministische Perspektiven auf neue Ein- und Ausschlüsse)*. Münster: Verlag Westfälisches Dampfboot.

Poutanen, S. & Kovalainen, A. (2016) 'Entrepreneurialism and Professionalism'. In M. Dent, I. Bourgeault, J.L. Denis and E. Kuhlmann (eds), *Routledge Companion on Professions and Professionalism*. London: Routledge. In press.

Poutanen, S. and Kovalainen, A. (2016) 'Intersectionality, Process Tokenism and Gendered Innovation'. In G. Alsos, E. Ljunggren and U. Hytti (eds.), *Handbook on Gender and Innovations*. Edward Elgar, Cheltenham. (In press).

Pringle, R. (1988) *Secretaries Talk: Sexuality, Power and Work*. London: Verso.

Propp, V. (1968) *The Morphology of the Folk Tale*. Austin, TX: University of Texas Press.

Puchta, C. and Potter, J. (2004) *Focus Group Practice*. London: SAGE.

Punch, K. (1998) *Introduction to Social Research: Quantitative and Qualitative Approaches*. London: SAGE.

Ram, M. (1994) *Managing to Survive: Working Lives in Small Firms*. Oxford: Blackwell.

Ram, M. (1999) 'Trading places: the ethnographic process in small firms' research'. *Entrepreneurship & Regional Development*, 11(2): 95–108.

Ramazanoglu, C. and Holland, J. (2002) *Feminist Methodology. Challenges and Choices*. London: SAGE.

Ramologlou, S. (2013) 'Who is a "non-entrepreneur"?: Taking the "others" of entrepreneurship seriously'. *International Small Business Journal*, 31(4): 432–53.

Rappaport, J. (1995) 'Empowerment meets narrative: listening to stories and creating settings'. *American Journal of Community Psychology*, 23(5): 795–807.

Reed, M. (2005) 'Reflections on the "realist turn" in organization and management studies'. *Journal of Management Studies*, 42(8): 1621–44.

Reinharz, S. (1992) *Feminist Methods in Social Research*. New York, NY: Oxford University Press.

Riad, S. (2005) 'The power of organizational culture as a discursive formation in merger integration'. *Organization Studies*, 26(10): 1529–54.

Richardson, L. (1990) *Writing Strategies: Reaching Diverse Audiences*. Newbury Park, CA: SAGE.

Richardson, L. (1994) 'Writing: a method of inquiry'. In N.K. Denzin and Y.S. Lincoln (eds), *Handbook of Qualitative Research*. London: SAGE. pp. 516–29.

Richardson, L. (1995) 'Narrative and sociology'. In J. van Maanen (ed.), *Representation in Ethnography*. Thousand Oaks, CA: SAGE. pp. 198–221.

Richardson, L. and Adams St Pierre, E. (2005) 'Writing: a method of inquiry'. In N.K. Denzin and Y.S. Lincoln (eds), *Handbook of Qualitative Research*, London: SAGE. pp. 959–78.

Ridley, D. (2012) *The Literature Review: A Step-By-Step Guide for Students*. London: SAGE.

Riessman, C. (1993) *Narrative Analysis. Qualitative Research Methods Series, No. 30.* Newbury Park, CA: SAGE.

Riessman, C. (2002) 'Analysis of personal narratives'. In J. Gubrium and J. Holstein (eds), *Handbook of Interview Research: Context and Method*. Newbury Park, CA: SAGE pp. 695–711.

Riessman, C. (2004) 'Narrative analysis'. In M.S. Lewis-Beck, A. Bryman and T. Futing Liao (eds), *Encyclopedia of Social Science Research Methods*. London: SAGE.

Rogers, R. (2013) *Digital Methods*. Boston: MIT Press.

Rose, G. (2012) *Visual Methodologies. An Introduction to Researching with Visual Materials*. London: SAGE.

Rosen, M. (1991) 'Coming to terms with the field: understanding and doing organizational ethnography'. *Journal of Management Studies*, 28(1): 1–24.

Rosen, M. (2000) *Turning Words, Spinning Worlds: Chapters in Organizational Ethnography*. London: Routledge.

Ryan, B., Scapens, R. and Theobald, M. (1992) *Research Method and Methodology in Finance and Accounting*. London: Academic Press.

Ryan, B., Scapens, R. and Theobald, M. (2002) *Research Method and Methodology in Finance and Accounting*. London: Thompson.

Saldaña, J. (2012) *The Coding Manual for Qualitative Researchers*. 2nd edn. London: SAGE.

Samra-Fredericks, D. (2003) 'Strategizing as lived experience and strategists' everyday efforts to shape strategic direction'. *Journal of Management Studies*, 40(1): 141–74.

Sayer, A. (2013) 'Abstraction: a realist interpretation'. In M. Archer, R. Bhaskar, A. Collier, T. Lawson and A. Norrie (eds), *Critical Realism: Essential Readings*. Abingdon, Oxon: Routledge. pp. 120–143.

Schein, E. (1995) 'Process consultation, action research and clinical inquiry, are they the same?' *Journal of Managerial Psychology*, 10(6): 14–19.

Schein, E. (1999) *Process Consultation Revisited: Building the Helping Relationship*. Reading, MA: Addison-Wesley.

Schwandt, T.A. (2001) *Dictionary of Qualitative Inquiry*. London: SAGE.

Schweingruber, D. and Berns, N. (2005) 'Shaping the selves of young salespeople through emotion management'. *Journal of Contemporary Ethnography*, 34: 679–706.

Segal, L. (2010) 'Genders'. In M. Wetherell and C. Talpade Mohanty (eds), *The SAGE Handbook of Identities*. London: SAGE.

Shank, G. (2002) *Qualitative Research. A Personal Skills Approach*. Upper Saddle River, NJ: Merrill Prentice Hall.

Shin Rohani, L., Aung, M. and Rohani, K. (2014) One step closer to the field: visual methods in marketing and consumer research. *Qualitative Market Research*, 17(4): 300–318

Silver, C. and Lewins, A. (2014) *Using Software in Qualitative Research: A Step-By-Step Guide*. London: SAGE.

Silverman, D. (2005) *Doing Qualitative Research: A Practical Handbook*. London: SAGE.

Silverman, D. (2011) *Interpreting Qualitative Data: Methods for Analysing Talk, Text and Interaction*. London: SAGE.

Silverman, D. (2013) *Doing Qualitative Research*. London: SAGE.

Skeggs, B. and Wood, H. (2012) *Reacting to Reality Television: Performance, Audience and Value*. London: Routledge.

Snell, J. (2011) Interrogating video data: systematic quantitative analysis versus micro-ethnographic analysis. *International Journal of Social Research Methodology*, 14(3): 253–8.

Somers, M. (1994) 'The narrative constitution of identity: a relational and network approach'. *Theory and Society*, 23(5): 605–49.

Spradley, J. (1979) *The Ethnographic Interview*. New York, NY: Holt, Rinehart and Winston.

Spradley, J. (1980) *Participant Observation*. New York, NY: Holt, Rinehart and Winston.

Staat, W. (1993) 'On abduction, deduction, induction and the categories'. *Transactions of the Charles S. Peirce Society*, 29: 225–37.

Stake, R. (1995) *The Art of Case Study Research*. Thousand Oaks, CA: SAGE.

Stake, R. (2005) 'Case studies'. In N.K. Denzin and Y.S. Lincoln (eds), *Handbook of Qualitative Research*. Thousand Oaks, CA: SAGE. pp. 435–54.

Stake, R.E. (2013) *Multiple Case Study Analysis*. New York: Guilford Press.

Stanley, L. and Wise, S. (1990) 'Method, methodology and epistemology in feminist research processes'. In L. Stanley (ed.), *Feminist Praxis*. London: Routledge.

Starkey, K. and Crane, A. (2003) 'Toward green narrative: management and the evolutionary epic'. *Academy of Management Review*, 28(2): 220–37.

Stewart, D.W. and Shamdasani, P.N. (2014) *Focus Groups*. London: SAGE.

Stoecker, R. (1991) 'Evaluating and rethinking the case study'. *Sociological Review*, 39(1): 88–112.

Stokoe, E. and Edwards, D. (2009) 'Accomplishing social action with identity categories: Mediating neighbour complaints'. In M. Wetherell (ed.), *Theorizing Identities and Social Action*. London: SAGE. pp. 95–115.

Strauss, A. (1987) *Qualitative Analysis for Social Scientists*. New York, NY: Cambridge University Press.

Strauss, A. (1990) *Qualitative Analysis for Social Scientists*. 2nd edn. New York, NY: Cambridge University Press.

Strauss, A. and Corbin, J. (1998) *Basics of Qualitative Research*. Thousand Oaks, CA: SAGE.

Suddaby, R. and Greenwood, R. (2005) Rhetorical strategies of legitimacy. *Administrative Science Quarterly*, 50(1): 35–67.

Suddaby, R., Hardy, C. and Huy, Q.N. (2011) 'Where are the new theories of organization?'. *Academy of Management Review*, 36(2): 236–46.

Suter, E. (2000) 'Focus groups in ethnography of communication: expanding topics of inquiry beyond participant observation'. *The Qualitative Report*, 5(1–2). www.nova.edu/ssss/QR/QR5–1/suter.html

Swan, E. (2010) 'Commodity diversity: smiling faces as a strategy of containment'. *Organization*, 17(1): 77–100.

Sweet, C. (2001) 'Designing and conducting virtual focus groups'. *Qualitative Market Research: An International Journal*, 4(3): 130–5.

Sword, H. (2012) *Stylish Academic Writing*. Boston: Harvard University Press.

Tadajewski, M. (2010) 'Towards a history of critical marketing studies'. *Journal of Marketing Management*, 26(9–10): 773–824.

Tashakkori, A. and Teddlie, C. (eds) (2010) *SAGE Handbook of Mixed Methods in Social and Behavioral Research*. London: SAGE.

Taylor, S. (2001) 'Evaluating and applying discourse analytic research'. In M. Wetherell, S. Taylor and S.J. Yates (eds), *Discourse as Data: A Guide to Analysis*. London: SAGE. pp. 311–30.

Thomas, G. (2010) *How To Do Your Case Study*. London: SAGE.

Thomson, P. and Kamler, B. (2013) *Writing for Peer Reviewed Journals: Strategies for Getting Published*. Abingdon: Routledge.

Thompson, P., Warhurst, C. and Callaghan, G. (2000) 'Human capital or capitalizing on humanity? Knowledge, skills and competencies in interactive service work'. In C. Prichard, M. Chumer, H. Willmott and R. Hull (eds), *Managing Knowledge*. London: Palgrave. pp. 122–40.

Thornberg, R. (2012) 'Informed grounded theory'. *Scandinavian Journal of Educational Research*, 56(3): 243–59.

Thornberg, R., Halldin, K., Bolmsjö, N. and Petterson, A. (2013) 'Victimizing of school bullying: A grounded theory'. *Research Papers in Education*, 28(3): 309–29.

Timmermans, S. and Tavory, I. (2007) 'Advancing ethnographic research through grounded theory practice'. In A. Bryant and K. Charmaz (eds), *Handbook of Grounded Theory*. London: SAGE. pp. 493–513.

Tourish, D. (2013) '"Evidence based management", or "evidence oriented organizing"? A critical realist perspective'. *Organization*, 20(2): 173–92.

Townley, B. (1993) 'Foucault, power/knowledge, and its relevance for human resource management'. *Academy of Management Review*, 18(3): 518–45.

Trist, E. and Murray, H. (1993) *The Social Engagement of Social Science: A Tavistock Anthology*. Philadelphia, PA: University of Pennsylvania Press.

Vaara, E. and Tienari, J. (2002) 'Justification, legitimization and naturalization of mergers and acquisitions: a critical discourse analysis of media texts'. *Organization*, 9(2): 275–304.

Vanderstaay, S. (2005) 'One hundred dollars and a dead man. Ethical decision making in ethnographic fieldwork'. *Journal of Contemporary Ethnography*, 34: 371–409.

Van Dijk, T. (1995) 'Discourse semantics and ideology'. *Discourse & Society*, 6(2): 243–89.

Van Dijk, T. (1998) *Ideology*. London: SAGE.

Van Dijk, T. (2001) 'The principles of critical discourse analysis'. In M. Wetherell, S. Taylor and S. Yates (eds), *Discourse Theory and Practice: A Reader*. London: SAGE. pp. 300–17.

van Leeuwen, T. and Jewitt, C. (2001) 'Introduction'. In T. van Leeuwen and C. Jewitt (eds), *Handbook of Visual Analysis*. London: SAGE.

Van Leunen, M.-C. (1978) *A Handbook for Scholars*. New York, NY: Alfred A. Knopf.

Van Maanen, J. (ed.) (1995) *Representation in Ethnography*. London: SAGE.

Van Maanen, J. (2011) *Tales of the Field: On Writing Ethnography*. Chicago, IL: University of Chicago Press.

van Marrewijk, A.H. (2014) 'Exceptional luck? Conducting ethnographies in business organizations'. *Anthropologist*, 18(1): 33–42.

Vincent, S. (2005) 'Really dealing. A critical perspective to inter-organizational exchange networks'. *Work, Employment & Society*, 19(1): 47–65.

Wadham, H. and Warren, R.C. (2014) 'Telling organizational tales. The extended case method in practice'. *Organizational Research Methods*, 17(1): 5–22.

Wallace, M. (1986) *Recent Theories of Narrative*. Ithaca, NY: Cornell University Press.

Wapshott, R. and Mallett, O. (2013) 'The unspoken side of mutual adjustment: understanding intersubjective negotiation in small professional service firms'. *International Small Business Journal*, 31(8): 978–96.

Watson, T. (1994) *In Search of Management: Culture, Chaos and Control in Managerial Work*. London: Routledge.

Webb, E.J., Campbell, T.D., Schwartz, R.D. and Sechrest, L. (1966) *Unobtrusive Measures. Nonreactive Measures in Social Sciences*. Chicago: Rand McNally.

Wengraf, T. (2001) *Qualitative Research Interviewing: Biographic Narrative and Semi-Structured Methods*. London: SAGE.

West, C. and Zimmerman, D.H. (1987) 'Doing gender'. *Gender & Society*, 1: 125–51.

Wetherell, M. (2001) 'Debates in discourse research'. In M. Wetherell, S. Taylor and S. Yates (eds), *Discourse Theory and Practice: A Reader*. London: SAGE. pp. 380–99.

Wetherell, M. and Edley, J. (2008) 'Masculinity manoeuvres: critical discourse psychology and the analysis of identity strategies'. In N. Coupland and A. Jaworski (eds), *The New Sociolinguistics Reader*. Basingstoke: Palgrave Macmillan. pp. 201–214.

Wetherell, M. and Potter, J. (1988) 'Discourse analysis and the identification of interpretive repertoires'. In C. Antaki (ed.), *Analysing Everyday Explanation: A Casebook of Methods*. Newbury Park, CA: SAGE. pp. 168–83.

Wetherell, M., Taylor, S. and Yates, S. (2001a) *Discourse Theory and Practice: A Reader*. London: SAGE.

Wetherell, M., Taylor, S. and Yates, S. (2001b) *Discourse as Data: A Guide for Analysts*. London: SAGE.

Wilkinson, S. (2004) 'Focus group research'. In D. Silverman (ed.), *Qualitative Research: Theory, Method and Practice*. London: SAGE. pp. 177–99.

Williamson, G.R., Bellman, L. and Webster, J. (2012) *Action Research in Nursing and Healthcare*. SAGE: London.

Willmott, H. (1997) 'Rethinking management and managerial work: capitalism, control and subjectivity'. *Human Relations*, 50(11): 1329–59.

Wilson, E. (2001) 'Organizational behaviour and gender'. In E. Wilson (ed.), *Organisational Behaviour Reassessed: The Impact of Gender*. London: SAGE. pp. 1–16.

Wodak, R. (1996) *Disorders of Discourse*. London: Longman.

Wodak, R. (1997) 'What CDA is about – a summary of its history, important concepts and its developments'. In R. Wodak and M. Meyer (eds), *Methods of Critical Discourse*. London: SAGE.

Wodak, R. and Mayer, M. (2001) *Methods of Critical Discourse Analysis*. London: SAGE.

Wolcott, H. (2005) *The Art of Fieldwork*. Oxford: AltaMira Press.

Wolcott, H. (2009) *Writing up Qualitative Research*. Thousand Oaks, CA: SAGE.

Woods, P. (2006) *Successful Writing for Qualitative Researchers*. London: Routledge.

Woodside, A. and Wilson, E. (2003) 'Case study research methods for theory building'. *Journal of Business and Industrial Marketing*, 18(6–7): 493–508.

Xu, O. (2000) 'On the way to knowledge: making a discourse at quality'. *Organization*, 7(3): 427–53.

Yanow, D., Ybema, S. and van Hulst, M. (2012) 'Practising organizational ethnography'. In G. Symon and C. Cassell (eds), *Qualitative Organizational Research: Core Methods and Current Challenges*. London: SAGE. pp. 351–72.

Yin, R. (2014) *Case Study Research*. Thousand Oaks, CA: SAGE.

Zalan, T. and Lewis, G. (2004) 'Writing about methods in qualitative research: towards a more transparent approach'. In R. Marschan-Piekkari and C. Welch (eds), *Handbook of Qualitative Methods for International Business*. Cheltenham: Edward Elgar.

Zanoni, P. and Janssens, M. (2003) 'Deconstructing difference: the rhetoric of human resources manager's diversity discourses'. *Organization Studies*, 25(1): 55–74.

Zelizer, V. (2011) *Economic Lives: How Culture Shapes the Economy*. Princeton, NJ: Princeton University Press.

INDEX

Boxes are indicated by page numbers printed in bold. The abbreviation 'bib' after a page number indicates bibliographical information in the Further Reading sections.